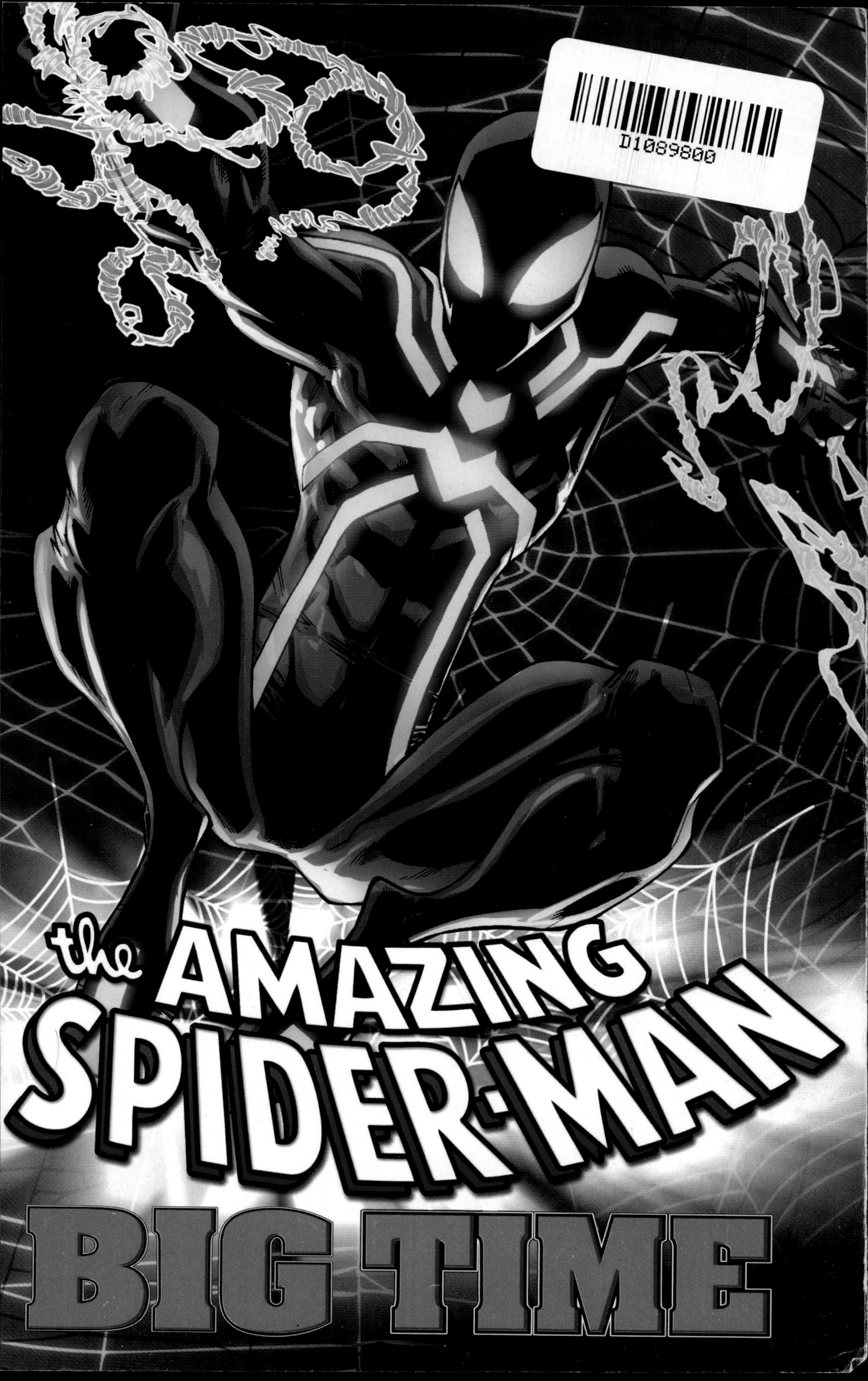
the AMAZING
SPIDER-MAN
BIG TIME

the AMAZING SPIDER-MAN

BIG TIME

Writer: **DAN SLOTT**
Penciler: **HUMBERTO RAMOS**
Inker: **CARLOS CUEVAS**
WITH **JOSEPH DAMON** & **VICTOR OLAZABA**
Colorist: **EDGAR DELGADO**
Letterer: **VC'S JOE CARAMAGNA**

"THE FINAL LESSON"
Writer: **DAN SLOTT**
Penciler: **NEIL EDWARDS**
Inker: **SCOTT HANNA**
Colorist: **MORRY HOLLOWELL**
Letterer: **VC'S CHRIS ELIOPOULOS**

"THE STING THAT NEVER GOES AWAY"
Writer: **DAN SLOTT**
Artist: **STEFANO CASELLI**
Colorist: **EDGAR DELGADO**
Letterer: **VC'S JOE CARAMAGNA**

Assistant Editor: **ELLIE PYLE** • Associate Editor: **THOMAS BRENNAN** • Senior Editor: **STEPHEN WACKER**

Collection Editor: **JENNIFER GRÜNWALD** • Editorial Assistants: **JAMES EMMETT** & **JOE HOCHSTEIN**
Assistant Editors: **ALEX STARBUCK** & **NELSON RIBEIRO** • Editor, Special Projects: **MARK D. BEAZLEY**
Senior Editor, Special Projects: **JEFF YOUNGQUIST** • Senior Vice President of Sales: **DAVID GABRIEL**

Editor in Chief: **JOE QUESADA** • Publisher: **DAN BUCKLEY** • Executive Producer: **ALAN FINE**

SPIDER-MAN: BIG TIME. Contains material originally published in magazine form as AMAZING SPIDER-MAN #648-651. First printing 2011. Hardcover: ISBN# 978-0-7851-4623-0. Softcover ISBN# 978-0-7851-4624-7. Published by MARVEL WORLDWIDE, INC., a subsidiary of MARVEL ENTERTAINMENT, LLC. OFFICE OF PUBLICATION: 135 West 50th Street, New York, NY 10020. Copyright © 2010 and 2011 Marvel Characters, Inc. All rights reserved. Hardcover: $19.99 per copy in the U.S. and $22.50 in Canada (GST #R127032852). Softcover: $14.99 per copy in the U.S. and $16.99 in Canada (GST #R127032852). Canadian Agreement #40668537. All characters featured in this issue and the distinctive names and likenesses thereof, and all related indicia are trademarks of Marvel Characters, Inc. No similarity between any of the names, characters, persons, and/or institutions in this magazine with those of any living or dead person or institution is intended, and any such similarity which may exist is purely coincidental. **Printed in the U.S.** ALAN FINE, EVP - Office of the President, Marvel Worldwide, Inc. and EVP & CMO Marvel Characters B.V.; DAN BUCKLEY, Chief Executive Officer and Publisher - Print, Animation & Digital Media; JIM SOKOLOWSKI, Chief Operating Officer; DAVID GABRIEL, SVP of Publishing Sales & Circulation; DAVID BOGART, SVP of Business Affairs & Talent Management; MICHAEL PASCIULLO, VP Merchandising & Communications; JIM O'KEEFE, VP of Operations & Logistics; DAN CARR, Executive Director of Publishing Technology; JUSTIN F. GABRIE, Director of Publishing & Editorial Operations; SUSAN CRESPI, Editorial Operations Manager; ALEX MORALES, Publishing Operations Manager; STAN LEE, Chairman Emeritus. For information regarding advertising in Marvel Comics or on Marvel.com, please contact Ron Stern, VP of Business Development, at rstern@marvel.com. For Marvel subscription inquiries, please call 800-217-9158. **Manufactured between 12/13/2010 and 1/17/2011 (hardcover), and 12/13/2010 and 7/18/2011 (softcover), by R.R. DONNELLEY, INC., SALEM, VA, USA.**

10 9 8 7 6 5 4 3 2 1

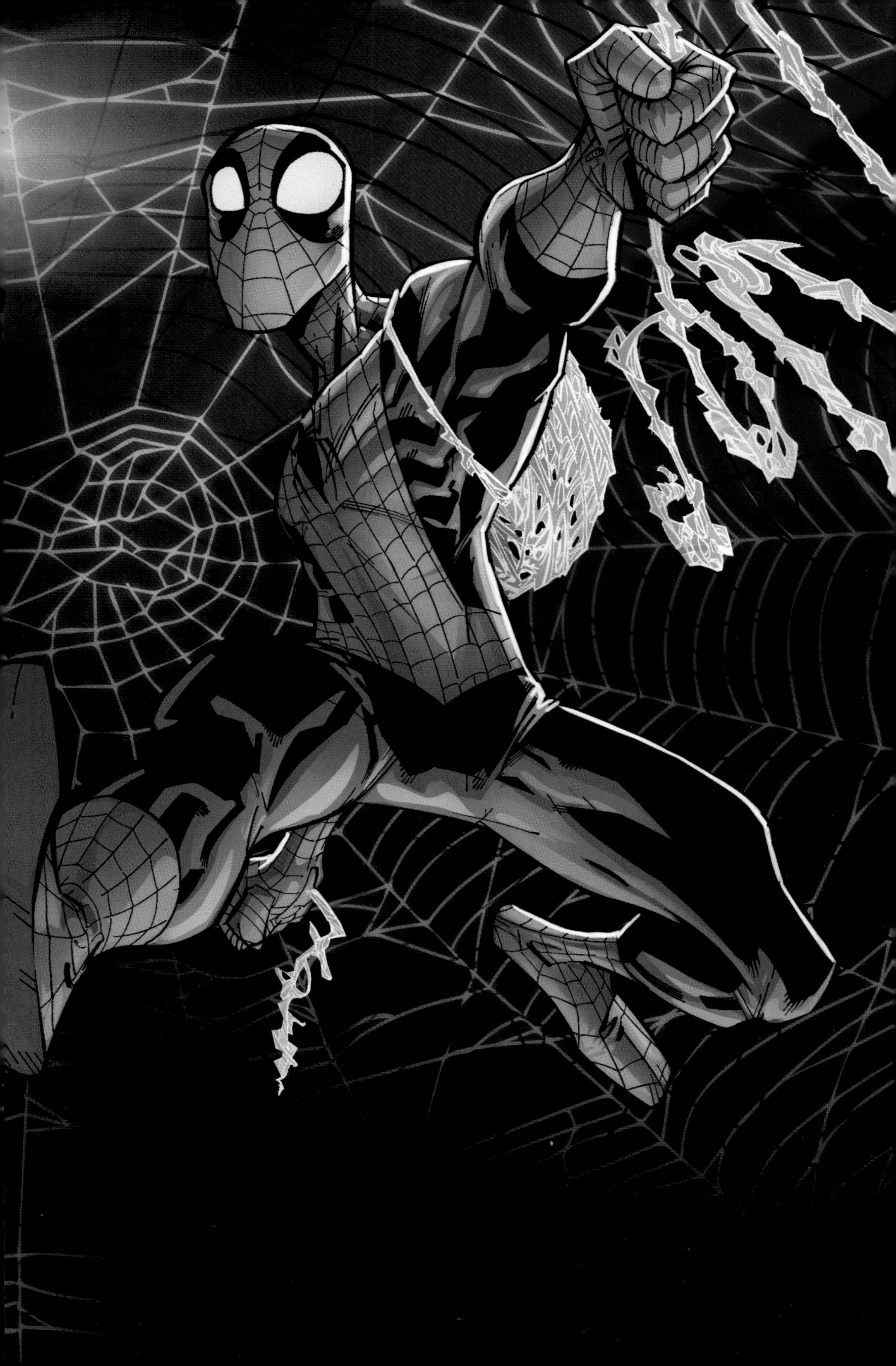

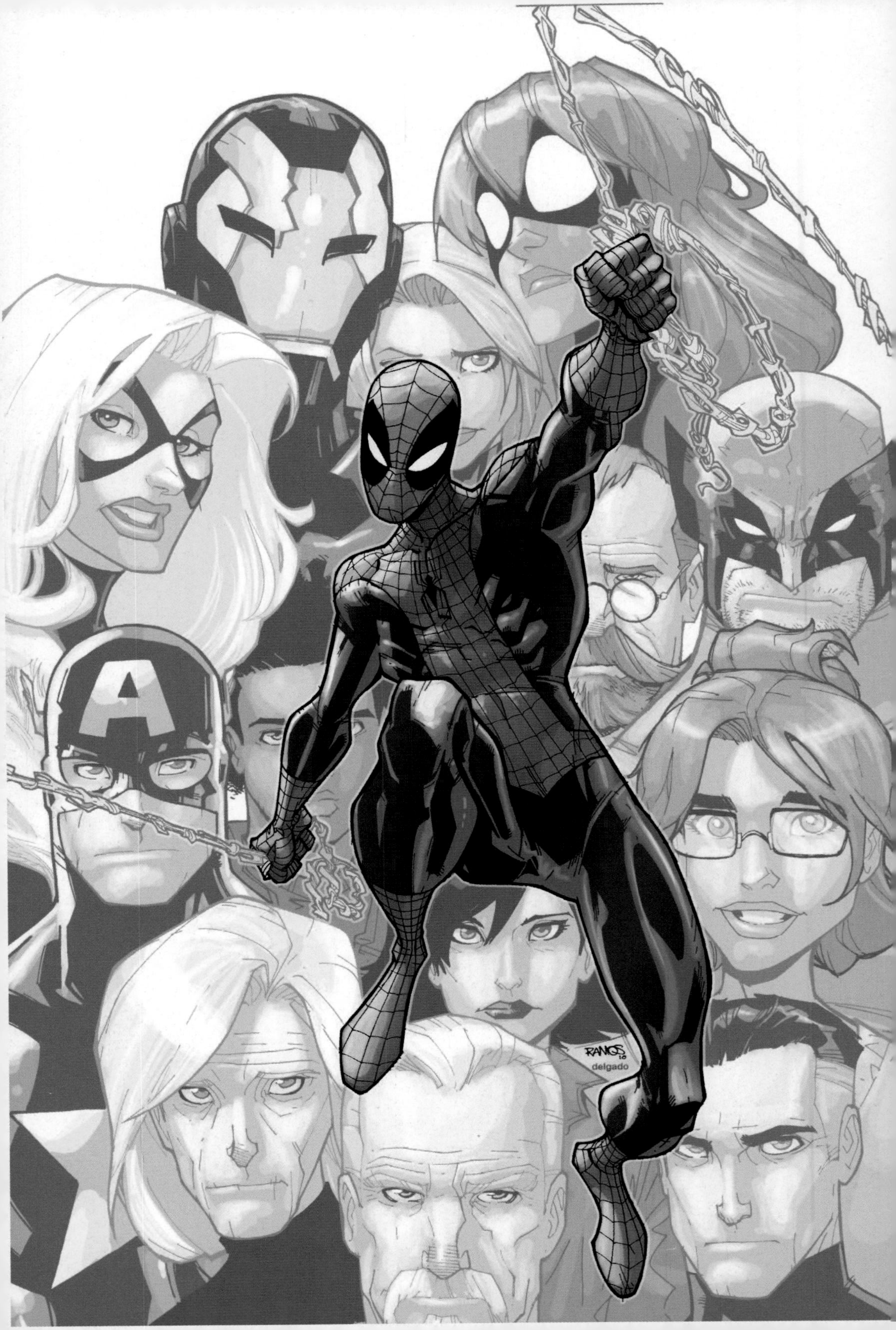
delgado

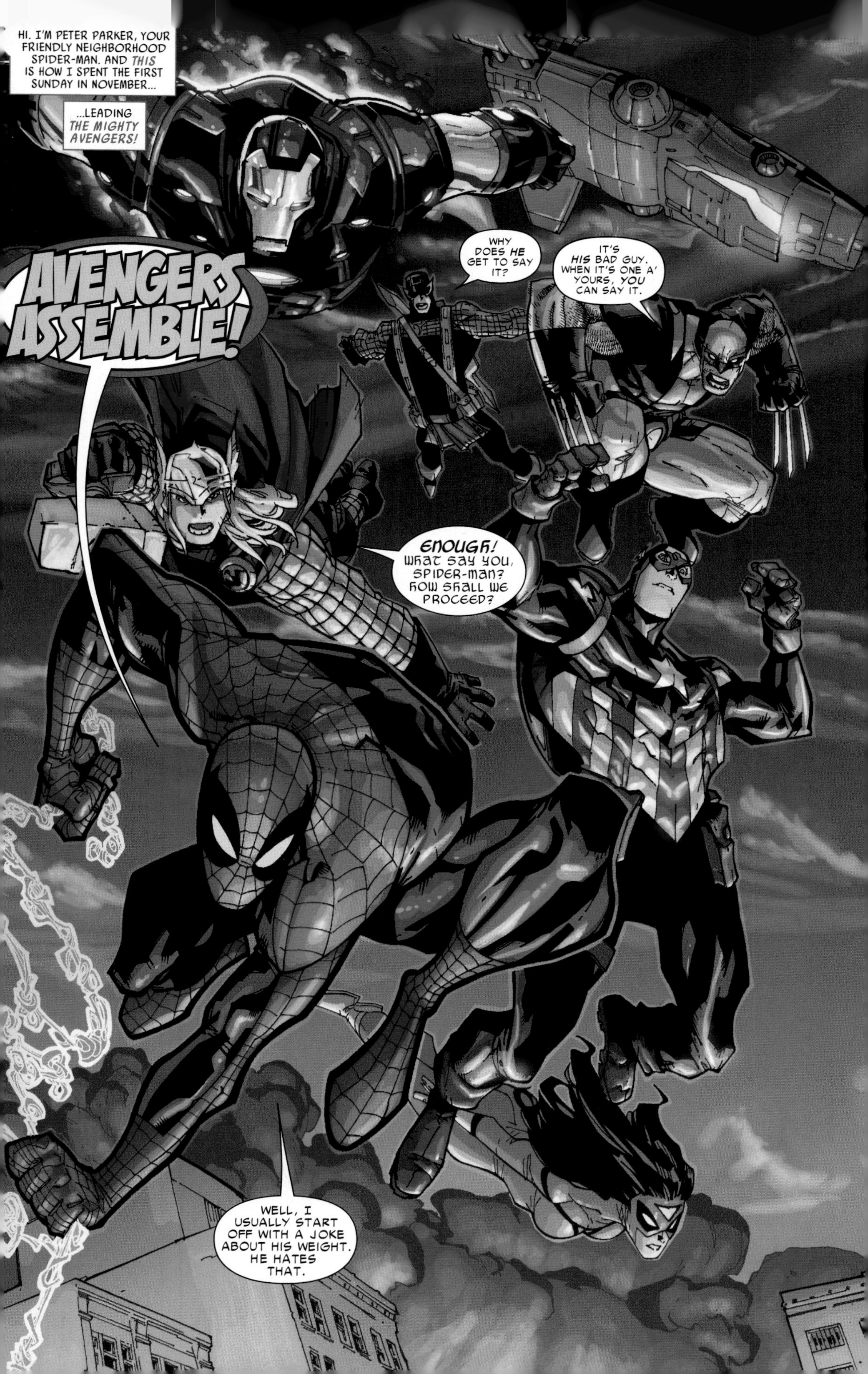
HI. I'M PETER PARKER, YOUR FRIENDLY NEIGHBORHOOD SPIDER-MAN. AND THIS IS HOW I SPENT THE FIRST SUNDAY IN NOVEMBER...
...LEADING THE MIGHTY AVENGERS!
AVENGERS ASSEMBLE!
WHY DOES HE GET TO SAY IT?
IT'S HIS BAD GUY. WHEN IT'S ONE A' YOURS, YOU CAN SAY IT.
ENOUGH! WHAT SAY YOU, SPIDER-MAN? HOW SHALL WE PROCEED?
WELL, I USUALLY START OFF WITH A JOKE ABOUT HIS WEIGHT. HE HATES THAT.

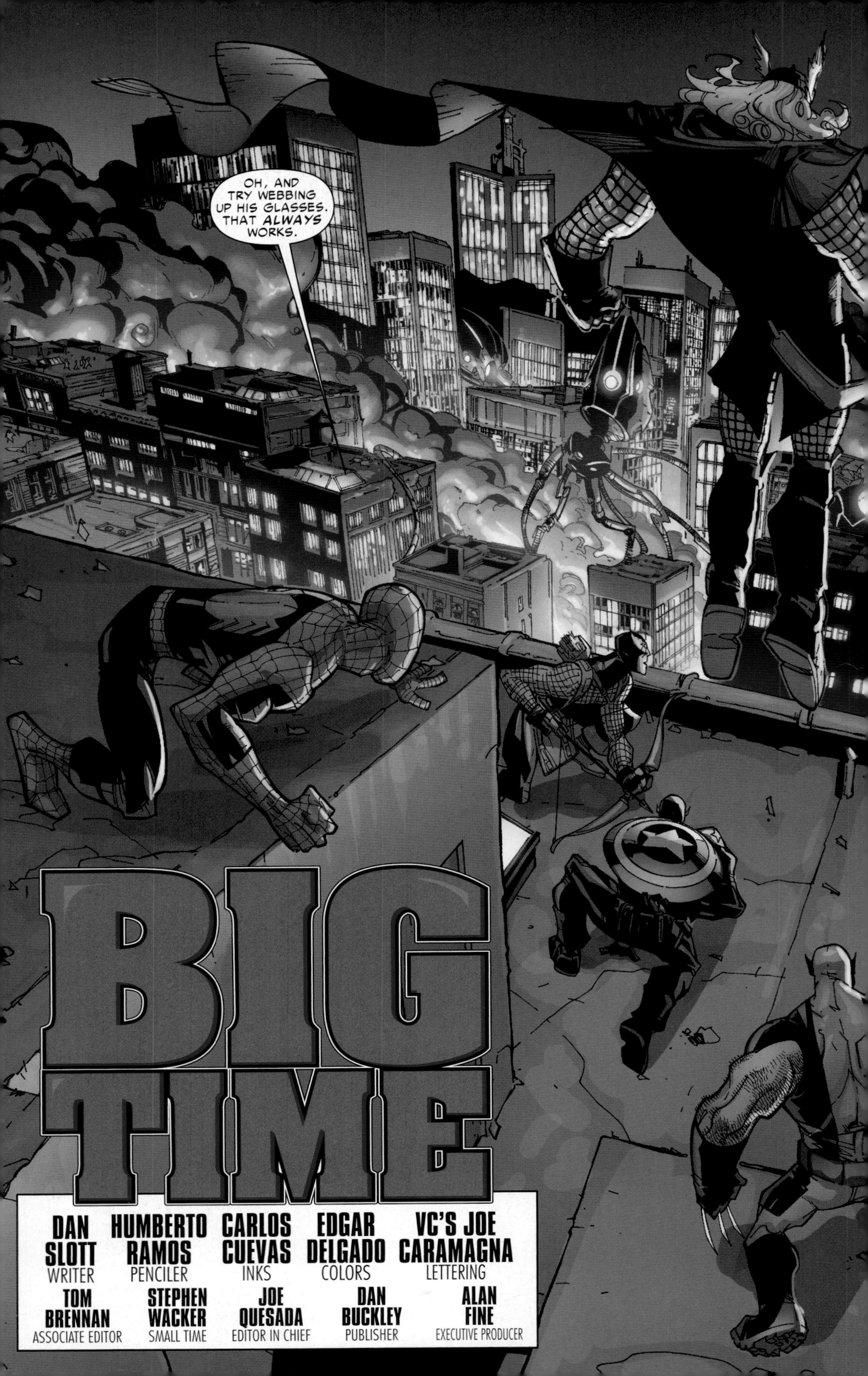
OH, AND TRY WEBBING UP HIS GLASSES. THAT ALWAYS WORKS.
BIG TIME
DAN SLOTT WRITER
HUMBERTO RAMOS PENCILER
CARLOS CUEVAS INKS
EDGAR DELGADO COLORS
VC'S JOE CARAMAGNA LETTERING
TOM BRENNAN ASSOCIATE EDITOR
STEPHEN WACKER SMALL TIME
JOE QUESADA EDITOR IN CHIEF
DAN BUCKLEY PUBLISHER
ALAN FINE EXECUTIVE PRODUCER

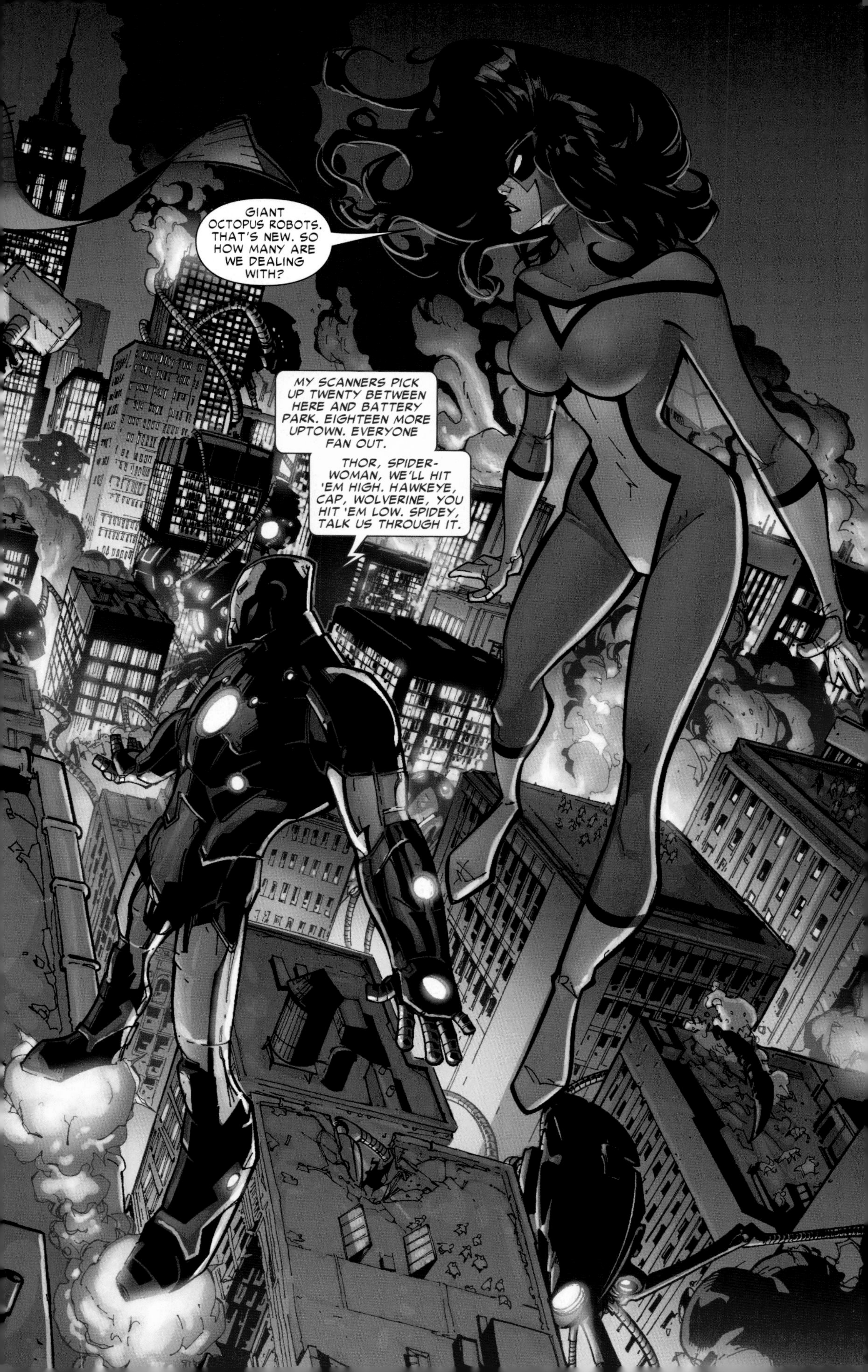
GIANT OCTOPUS ROBOTS. THAT'S NEW. SO HOW MANY ARE WE DEALING WITH?
MY SCANNERS PICK UP TWENTY BETWEEN HERE AND BATTERY PARK. EIGHTEEN MORE UPTOWN. EVERYONE FAN OUT.
THOR, SPIDER-WOMAN, WE'LL HIT 'EM HIGH. HAWKEYE, CAP, WOLVERINE, YOU HIT 'EM LOW. SPIDEY, TALK US THROUGH IT.

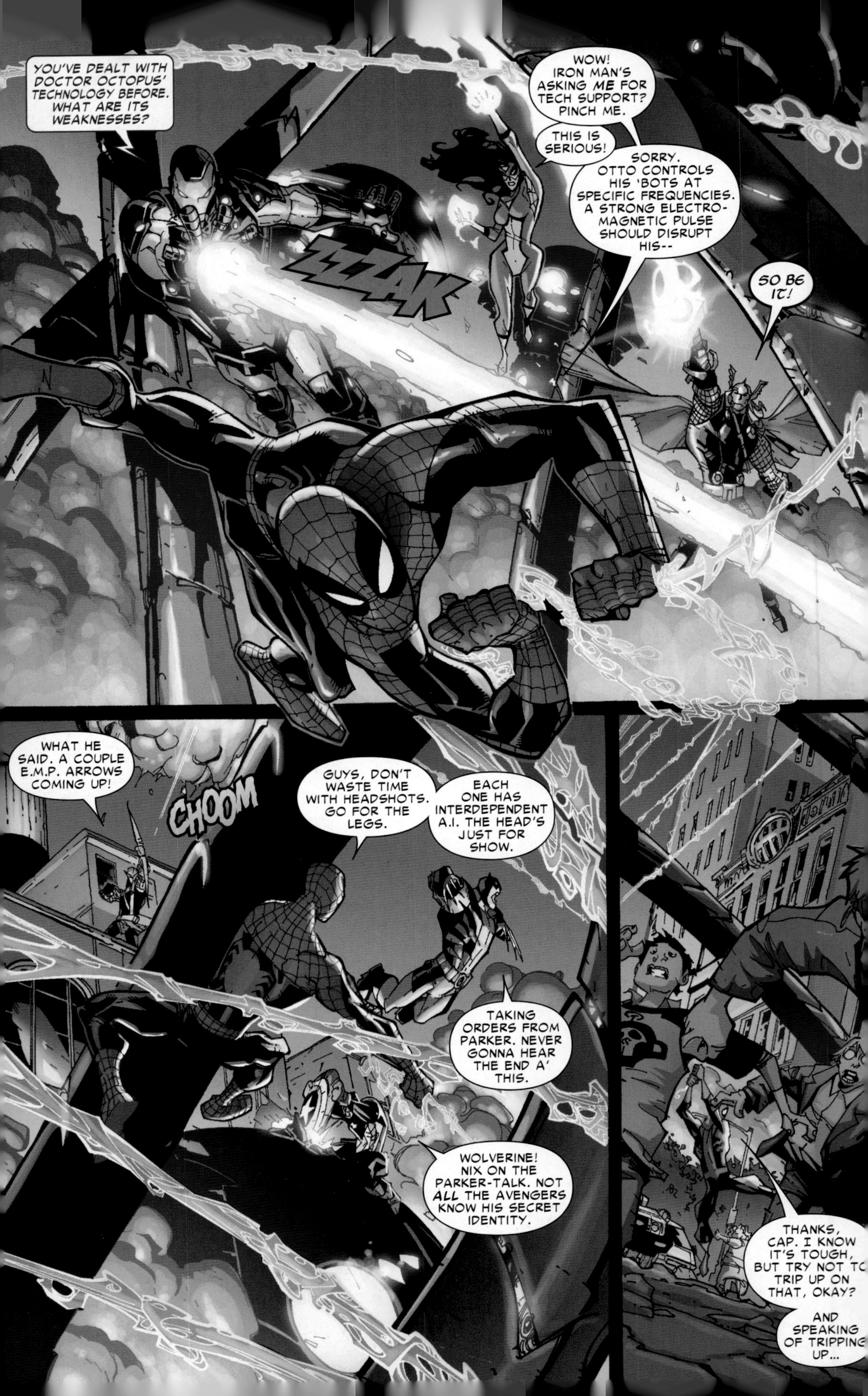
YOU'VE DEALT WITH DOCTOR OCTOPUS' TECHNOLOGY BEFORE. WHAT ARE ITS WEAKNESSES?
WOW! IRON MAN'S ASKING ME FOR TECH SUPPORT? PINCH ME.
THIS IS SERIOUS!
SORRY. OTTO CONTROLS HIS 'BOTS AT SPECIFIC FREQUENCIES. A STRONG ELECTRO-MAGNETIC PULSE SHOULD DISRUPT HIS--
ZZZAK
SO BE IT!
WHAT HE SAID. A COUPLE E.M.P. ARROWS COMING UP!
CHOOM
GUYS, DON'T WASTE TIME WITH HEADSHOTS. GO FOR THE LEGS.
EACH ONE HAS INTERDEPENDENT A.I. THE HEAD'S JUST FOR SHOW.
TAKING ORDERS FROM PARKER. NEVER GONNA HEAR THE END A' THIS.
WOLVERINE! NIX ON THE PARKER-TALK. NOT ALL THE AVENGERS KNOW HIS SECRET IDENTITY.
THANKS, CAP. I KNOW IT'S TOUGH, BUT TRY NOT TO TRIP UP ON THAT, OKAY?
AND SPEAKING OF TRIPPING UP...

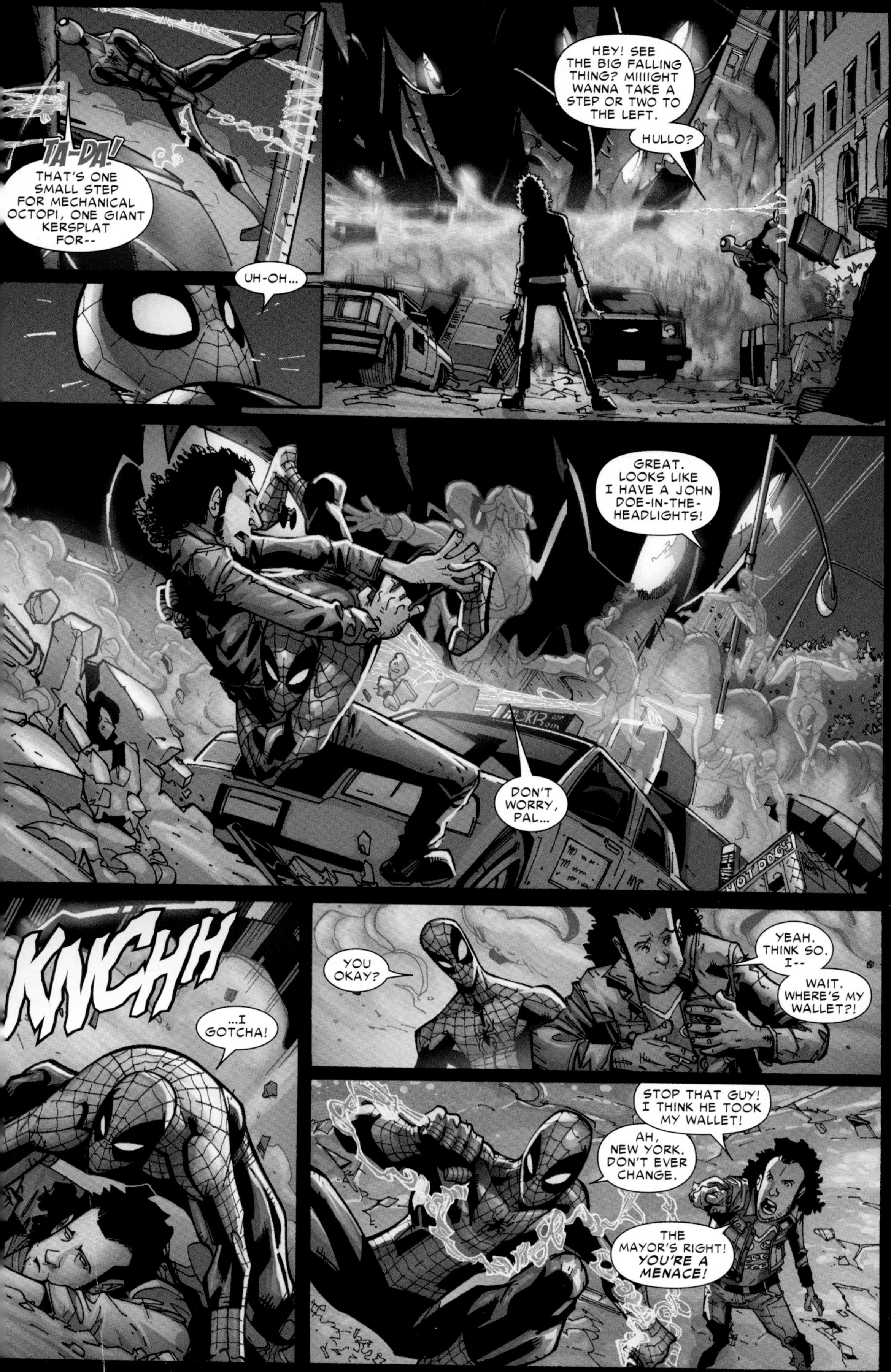
TA-DA!
THAT'S ONE SMALL STEP FOR MECHANICAL OCTOPI, ONE GIANT KERSPLAT FOR--
UH-OH...
HEY! SEE THE BIG FALLING THING? MIIIIGHT WANNA TAKE A STEP OR TWO TO THE LEFT.
HULLO?
GREAT. LOOKS LIKE I HAVE A JOHN DOE-IN-THE-HEADLIGHTS!
DON'T WORRY, PAL...
HOT DOGS
KNCHH
...I GOTCHA!
YOU OKAY?
YEAH. THINK SO. I--
WAIT. WHERE'S MY WALLET?!
STOP THAT GUY! I THINK HE TOOK MY WALLET!
AH, NEW YORK. DON'T EVER CHANGE.
THE MAYOR'S RIGHT! *YOU'RE A MENACE!*

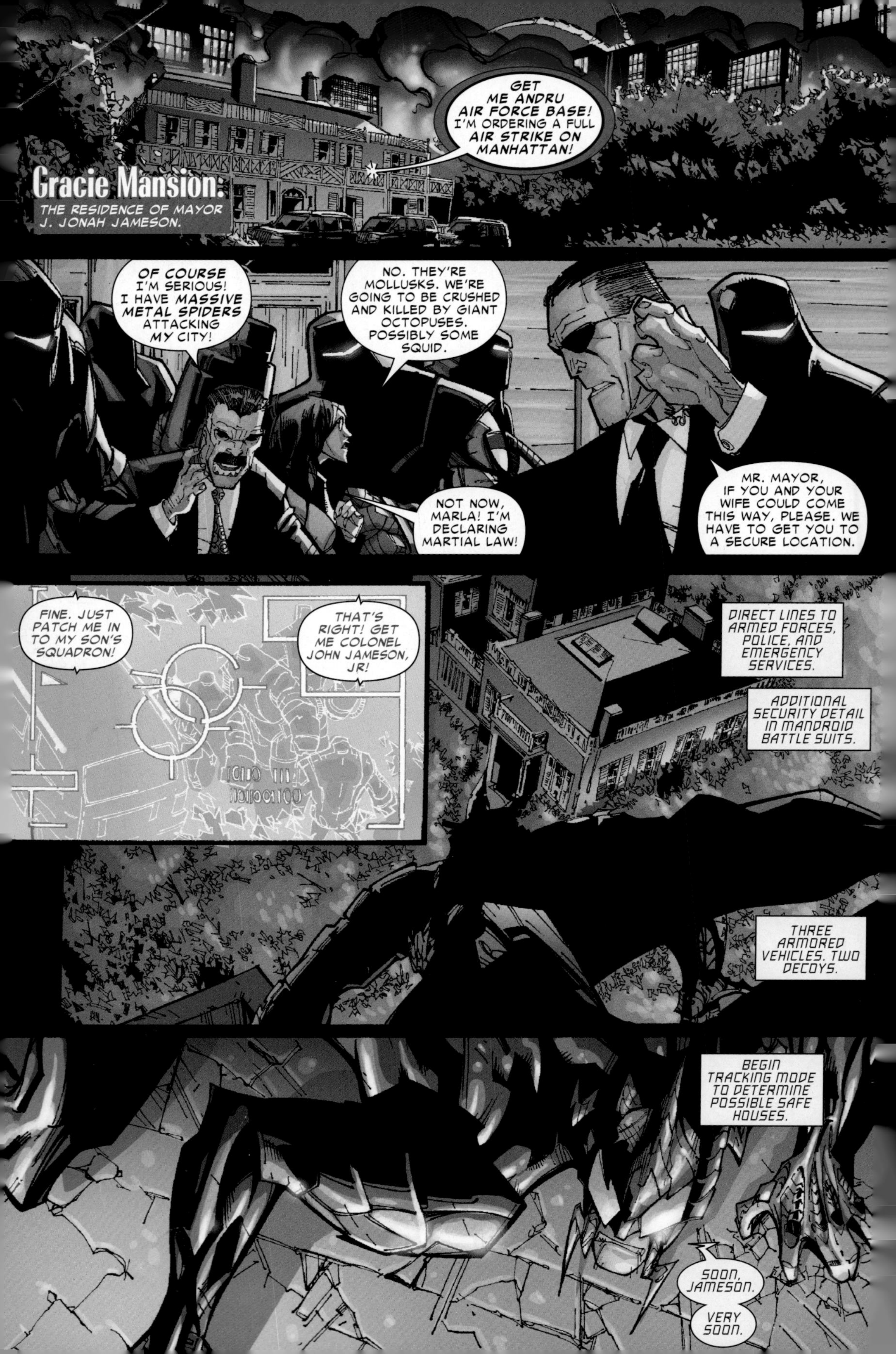
Gracie Mansion:
THE RESIDENCE OF MAYOR J. JONAH JAMESON.
GET ME ANDRU AIR FORCE BASE! I'M ORDERING A FULL AIR STRIKE ON MANHATTAN!
OF COURSE I'M SERIOUS! I HAVE MASSIVE METAL SPIDERS ATTACKING MY CITY!
NO. THEY'RE MOLLUSKS. WE'RE GOING TO BE CRUSHED AND KILLED BY GIANT OCTOPUSES. POSSIBLY SOME SQUID.
NOT NOW, MARLA! I'M DECLARING MARTIAL LAW!
MR. MAYOR, IF YOU AND YOUR WIFE COULD COME THIS WAY, PLEASE. WE HAVE TO GET YOU TO A SECURE LOCATION.
FINE. JUST PATCH ME IN TO MY SON'S SQUADRON!
THAT'S RIGHT! GET ME COLONEL JOHN JAMESON, JR!
DIRECT LINES TO ARMED FORCES, POLICE, AND EMERGENCY SERVICES.
ADDITIONAL SECURITY DETAIL IN MANDROID BATTLE SUITS.
THREE ARMORED VEHICLES. TWO DECOYS.
BEGIN TRACKING MODE TO DETERMINE POSSIBLE SAFE HOUSES.
SOON, JAMESON.
VERY SOON.

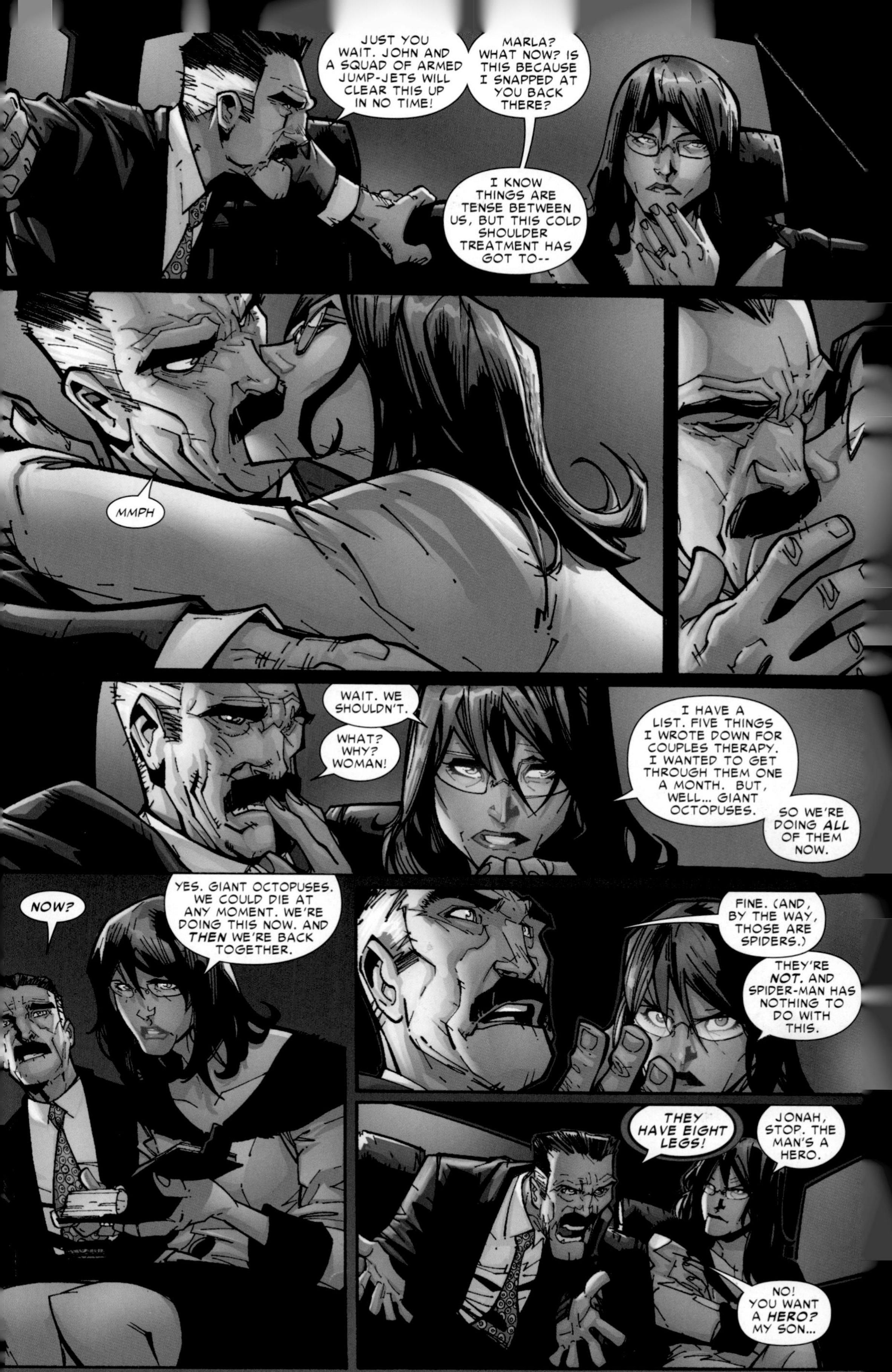
JUST YOU WAIT. JOHN AND A SQUAD OF ARMED JUMP-JETS WILL CLEAR THIS UP IN NO TIME!
MARLA? WHAT NOW? IS THIS BECAUSE I SNAPPED AT YOU BACK THERE?
I KNOW THINGS ARE TENSE BETWEEN US, BUT THIS COLD SHOULDER TREATMENT HAS GOT TO--
MMPH
WAIT. WE SHOULDN'T.
WHAT? WHY? WOMAN!
I HAVE A LIST. FIVE THINGS I WROTE DOWN FOR COUPLES THERAPY. I WANTED TO GET THROUGH THEM ONE A MONTH. BUT, WELL... GIANT OCTOPUSES.
SO WE'RE DOING ALL OF THEM NOW.
NOW?
YES. GIANT OCTOPUSES. WE COULD DIE AT ANY MOMENT. WE'RE DOING THIS NOW. AND THEN WE'RE BACK TOGETHER.
FINE. (AND, BY THE WAY, THOSE ARE SPIDERS.)
THEY'RE NOT. AND SPIDER-MAN HAS NOTHING TO DO WITH THIS.
THEY HAVE EIGHT LEGS!
JONAH, STOP. THE MAN'S A HERO.
NO! YOU WANT A HERO? MY SON...

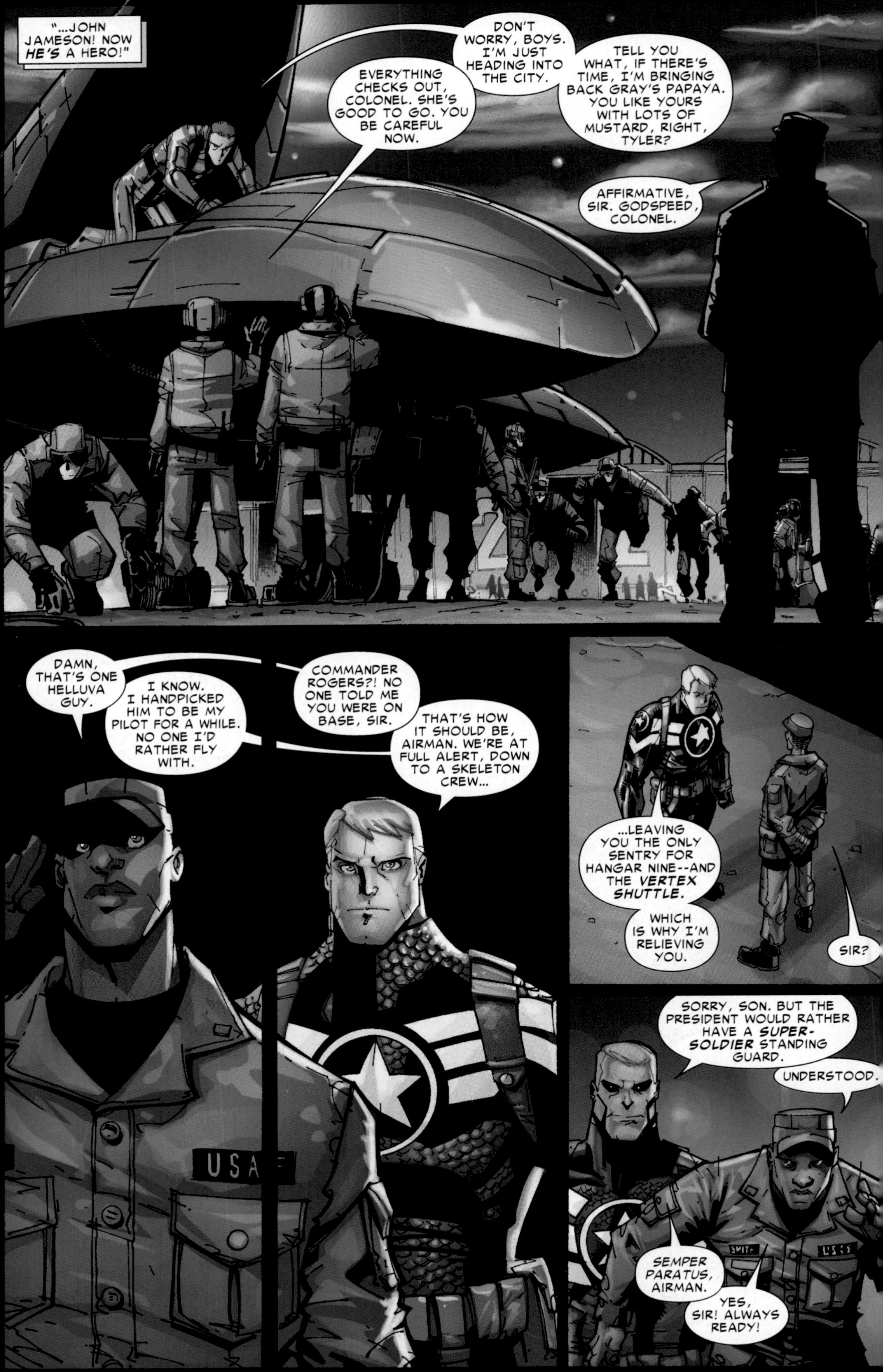
"...JOHN JAMESON! NOW HE'S A HERO!"
EVERYTHING CHECKS OUT, COLONEL. SHE'S GOOD TO GO. YOU BE CAREFUL NOW.
DON'T WORRY, BOYS. I'M JUST HEADING INTO THE CITY.
TELL YOU WHAT, IF THERE'S TIME, I'M BRINGING BACK GRAY'S PAPAYA. YOU LIKE YOURS WITH LOTS OF MUSTARD, RIGHT, TYLER?
AFFIRMATIVE, SIR. GODSPEED, COLONEL.
DAMN, THAT'S ONE HELLUVA GUY.
I KNOW. I HANDPICKED HIM TO BE MY PILOT FOR A WHILE. NO ONE I'D RATHER FLY WITH.
COMMANDER ROGERS?! NO ONE TOLD ME YOU WERE ON BASE, SIR.
THAT'S HOW IT SHOULD BE, AIRMAN. WE'RE AT FULL ALERT, DOWN TO A SKELETON CREW...
USA
...LEAVING YOU THE ONLY SENTRY FOR HANGAR NINE--AND THE VERTEX SHUTTLE.
WHICH IS WHY I'M RELIEVING YOU.
SIR?
SORRY, SON. BUT THE PRESIDENT WOULD RATHER HAVE A SUPER-SOLDIER STANDING GUARD.
UNDERSTOOD.
SEMPER PARATUS, AIRMAN.
YES, SIR! ALWAYS READY!

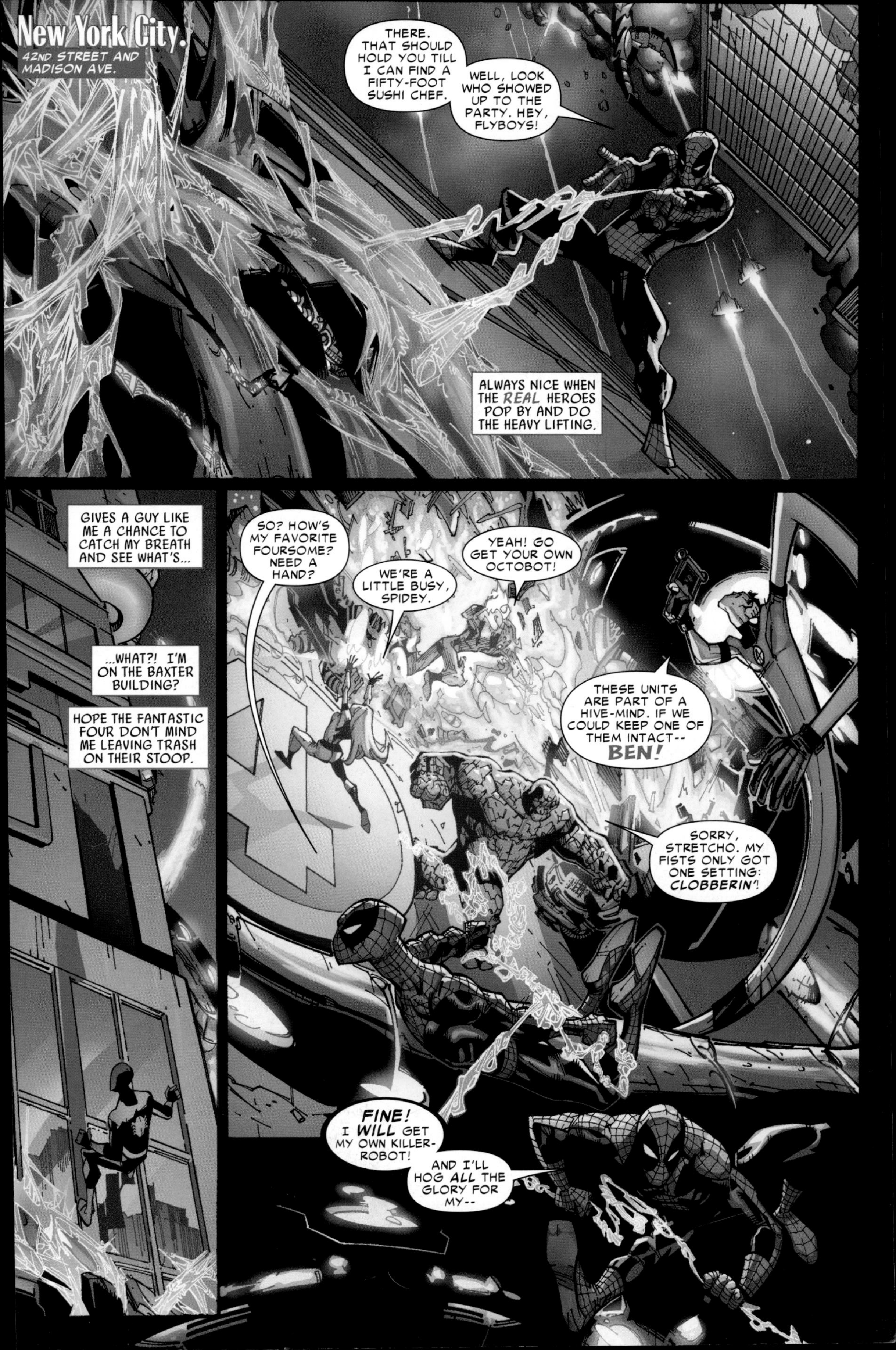
New York City.
42ND STREET AND MADISON AVE.
THERE. THAT SHOULD HOLD YOU TILL I CAN FIND A FIFTY-FOOT SUSHI CHEF.
WELL, LOOK WHO SHOWED UP TO THE PARTY. HEY, FLYBOYS!
ALWAYS NICE WHEN THE REAL HEROES POP BY AND DO THE HEAVY LIFTING.
GIVES A GUY LIKE ME A CHANCE TO CATCH MY BREATH AND SEE WHAT'S...
...WHAT?! I'M ON THE BAXTER BUILDING?
HOPE THE FANTASTIC FOUR DON'T MIND ME LEAVING TRASH ON THEIR STOOP.
SO? HOW'S MY FAVORITE FOURSOME? NEED A HAND?
WE'RE A LITTLE BUSY, SPIDEY.
YEAH! GO GET YOUR OWN OCTOBOT!
THESE UNITS ARE PART OF A HIVE-MIND. IF WE COULD KEEP ONE OF THEM INTACT-- BEN!
SORRY, STRETCHO. MY FISTS ONLY GOT ONE SETTING: CLOBBERIN'!
FINE! I WILL GET MY OWN KILLER-ROBOT!
AND I'LL HOG ALL THE GLORY FOR MY--

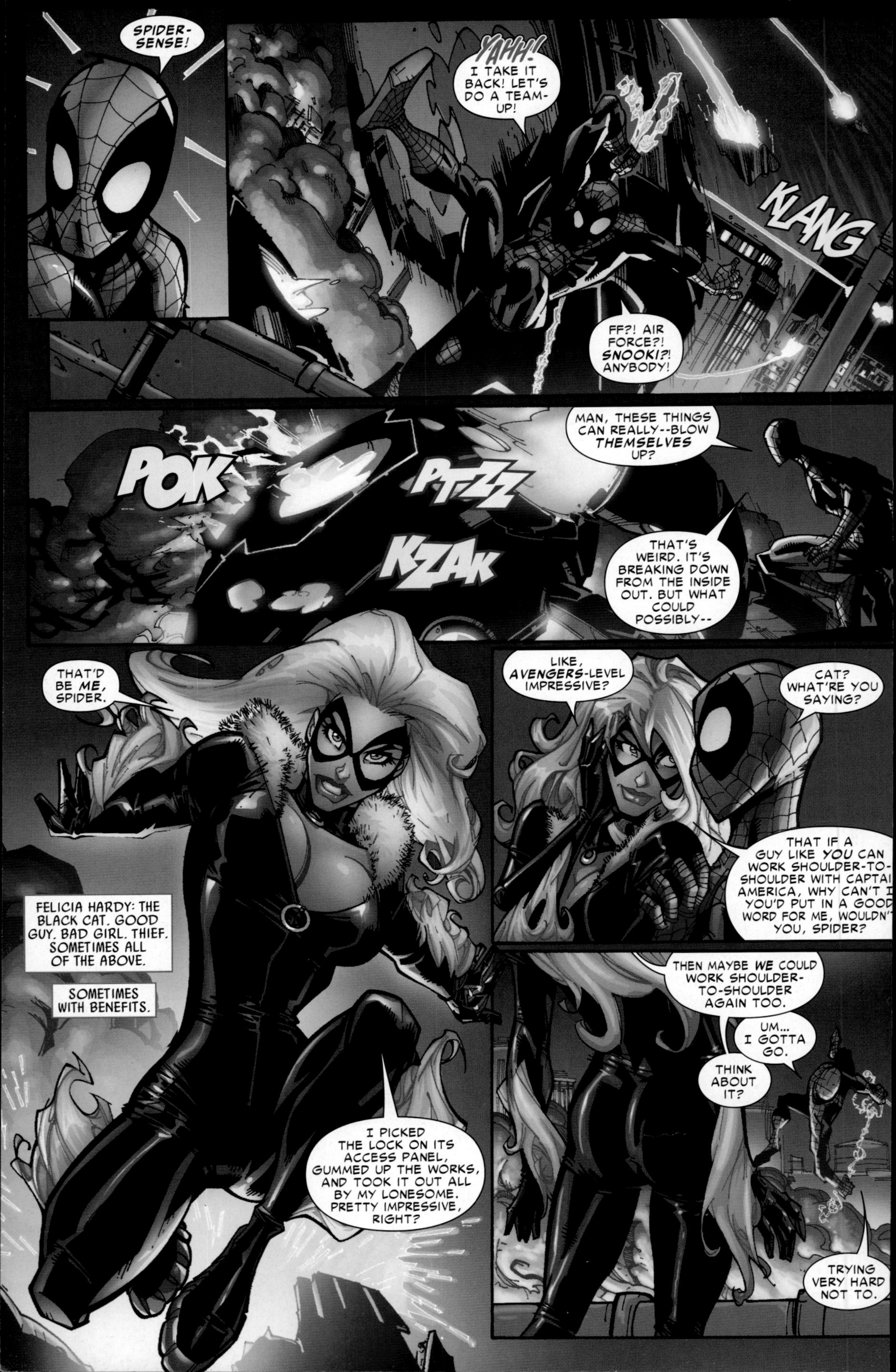
SPIDER-SENSE!
YAHH! I TAKE IT BACK! LET'S DO A TEAM-UP!
KLANG
FF?! AIR FORCE?! SNOOKI?! ANYBODY!
POK
PTZZZ
KZAK
MAN, THESE THINGS CAN REALLY--BLOW THEMSELVES UP?
THAT'S WEIRD. IT'S BREAKING DOWN FROM THE INSIDE OUT. BUT WHAT COULD POSSIBLY--
THAT'D BE ME, SPIDER.
FELICIA HARDY: THE BLACK CAT. GOOD GUY. BAD GIRL. THIEF. SOMETIMES ALL OF THE ABOVE.
SOMETIMES WITH BENEFITS.
I PICKED THE LOCK ON ITS ACCESS PANEL, GUMMED UP THE WORKS, AND TOOK IT OUT ALL BY MY LONESOME. PRETTY IMPRESSIVE, RIGHT?
LIKE, AVENGERS-LEVEL IMPRESSIVE?
CAT? WHAT'RE YOU SAYING?
THAT IF A GUY LIKE YOU CAN WORK SHOULDER-TO-SHOULDER WITH CAPTAI AMERICA, WHY CAN'T I YOU'D PUT IN A GOOD WORD FOR ME, WOULDN' YOU, SPIDER?
THEN MAYBE WE COULD WORK SHOULDER-TO-SHOULDER AGAIN TOO.
UM... I GOTTA GO.
THINK ABOUT IT?
TRYING VERY HARD NOT TO.

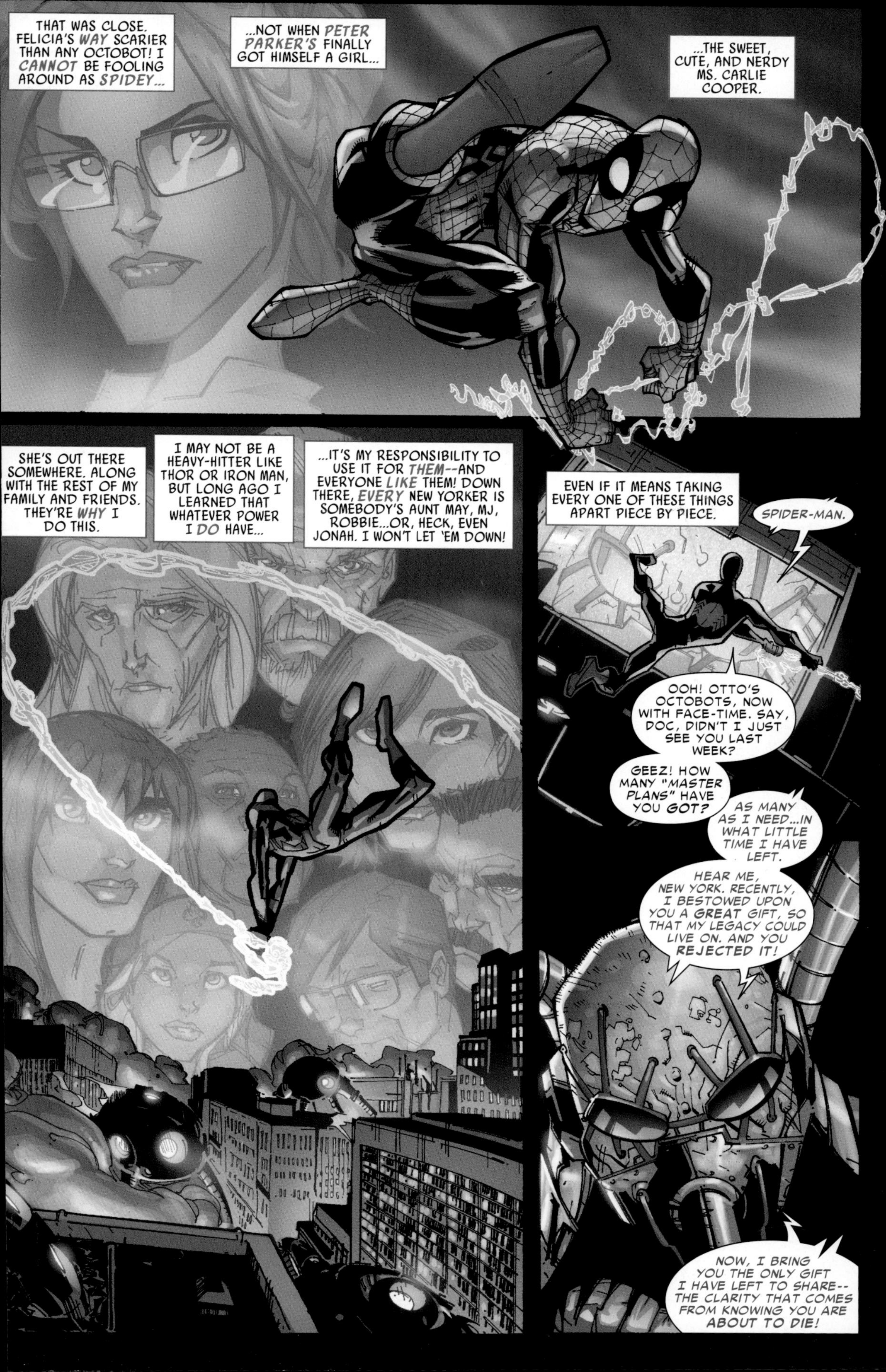
THAT WAS CLOSE. FELICIA'S WAY SCARIER THAN ANY OCTOBOT! I CANNOT BE FOOLING AROUND AS SPIDEY...
...NOT WHEN PETER PARKER'S FINALLY GOT HIMSELF A GIRL...
...THE SWEET, CUTE, AND NERDY MS. CARLIE COOPER.
SHE'S OUT THERE SOMEWHERE. ALONG WITH THE REST OF MY FAMILY AND FRIENDS. THEY'RE WHY I DO THIS.
I MAY NOT BE A HEAVY-HITTER LIKE THOR OR IRON MAN, BUT LONG AGO I LEARNED THAT WHATEVER POWER I DO HAVE...
...IT'S MY RESPONSIBILITY TO USE IT FOR THEM--AND EVERYONE LIKE THEM! DOWN THERE, EVERY NEW YORKER IS SOMEBODY'S AUNT MAY, MJ, ROBBIE...OR, HECK, EVEN JONAH. I WON'T LET 'EM DOWN!
EVEN IF IT MEANS TAKING EVERY ONE OF THESE THINGS APART PIECE BY PIECE.
SPIDER-MAN.
OOH! OTTO'S OCTOBOTS, NOW WITH FACE-TIME. SAY, DOC, DIDN'T I JUST SEE YOU LAST WEEK?
GEEZ! HOW MANY "MASTER PLANS" HAVE YOU GOT?
AS MANY AS I NEED...IN WHAT LITTLE TIME I HAVE LEFT.
HEAR ME, NEW YORK. RECENTLY, I BESTOWED UPON YOU A GREAT GIFT, SO THAT MY LEGACY COULD LIVE ON. AND YOU REJECTED IT!
NOW, I BRING YOU THE ONLY GIFT I HAVE LEFT TO SHARE--THE CLARITY THAT COMES FROM KNOWING YOU ARE ABOUT TO DIE!

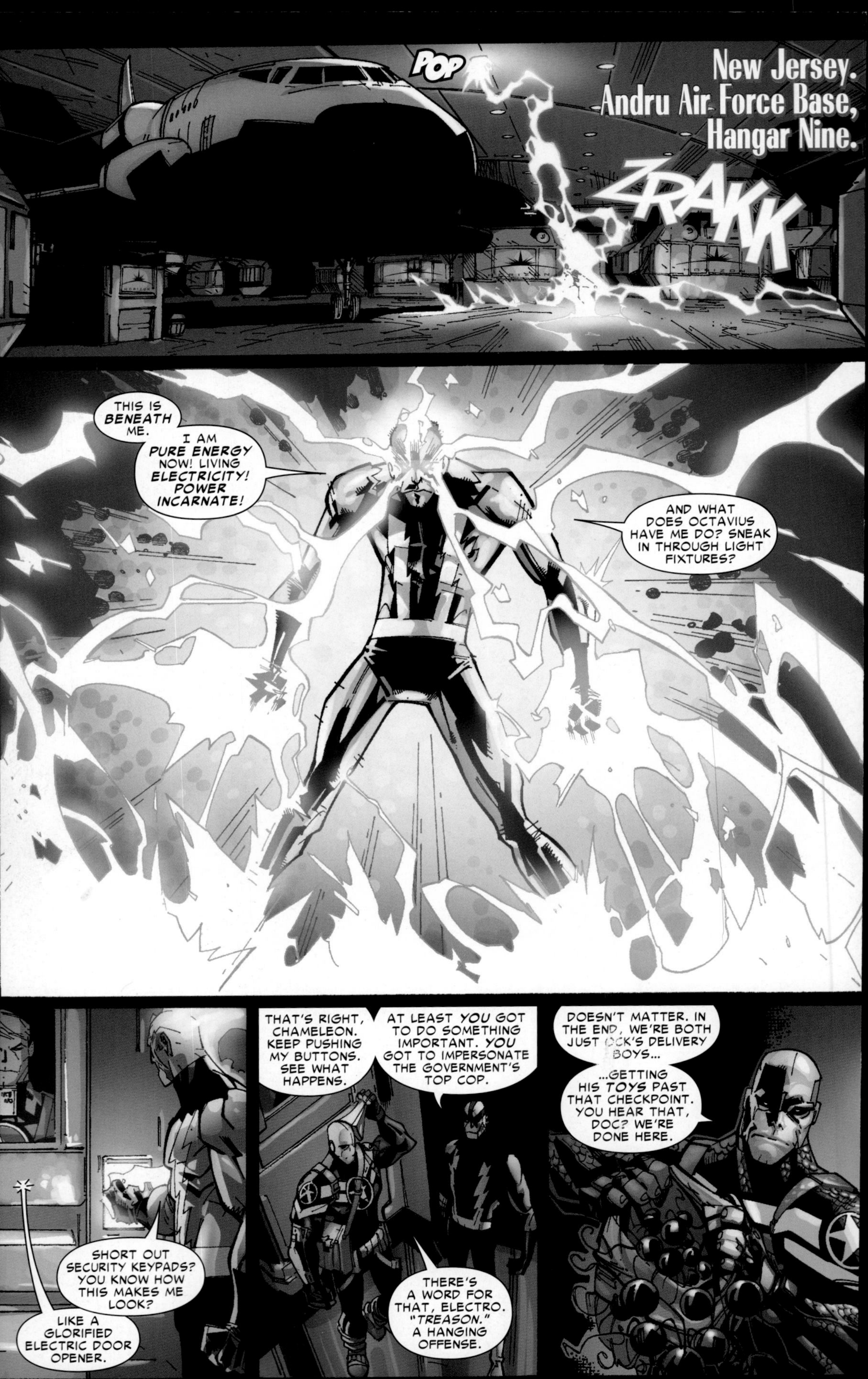
POP
New Jersey. Andru Air Force Base, Hangar Nine.
ZRAKK
THIS IS *BENEATH* ME.
I AM *PURE ENERGY* NOW! LIVING *ELECTRICITY*! *POWER INCARNATE*!
AND WHAT DOES OCTAVIUS HAVE ME DO? SNEAK IN THROUGH LIGHT FIXTURES?
SHORT OUT SECURITY KEYPADS? YOU KNOW HOW THIS MAKES ME LOOK?
LIKE A GLORIFIED ELECTRIC DOOR OPENER.
THAT'S RIGHT, CHAMELEON. KEEP PUSHING MY BUTTONS. SEE WHAT HAPPENS.
AT LEAST *YOU* GOT TO DO SOMETHING IMPORTANT. *YOU* GOT TO IMPERSONATE THE GOVERNMENT'S TOP COP.
THERE'S A WORD FOR THAT, ELECTRO. "*TREASON*." A HANGING OFFENSE.
DOESN'T MATTER. IN THE END, WE'RE BOTH JUST OCK'S DELIVERY BOYS...
...GETTING HIS *TOYS* PAST THAT CHECKPOINT. YOU HEAR THAT, DOC? WE'RE DONE HERE.

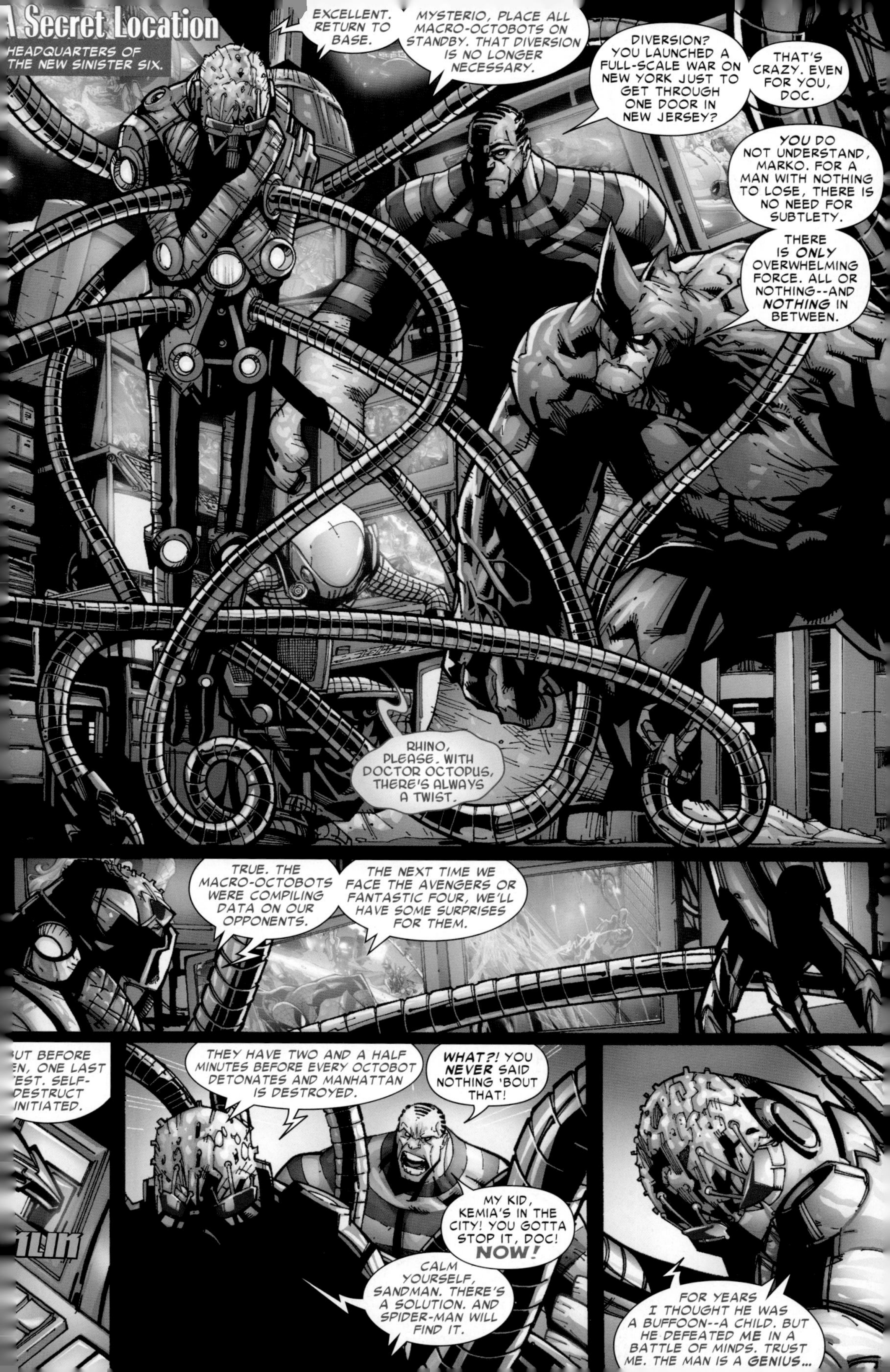
A Secret Location
HEADQUARTERS OF THE NEW SINISTER SIX.
EXCELLENT. RETURN TO BASE.
MYSTERIO, PLACE ALL MACRO-OCTOBOTS ON STANDBY. THAT DIVERSION IS NO LONGER NECESSARY.
DIVERSION? YOU LAUNCHED A FULL-SCALE WAR ON NEW YORK JUST TO GET THROUGH ONE DOOR IN NEW JERSEY?
THAT'S CRAZY. EVEN FOR YOU, DOC.
YOU DO NOT UNDERSTAND, MARKO. FOR A MAN WITH NOTHING TO LOSE, THERE IS NO NEED FOR SUBTLETY.
THERE IS ONLY OVERWHELMING FORCE. ALL OR NOTHING--AND NOTHING IN BETWEEN.
RHINO, PLEASE. WITH DOCTOR OCTOPUS, THERE'S ALWAYS A TWIST.
TRUE. THE MACRO-OCTOBOTS WERE COMPILING DATA ON OUR OPPONENTS.
THE NEXT TIME WE FACE THE AVENGERS OR FANTASTIC FOUR, WE'LL HAVE SOME SURPRISES FOR THEM.
UT BEFORE EN, ONE LAST TEST. SELF-DESTRUCT INITIATED.
THEY HAVE TWO AND A HALF MINUTES BEFORE EVERY OCTOBOT DETONATES AND MANHATTAN IS DESTROYED.
WHAT?! YOU NEVER SAID NOTHING 'BOUT THAT!
MY KID, KEMIA'S IN THE CITY! YOU GOTTA STOP IT, DOC! NOW!
CALM YOURSELF, SANDMAN. THERE'S A SOLUTION. AND SPIDER-MAN WILL FIND IT.
FOR YEARS I THOUGHT HE WAS A BUFFOON--A CHILD. BUT HE DEFEATED ME IN A BATTLE OF MINDS. TRUST ME. THE MAN IS A GENIUS...

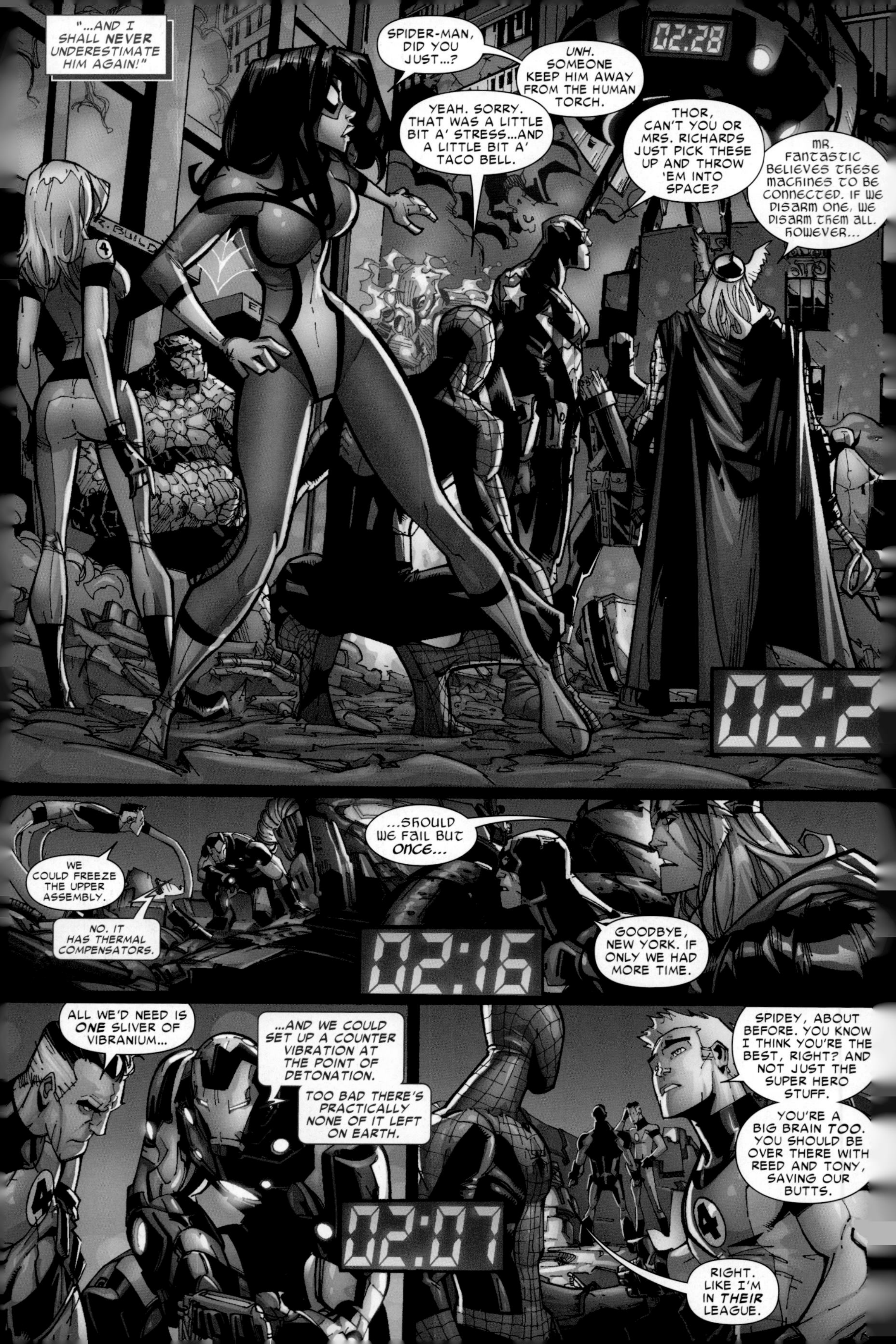
"...AND I SHALL NEVER UNDERESTIMATE HIM AGAIN!"
02:28
SPIDER-MAN, DID YOU JUST...?
UNH. SOMEONE KEEP HIM AWAY FROM THE HUMAN TORCH.
YEAH. SORRY. THAT WAS A LITTLE BIT A' STRESS...AND A LITTLE BIT A' TACO BELL.
THOR, CAN'T YOU OR MRS. RICHARDS JUST PICK THESE UP AND THROW 'EM INTO SPACE?
MR. FANTASTIC BELIEVES THESE MACHINES TO BE CONNECTED. IF WE DISARM ONE, WE DISARM THEM ALL. HOWEVER...
WE COULD FREEZE THE UPPER ASSEMBLY.
NO. IT HAS THERMAL COMPENSATORS.
...SHOULD WE FAIL BUT ONCE...
GOODBYE, NEW YORK. IF ONLY WE HAD MORE TIME.
02:16
ALL WE'D NEED IS ONE SLIVER OF VIBRANIUM...
...AND WE COULD SET UP A COUNTER VIBRATION AT THE POINT OF DETONATION.
TOO BAD THERE'S PRACTICALLY NONE OF IT LEFT ON EARTH.
02:07
SPIDEY, ABOUT BEFORE. YOU KNOW I THINK YOU'RE THE BEST, RIGHT? AND NOT JUST THE SUPER HERO STUFF.
YOU'RE A BIG BRAIN TOO. YOU SHOULD BE OVER THERE WITH REED AND TONY, SAVING OUR BUTTS.
RIGHT. LIKE I'M IN THEIR LEAGUE.

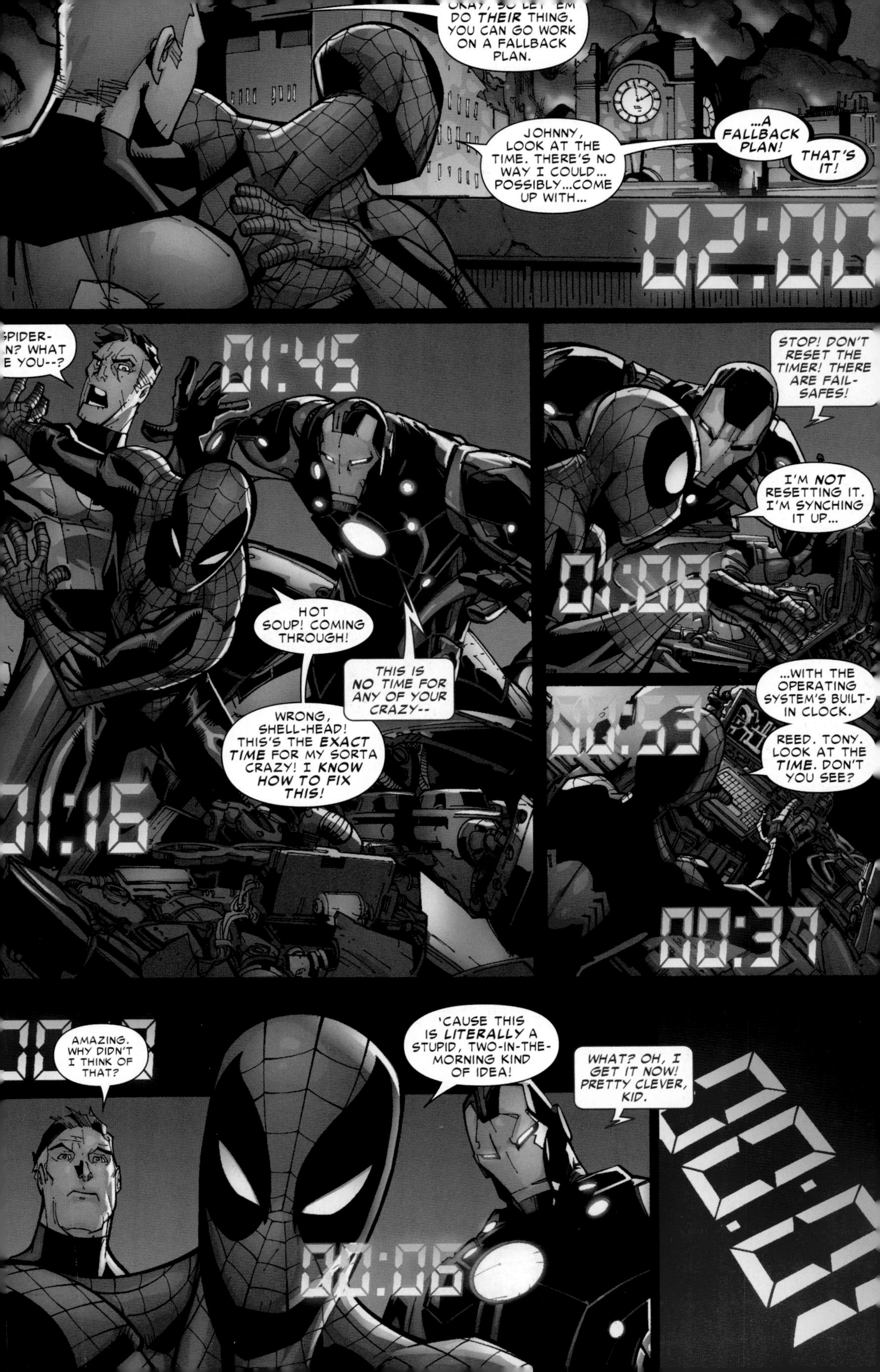
OKAY, SO LET 'EM DO THEIR THING. YOU CAN GO WORK ON A FALLBACK PLAN.
JOHNNY, LOOK AT THE TIME. THERE'S NO WAY I COULD... POSSIBLY...COME UP WITH...
...A FALLBACK PLAN!
THAT'S IT!
02:00
SPIDER-MAN? WHAT ARE YOU--?
01:45
HOT SOUP! COMING THROUGH!
THIS IS NO TIME FOR ANY OF YOUR CRAZY--
WRONG, SHELL-HEAD! THIS'S THE EXACT TIME FOR MY SORTA CRAZY! I KNOW HOW TO FIX THIS!
01:16
STOP! DON'T RESET THE TIMER! THERE ARE FAIL-SAFES!
I'M NOT RESETTING IT. I'M SYNCHING IT UP...
01:08
...WITH THE OPERATING SYSTEM'S BUILT-IN CLOCK.
REED. TONY. LOOK AT THE TIME. DON'T YOU SEE?
00:37
AMAZING. WHY DIDN'T I THINK OF THAT?
'CAUSE THIS IS LITERALLY A STUPID, TWO-IN-THE-MORNING KIND OF IDEA!
WHAT? OH, I GET IT NOW! PRETTY CLEVER, KID.
00:06

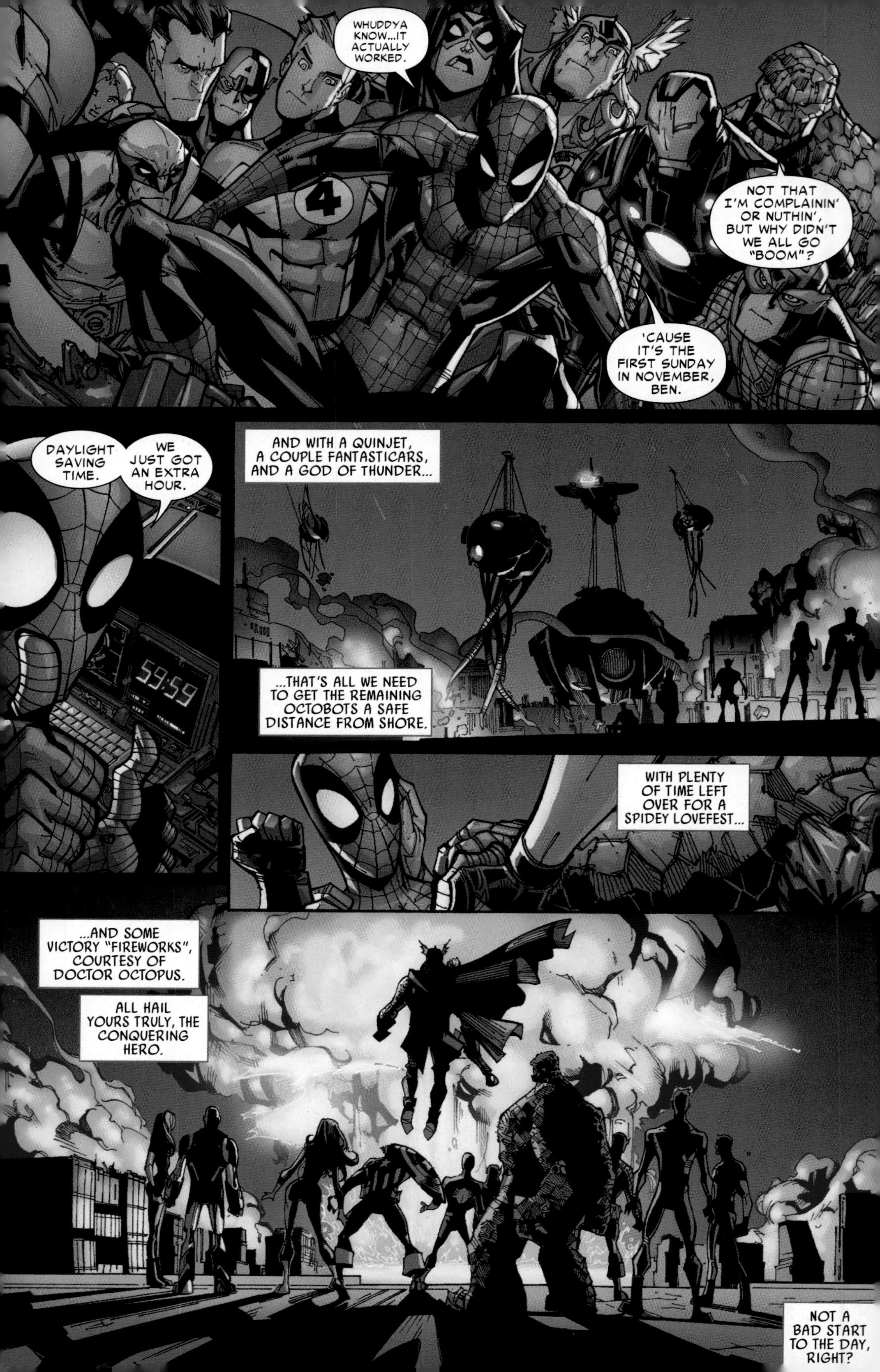
WHUDDYA KNOW...IT ACTUALLY WORKED.
NOT THAT I'M COMPLAININ' OR NUTHIN', BUT WHY DIDN'T WE ALL GO "BOOM"?
'CAUSE IT'S THE FIRST SUNDAY IN NOVEMBER, BEN.
DAYLIGHT SAVING TIME.
WE JUST GOT AN EXTRA HOUR.
59:59
AND WITH A QUINJET, A COUPLE FANTASTICARS, AND A GOD OF THUNDER...
...THAT'S ALL WE NEED TO GET THE REMAINING OCTOBOTS A SAFE DISTANCE FROM SHORE.
WITH PLENTY OF TIME LEFT OVER FOR A SPIDEY LOVEFEST...
...AND SOME VICTORY "FIREWORKS", COURTESY OF DOCTOR OCTOPUS.
ALL HAIL YOURS TRULY, THE CONQUERING HERO.
NOT A BAD START TO THE DAY, RIGHT?

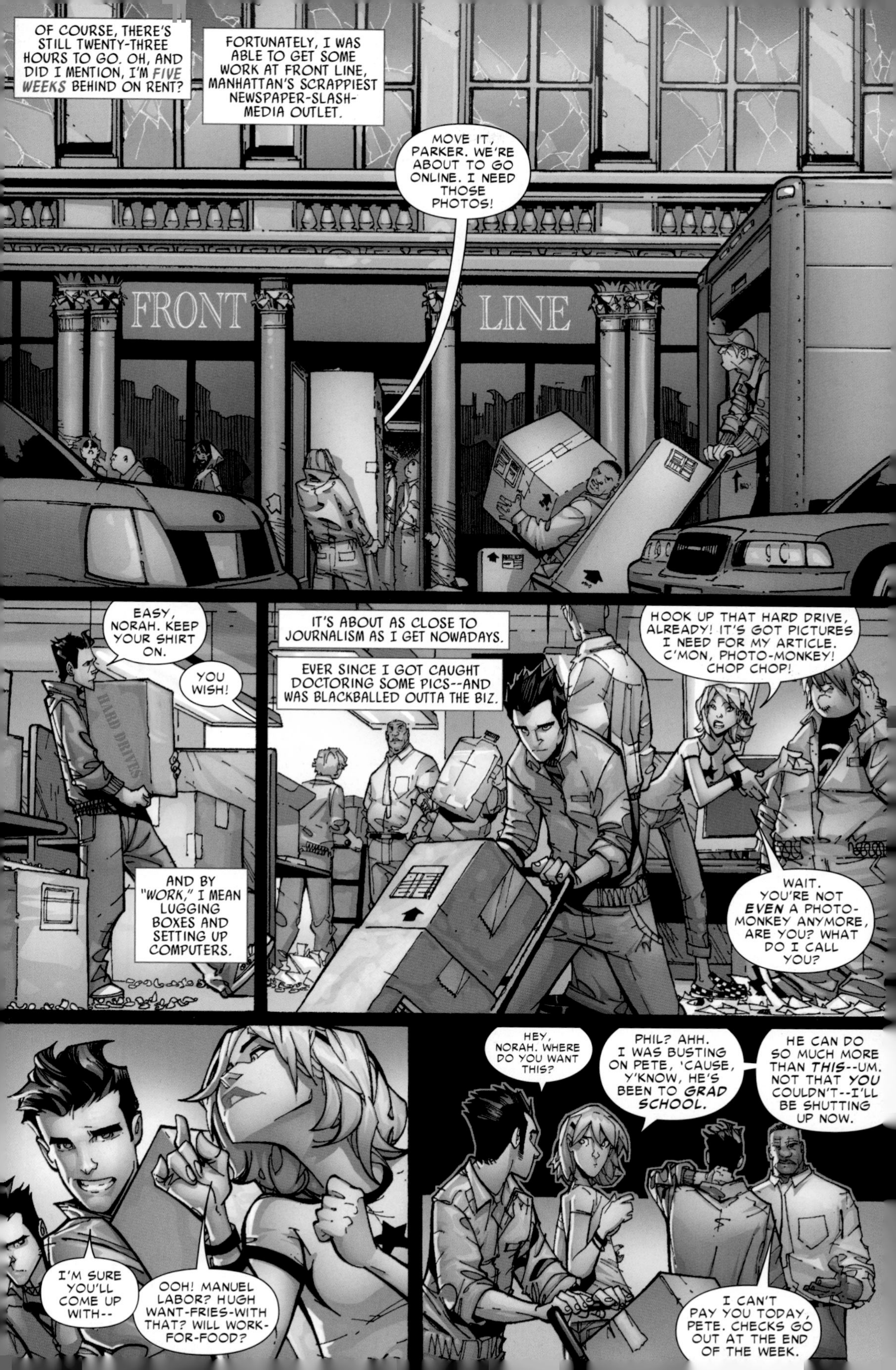

OF COURSE, THERE'S STILL TWENTY-THREE HOURS TO GO. OH, AND DID I MENTION, I'M *FIVE WEEKS* BEHIND ON RENT?
FORTUNATELY, I WAS ABLE TO GET SOME WORK AT FRONT LINE, MANHATTAN'S SCRAPPIEST NEWSPAPER-SLASH-MEDIA OUTLET.
MOVE IT, PARKER. WE'RE ABOUT TO GO ONLINE. I NEED THOSE PHOTOS!
FRONT LINE
EASY, NORAH. KEEP YOUR SHIRT ON.
YOU WISH!
HARD DRIVES
AND BY "*WORK*," I MEAN LUGGING BOXES AND SETTING UP COMPUTERS.
IT'S ABOUT AS CLOSE TO JOURNALISM AS I GET NOWADAYS.
EVER SINCE I GOT CAUGHT DOCTORING SOME PICS--AND WAS BLACKBALLED OUTTA THE BIZ.
HOOK UP THAT HARD DRIVE, ALREADY! IT'S GOT PICTURES I NEED FOR MY ARTICLE. C'MON, PHOTO-MONKEY! CHOP CHOP!
WAIT. YOU'RE NOT *EVEN* A PHOTO-MONKEY ANYMORE, ARE YOU? WHAT DO I CALL YOU?
I'M SURE YOU'LL COME UP WITH--
OOH! MANUEL LABOR? HUGH WANT-FRIES-WITH THAT? WILL WORK-FOR-FOOD?
HEY, NORAH. WHERE DO YOU WANT THIS?
PHIL? AHH. I WAS BUSTING ON PETE, 'CAUSE, Y'KNOW, HE'S BEEN TO *GRAD SCHOOL.*
HE CAN DO SO MUCH MORE THAN *THIS*--UM. NOT THAT *YOU* COULDN'T--I'LL BE SHUTTING UP NOW.
I CAN'T PAY YOU TODAY, PETE. CHECKS GO OUT AT THE END OF THE WEEK.

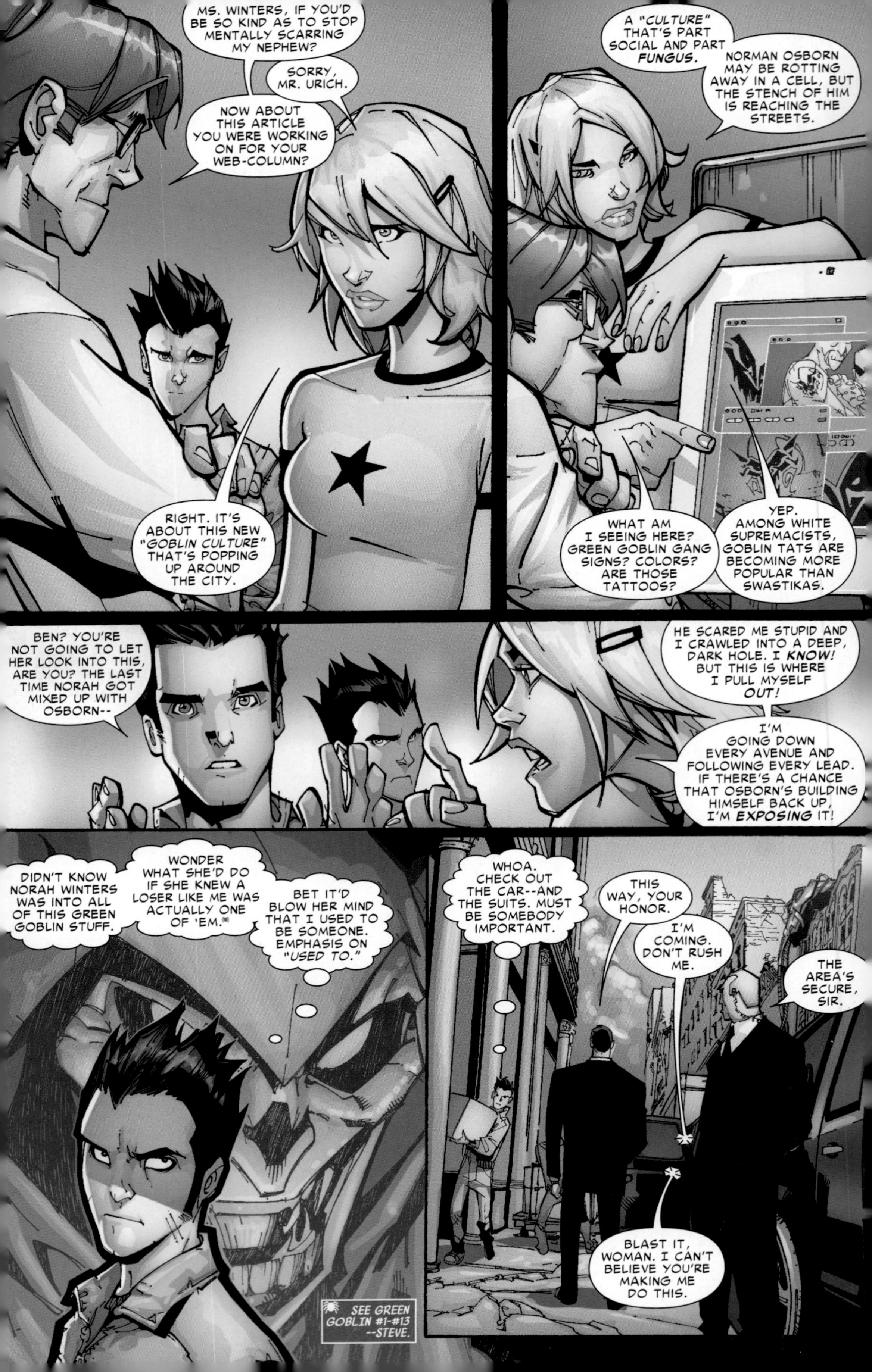
MS. WINTERS, IF YOU'D BE SO KIND AS TO STOP MENTALLY SCARRING MY NEPHEW?
SORRY, MR. URICH.
NOW ABOUT THIS ARTICLE YOU WERE WORKING ON FOR YOUR WEB-COLUMN?
RIGHT. IT'S ABOUT THIS NEW "GOBLIN CULTURE" THAT'S POPPING UP AROUND THE CITY.
A "CULTURE" THAT'S PART SOCIAL AND PART FUNGUS.
NORMAN OSBORN MAY BE ROTTING AWAY IN A CELL, BUT THE STENCH OF HIM IS REACHING THE STREETS.
WHAT AM I SEEING HERE? GREEN GOBLIN GANG SIGNS? COLORS? ARE THOSE TATTOOS?
YEP. AMONG WHITE SUPREMACISTS, GOBLIN TATS ARE BECOMING MORE POPULAR THAN SWASTIKAS.
BEN? YOU'RE NOT GOING TO LET HER LOOK INTO THIS, ARE YOU? THE LAST TIME NORAH GOT MIXED UP WITH OSBORN--
HE SCARED ME STUPID AND I CRAWLED INTO A DEEP, DARK HOLE. I KNOW! BUT THIS IS WHERE I PULL MYSELF OUT!
I'M GOING DOWN EVERY AVENUE AND FOLLOWING EVERY LEAD. IF THERE'S A CHANCE THAT OSBORN'S BUILDING HIMSELF BACK UP, I'M EXPOSING IT!
DIDN'T KNOW NORAH WINTERS WAS INTO ALL OF THIS GREEN GOBLIN STUFF.
WONDER WHAT SHE'D DO IF SHE KNEW A LOSER LIKE ME WAS ACTUALLY ONE OF 'EM.*
BET IT'D BLOW HER MIND THAT I USED TO BE SOMEONE. EMPHASIS ON "USED TO."
*SEE GREEN GOBLIN #1-#13 --STEVE.
WHOA. CHECK OUT THE CAR--AND THE SUITS. MUST BE SOMEBODY IMPORTANT.
THIS WAY, YOUR HONOR.
I'M COMING. DON'T RUSH ME.
THE AREA'S SECURE, SIR.
BLAST IT, WOMAN. I CAN'T BELIEVE YOU'RE MAKING ME DO THIS.

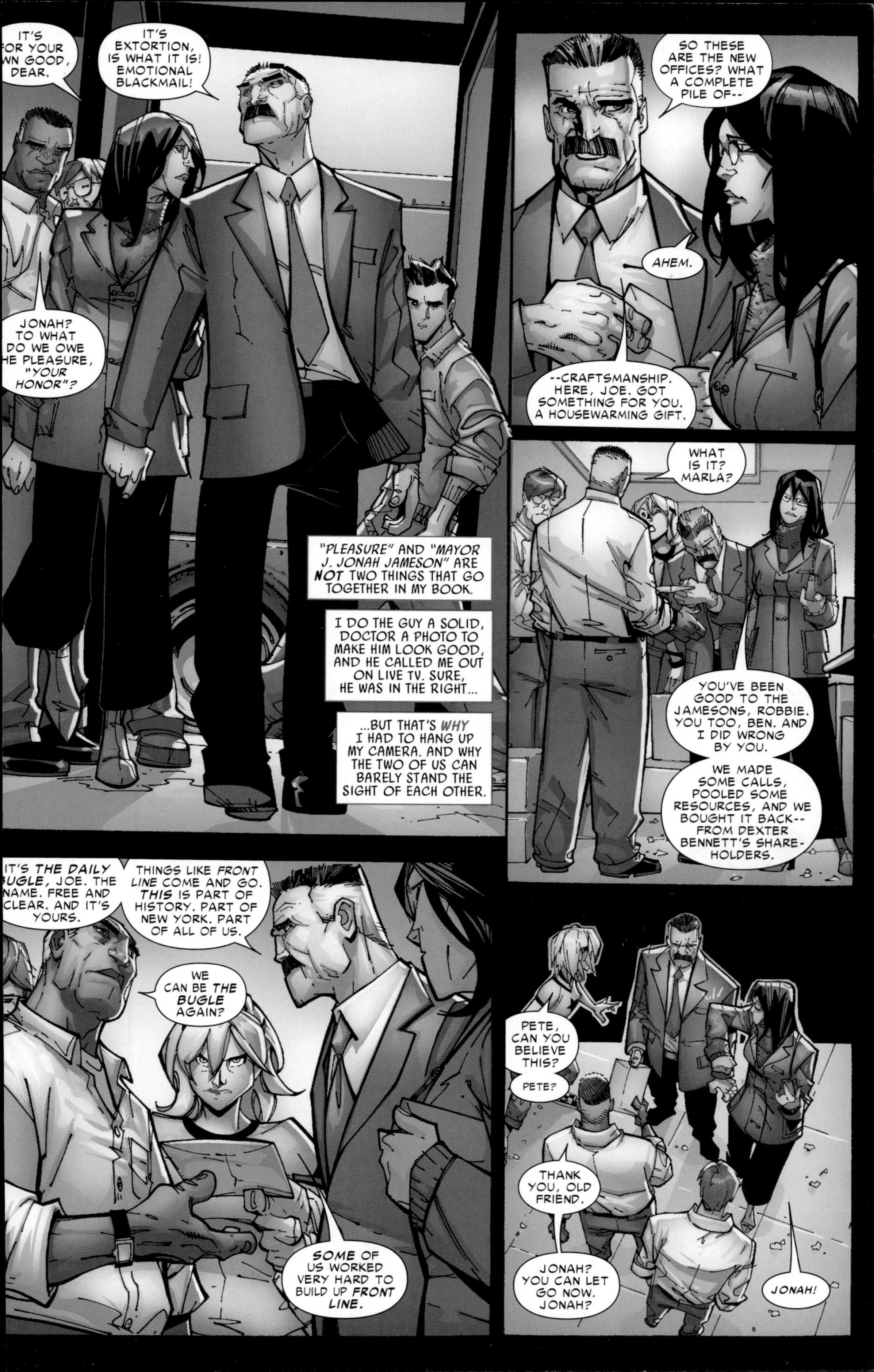

IT'S FOR YOUR OWN GOOD, DEAR.
IT'S EXTORTION, IS WHAT IT IS! EMOTIONAL BLACKMAIL!
JONAH? TO WHAT DO WE OWE THE PLEASURE, "YOUR HONOR"?
"PLEASURE" AND "MAYOR J. JONAH JAMESON" ARE NOT TWO THINGS THAT GO TOGETHER IN MY BOOK.
I DO THE GUY A SOLID, DOCTOR A PHOTO TO MAKE HIM LOOK GOOD, AND HE CALLED ME OUT ON LIVE TV. SURE, HE WAS IN THE RIGHT...
...BUT THAT'S WHY I HAD TO HANG UP MY CAMERA. AND WHY THE TWO OF US CAN BARELY STAND THE SIGHT OF EACH OTHER.
SO THESE ARE THE NEW OFFICES? WHAT A COMPLETE PILE OF--
AHEM.
--CRAFTSMANSHIP. HERE, JOE. GOT SOMETHING FOR YOU. A HOUSEWARMING GIFT.
WHAT IS IT? MARLA?
YOU'VE BEEN GOOD TO THE JAMESONS, ROBBIE. YOU TOO, BEN. AND I DID WRONG BY YOU.
WE MADE SOME CALLS, POOLED SOME RESOURCES, AND WE BOUGHT IT BACK-- FROM DEXTER BENNETT'S SHARE-HOLDERS.
IT'S THE DAILY BUGLE, JOE. THE NAME. FREE AND CLEAR. AND IT'S YOURS.
THINGS LIKE FRONT LINE COME AND GO. THIS IS PART OF HISTORY. PART OF NEW YORK. PART OF ALL OF US.
WE CAN BE THE BUGLE AGAIN?
SOME OF US WORKED VERY HARD TO BUILD UP FRONT LINE.
PETE, CAN YOU BELIEVE THIS?
PETE?
THANK YOU, OLD FRIEND.
JONAH? YOU CAN LET GO NOW. JONAH?
JONAH!

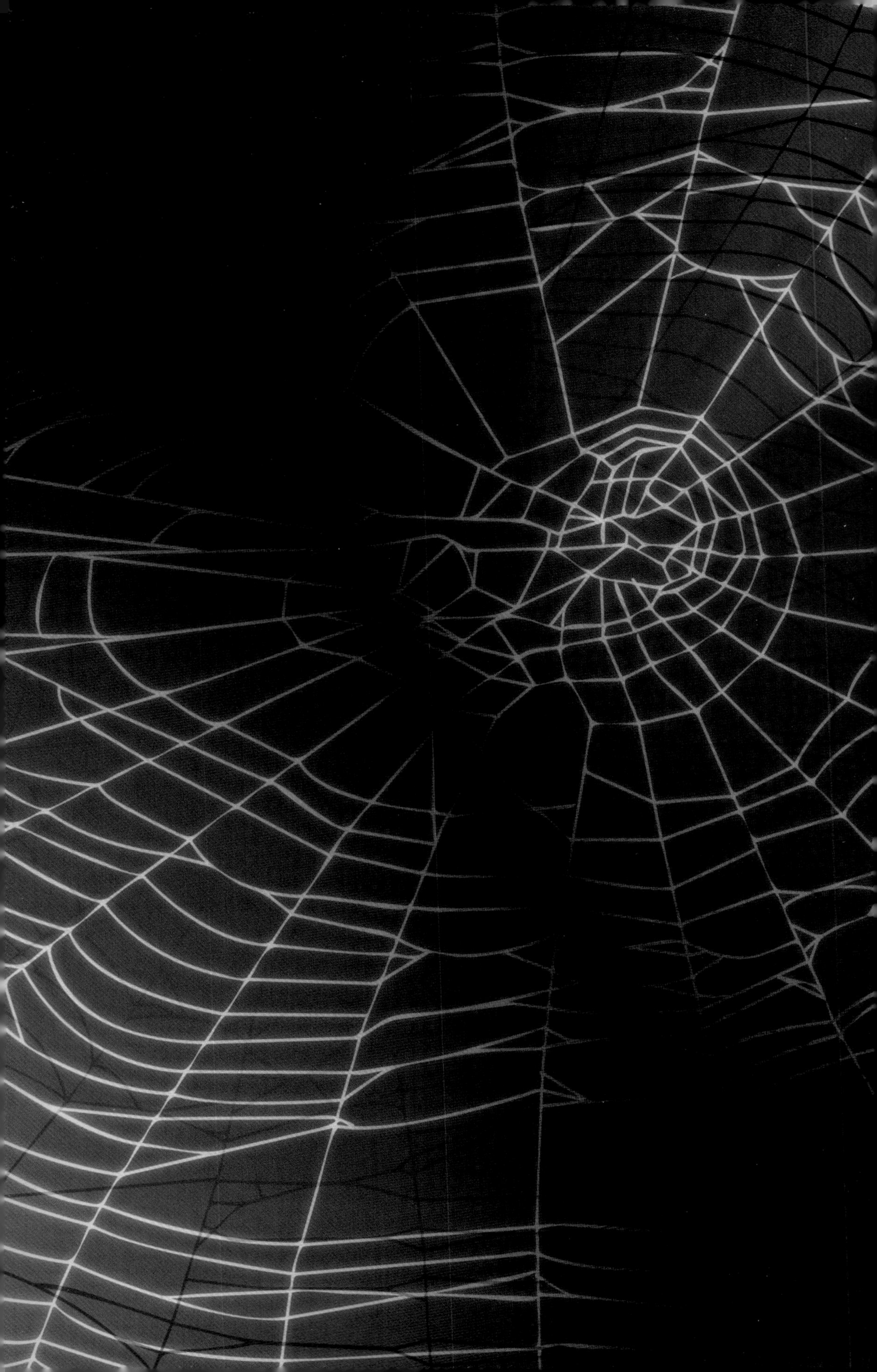

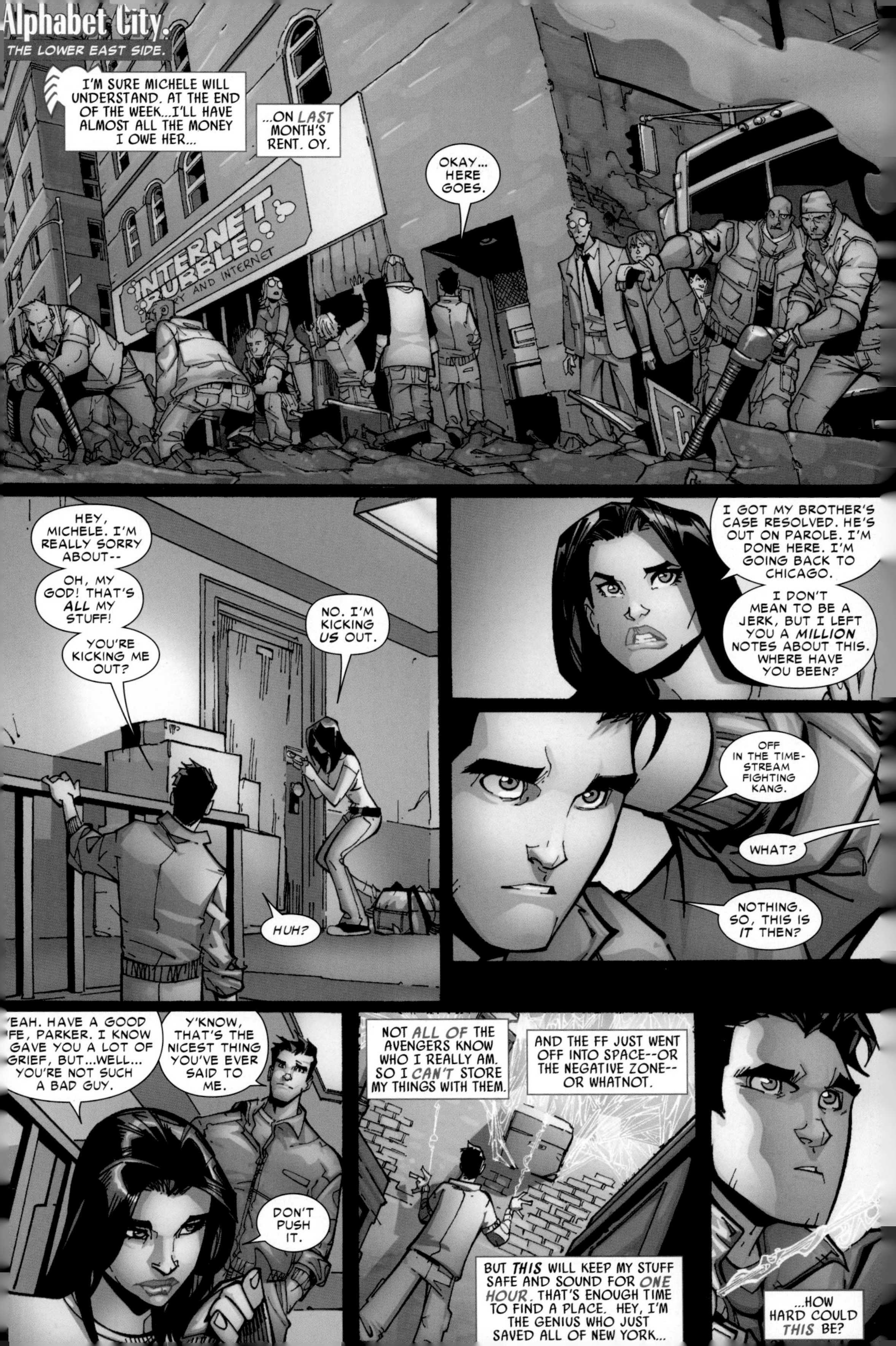
Alphabet City.
THE LOWER EAST SIDE.
I'M SURE MICHELE WILL UNDERSTAND. AT THE END OF THE WEEK...I'LL HAVE ALMOST ALL THE MONEY I OWE HER...
...ON LAST MONTH'S RENT. OY.
OKAY... HERE GOES.
INTERNET BUBBLE.
HEY, MICHELE. I'M REALLY SORRY ABOUT--
OH, MY GOD! THAT'S ALL MY STUFF!
YOU'RE KICKING ME OUT?
NO. I'M KICKING US OUT.
HUH?
I GOT MY BROTHER'S CASE RESOLVED. HE'S OUT ON PAROLE. I'M DONE HERE. I'M GOING BACK TO CHICAGO.
I DON'T MEAN TO BE A JERK, BUT I LEFT YOU A MILLION NOTES ABOUT THIS. WHERE HAVE YOU BEEN?
OFF IN THE TIME-STREAM FIGHTING KANG.
WHAT?
NOTHING. SO, THIS IS IT THEN?
YEAH. HAVE A GOOD LIFE, PARKER. I KNOW I GAVE YOU A LOT OF GRIEF, BUT...WELL... YOU'RE NOT SUCH A BAD GUY.
Y'KNOW, THAT'S THE NICEST THING YOU'VE EVER SAID TO ME.
DON'T PUSH IT.
NOT ALL OF THE AVENGERS KNOW WHO I REALLY AM. SO I CAN'T STORE MY THINGS WITH THEM.
AND THE FF JUST WENT OFF INTO SPACE--OR THE NEGATIVE ZONE--OR WHATNOT.
BUT THIS WILL KEEP MY STUFF SAFE AND SOUND FOR ONE HOUR. THAT'S ENOUGH TIME TO FIND A PLACE. HEY, I'M THE GENIUS WHO JUST SAVED ALL OF NEW YORK...
...HOW HARD COULD THIS BE?

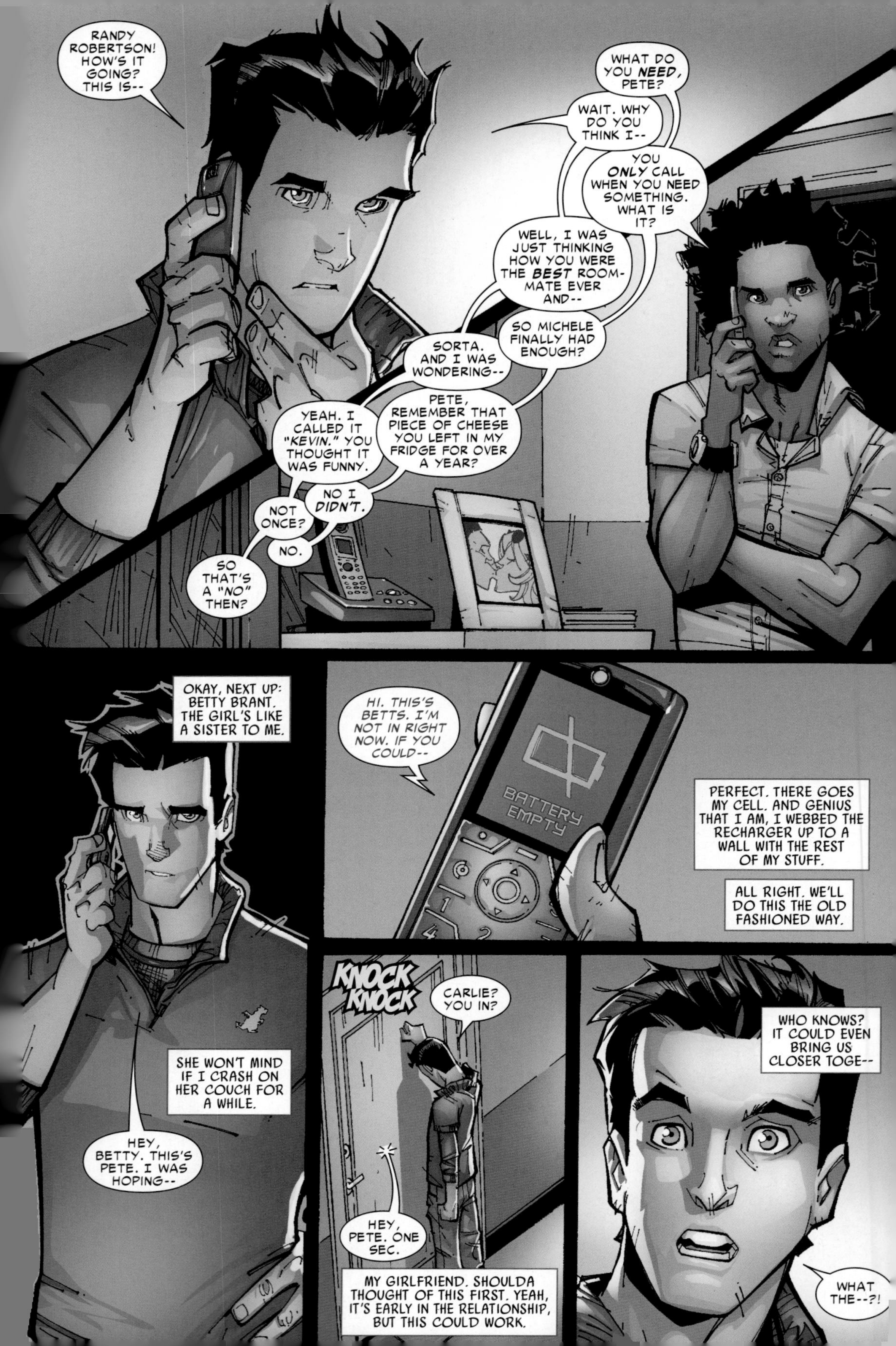
RANDY ROBERTSON! HOW'S IT GOING? THIS IS--
WHAT DO YOU NEED, PETE?
WAIT. WHY DO YOU THINK I--
YOU ONLY CALL WHEN YOU NEED SOMETHING. WHAT IS IT?
WELL, I WAS JUST THINKING HOW YOU WERE THE BEST ROOMMATE EVER AND--
SO MICHELE FINALLY HAD ENOUGH?
SORTA. AND I WAS WONDERING--
PETE, REMEMBER THAT PIECE OF CHEESE YOU LEFT IN MY FRIDGE FOR OVER A YEAR?
YEAH. I CALLED IT "KEVIN." YOU THOUGHT IT WAS FUNNY.
NO I DIDN'T.
NOT ONCE?
NO.
SO THAT'S A "NO" THEN?
OKAY, NEXT UP: BETTY BRANT. THE GIRL'S LIKE A SISTER TO ME.
SHE WON'T MIND IF I CRASH ON HER COUCH FOR A WHILE.
HEY, BETTY. THIS'S PETE. I WAS HOPING--
HI. THIS'S BETTS. I'M NOT IN RIGHT NOW. IF YOU COULD--
BATTERY EMPTY
PERFECT. THERE GOES MY CELL. AND GENIUS THAT I AM, I WEBBED THE RECHARGER UP TO A WALL WITH THE REST OF MY STUFF.
ALL RIGHT. WE'LL DO THIS THE OLD FASHIONED WAY.
KNOCK KNOCK
CARLIE? YOU IN?
HEY, PETE. ONE SEC.
MY GIRLFRIEND. SHOULDA THOUGHT OF THIS FIRST. YEAH, IT'S EARLY IN THE RELATIONSHIP, BUT THIS COULD WORK.
WHO KNOWS? IT COULD EVEN BRING US CLOSER TOGE--
WHAT THE--?!

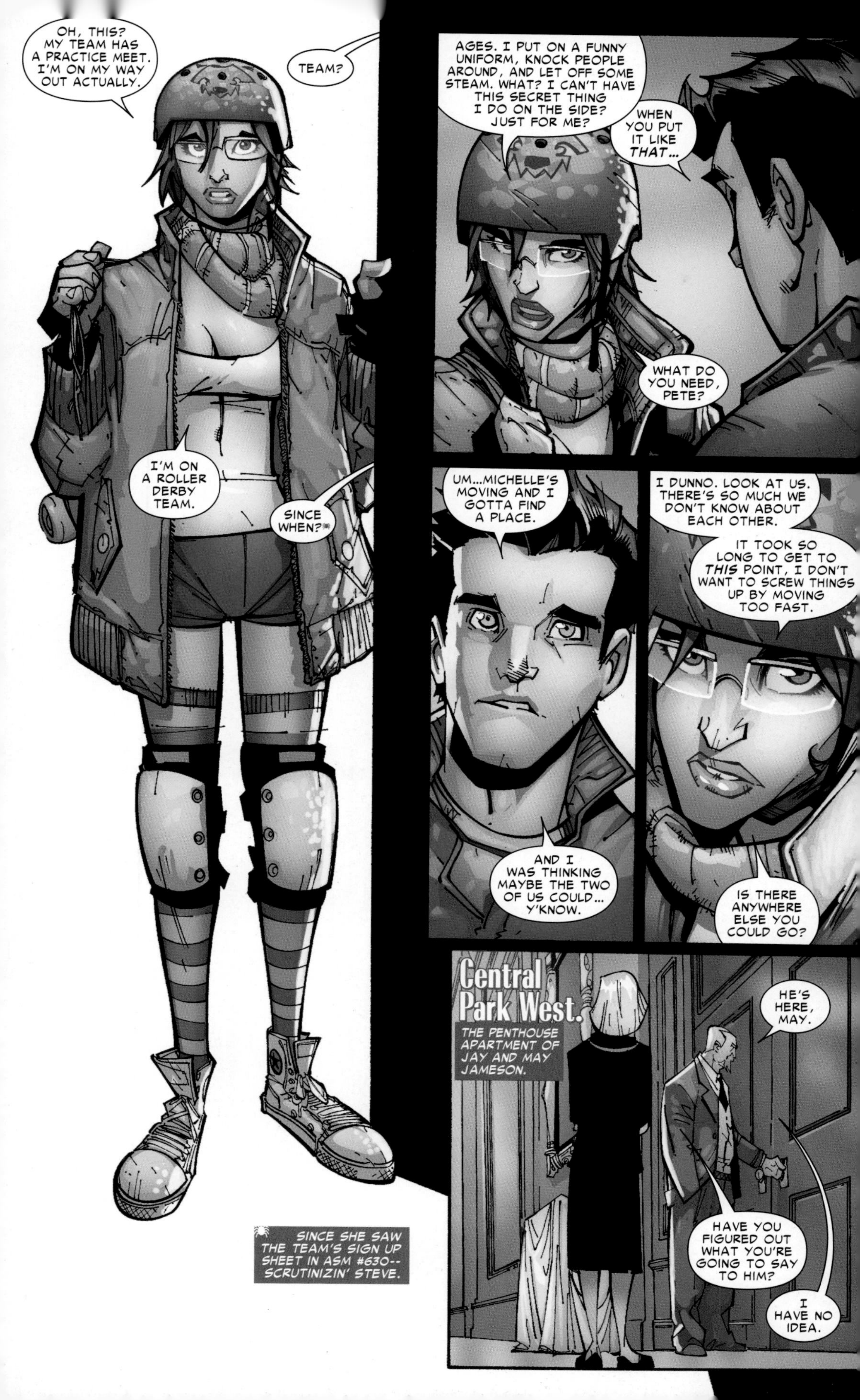
OH, THIS? MY TEAM HAS A PRACTICE MEET. I'M ON MY WAY OUT ACTUALLY.
TEAM?
I'M ON A ROLLER DERBY TEAM.
SINCE WHEN?
SINCE SHE SAW THE TEAM'S SIGN UP SHEET IN ASM #630-- SCRUTINIZIN' STEVE.
AGES. I PUT ON A FUNNY UNIFORM, KNOCK PEOPLE AROUND, AND LET OFF SOME STEAM. WHAT? I CAN'T HAVE THIS SECRET THING I DO ON THE SIDE? JUST FOR ME?
WHEN YOU PUT IT LIKE *THAT*...
WHAT DO YOU NEED, PETE?
UM...MICHELLE'S MOVING AND I GOTTA FIND A PLACE.
AND I WAS THINKING MAYBE THE TWO OF US COULD... Y'KNOW.
I DUNNO. LOOK AT US. THERE'S SO MUCH WE DON'T KNOW ABOUT EACH OTHER.
IT TOOK SO LONG TO GET TO ***THIS*** POINT, I DON'T WANT TO SCREW THINGS UP BY MOVING TOO FAST.
IS THERE ANYWHERE ELSE YOU COULD GO?
Central Park West.
THE PENTHOUSE APARTMENT OF JAY AND MAY JAMESON.
HE'S HERE, MAY.
HAVE YOU FIGURED OUT WHAT YOU'RE GOING TO SAY TO HIM?
I HAVE NO IDEA.

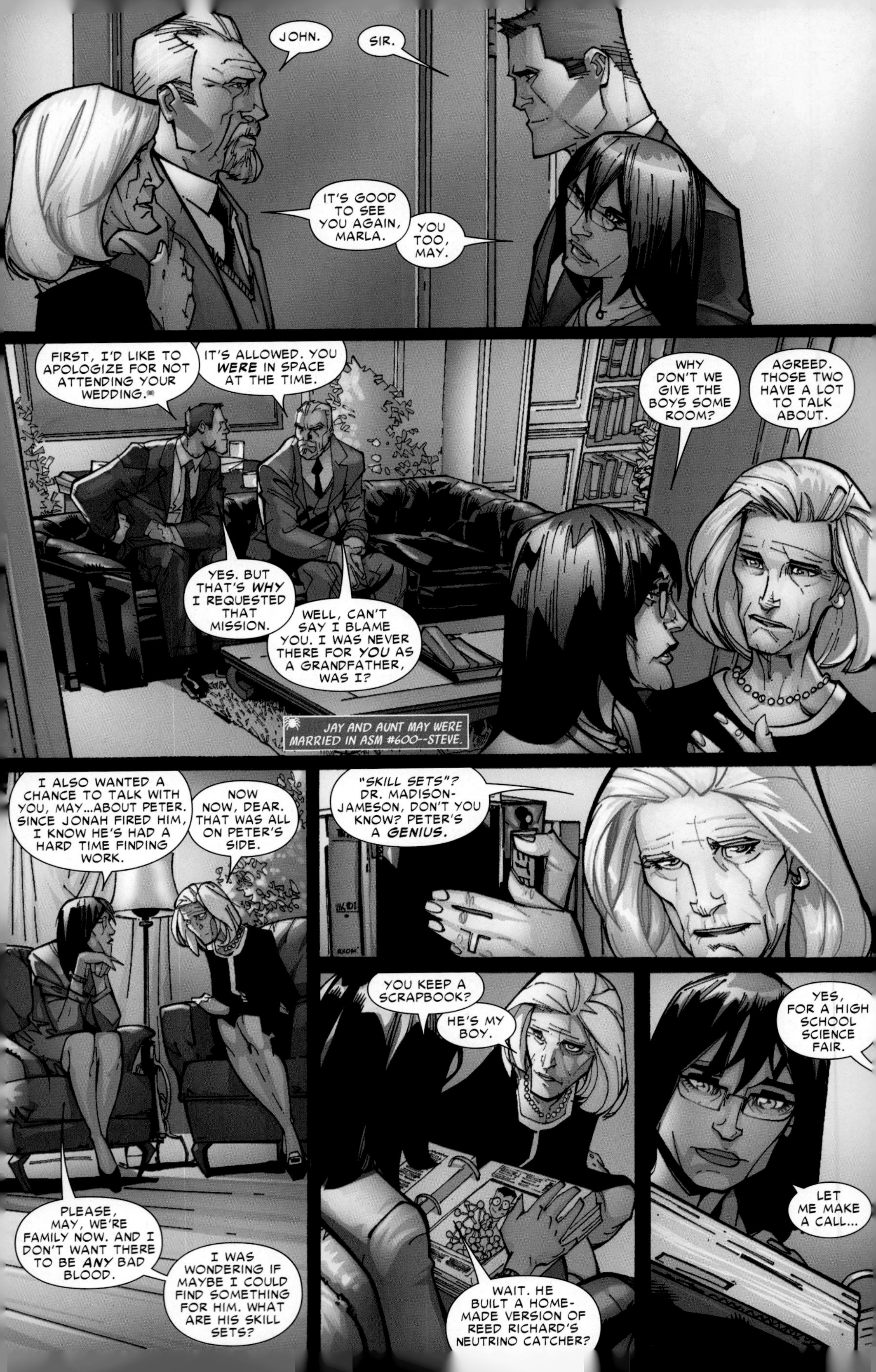
JOHN.
SIR.
IT'S GOOD TO SEE YOU AGAIN, MARLA.
YOU TOO, MAY.
FIRST, I'D LIKE TO APOLOGIZE FOR NOT ATTENDING YOUR WEDDING.
IT'S ALLOWED. YOU WERE IN SPACE AT THE TIME.
WHY DON'T WE GIVE THE BOYS SOME ROOM?
AGREED. THOSE TWO HAVE A LOT TO TALK ABOUT.
YES. BUT THAT'S WHY I REQUESTED THAT MISSION.
WELL, CAN'T SAY I BLAME YOU. I WAS NEVER THERE FOR YOU AS A GRANDFATHER, WAS I?
JAY AND AUNT MAY WERE MARRIED IN ASM #600--STEVE.
I ALSO WANTED A CHANCE TO TALK WITH YOU, MAY...ABOUT PETER. SINCE JONAH FIRED HIM, I KNOW HE'S HAD A HARD TIME FINDING WORK.
NOW NOW, DEAR. THAT WAS ALL ON PETER'S SIDE.
PLEASE, MAY, WE'RE FAMILY NOW. AND I DON'T WANT THERE TO BE ANY BAD BLOOD.
I WAS WONDERING IF MAYBE I COULD FIND SOMETHING FOR HIM. WHAT ARE HIS SKILL SETS?
"SKILL SETS"? DR. MADISON-JAMESON, DON'T YOU KNOW? PETER'S A GENIUS.
YOU KEEP A SCRAPBOOK?
HE'S MY BOY.
WAIT. HE BUILT A HOME-MADE VERSION OF REED RICHARD'S NEUTRINO CATCHER?
YES, FOR A HIGH SCHOOL SCIENCE FAIR.
LET ME MAKE A CALL...

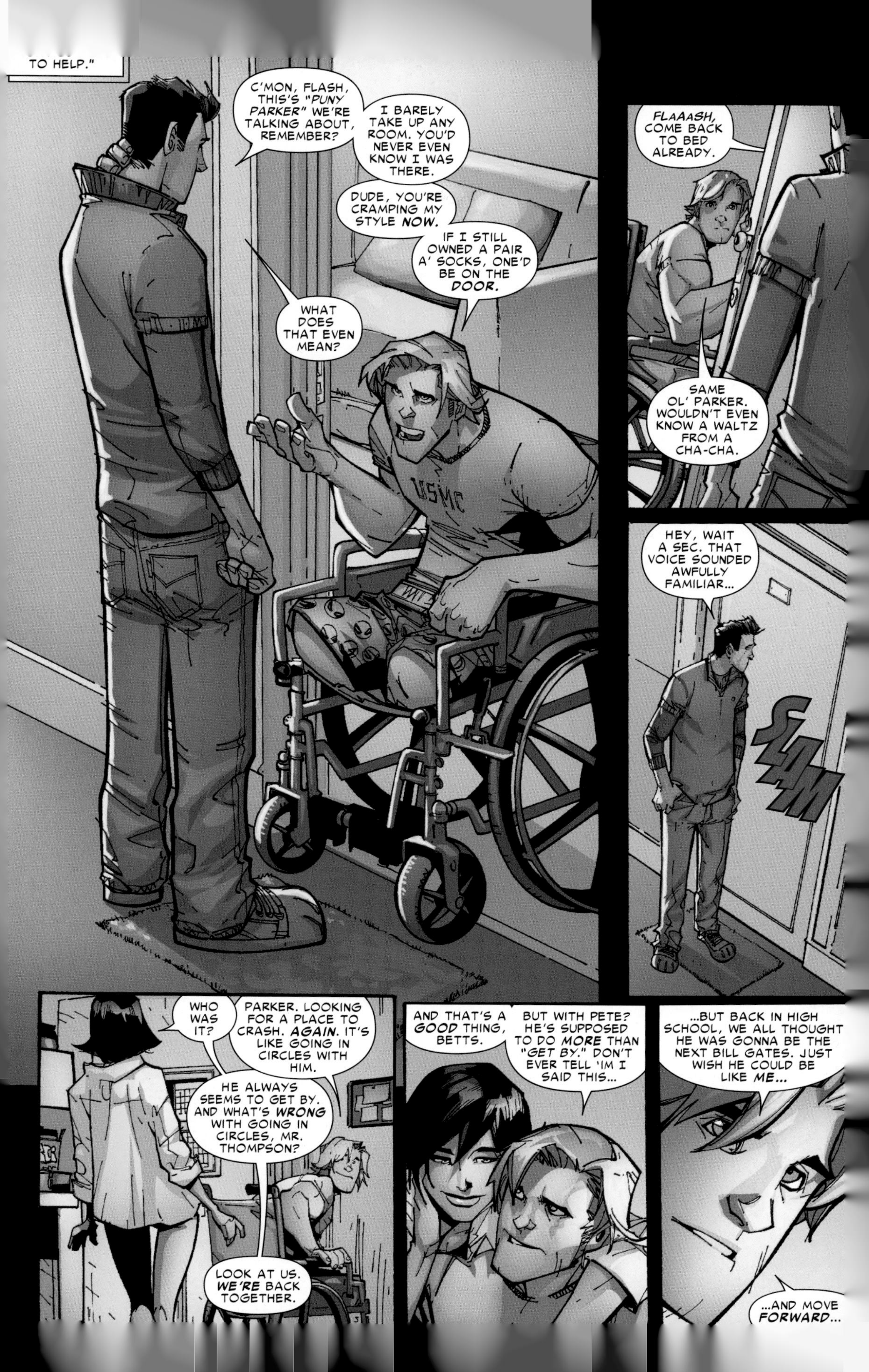

TO HELP."
C'MON, FLASH, THIS'S "PUNY PARKER" WE'RE TALKING ABOUT, REMEMBER?
I BARELY TAKE UP ANY ROOM. YOU'D NEVER EVEN KNOW I WAS THERE.
DUDE, YOU'RE CRAMPING MY STYLE NOW.
IF I STILL OWNED A PAIR A' SOCKS, ONE'D BE ON THE DOOR.
WHAT DOES THAT EVEN MEAN?
USMC
FLAAASH, COME BACK TO BED ALREADY.
SAME OL' PARKER. WOULDN'T EVEN KNOW A WALTZ FROM A CHA-CHA.
HEY, WAIT A SEC. THAT VOICE SOUNDED AWFULLY FAMILIAR...
SLAM
WHO WAS IT?
PARKER. LOOKING FOR A PLACE TO CRASH. AGAIN. IT'S LIKE GOING IN CIRCLES WITH HIM.
HE ALWAYS SEEMS TO GET BY. AND WHAT'S WRONG WITH GOING IN CIRCLES, MR. THOMPSON?
LOOK AT US. WE'RE BACK TOGETHER.
AND THAT'S A GOOD THING, BETTS.
BUT WITH PETE? HE'S SUPPOSED TO DO MORE THAN "GET BY." DON'T EVER TELL 'IM I SAID THIS...
...BUT BACK IN HIGH SCHOOL, WE ALL THOUGHT HE WAS GONNA BE THE NEXT BILL GATES. JUST WISH HE COULD BE LIKE ME...
...AND MOVE FORWARD...

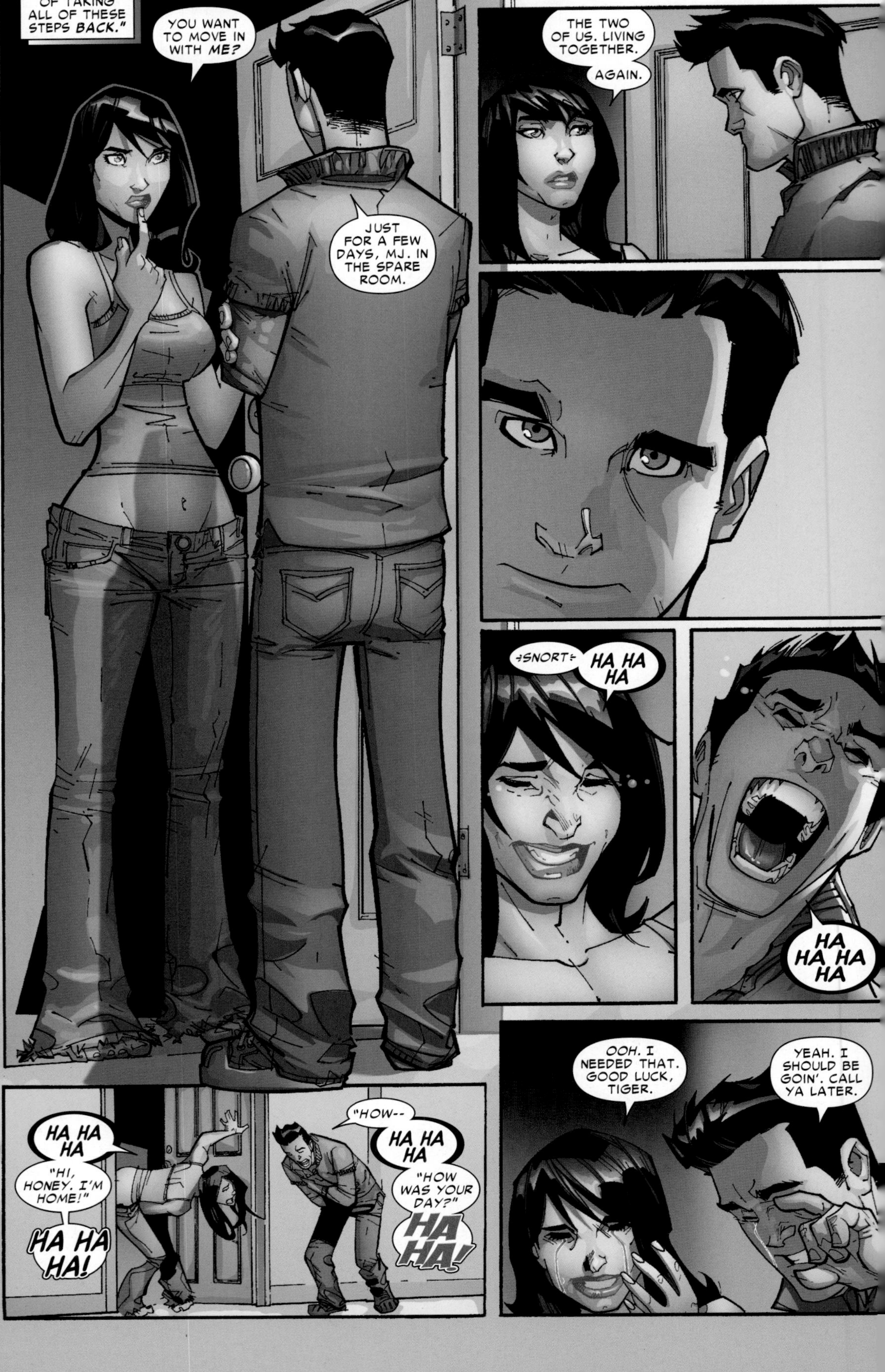
"...INSTEAD OF TAKING ALL OF THESE STEPS BACK."
YOU WANT TO MOVE IN WITH ME?
JUST FOR A FEW DAYS, MJ. IN THE SPARE ROOM.
THE TWO OF US. LIVING TOGETHER.
AGAIN.
=SNORT=
HA HA HA
HA HA HA HA
HA HA HA
"HI, HONEY. I'M HOME!"
HA HA HA!
"HOW--
HA HA HA
"HOW WAS YOUR DAY?"
HA HA!
OOH. I NEEDED THAT. GOOD LUCK, TIGER.
YEAH. I SHOULD BE GOIN'. CALL YA LATER.

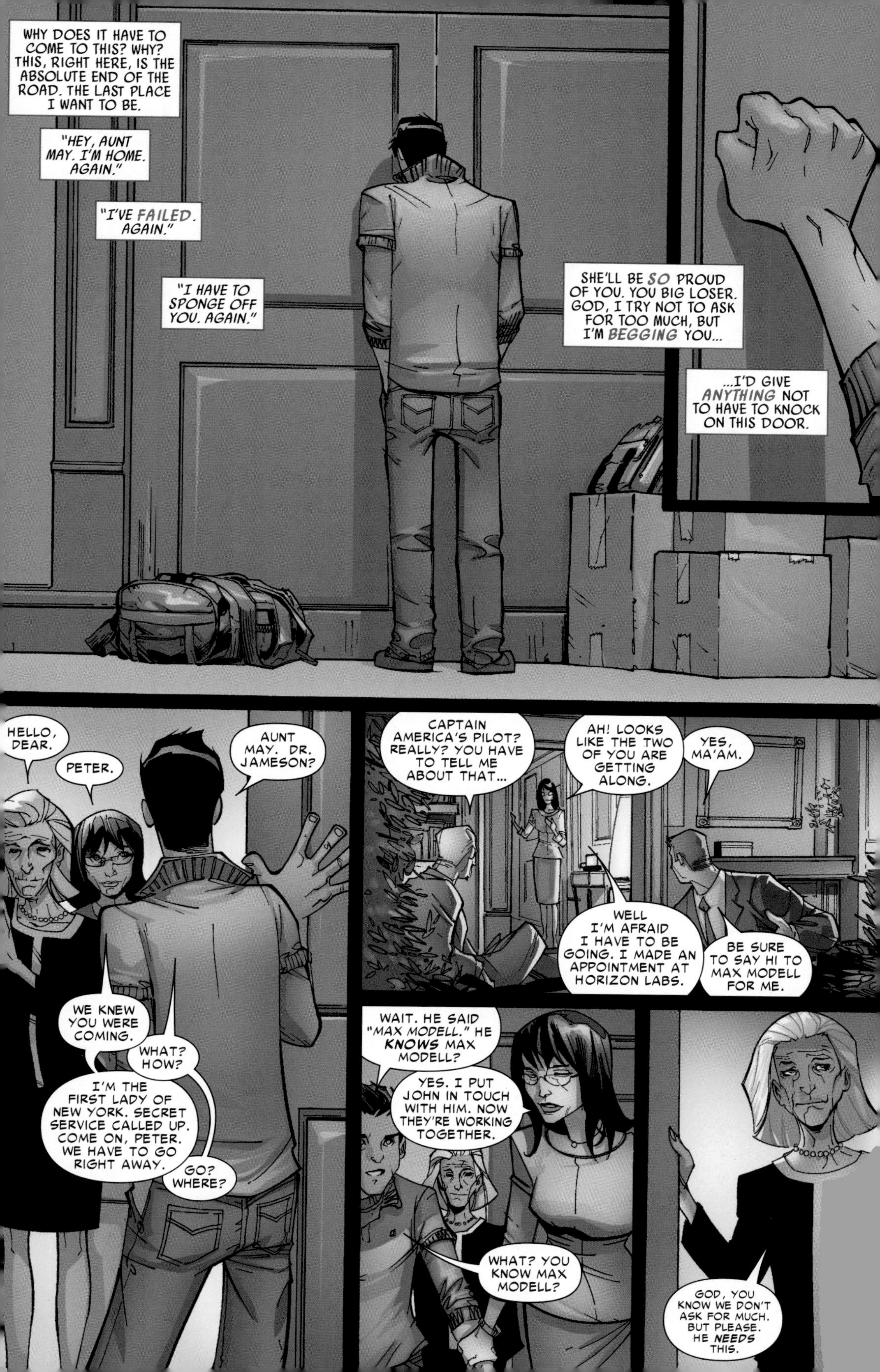
WHY DOES IT HAVE TO COME TO THIS? WHY? THIS, RIGHT HERE, IS THE ABSOLUTE END OF THE ROAD. THE LAST PLACE I WANT TO BE.
"HEY, AUNT MAY. I'M HOME. AGAIN."
"I'VE FAILED. AGAIN."
"I HAVE TO SPONGE OFF YOU. AGAIN."
SHE'LL BE SO PROUD OF YOU. YOU BIG LOSER. GOD, I TRY NOT TO ASK FOR TOO MUCH, BUT I'M BEGGING YOU...
...I'D GIVE ANYTHING NOT TO HAVE TO KNOCK ON THIS DOOR.
HELLO, DEAR.
PETER.
AUNT MAY. DR. JAMESON?
WE KNEW YOU WERE COMING.
WHAT? HOW?
I'M THE FIRST LADY OF NEW YORK. SECRET SERVICE CALLED UP. COME ON, PETER. WE HAVE TO GO RIGHT AWAY.
GO? WHERE?
CAPTAIN AMERICA'S PILOT? REALLY? YOU HAVE TO TELL ME ABOUT THAT...
AH! LOOKS LIKE THE TWO OF YOU ARE GETTING ALONG.
YES, MA'AM.
WELL I'M AFRAID I HAVE TO BE GOING. I MADE AN APPOINTMENT AT HORIZON LABS.
BE SURE TO SAY HI TO MAX MODELL FOR ME.
WAIT. HE SAID "MAX MODELL." HE KNOWS MAX MODELL?
YES. I PUT JOHN IN TOUCH WITH HIM. NOW THEY'RE WORKING TOGETHER.
WHAT? YOU KNOW MAX MODELL?
GOD, YOU KNOW WE DON'T ASK FOR MUCH. BUT PLEASE. HE NEEDS THIS.

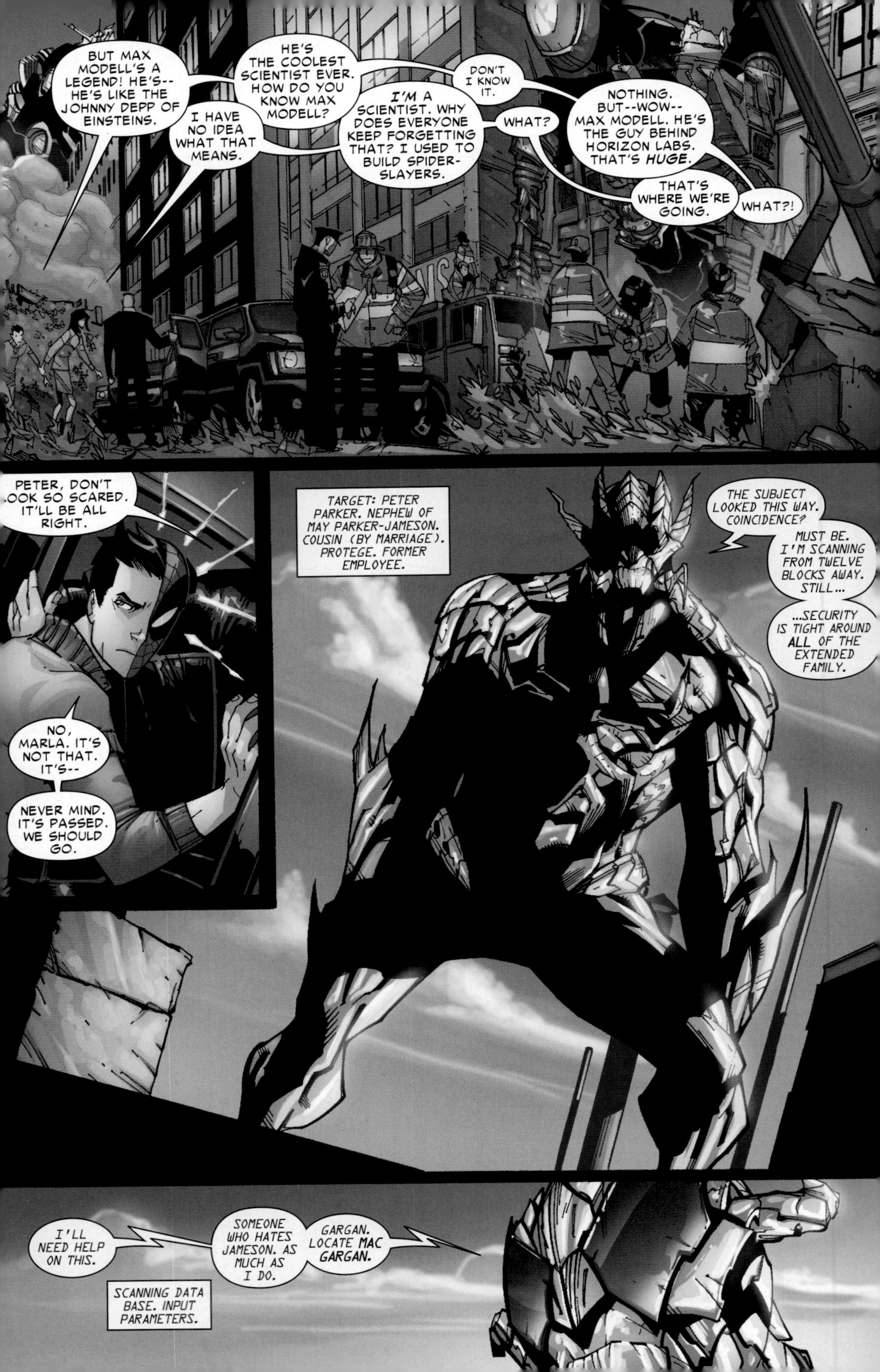
BUT MAX MODELL'S A LEGEND! HE'S--HE'S LIKE THE JOHNNY DEPP OF EINSTEINS.
I HAVE NO IDEA WHAT THAT MEANS.
HE'S THE COOLEST SCIENTIST EVER. HOW DO YOU KNOW MAX MODELL?
I'M A SCIENTIST. WHY DOES EVERYONE KEEP FORGETTING THAT? I USED TO BUILD SPIDER-SLAYERS.
DON'T I KNOW IT.
WHAT?
NOTHING. BUT--WOW--MAX MODELL. HE'S THE GUY BEHIND HORIZON LABS. THAT'S HUGE.
THAT'S WHERE WE'RE GOING.
WHAT?!
PETER, DON'T LOOK SO SCARED. IT'LL BE ALL RIGHT.
NO, MARLA. IT'S NOT THAT. IT'S--
NEVER MIND. IT'S PASSED. WE SHOULD GO.
TARGET: PETER PARKER. NEPHEW OF MAY PARKER-JAMESON. COUSIN (BY MARRIAGE). PROTEGE. FORMER EMPLOYEE.
THE SUBJECT LOOKED THIS WAY. COINCIDENCE?
MUST BE. I'M SCANNING FROM TWELVE BLOCKS AWAY. STILL...
...SECURITY IS TIGHT AROUND ALL OF THE EXTENDED FAMILY.
I'LL NEED HELP ON THIS.
SCANNING DATA BASE. INPUT PARAMETERS.
SOMEONE WHO HATES JAMESON. AS MUCH AS I DO.
GARGAN. LOCATE MAC GARGAN.

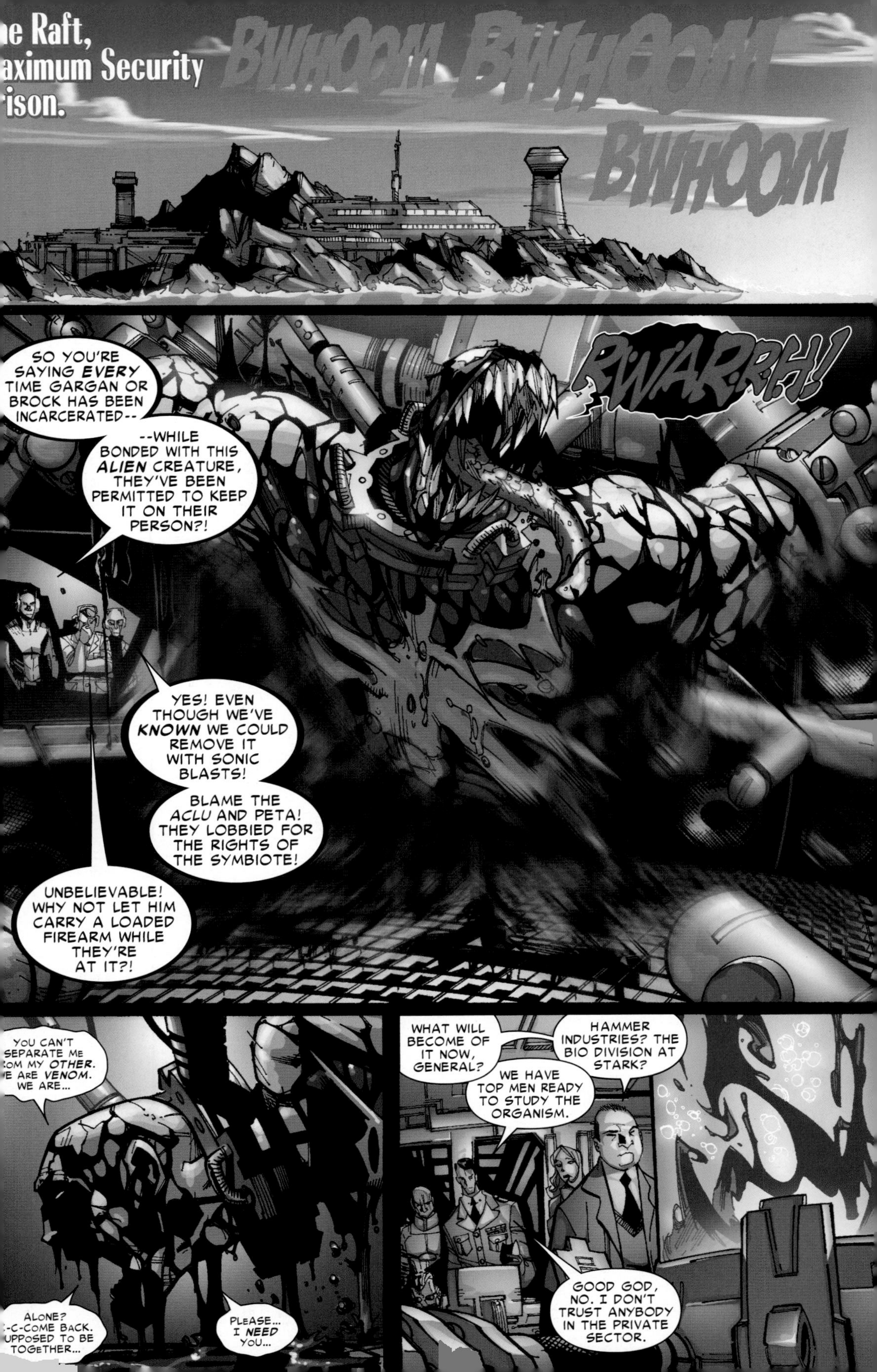

e Raft,
aximum Security
rison.
BWHOOM BWHOOM
BWHOOM
RWARRH!!
SO YOU'RE SAYING EVERY TIME GARGAN OR BROCK HAS BEEN INCARCERATED--
--WHILE BONDED WITH THIS ALIEN CREATURE, THEY'VE BEEN PERMITTED TO KEEP IT ON THEIR PERSON?!
YES! EVEN THOUGH WE'VE KNOWN WE COULD REMOVE IT WITH SONIC BLASTS!
BLAME THE ACLU AND PETA! THEY LOBBIED FOR THE RIGHTS OF THE SYMBIOTE!
UNBELIEVABLE! WHY NOT LET HIM CARRY A LOADED FIREARM WHILE THEY'RE AT IT?!
YOU CAN'T SEPARATE ME ROM MY OTHER. E ARE VENOM. WE ARE...
ALONE? -C-COME BACK. UPPOSED TO BE TOGETHER...
PLEASE... I NEED YOU...
WHAT WILL BECOME OF IT NOW, GENERAL?
HAMMER INDUSTRIES? THE BIO DIVISION AT STARK?
WE HAVE TOP MEN READY TO STUDY THE ORGANISM.
GOOD GOD, NO. I DON'T TRUST ANYBODY IN THE PRIVATE SECTOR.

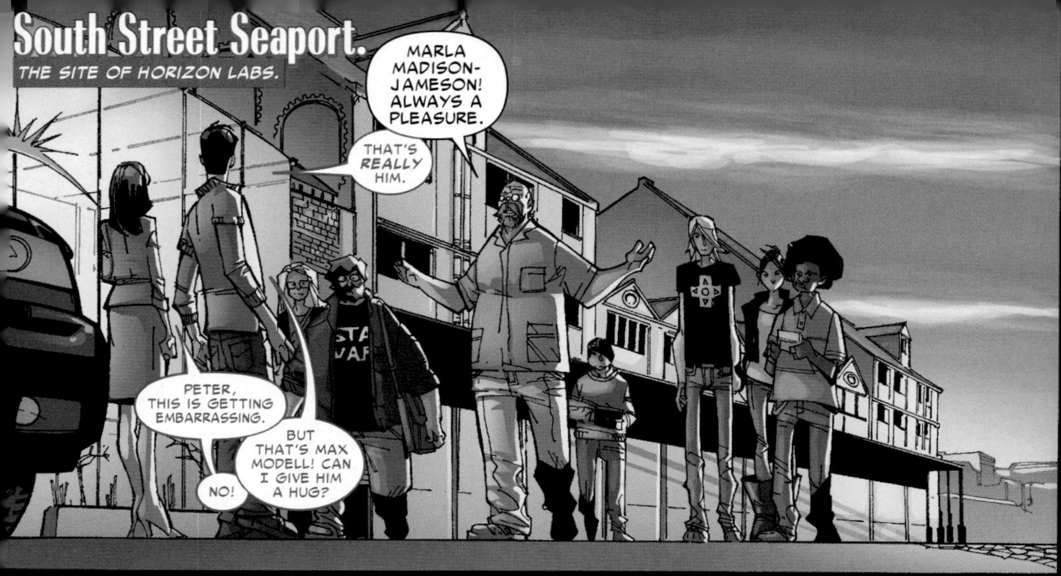
South Street Seaport.
THE SITE OF HORIZON LABS.
MARLA MADISON-JAMESON! ALWAYS A PLEASURE.
THAT'S REALLY HIM.
PETER, THIS IS GETTING EMBARRASSING.
BUT THAT'S MAX MODELL! CAN I GIVE HIM A HUG?
NO!

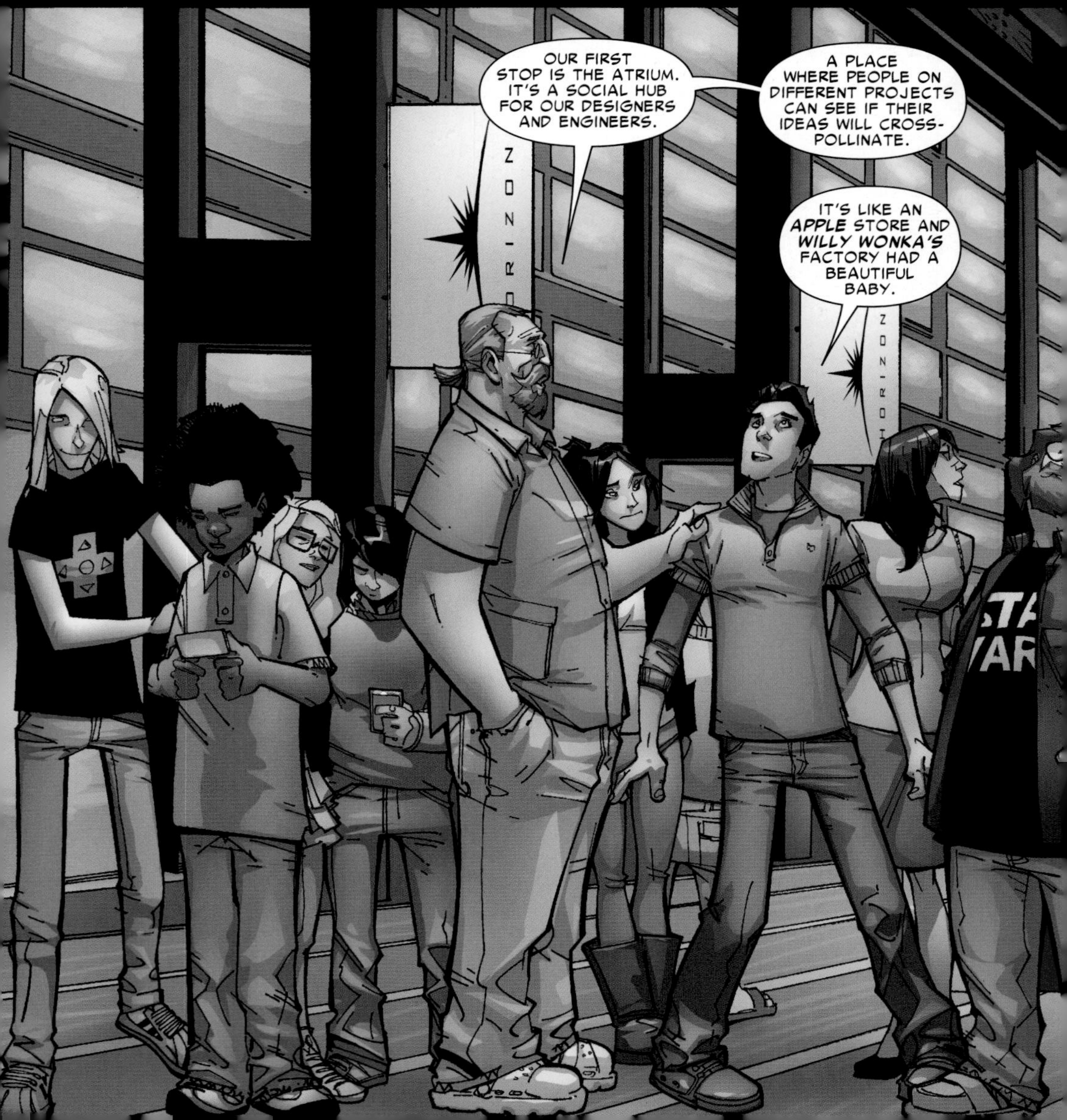
OUR FIRST STOP IS THE ATRIUM. IT'S A SOCIAL HUB FOR OUR DESIGNERS AND ENGINEERS.
A PLACE WHERE PEOPLE ON DIFFERENT PROJECTS CAN SEE IF THEIR IDEAS WILL CROSS-POLLINATE.
IT'S LIKE AN APPLE STORE AND WILLY WONKA'S FACTORY HAD A BEAUTIFUL BABY.
HORIZON

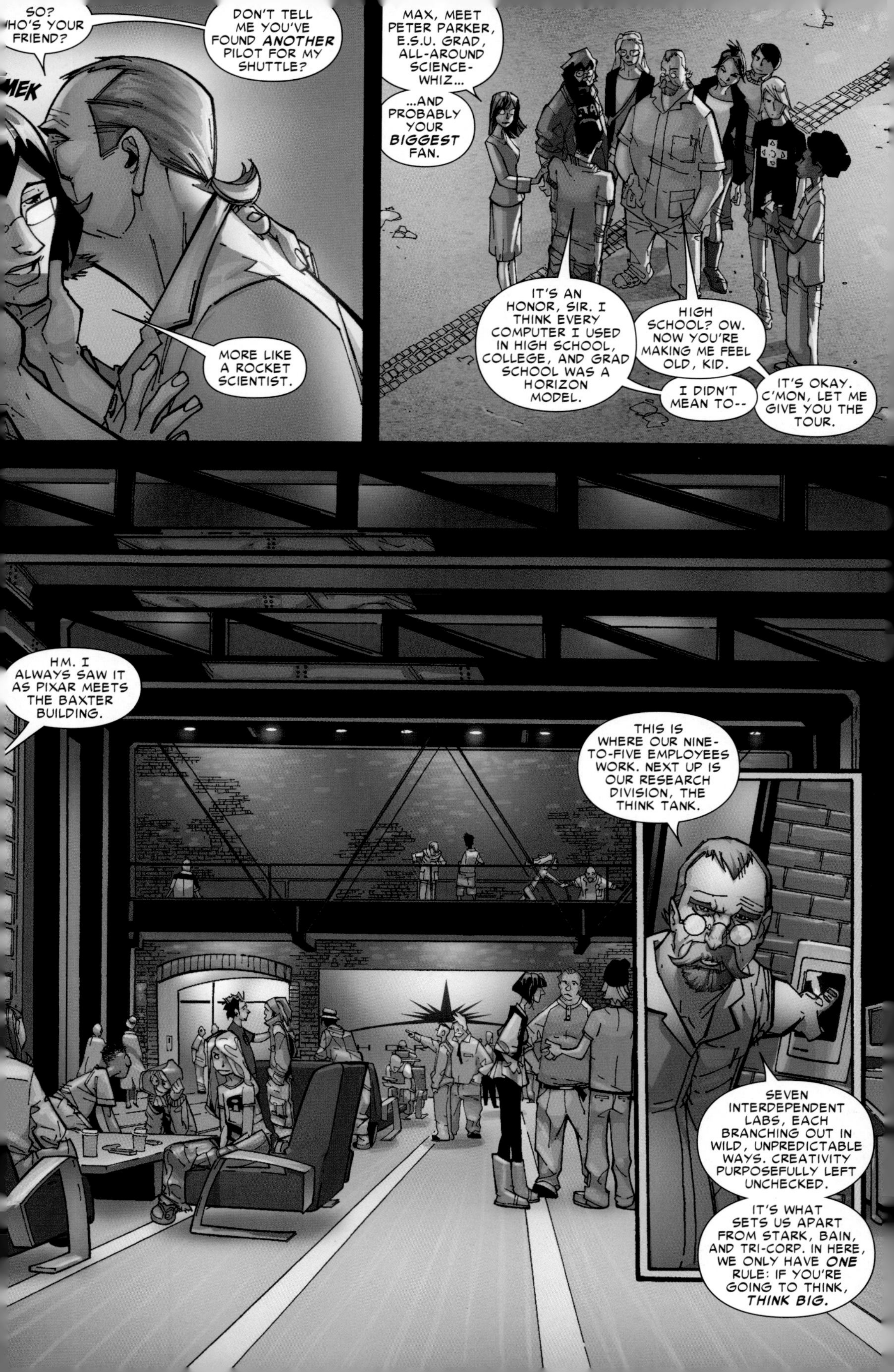
SO? WHO'S YOUR FRIEND?
MEK
DON'T TELL ME YOU'VE FOUND ANOTHER PILOT FOR MY SHUTTLE?
MORE LIKE A ROCKET SCIENTIST.
MAX, MEET PETER PARKER, E.S.U. GRAD, ALL-AROUND SCIENCE-WHIZ...
...AND PROBABLY YOUR BIGGEST FAN.
IT'S AN HONOR, SIR. I THINK EVERY COMPUTER I USED IN HIGH SCHOOL, COLLEGE, AND GRAD SCHOOL WAS A HORIZON MODEL.
HIGH SCHOOL? OW. NOW YOU'RE MAKING ME FEEL OLD, KID.
I DIDN'T MEAN TO--
IT'S OKAY. C'MON, LET ME GIVE YOU THE TOUR.
HM. I ALWAYS SAW IT AS PIXAR MEETS THE BAXTER BUILDING.
THIS IS WHERE OUR NINE-TO-FIVE EMPLOYEES WORK. NEXT UP IS OUR RESEARCH DIVISION, THE THINK TANK.
SEVEN INTERDEPENDENT LABS, EACH BRANCHING OUT IN WILD, UNPREDICTABLE WAYS. CREATIVITY PURPOSEFULLY LEFT UNCHECKED.
IT'S WHAT SETS US APART FROM STARK, BAIN, AND TRI-CORP. IN HERE, WE ONLY HAVE ONE RULE: IF YOU'RE GOING TO THINK, THINK BIG.

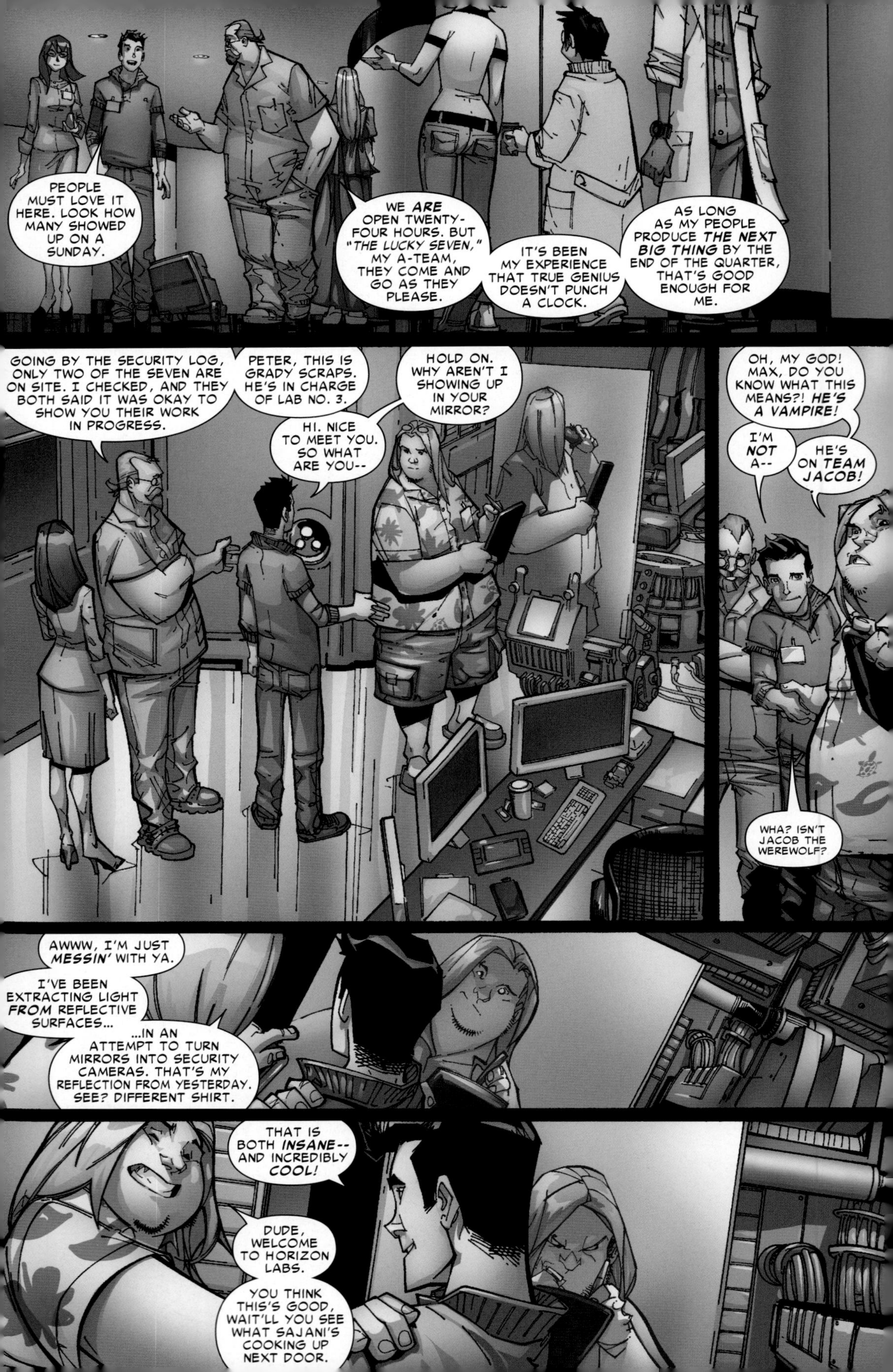
PEOPLE MUST LOVE IT HERE. LOOK HOW MANY SHOWED UP ON A SUNDAY.
WE *ARE* OPEN TWENTY-FOUR HOURS. BUT *"THE LUCKY SEVEN,"* MY A-TEAM, THEY COME AND GO AS THEY PLEASE.
IT'S BEEN MY EXPERIENCE THAT TRUE GENIUS DOESN'T PUNCH A CLOCK.
AS LONG AS MY PEOPLE PRODUCE *THE NEXT BIG THING* BY THE END OF THE QUARTER, THAT'S GOOD ENOUGH FOR ME.
GOING BY THE SECURITY LOG, ONLY TWO OF THE SEVEN ARE ON SITE. I CHECKED, AND THEY BOTH SAID IT WAS OKAY TO SHOW YOU THEIR WORK IN PROGRESS.
PETER, THIS IS GRADY SCRAPS. HE'S IN CHARGE OF LAB NO. 3.
HI. NICE TO MEET YOU. SO WHAT ARE YOU--
HOLD ON. WHY AREN'T I SHOWING UP IN YOUR MIRROR?
OH, MY GOD! MAX, DO YOU KNOW WHAT THIS MEANS?! *HE'S A VAMPIRE!*
I'M *NOT* A--
HE'S ON *TEAM JACOB!*
WHA? ISN'T JACOB THE WEREWOLF?
AWWW, I'M JUST *MESSIN'* WITH YA.
I'VE BEEN EXTRACTING LIGHT *FROM* REFLECTIVE SURFACES...
...IN AN ATTEMPT TO TURN MIRRORS INTO SECURITY CAMERAS. THAT'S MY REFLECTION FROM YESTERDAY. SEE? DIFFERENT SHIRT.
THAT IS BOTH *INSANE*-- AND INCREDIBLY *COOL!*
DUDE, WELCOME TO HORIZON LABS.
YOU THINK THIS'S GOOD, WAIT'LL YOU SEE WHAT SAJANI'S COOKING UP NEXT DOOR.

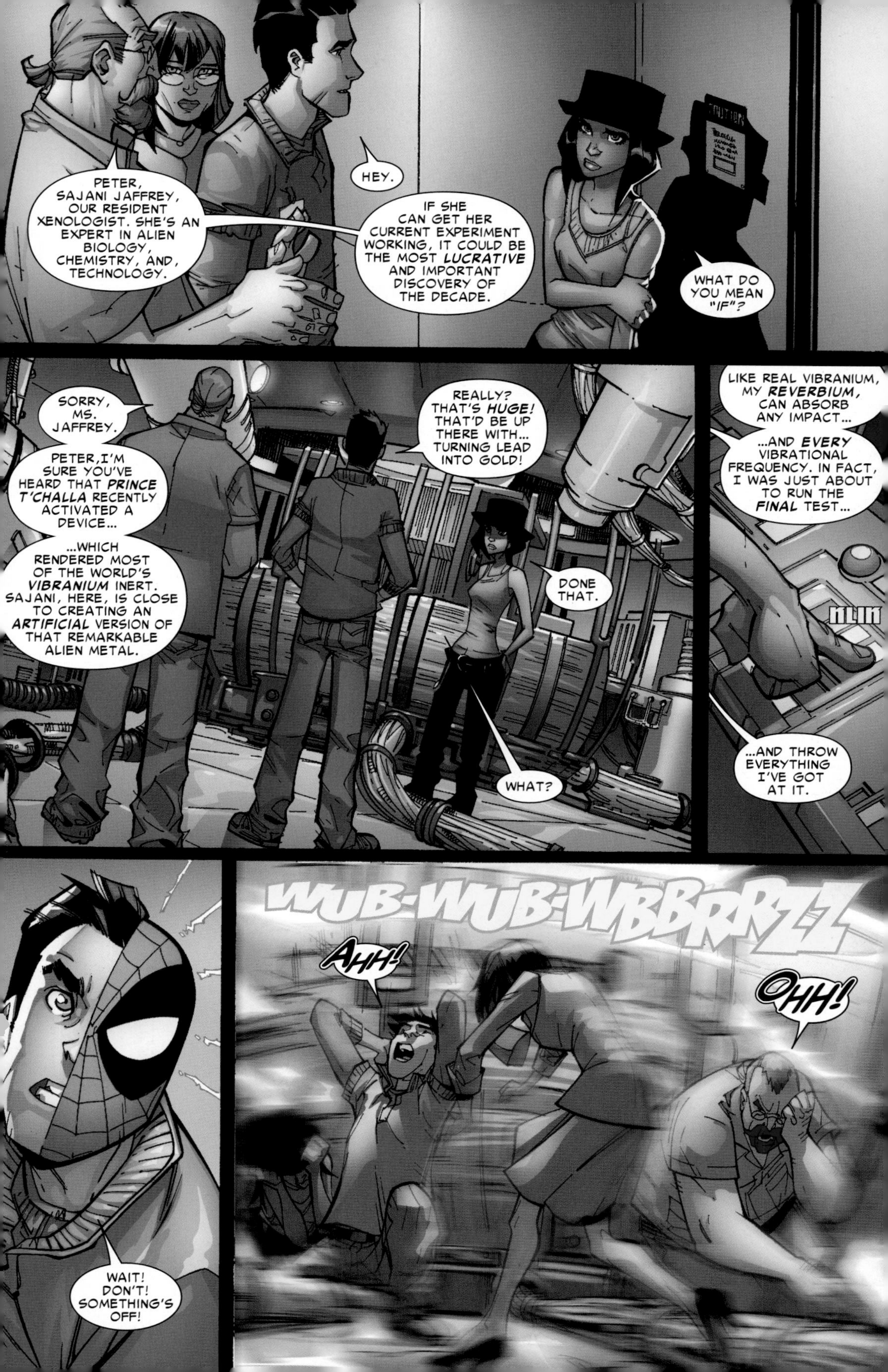

PETER, SAJANI JAFFREY, OUR RESIDENT XENOLOGIST. SHE'S AN EXPERT IN ALIEN BIOLOGY, CHEMISTRY, AND, TECHNOLOGY.
HEY.
IF SHE CAN GET HER CURRENT EXPERIMENT WORKING, IT COULD BE THE MOST LUCRATIVE AND IMPORTANT DISCOVERY OF THE DECADE.
WHAT DO YOU MEAN "IF"?
SORRY, MS. JAFFREY.
PETER, I'M SURE YOU'VE HEARD THAT PRINCE T'CHALLA RECENTLY ACTIVATED A DEVICE...
...WHICH RENDERED MOST OF THE WORLD'S VIBRANIUM INERT. SAJANI, HERE, IS CLOSE TO CREATING AN ARTIFICIAL VERSION OF THAT REMARKABLE ALIEN METAL.
REALLY? THAT'S HUGE! THAT'D BE UP THERE WITH... TURNING LEAD INTO GOLD!
DONE THAT.
WHAT?
LIKE REAL VIBRANIUM, MY REVERBIUM, CAN ABSORB ANY IMPACT...
...AND EVERY VIBRATIONAL FREQUENCY. IN FACT, I WAS JUST ABOUT TO RUN THE FINAL TEST...
NLIN
...AND THROW EVERYTHING I'VE GOT AT IT.
WAIT! DON'T! SOMETHING'S OFF!
WUB-WUB-WBBRRZZ
AHH!
OHH!

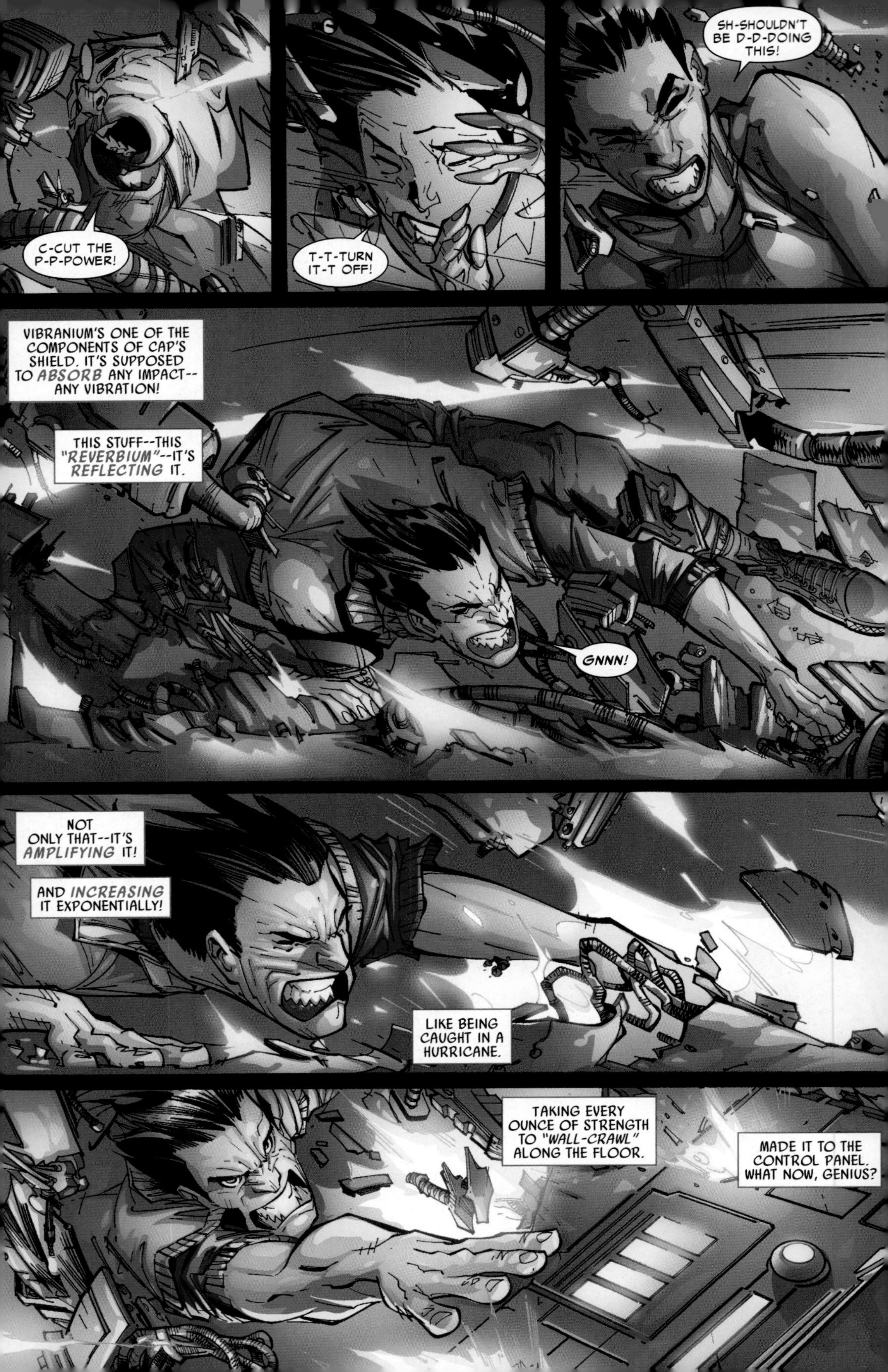
C-CUT THE P-P-POWER!
T-T-TURN IT-T OFF!
SH-SHOULDN'T BE D-D-DOING THIS!
VIBRANIUM'S ONE OF THE COMPONENTS OF CAP'S SHIELD. IT'S SUPPOSED TO ABSORB ANY IMPACT--ANY VIBRATION!
THIS STUFF--THIS "REVERBIUM"--IT'S REFLECTING IT.
GNNN!
NOT ONLY THAT--IT'S AMPLIFYING IT!
AND INCREASING IT EXPONENTIALLY!
LIKE BEING CAUGHT IN A HURRICANE.
TAKING EVERY OUNCE OF STRENGTH TO "WALL-CRAWL" ALONG THE FLOOR.
MADE IT TO THE CONTROL PANEL. WHAT NOW, GENIUS?

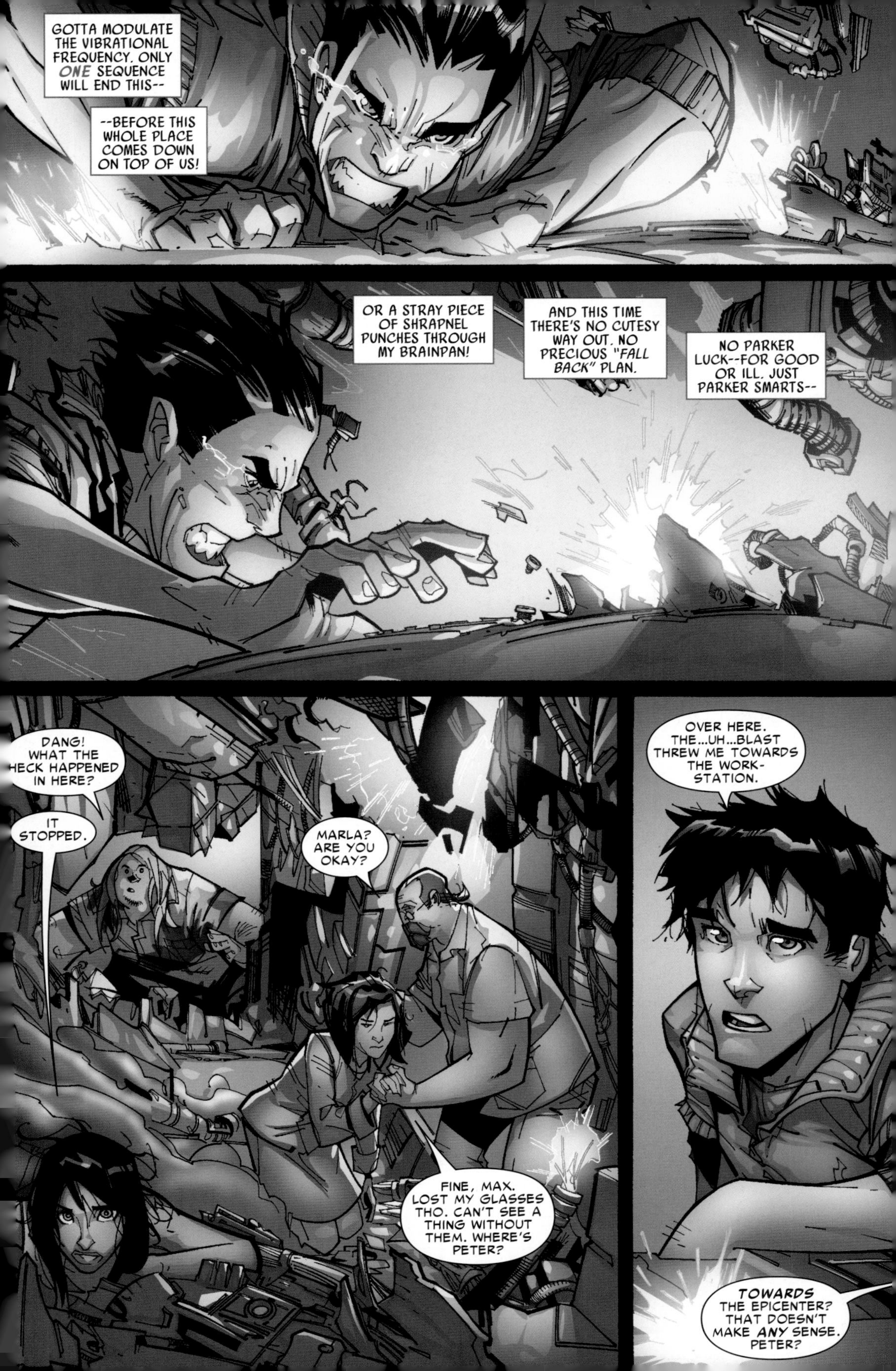
GOTTA MODULATE THE VIBRATIONAL FREQUENCY. ONLY ONE SEQUENCE WILL END THIS--
--BEFORE THIS WHOLE PLACE COMES DOWN ON TOP OF US!
OR A STRAY PIECE OF SHRAPNEL PUNCHES THROUGH MY BRAINPAN!
AND THIS TIME THERE'S NO CUTESY WAY OUT. NO PRECIOUS "FALL BACK" PLAN.
NO PARKER LUCK--FOR GOOD OR ILL. JUST PARKER SMARTS--
DANG! WHAT THE HECK HAPPENED IN HERE?
IT STOPPED.
MARLA? ARE YOU OKAY?
FINE, MAX. LOST MY GLASSES THO. CAN'T SEE A THING WITHOUT THEM. WHERE'S PETER?
OVER HERE. THE...UH...BLAST THREW ME TOWARDS THE WORK-STATION.
TOWARDS THE EPICENTER? THAT DOESN'T MAKE ANY SENSE. PETER?

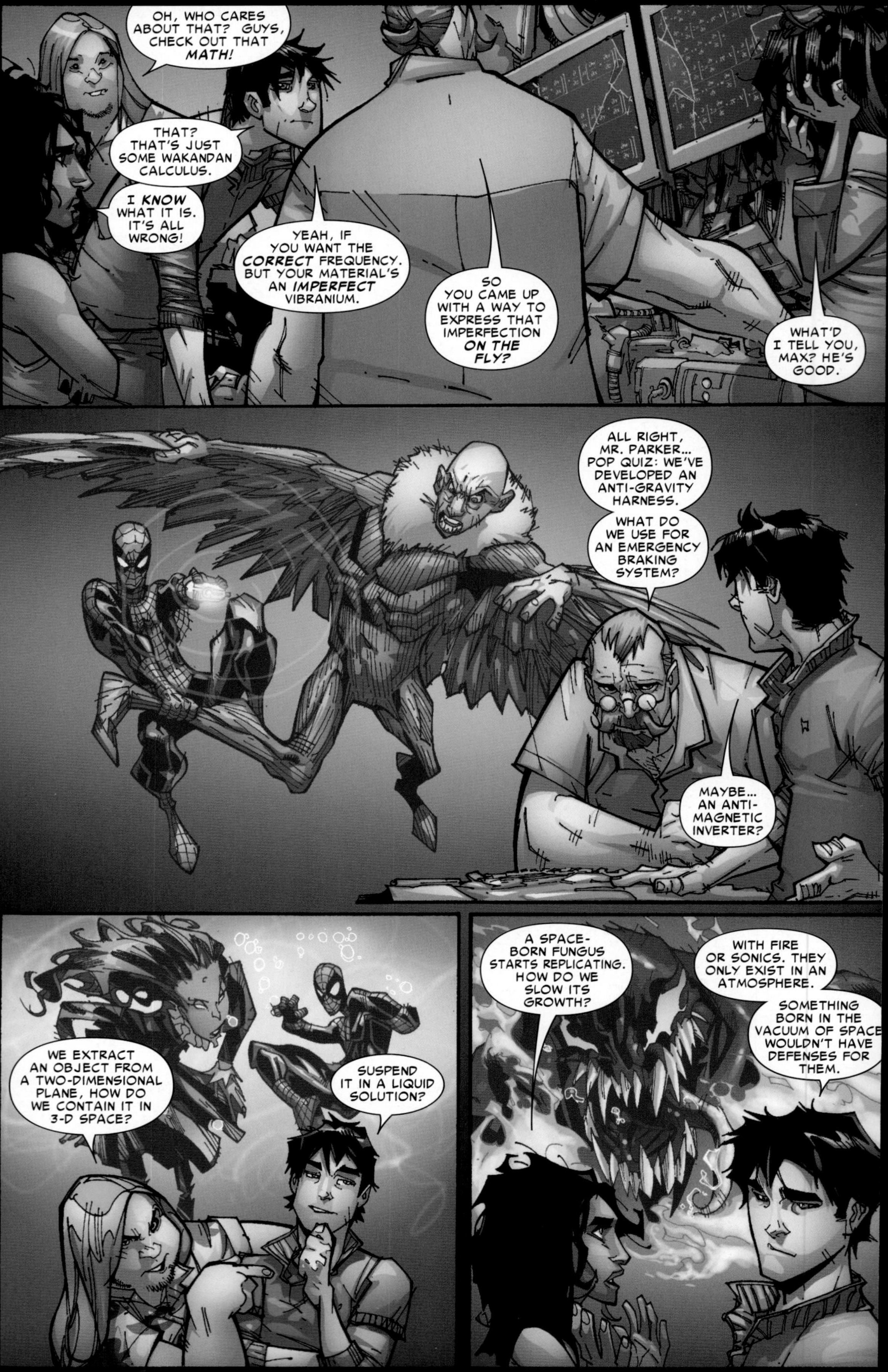

OH, WHO CARES ABOUT THAT? GUYS, CHECK OUT THAT MATH!
THAT? THAT'S JUST SOME WAKANDAN CALCULUS.
I KNOW WHAT IT IS. IT'S ALL WRONG!
YEAH, IF YOU WANT THE CORRECT FREQUENCY. BUT YOUR MATERIAL'S AN IMPERFECT VIBRANIUM.
SO YOU CAME UP WITH A WAY TO EXPRESS THAT IMPERFECTION ON THE FLY?
WHAT'D I TELL YOU, MAX? HE'S GOOD.
ALL RIGHT, MR. PARKER... POP QUIZ: WE'VE DEVELOPED AN ANTI-GRAVITY HARNESS.
WHAT DO WE USE FOR AN EMERGENCY BRAKING SYSTEM?
MAYBE... AN ANTI-MAGNETIC INVERTER?
WE EXTRACT AN OBJECT FROM A TWO-DIMENSIONAL PLANE, HOW DO WE CONTAIN IT IN 3-D SPACE?
SUSPEND IT IN A LIQUID SOLUTION?
A SPACE-BORN FUNGUS STARTS REPLICATING. HOW DO WE SLOW ITS GROWTH?
WITH FIRE OR SONICS. THEY ONLY EXIST IN AN ATMOSPHERE.
SOMETHING BORN IN THE VACUUM OF SPACE WOULDN'T HAVE DEFENSES FOR THEM.

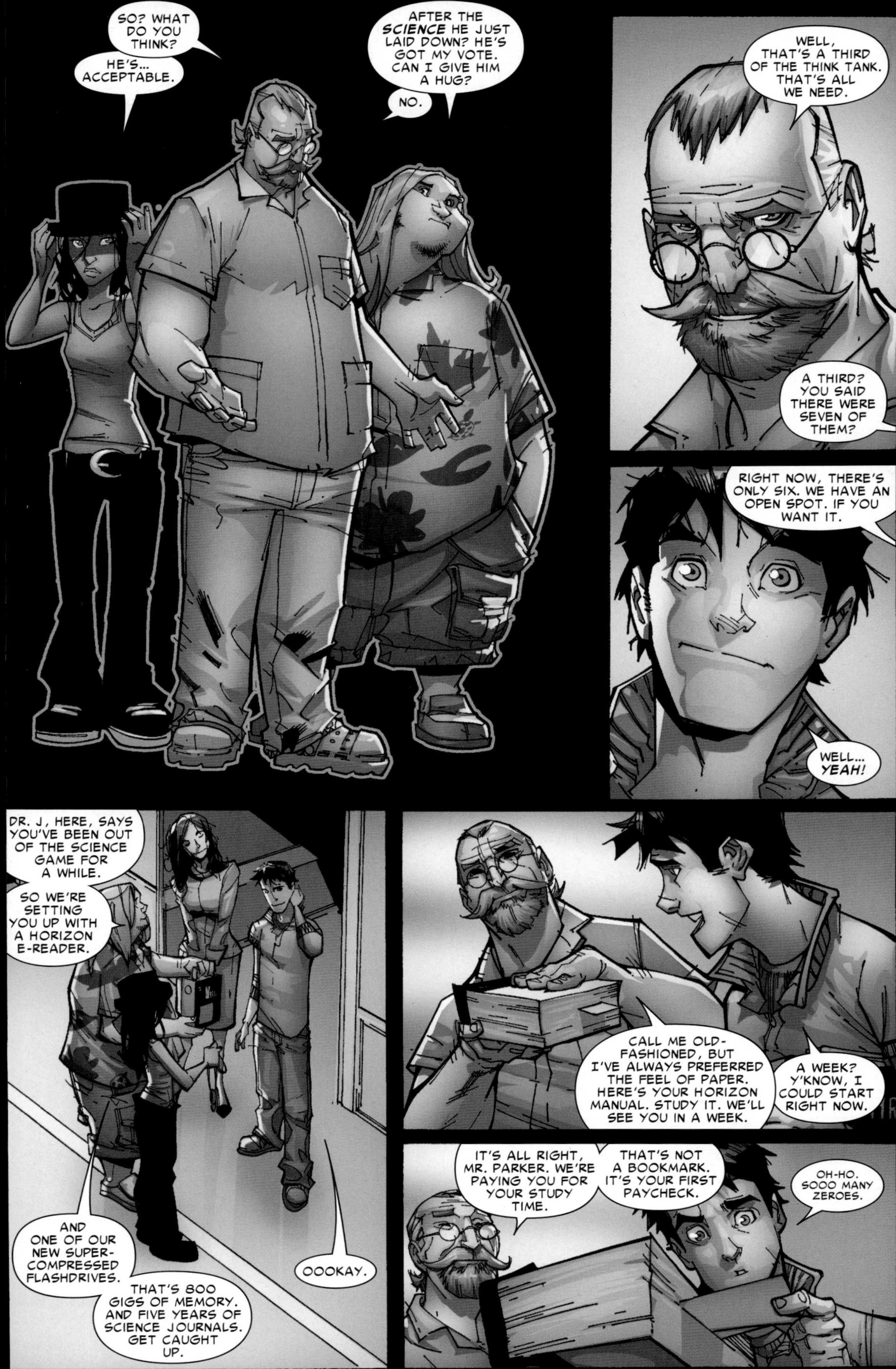
SO? WHAT DO YOU THINK?
HE'S... ACCEPTABLE.
AFTER THE SCIENCE HE JUST LAID DOWN? HE'S GOT MY VOTE. CAN I GIVE HIM A HUG?
NO.
WELL, THAT'S A THIRD OF THE THINK TANK. THAT'S ALL WE NEED.
A THIRD? YOU SAID THERE WERE SEVEN OF THEM?
RIGHT NOW, THERE'S ONLY SIX. WE HAVE AN OPEN SPOT. IF YOU WANT IT.
WELL... YEAH!
DR. J, HERE, SAYS YOU'VE BEEN OUT OF THE SCIENCE GAME FOR A WHILE.
SO WE'RE SETTING YOU UP WITH A HORIZON E-READER.
AND ONE OF OUR NEW SUPER-COMPRESSED FLASHDRIVES.
THAT'S 800 GIGS OF MEMORY. AND FIVE YEARS OF SCIENCE JOURNALS. GET CAUGHT UP.
OOOKAY.
CALL ME OLD-FASHIONED, BUT I'VE ALWAYS PREFERRED THE FEEL OF PAPER. HERE'S YOUR HORIZON MANUAL. STUDY IT. WE'LL SEE YOU IN A WEEK.
A WEEK? Y'KNOW, I COULD START RIGHT NOW.
IT'S ALL RIGHT, MR. PARKER. WE'RE PAYING YOU FOR YOUR STUDY TIME.
THAT'S NOT A BOOKMARK. IT'S YOUR FIRST PAYCHECK.
OH-HO. SOOO MANY ZEROES.

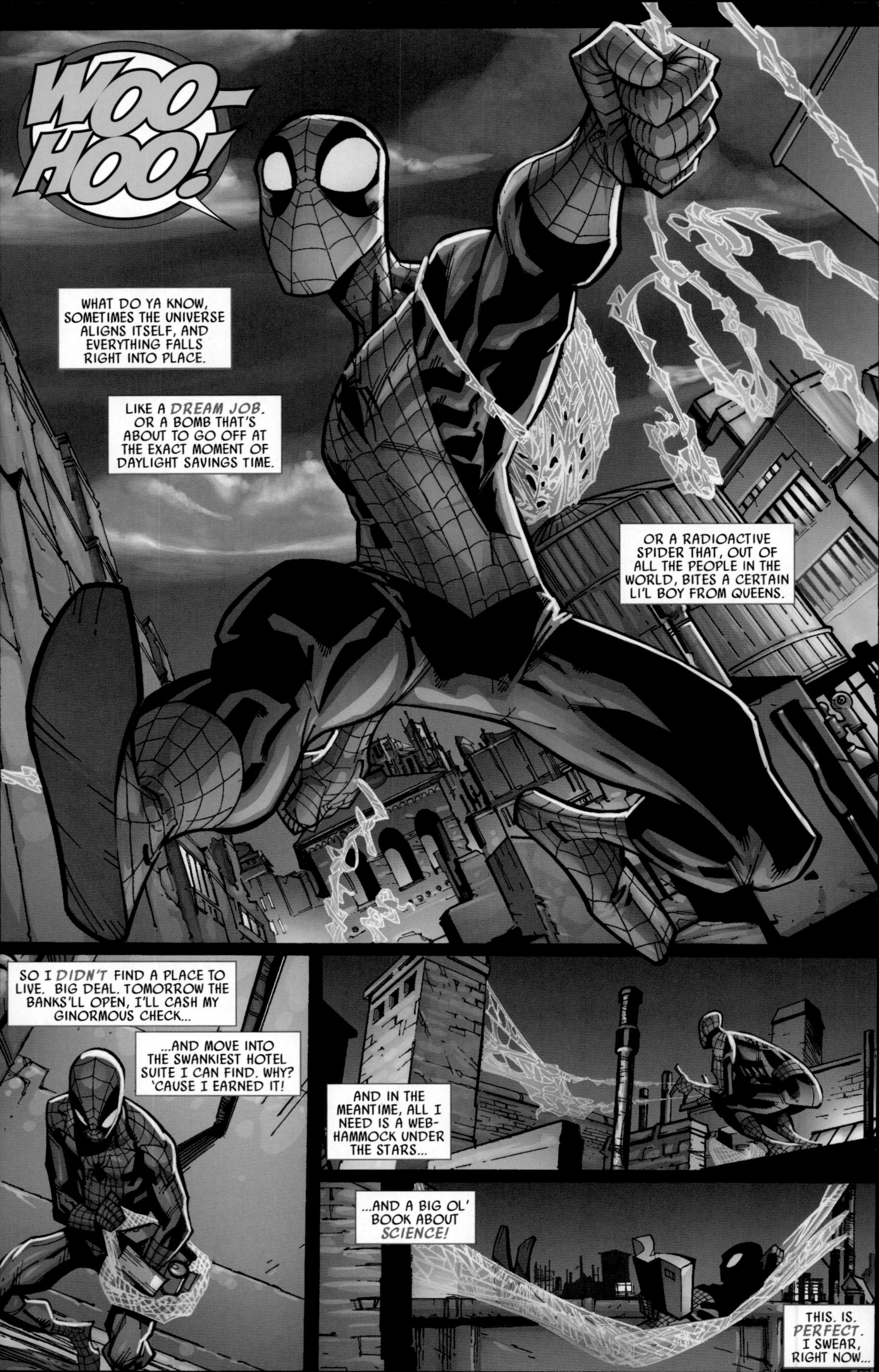
WOO-HOO!
WHAT DO YA KNOW, SOMETIMES THE UNIVERSE ALIGNS ITSELF, AND EVERYTHING FALLS RIGHT INTO PLACE.
LIKE A DREAM JOB. OR A BOMB THAT'S ABOUT TO GO OFF AT THE EXACT MOMENT OF DAYLIGHT SAVINGS TIME.
OR A RADIOACTIVE SPIDER THAT, OUT OF ALL THE PEOPLE IN THE WORLD, BITES A CERTAIN LI'L BOY FROM QUEENS.
SO I DIDN'T FIND A PLACE TO LIVE. BIG DEAL. TOMORROW THE BANKS'LL OPEN, I'LL CASH MY GINORMOUS CHECK...
...AND MOVE INTO THE SWANKIEST HOTEL SUITE I CAN FIND. WHY? 'CAUSE I EARNED IT!
AND IN THE MEANTIME, ALL I NEED IS A WEB-HAMMOCK UNDER THE STARS...
...AND A BIG OL' BOOK ABOUT SCIENCE!
THIS. IS. PERFECT. I SWEAR, RIGHT NOW...

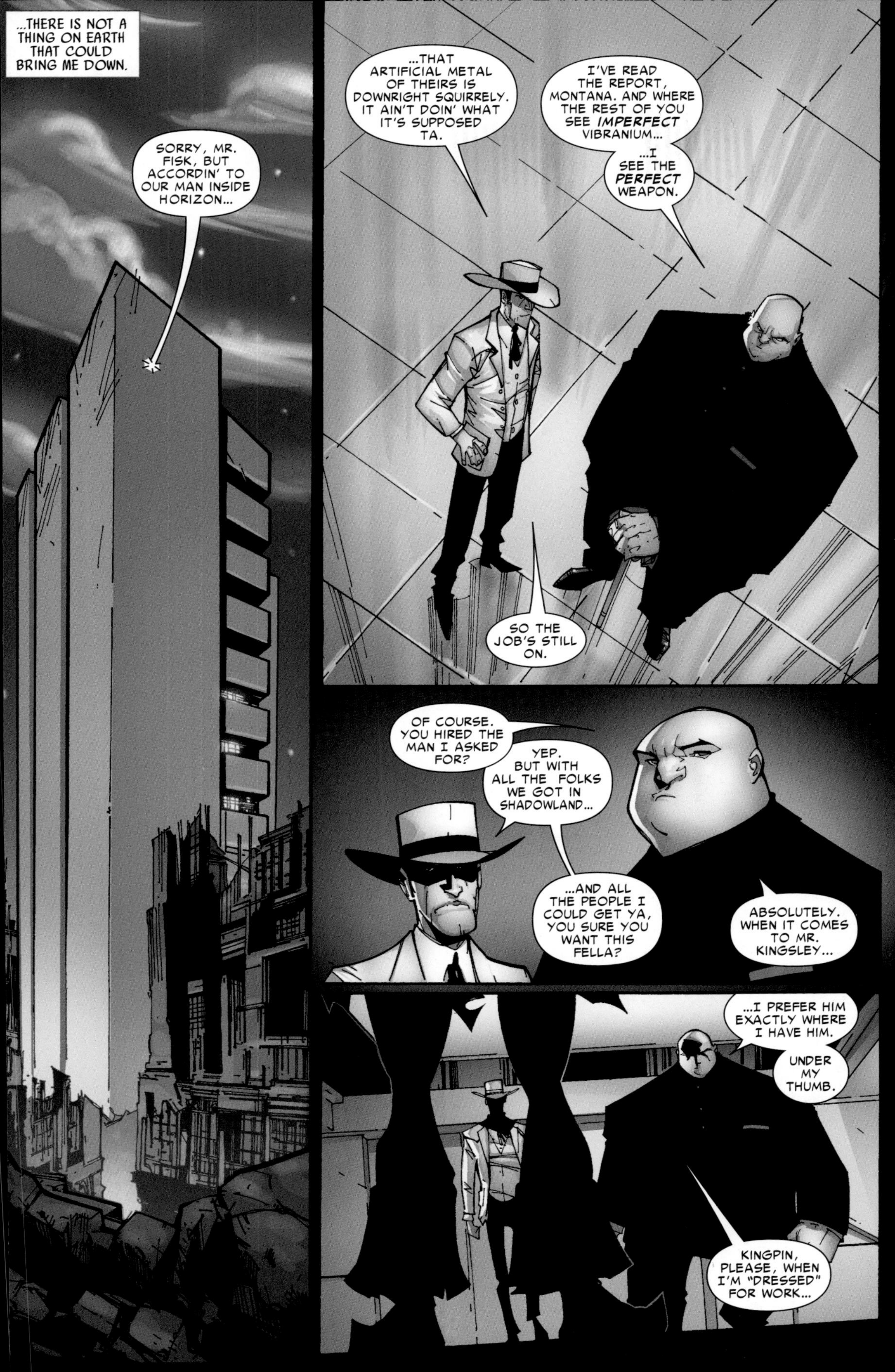
...THERE IS NOT A THING ON EARTH THAT COULD BRING ME DOWN.
SORRY, MR. FISK, BUT ACCORDIN' TO OUR MAN INSIDE HORIZON...
...THAT ARTIFICIAL METAL OF THEIRS IS DOWNRIGHT SQUIRRELY. IT AIN'T DOIN' WHAT IT'S SUPPOSED TA.
I'VE READ THE REPORT, MONTANA. AND WHERE THE REST OF YOU SEE IMPERFECT VIBRANIUM...
...I SEE THE PERFECT WEAPON.
SO THE JOB'S STILL ON.
OF COURSE. YOU HIRED THE MAN I ASKED FOR?
YEP. BUT WITH ALL THE FOLKS WE GOT IN SHADOWLAND...
...AND ALL THE PEOPLE I COULD GET YA, YOU SURE YOU WANT THIS FELLA?
ABSOLUTELY. WHEN IT COMES TO MR. KINGSLEY...
...I PREFER HIM EXACTLY WHERE I HAVE HIM.
UNDER MY THUMB.
KINGPIN, PLEASE, WHEN I'M "DRESSED" FOR WORK...

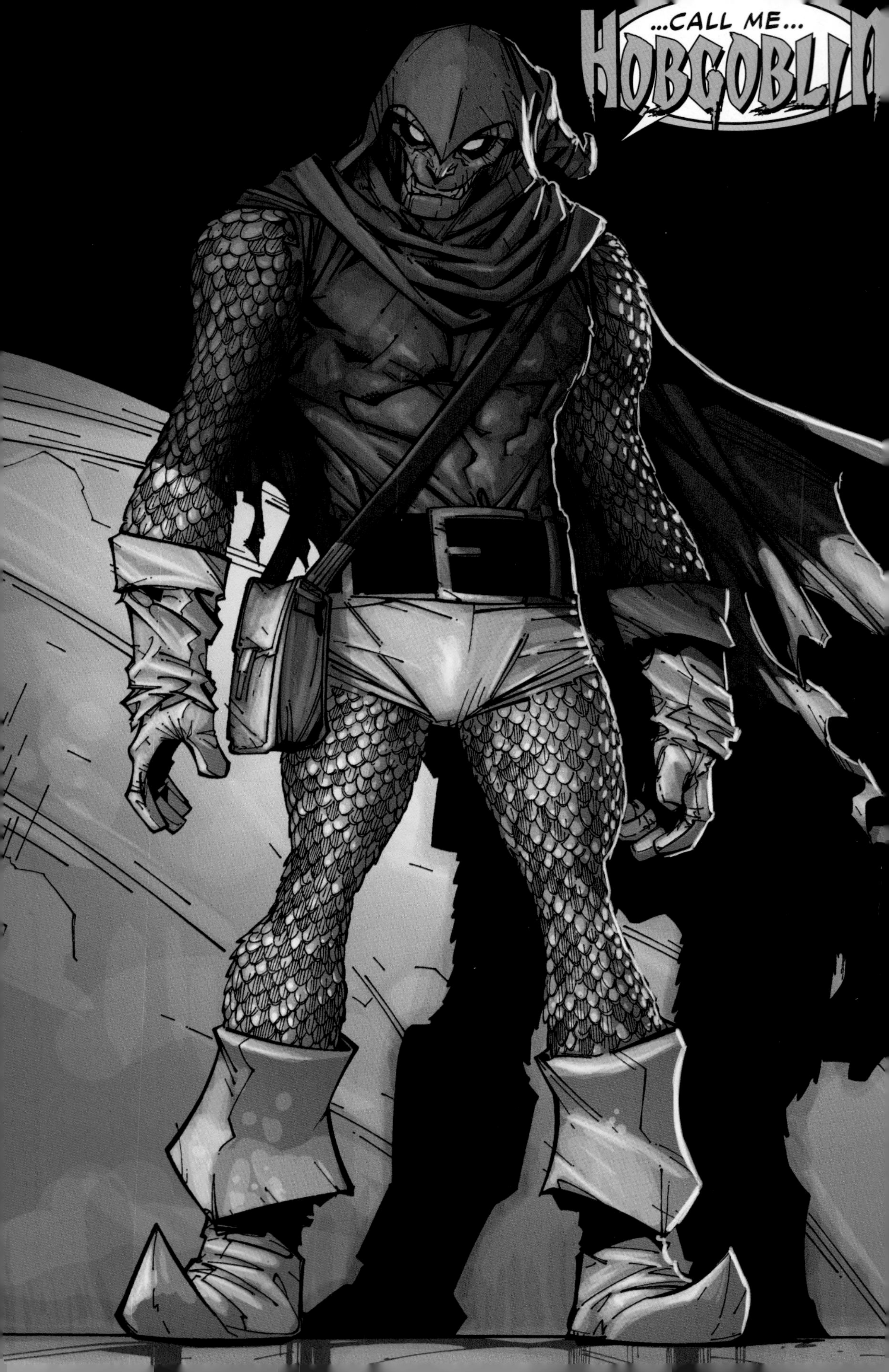
...CALL ME...
HOBGOBLIN

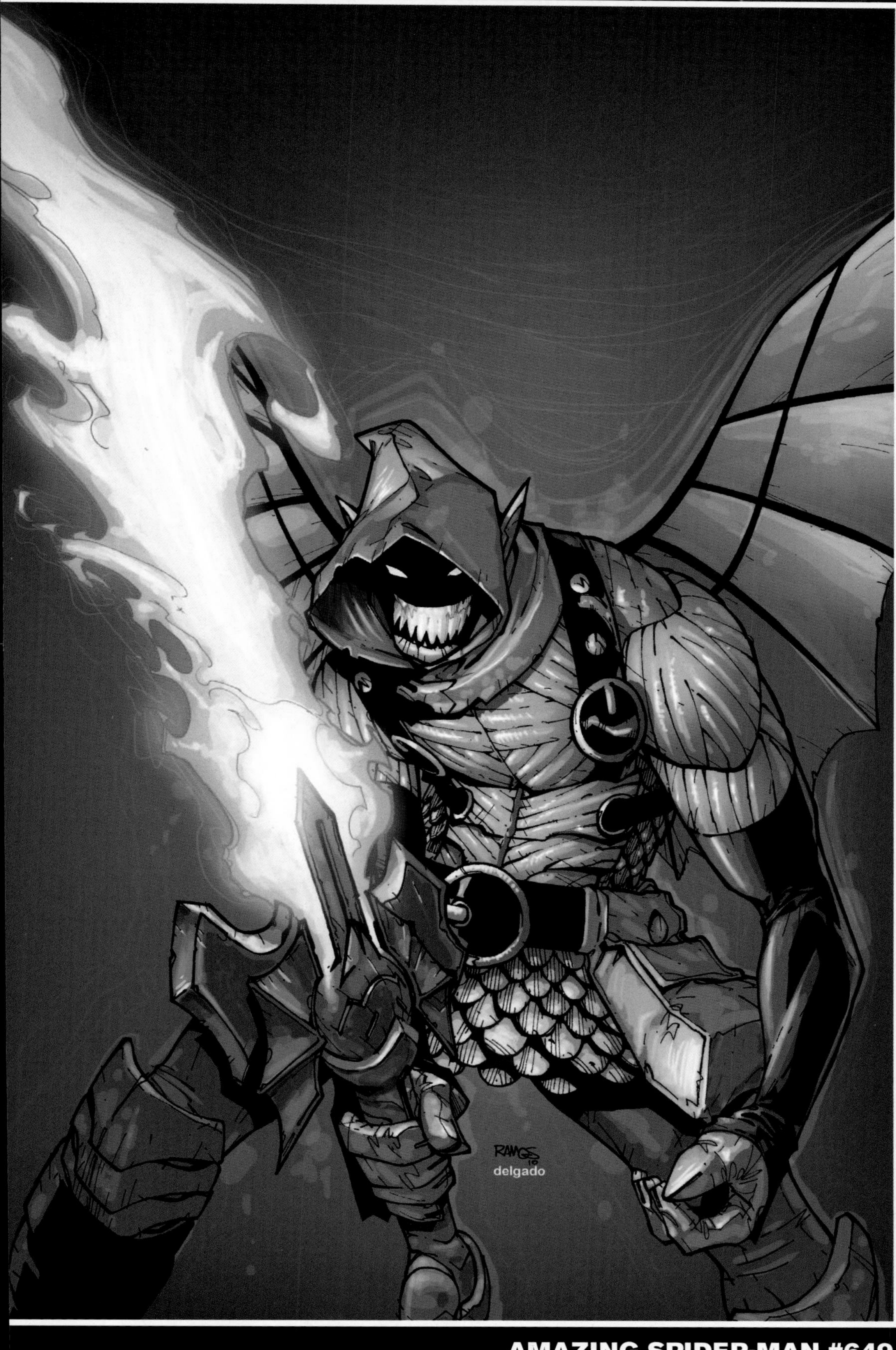
RAMOS 10
delgado

AMAZING SPIDER-MAN #649
COVER BY HUMBERTO RAMOS & EDGAR DELGADO

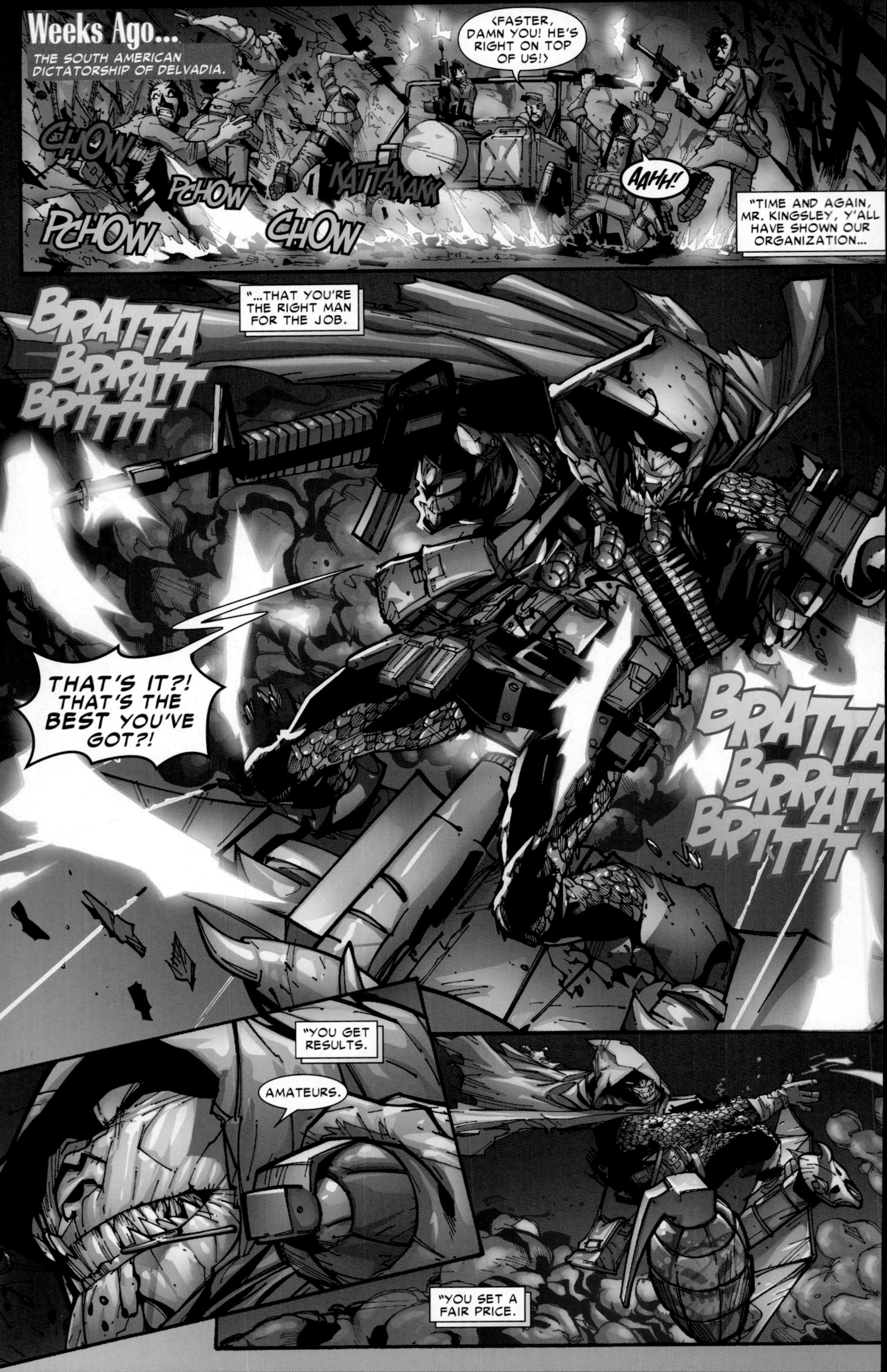
Weeks Ago...
THE SOUTH AMERICAN DICTATORSHIP OF DELVADIA.
‹FASTER, DAMN YOU! HE'S RIGHT ON TOP OF US!›
CHOW
PCHOW
KATTAKAKK
AAHH!
PCHOW
CHOW
"TIME AND AGAIN, MR. KINGSLEY, Y'ALL HAVE SHOWN OUR ORGANIZATION...
"...THAT YOU'RE THE RIGHT MAN FOR THE JOB.
BRATTA BRRATT BRTTTT
THAT'S IT?! THAT'S THE BEST YOU'VE GOT?!
BRATTA BRRATT BRTTTT
"YOU GET RESULTS.
AMATEURS.
"YOU SET A FAIR PRICE.

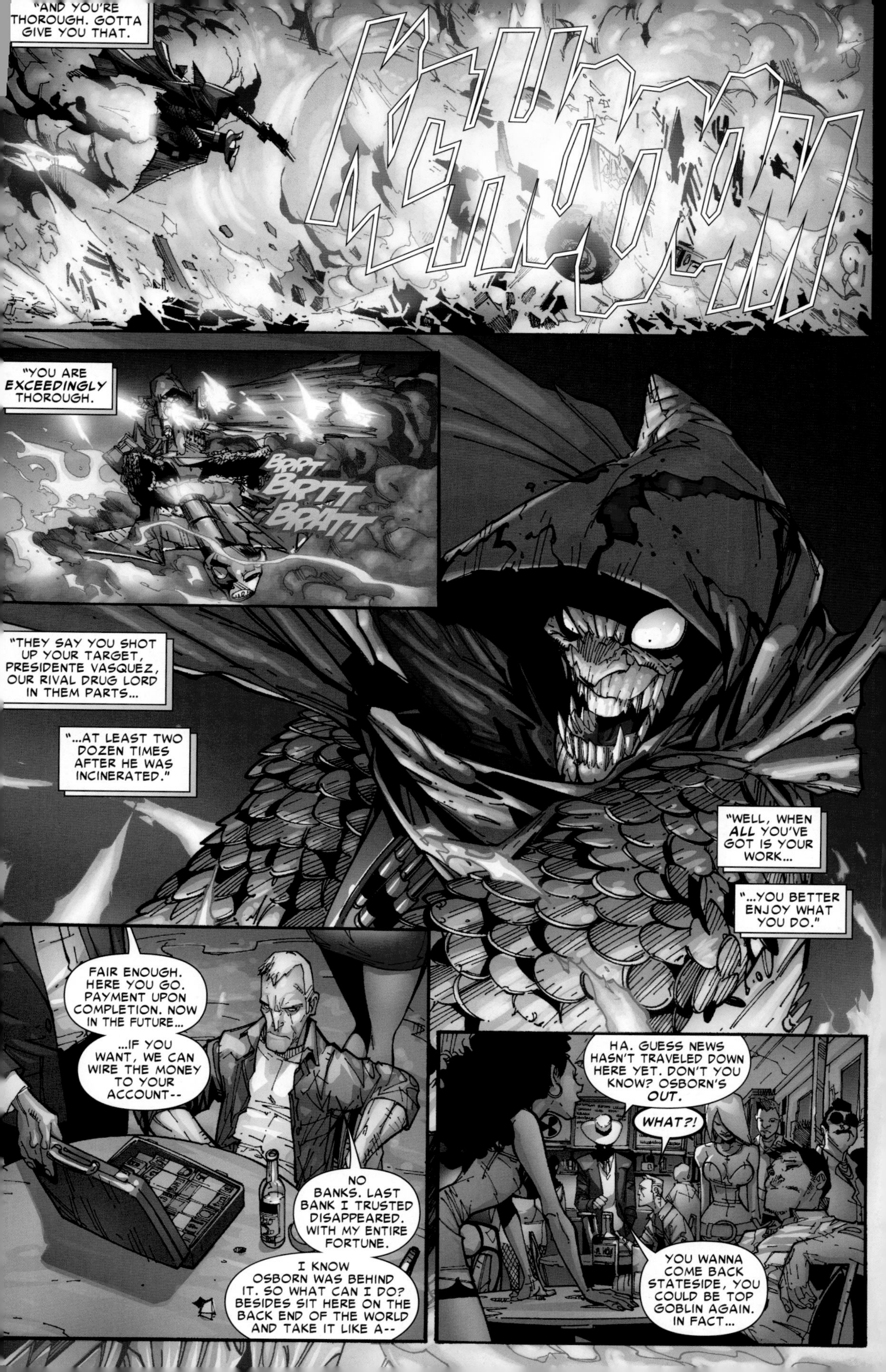
"AND YOU'RE THOROUGH. GOTTA GIVE YOU THAT.
KRUMM KALLOOM
"YOU ARE EXCEEDINGLY THOROUGH.
BRRPT BRTT BRATT
"THEY SAY YOU SHOT UP YOUR TARGET, PRESIDENTE VASQUEZ, OUR RIVAL DRUG LORD IN THEM PARTS...
"...AT LEAST TWO DOZEN TIMES AFTER HE WAS INCINERATED."
"WELL, WHEN ALL YOU'VE GOT IS YOUR WORK...
"...YOU BETTER ENJOY WHAT YOU DO."
FAIR ENOUGH. HERE YOU GO. PAYMENT UPON COMPLETION. NOW IN THE FUTURE...
...IF YOU WANT, WE CAN WIRE THE MONEY TO YOUR ACCOUNT--
NO BANKS. LAST BANK I TRUSTED DISAPPEARED. WITH MY ENTIRE FORTUNE.
I KNOW OSBORN WAS BEHIND IT. SO WHAT CAN I DO? BESIDES SIT HERE ON THE BACK END OF THE WORLD AND TAKE IT LIKE A--
HA. GUESS NEWS HASN'T TRAVELED DOWN HERE YET. DON'T YOU KNOW? OSBORN'S OUT.
WHAT?!
YOU WANNA COME BACK STATESIDE, YOU COULD BE TOP GOBLIN AGAIN. IN FACT...

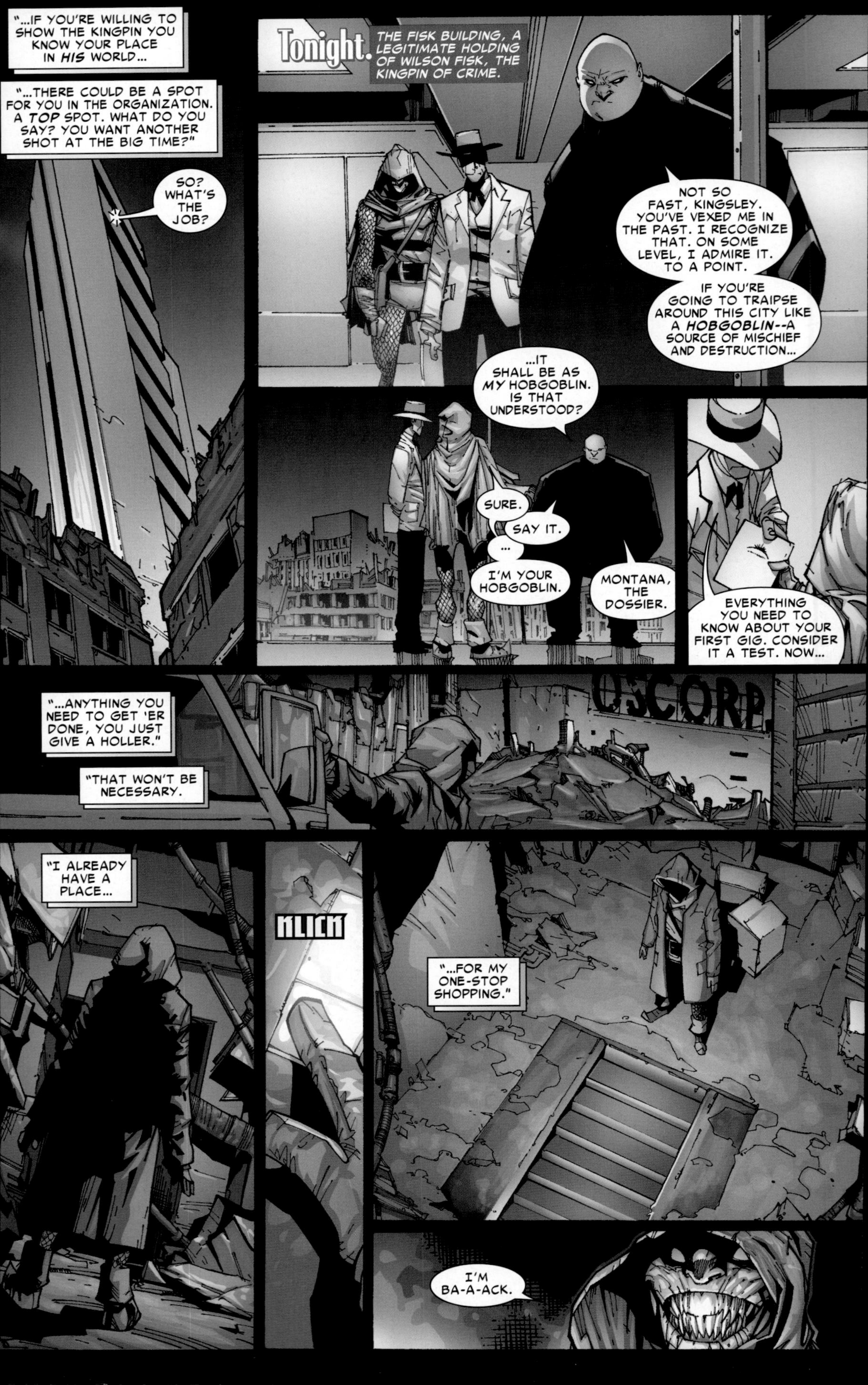
"...IF YOU'RE WILLING TO SHOW THE KINGPIN YOU KNOW YOUR PLACE IN HIS WORLD...
"...THERE COULD BE A SPOT FOR YOU IN THE ORGANIZATION. A TOP SPOT. WHAT DO YOU SAY? YOU WANT ANOTHER SHOT AT THE BIG TIME?"
SO? WHAT'S THE JOB?
Tonight.
THE FISK BUILDING, A LEGITIMATE HOLDING OF WILSON FISK, THE KINGPIN OF CRIME.
NOT SO FAST, KINGSLEY. YOU'VE VEXED ME IN THE PAST. I RECOGNIZE THAT. ON SOME LEVEL, I ADMIRE IT. TO A POINT.
IF YOU'RE GOING TO TRAIPSE AROUND THIS CITY LIKE A HOBGOBLIN--A SOURCE OF MISCHIEF AND DESTRUCTION...
...IT SHALL BE AS MY HOBGOBLIN. IS THAT UNDERSTOOD?
SURE.
SAY IT.
...
I'M YOUR HOBGOBLIN.
MONTANA, THE DOSSIER.
EVERYTHING YOU NEED TO KNOW ABOUT YOUR FIRST GIG. CONSIDER IT A TEST. NOW...
"...ANYTHING YOU NEED TO GET 'ER DONE, YOU JUST GIVE A HOLLER."
"THAT WON'T BE NECESSARY.
OSCORP
"I ALREADY HAVE A PLACE...
KLICK
"...FOR MY ONE-STOP SHOPPING."
I'M BA-A-ACK.

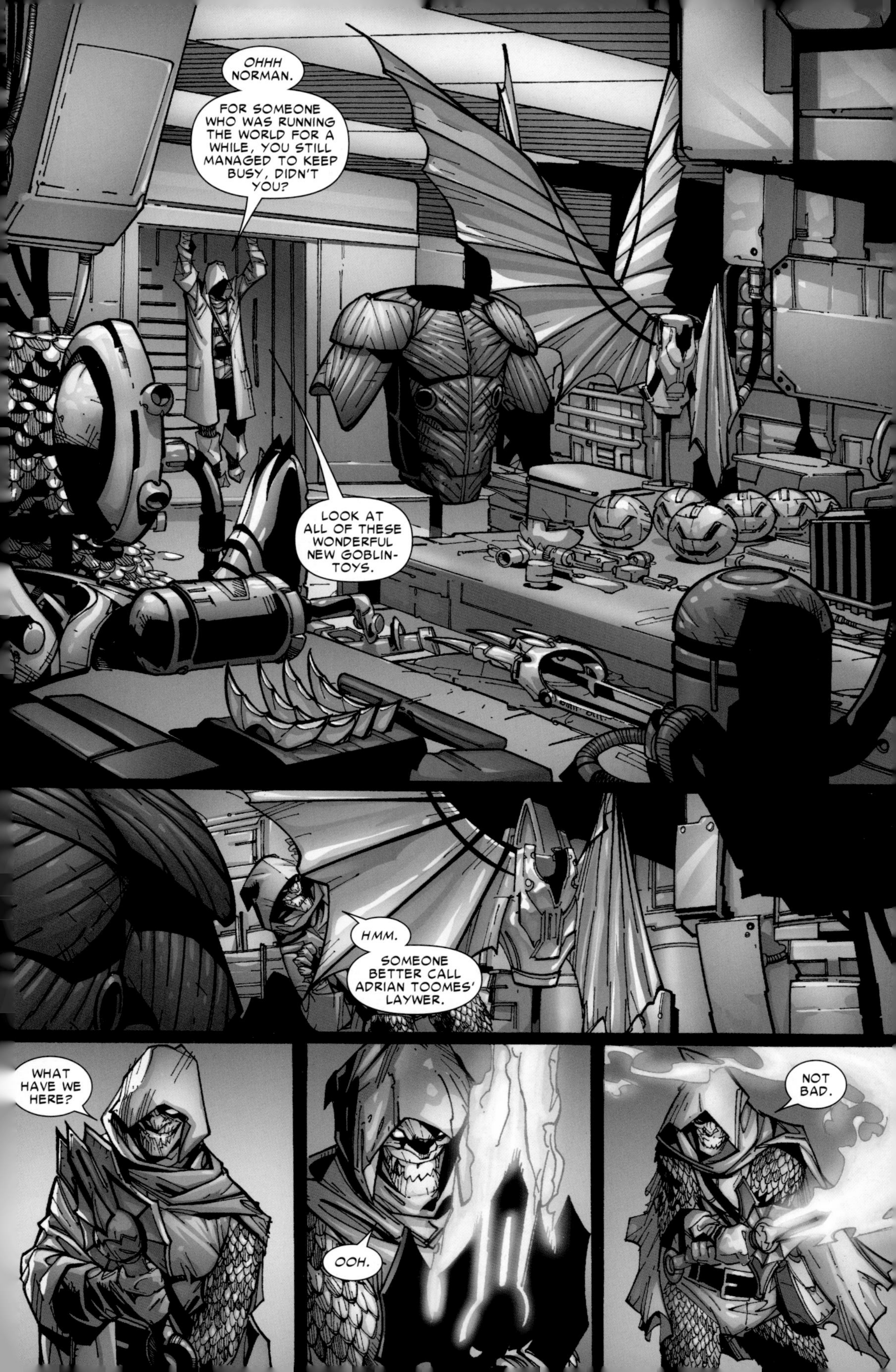
OHHH NORMAN.
FOR SOMEONE WHO WAS RUNNING THE WORLD FOR A WHILE, YOU STILL MANAGED TO KEEP BUSY, DIDN'T YOU?
LOOK AT ALL OF THESE WONDERFUL NEW GOBLIN-TOYS.
HMM.
SOMEONE BETTER CALL ADRIAN TOOMES' LAYWER.
WHAT HAVE WE HERE?
OOH.
NOT BAD.

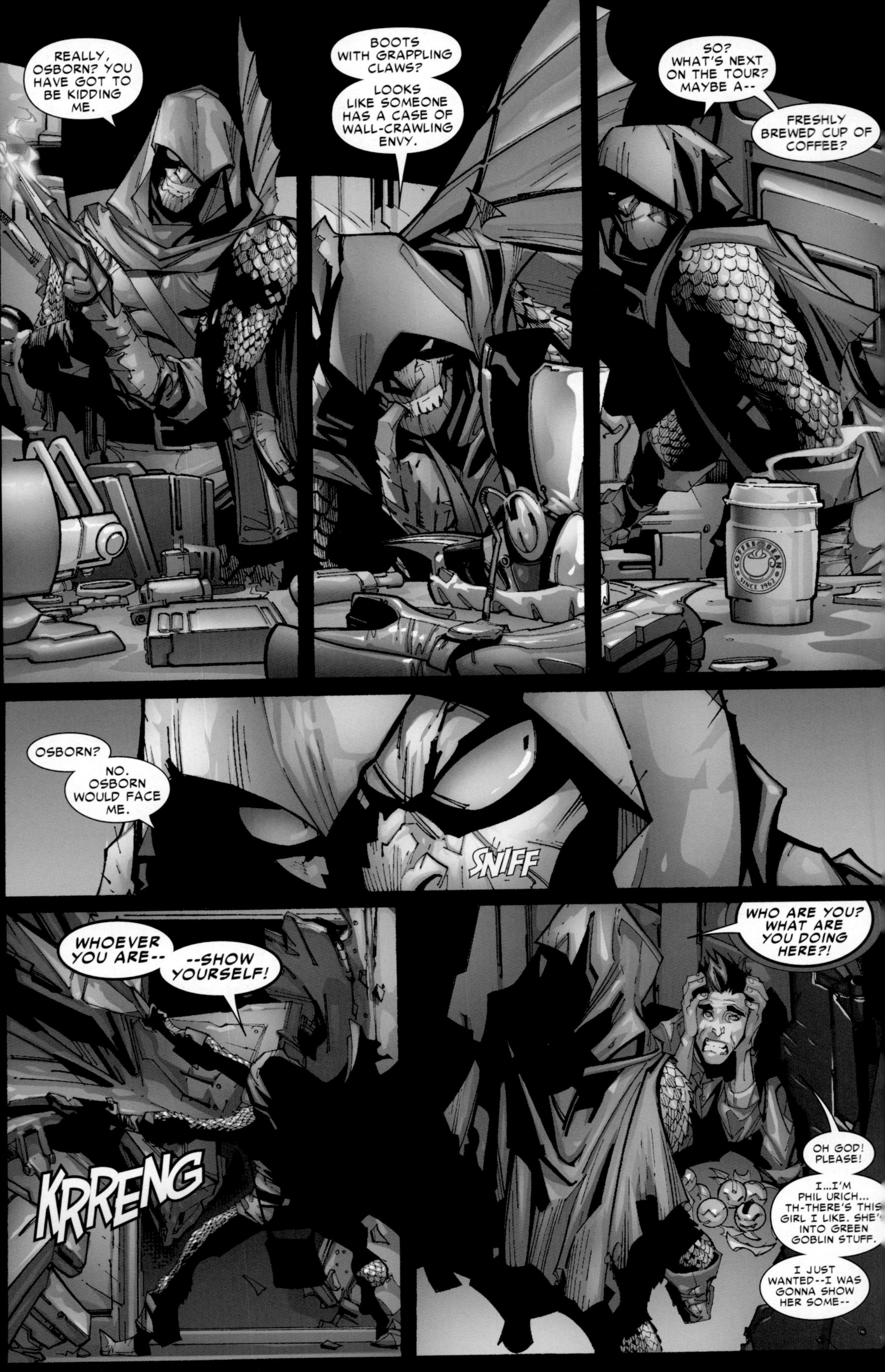
REALLY, OSBORN? YOU HAVE GOT TO BE KIDDING ME.
BOOTS WITH GRAPPLING CLAWS?
LOOKS LIKE SOMEONE HAS A CASE OF WALL-CRAWLING ENVY.
SO? WHAT'S NEXT ON THE TOUR? MAYBE A--
FRESHLY BREWED CUP OF COFFEE?
COFFEE BEAN
SINCE 1962
OSBORN?
NO. OSBORN WOULD FACE ME.
SNIFF
WHOEVER YOU ARE--
--SHOW YOURSELF!
KRRENG
WHO ARE YOU? WHAT ARE YOU DOING HERE?!
OH GOD! PLEASE!
I...I'M PHIL URICH... TH-THERE'S THIS GIRL I LIKE. SHE' INTO GREEN GOBLIN STUFF.
I JUST WANTED--I WAS GONNA SHOW HER SOME--

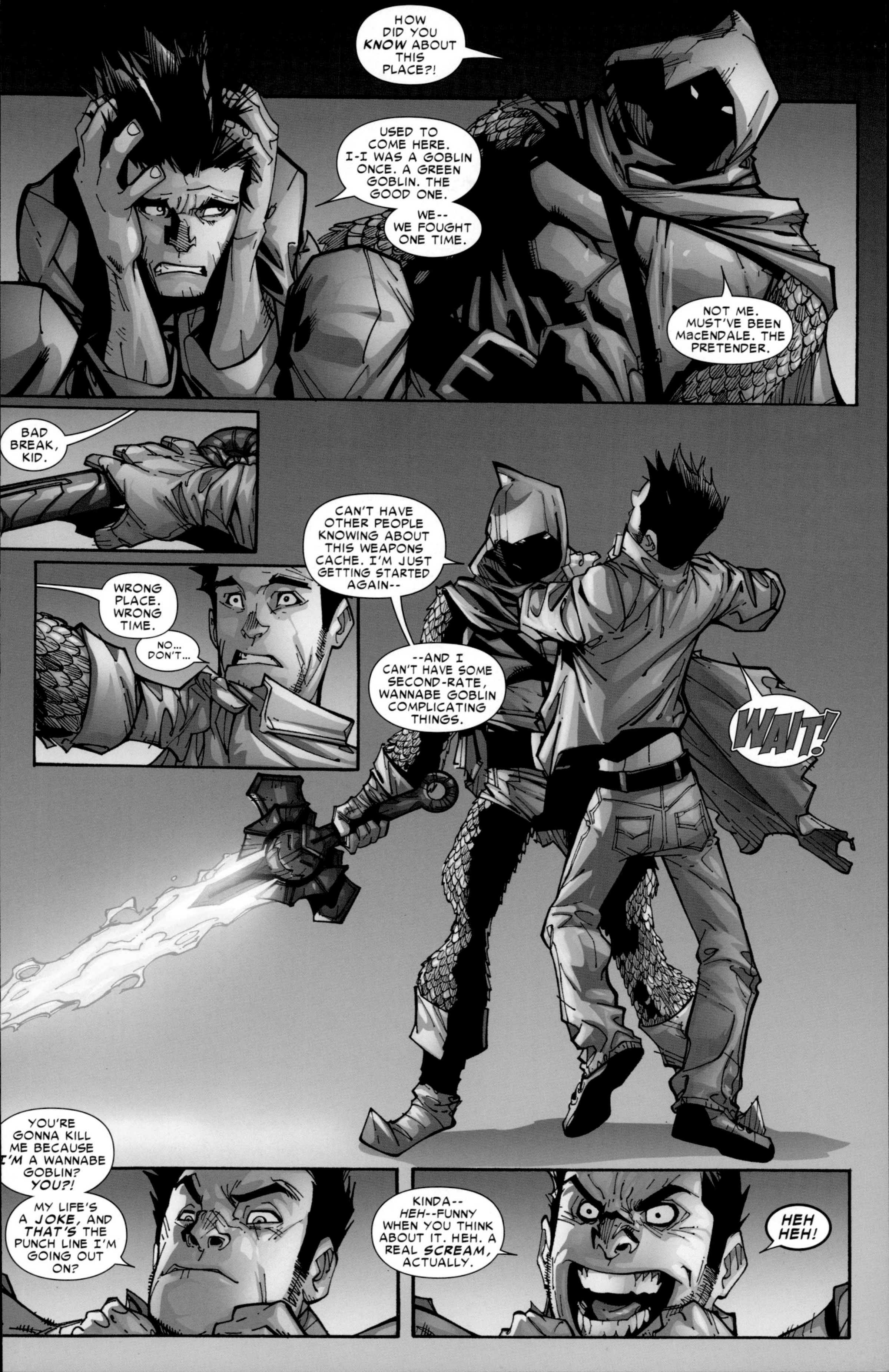
HOW DID YOU KNOW ABOUT THIS PLACE?!
USED TO COME HERE. I-I WAS A GOBLIN ONCE. A GREEN GOBLIN. THE GOOD ONE.
WE-- WE FOUGHT ONE TIME.
NOT ME. MUST'VE BEEN MacENDALE. THE PRETENDER.
BAD BREAK, KID.
WRONG PLACE. WRONG TIME.
NO... DON'T...
CAN'T HAVE OTHER PEOPLE KNOWING ABOUT THIS WEAPONS CACHE. I'M JUST GETTING STARTED AGAIN--
--AND I CAN'T HAVE SOME SECOND-RATE, WANNABE GOBLIN COMPLICATING THINGS.
WAIT!
YOU'RE GONNA KILL ME BECAUSE I'M A WANNABE GOBLIN? YOU?!
MY LIFE'S A JOKE, AND THAT'S THE PUNCH LINE I'M GOING OUT ON?
KINDA-- HEH--FUNNY WHEN YOU THINK ABOUT IT. HEH. A REAL SCREAM, ACTUALLY.
HEH HEH!

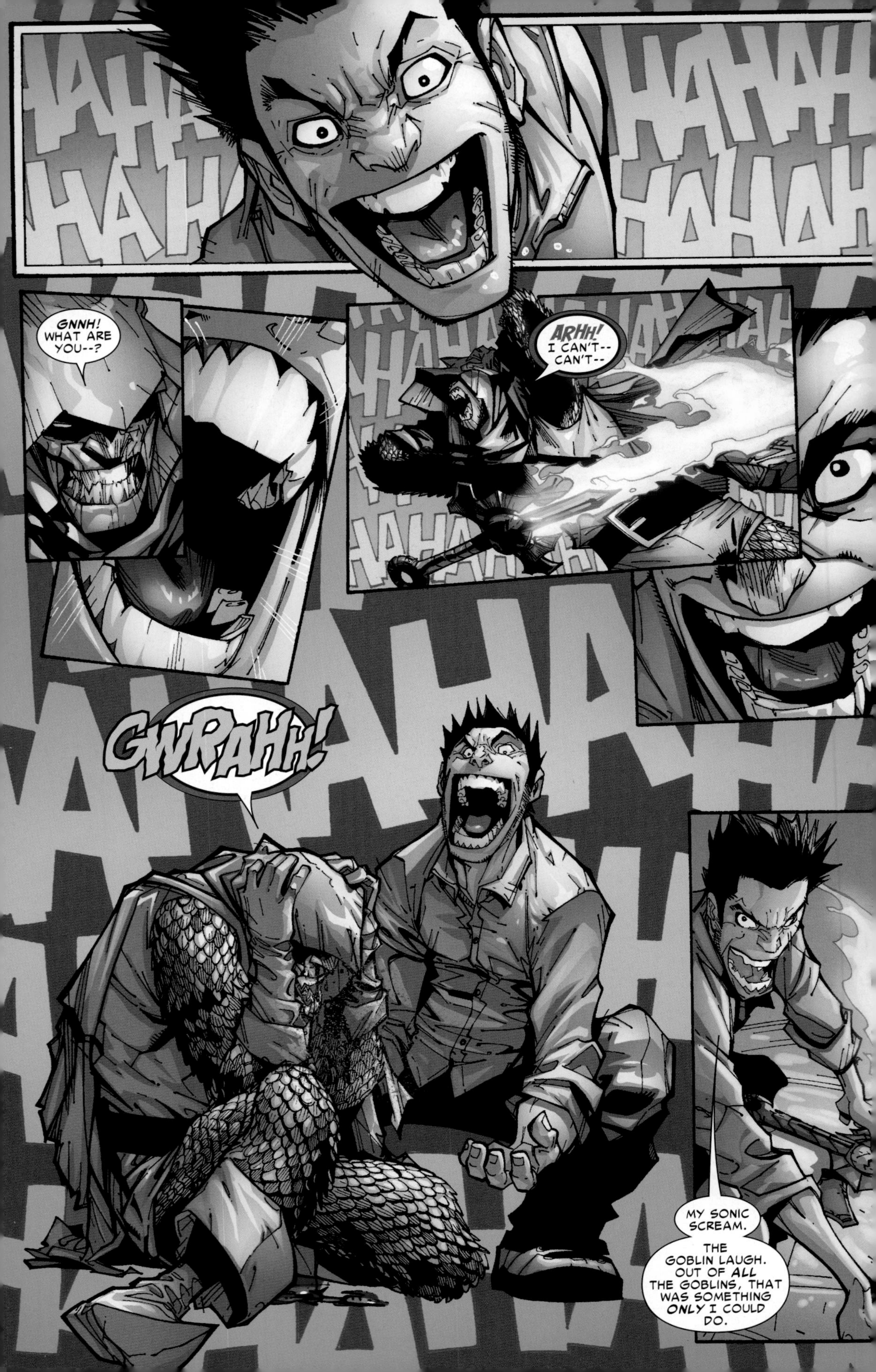
HAHAHAHAHA
GNNH! WHAT ARE YOU--?
ARHH! I CAN'T-- CAN'T--
GWRAHH!
MY SONIC SCREAM.
THE GOBLIN LAUGH. OUT OF ALL THE GOBLINS, THAT WAS SOMETHING ONLY I COULD DO.

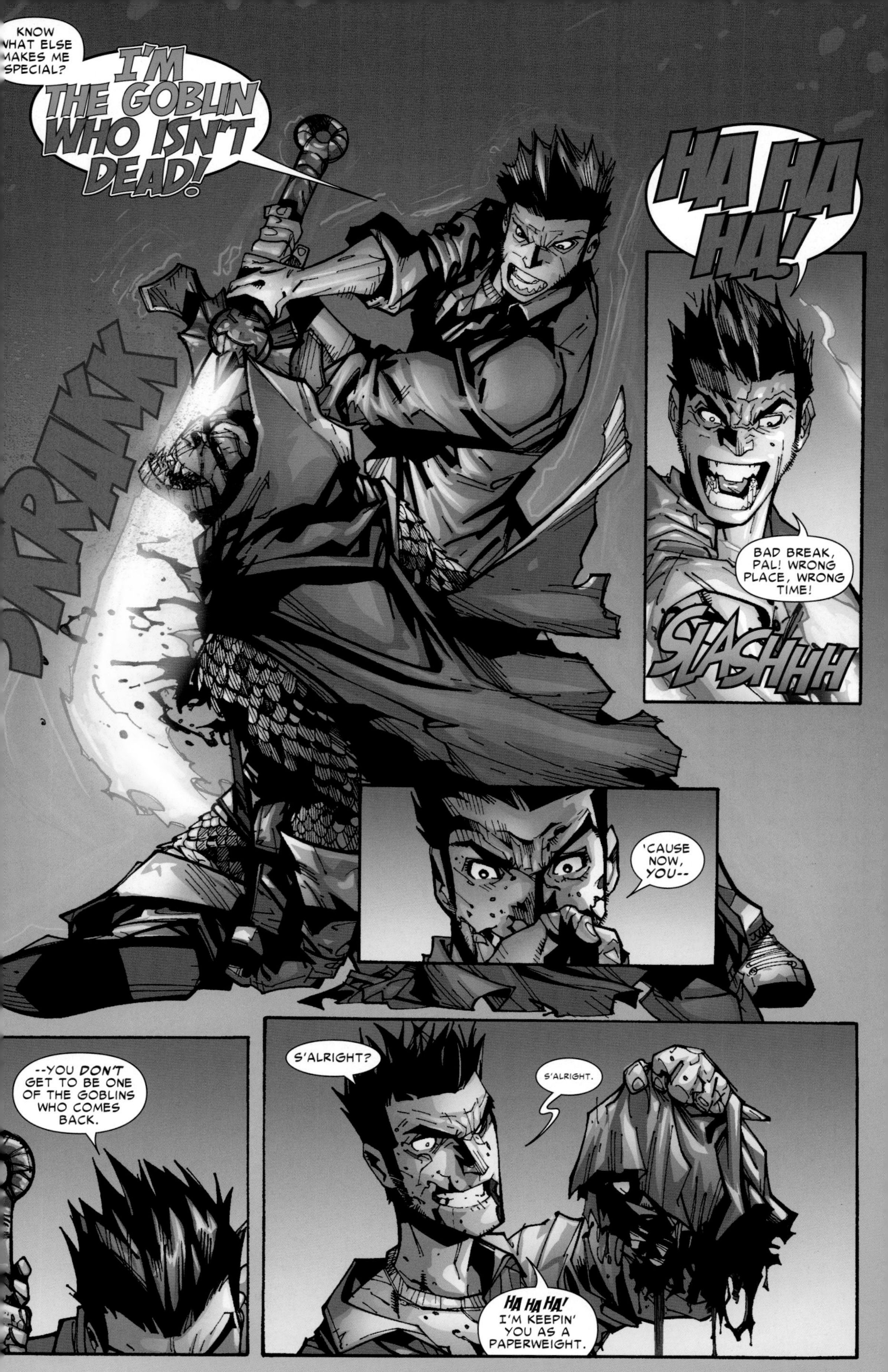
KNOW WHAT ELSE MAKES ME SPECIAL?
I'M THE GOBLIN WHO ISN'T DEAD!
DRAAK
HA HA HA!
BAD BREAK, PAL! WRONG PLACE, WRONG TIME!
SLASHHH
'CAUSE NOW, YOU--
--YOU DON'T GET TO BE ONE OF THE GOBLINS WHO COMES BACK.
S'ALRIGHT?
S'ALRIGHT.
HA HA HA! I'M KEEPIN' YOU AS A PAPERWEIGHT.

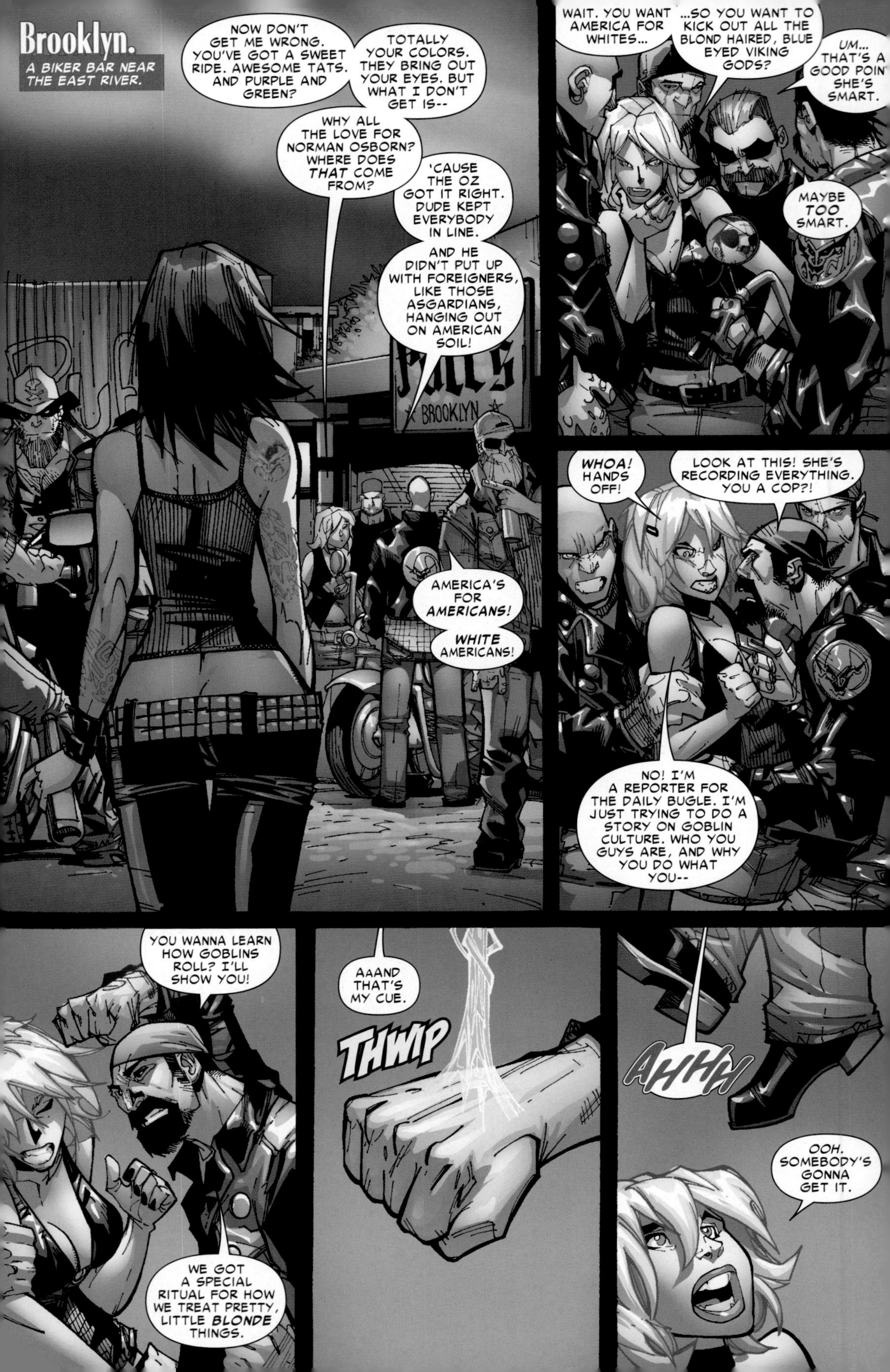
Brooklyn.
A BIKER BAR NEAR THE EAST RIVER.
NOW DON'T GET ME WRONG. YOU'VE GOT A SWEET RIDE. AWESOME TATS. AND PURPLE AND GREEN?
TOTALLY YOUR COLORS. THEY BRING OUT YOUR EYES. BUT WHAT I DON'T GET IS--
WHY ALL THE LOVE FOR NORMAN OSBORN? WHERE DOES THAT COME FROM?
'CAUSE THE OZ GOT IT RIGHT. DUDE KEPT EVERYBODY IN LINE.
AND HE DIDN'T PUT UP WITH FOREIGNERS, LIKE THOSE ASGARDIANS, HANGING OUT ON AMERICAN SOIL!
BROOKLYN
AMERICA'S FOR AMERICANS!
WHITE AMERICANS!
WAIT. YOU WANT AMERICA FOR WHITES...
...SO YOU WANT TO KICK OUT ALL THE BLOND HAIRED, BLUE EYED VIKING GODS?
UM... THAT'S A GOOD POIN' SHE'S SMART.
MAYBE TOO SMART.
WHOA! HANDS OFF!
LOOK AT THIS! SHE'S RECORDING EVERYTHING. YOU A COP?!
NO! I'M A REPORTER FOR THE DAILY BUGLE. I'M JUST TRYING TO DO A STORY ON GOBLIN CULTURE. WHO YOU GUYS ARE, AND WHY YOU DO WHAT YOU--
YOU WANNA LEARN HOW GOBLINS ROLL? I'LL SHOW YOU!
WE GOT A SPECIAL RITUAL FOR HOW WE TREAT PRETTY, LITTLE BLONDE THINGS.
AAAND THAT'S MY CUE.
THWIP
AHHH
OOH. SOMEBODY'S GONNA GET IT.

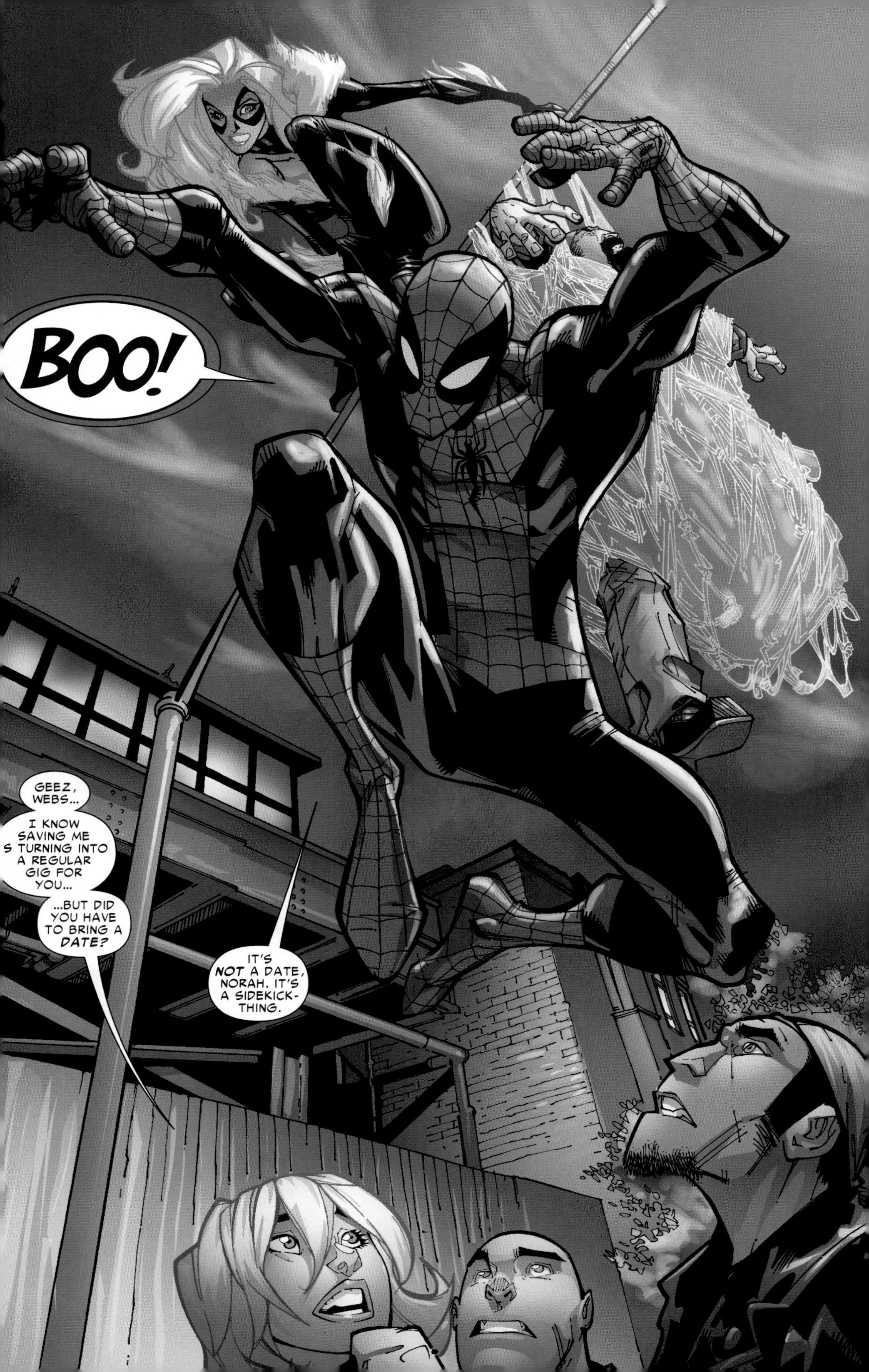
BOO!
GEEZ, WEBS...
I KNOW SAVING ME S TURNING INTO A REGULAR GIG FOR YOU...
...BUT DID YOU HAVE TO BRING A DATE?
IT'S NOT A DATE, NORAH. IT'S A SIDEKICK-THING.

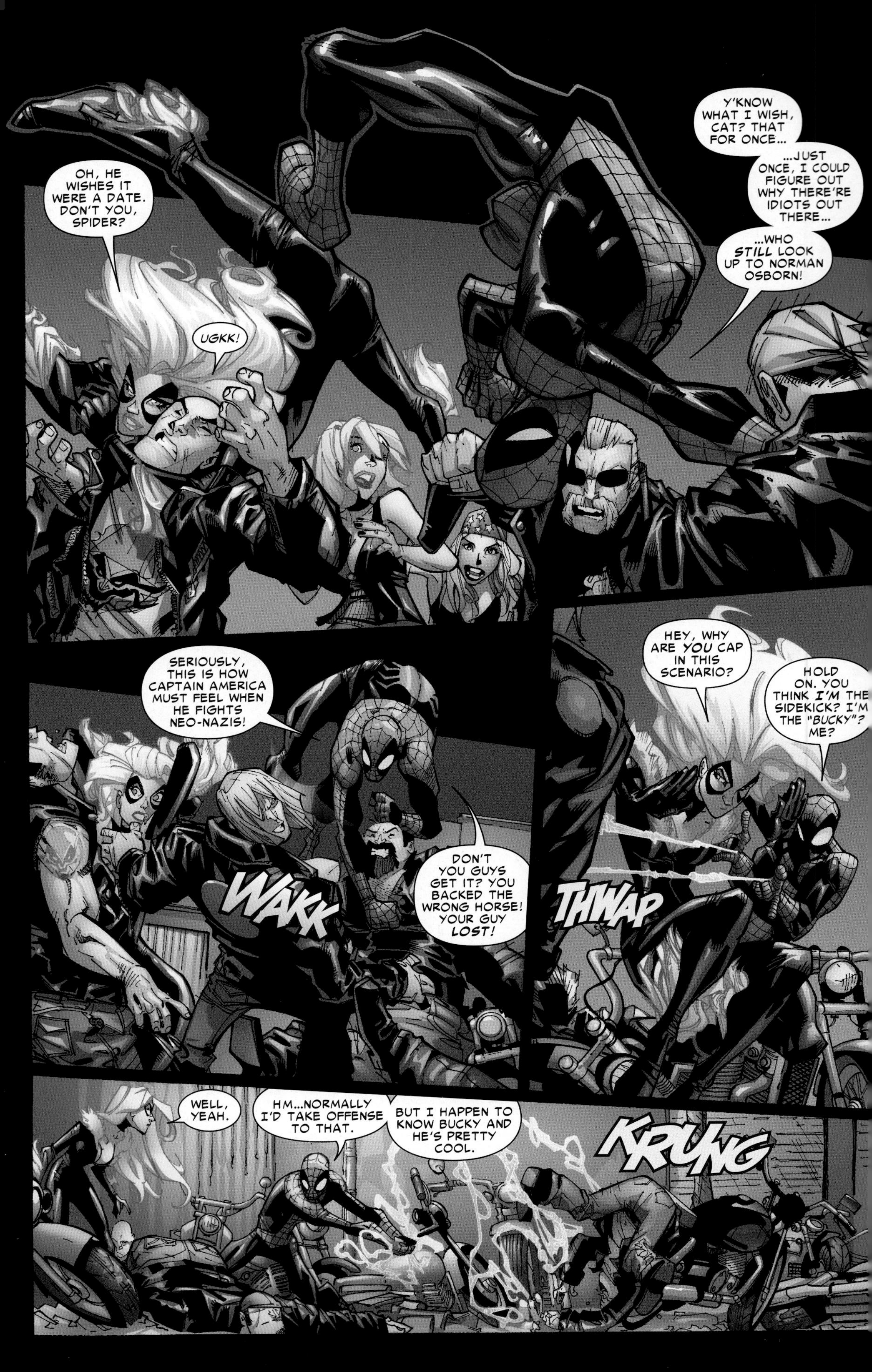

OH, HE WISHES IT WERE A DATE. DON'T YOU, SPIDER?
Y'KNOW WHAT I WISH, CAT? THAT FOR ONCE...
...JUST ONCE, I COULD FIGURE OUT WHY THERE'RE IDIOTS OUT THERE...
...WHO STILL LOOK UP TO NORMAN OSBORN!
UGKK!
SERIOUSLY, THIS IS HOW CAPTAIN AMERICA MUST FEEL WHEN HE FIGHTS NEO-NAZIS!
DON'T YOU GUYS GET IT? YOU BACKED THE WRONG HORSE! YOUR GUY LOST!
WAKK
HEY, WHY ARE YOU CAP IN THIS SCENARIO?
HOLD ON. YOU THINK I'M THE SIDEKICK? I'M THE "BUCKY"? ME?
THWAP
WELL, YEAH.
HM...NORMALLY I'D TAKE OFFENSE TO THAT.
BUT I HAPPEN TO KNOW BUCKY AND HE'S PRETTY COOL.
KRUNG

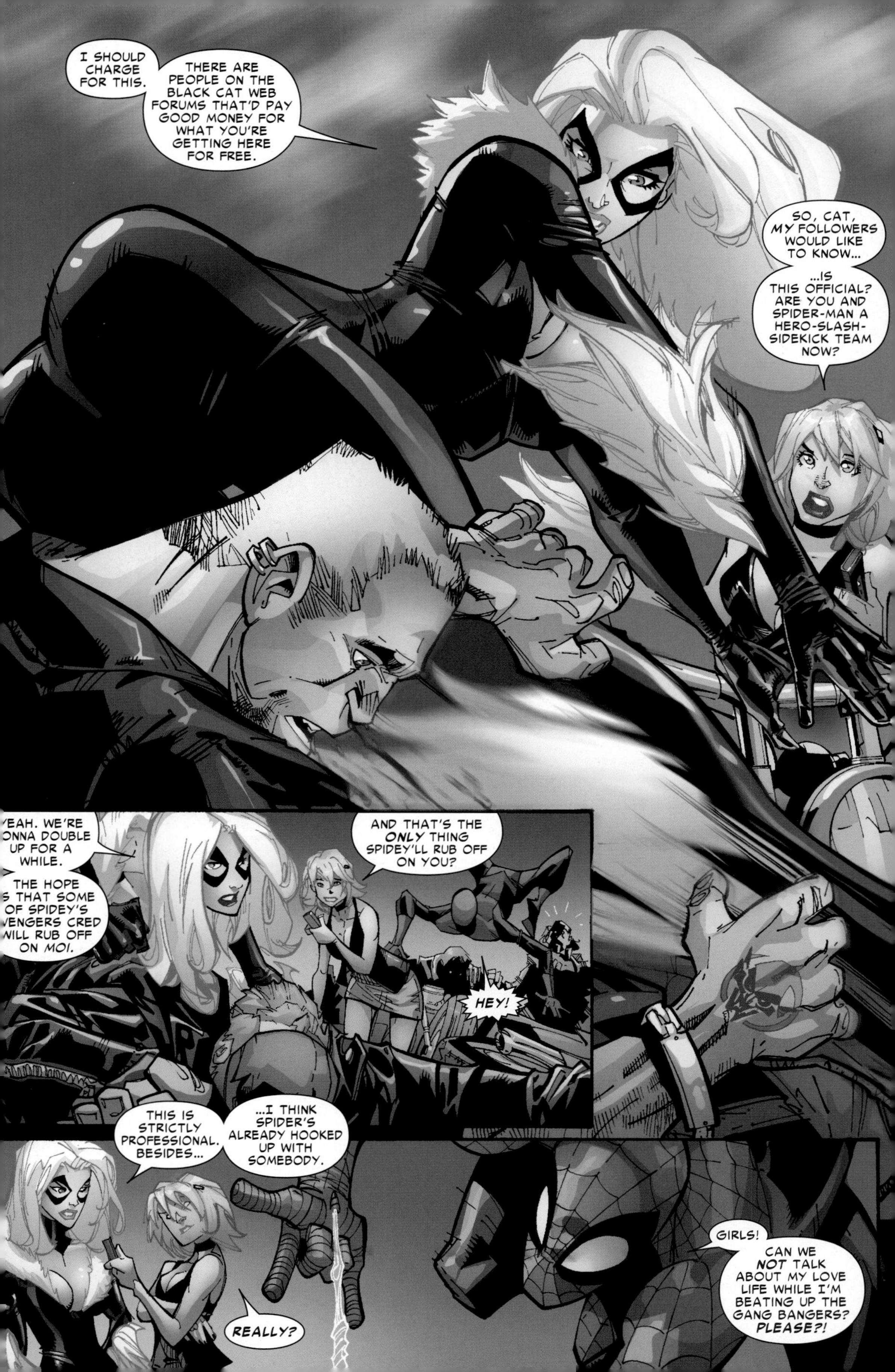
I SHOULD CHARGE FOR THIS.
THERE ARE PEOPLE ON THE BLACK CAT WEB FORUMS THAT'D PAY GOOD MONEY FOR WHAT YOU'RE GETTING HERE FOR FREE.
SO, CAT, MY FOLLOWERS WOULD LIKE TO KNOW...
...IS THIS OFFICIAL? ARE YOU AND SPIDER-MAN A HERO-SLASH-SIDEKICK TEAM NOW?
YEAH. WE'RE ONNA DOUBLE UP FOR A WHILE.
THE HOPE S THAT SOME OF SPIDEY'S VENGERS CRED WILL RUB OFF ON MOI.
AND THAT'S THE ONLY THING SPIDEY'LL RUB OFF ON YOU?
HEY!
THIS IS STRICTLY PROFESSIONAL. BESIDES...
...I THINK SPIDER'S ALREADY HOOKED UP WITH SOMEBODY.
REALLY?
GIRLS!
CAN WE NOT TALK ABOUT MY LOVE LIFE WHILE I'M BEATING UP THE GANG BANGERS? PLEASE?!

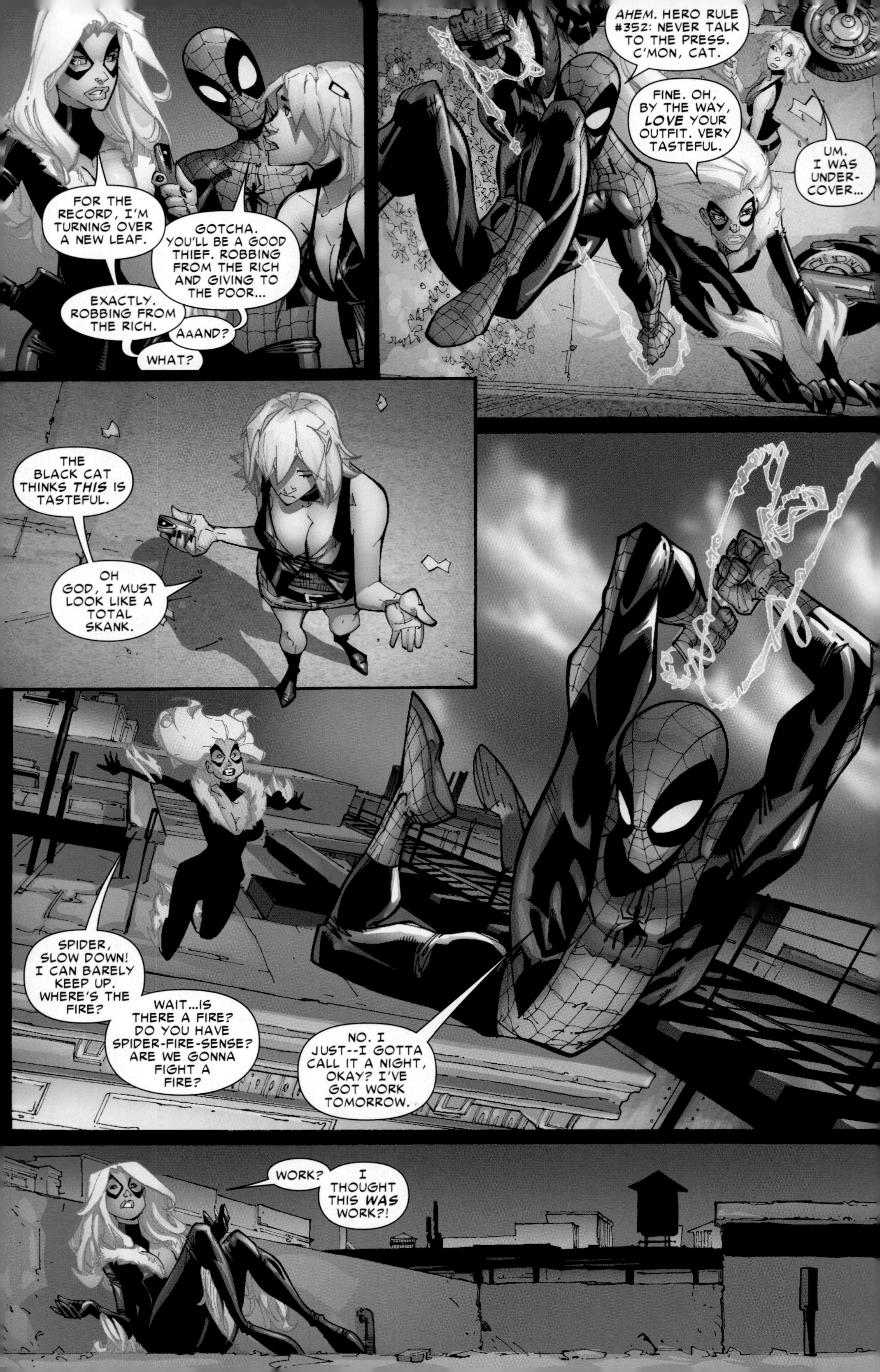
FOR THE RECORD, I'M TURNING OVER A NEW LEAF.
GOTCHA. YOU'LL BE A GOOD THIEF. ROBBING FROM THE RICH AND GIVING TO THE POOR...
EXACTLY. ROBBING FROM THE RICH.
AAAND?
WHAT?
AHEM. HERO RULE #352: NEVER TALK TO THE PRESS. C'MON, CAT.
FINE. OH, BY THE WAY, ***LOVE*** YOUR OUTFIT. VERY TASTEFUL.
UM. I WAS UNDER-COVER...
THE BLACK CAT THINKS ***THIS*** IS TASTEFUL.
OH GOD, I MUST LOOK LIKE A TOTAL SKANK.
SPIDER, SLOW DOWN! I CAN BARELY KEEP UP. WHERE'S THE FIRE?
WAIT...IS THERE A FIRE? DO YOU HAVE SPIDER-FIRE-SENSE? ARE WE GONNA FIGHT A FIRE?
NO. I JUST--I GOTTA CALL IT A NIGHT, OKAY? I'VE GOT WORK TOMORROW.
WORK?
I THOUGHT THIS ***WAS*** WORK?!

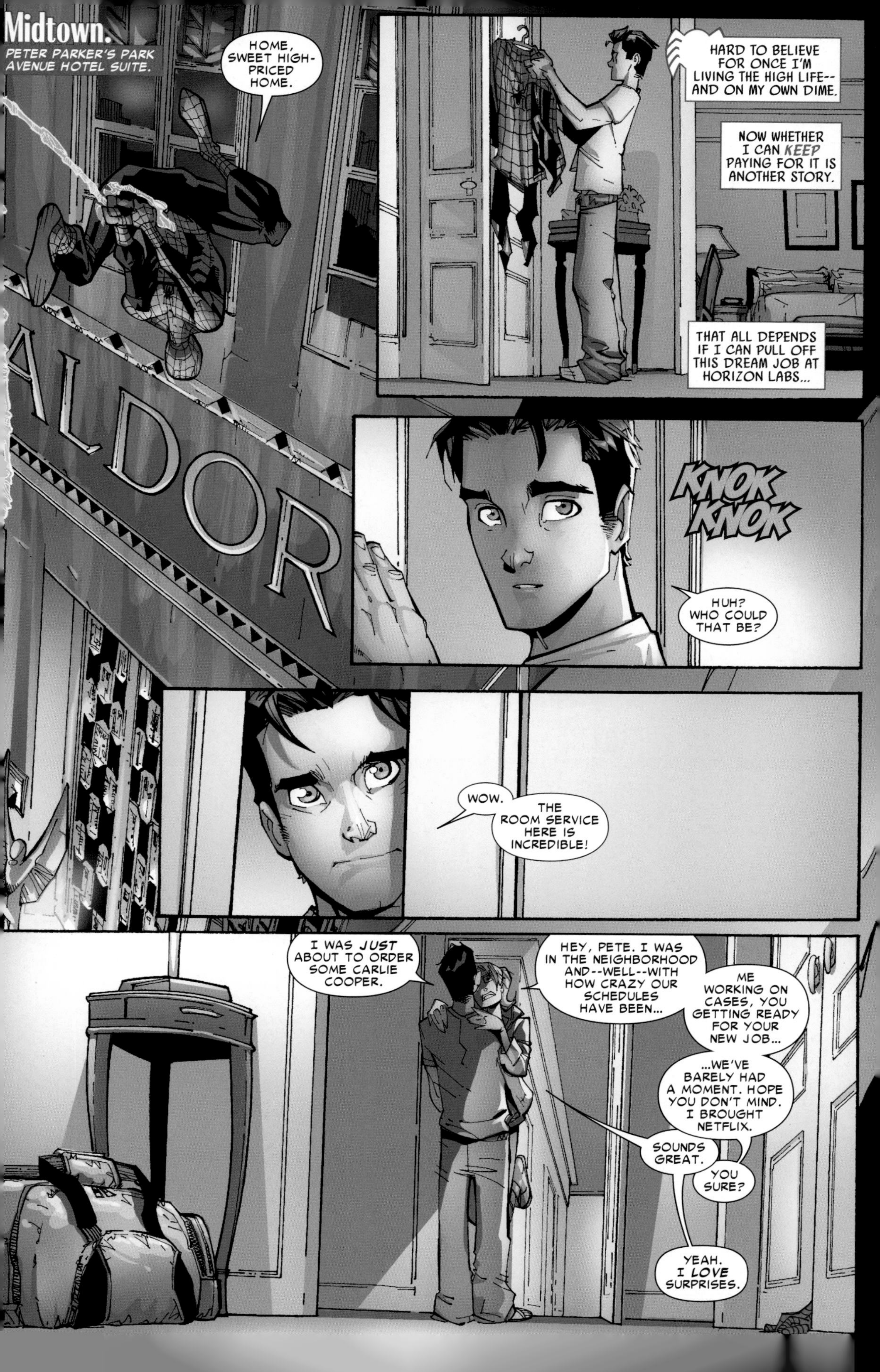

Midtown.
PETER PARKER'S PARK AVENUE HOTEL SUITE.
HOME, SWEET HIGH-PRICED HOME.
HARD TO BELIEVE FOR ONCE I'M LIVING THE HIGH LIFE--AND ON MY OWN DIME.
NOW WHETHER I CAN KEEP PAYING FOR IT IS ANOTHER STORY.
THAT ALL DEPENDS IF I CAN PULL OFF THIS DREAM JOB AT HORIZON LABS...
KNOK KNOK
HUH? WHO COULD THAT BE?
WOW.
THE ROOM SERVICE HERE IS INCREDIBLE!
I WAS JUST ABOUT TO ORDER SOME CARLIE COOPER.
HEY, PETE. I WAS IN THE NEIGHBORHOOD AND--WELL--WITH HOW CRAZY OUR SCHEDULES HAVE BEEN...
ME WORKING ON CASES, YOU GETTING READY FOR YOUR NEW JOB...
...WE'VE BARELY HAD A MOMENT. HOPE YOU DON'T MIND. I BROUGHT NETFLIX.
SOUNDS GREAT.
YOU SURE?
YEAH. I LOVE SURPRISES.

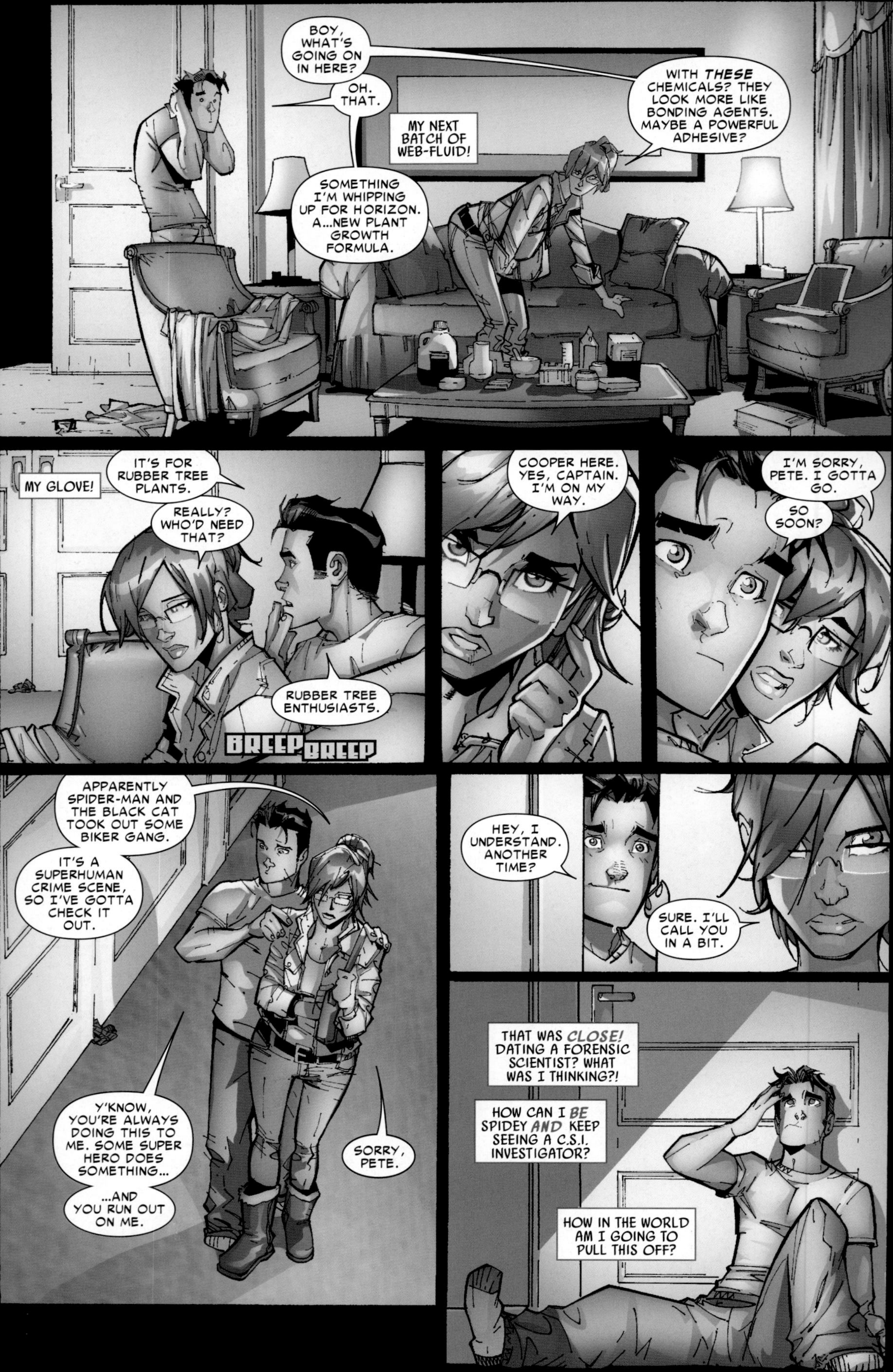
BOY, WHAT'S GOING ON IN HERE?
WITH THESE CHEMICALS? THEY LOOK MORE LIKE BONDING AGENTS. MAYBE A POWERFUL ADHESIVE?
OH. THAT.
MY NEXT BATCH OF WEB-FLUID!
SOMETHING I'M WHIPPING UP FOR HORIZON. A...NEW PLANT GROWTH FORMULA.
MY GLOVE!
IT'S FOR RUBBER TREE PLANTS.
REALLY? WHO'D NEED THAT?
RUBBER TREE ENTHUSIASTS.
BREEP BREEP
COOPER HERE. YES, CAPTAIN. I'M ON MY WAY.
I'M SORRY, PETE. I GOTTA GO.
SO SOON?
APPARENTLY SPIDER-MAN AND THE BLACK CAT TOOK OUT SOME BIKER GANG.
IT'S A SUPERHUMAN CRIME SCENE, SO I'VE GOTTA CHECK IT OUT.
Y'KNOW, YOU'RE ALWAYS DOING THIS TO ME. SOME SUPER HERO DOES SOMETHING...
...AND YOU RUN OUT ON ME.
SORRY, PETE.
HEY, I UNDERSTAND. ANOTHER TIME?
SURE. I'LL CALL YOU IN A BIT.
THAT WAS CLOSE! DATING A FORENSIC SCIENTIST? WHAT WAS I THINKING?!
HOW CAN I BE SPIDEY AND KEEP SEEING A C.S.I. INVESTIGATOR?
HOW IN THE WORLD AM I GOING TO PULL THIS OFF?

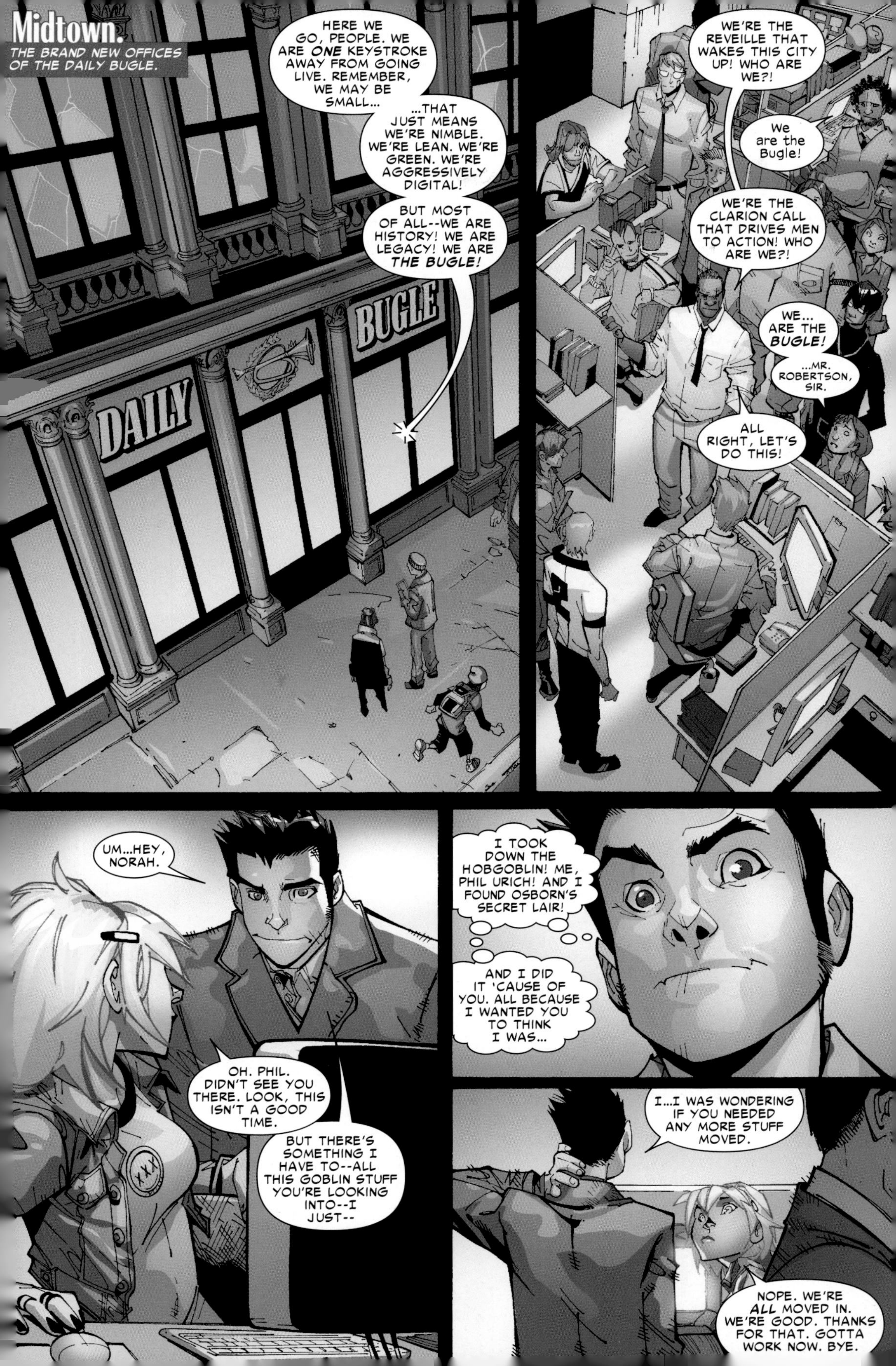
Midtown.
THE BRAND NEW OFFICES OF THE DAILY BUGLE.
HERE WE GO, PEOPLE. WE ARE ONE KEYSTROKE AWAY FROM GOING LIVE. REMEMBER, WE MAY BE SMALL...
...THAT JUST MEANS WE'RE NIMBLE. WE'RE LEAN. WE'RE GREEN. WE'RE AGGRESSIVELY DIGITAL!
BUT MOST OF ALL--WE ARE HISTORY! WE ARE LEGACY! WE ARE THE BUGLE!
DAILY BUGLE
WE'RE THE REVEILLE THAT WAKES THIS CITY UP! WHO ARE WE?!
We are the Bugle!
WE'RE THE CLARION CALL THAT DRIVES MEN TO ACTION! WHO ARE WE?!
WE... ARE THE BUGLE!
...MR. ROBERTSON, SIR.
ALL RIGHT, LET'S DO THIS!
UM...HEY, NORAH.
OH. PHIL. DIDN'T SEE YOU THERE. LOOK, THIS ISN'T A GOOD TIME.
BUT THERE'S SOMETHING I HAVE TO--ALL THIS GOBLIN STUFF YOU'RE LOOKING INTO--I JUST--
I TOOK DOWN THE HOBGOBLIN! ME, PHIL URICH! AND I FOUND OSBORN'S SECRET LAIR!
AND I DID IT 'CAUSE OF YOU. ALL BECAUSE I WANTED YOU TO THINK I WAS...
I...I WAS WONDERING IF YOU NEEDED ANY MORE STUFF MOVED.
NOPE. WE'RE ALL MOVED IN. WE'RE GOOD. THANKS FOR THAT. GOTTA WORK NOW. BYE.

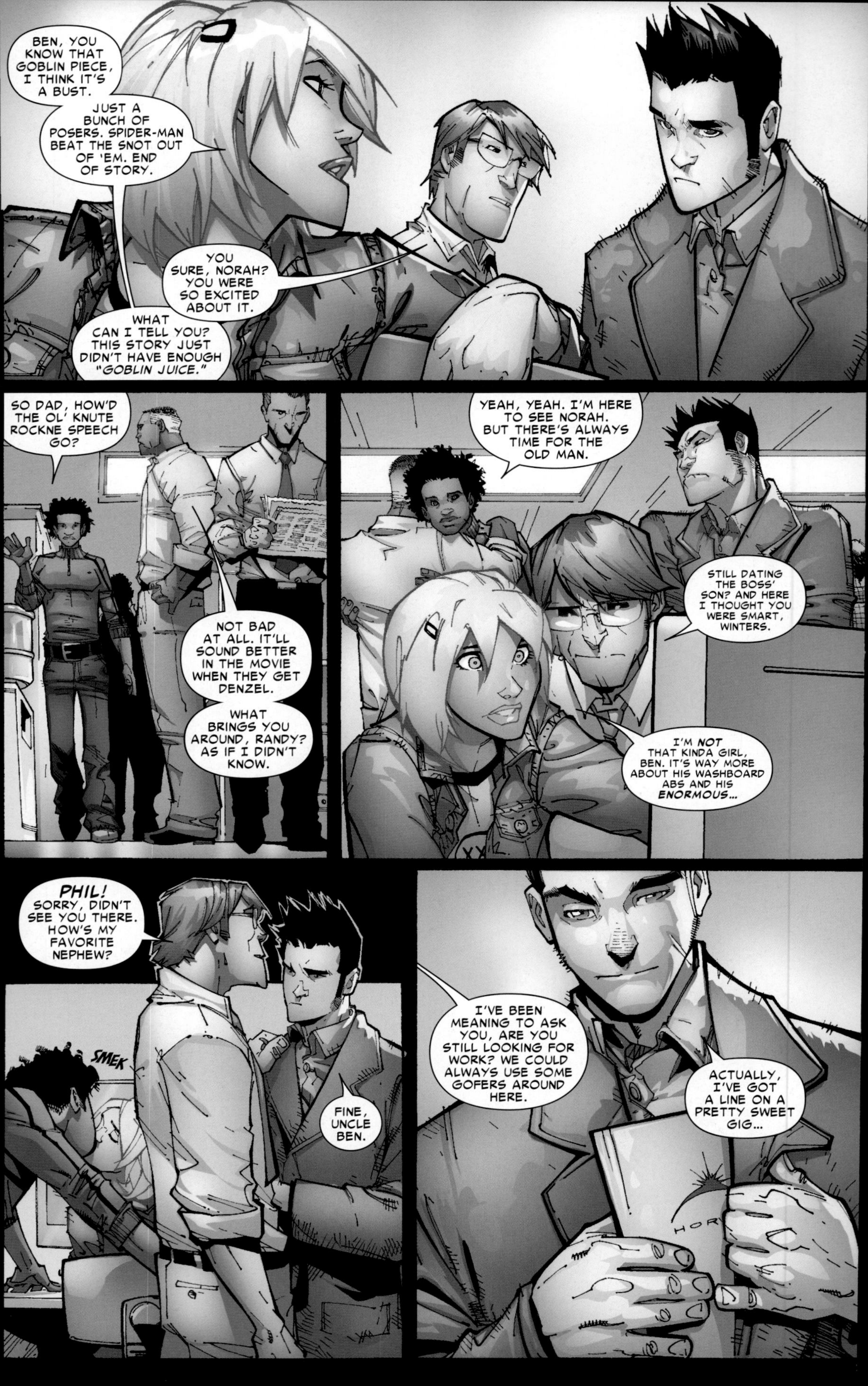

BEN, YOU KNOW THAT GOBLIN PIECE, I THINK IT'S A BUST.
JUST A BUNCH OF POSERS. SPIDER-MAN BEAT THE SNOT OUT OF 'EM. END OF STORY.
YOU SURE, NORAH? YOU WERE SO EXCITED ABOUT IT.
WHAT CAN I TELL YOU? THIS STORY JUST DIDN'T HAVE ENOUGH "GOBLIN JUICE."
SO DAD, HOW'D THE OL' KNUTE ROCKNE SPEECH GO?
NOT BAD AT ALL. IT'LL SOUND BETTER IN THE MOVIE WHEN THEY GET DENZEL.
WHAT BRINGS YOU AROUND, RANDY? AS IF I DIDN'T KNOW.
YEAH, YEAH. I'M HERE TO SEE NORAH. BUT THERE'S ALWAYS TIME FOR THE OLD MAN.
STILL DATING THE BOSS' SON? AND HERE I THOUGHT YOU WERE SMART, WINTERS.
I'M NOT THAT KINDA GIRL, BEN. IT'S WAY MORE ABOUT HIS WASHBOARD ABS AND HIS ENORMOUS...
PHIL! SORRY, DIDN'T SEE YOU THERE. HOW'S MY FAVORITE NEPHEW?
SMEK
FINE, UNCLE BEN.
I'VE BEEN MEANING TO ASK YOU, ARE YOU STILL LOOKING FOR WORK? WE COULD ALWAYS USE SOME GOFERS AROUND HERE.
ACTUALLY, I'VE GOT A LINE ON A PRETTY SWEET GIG...

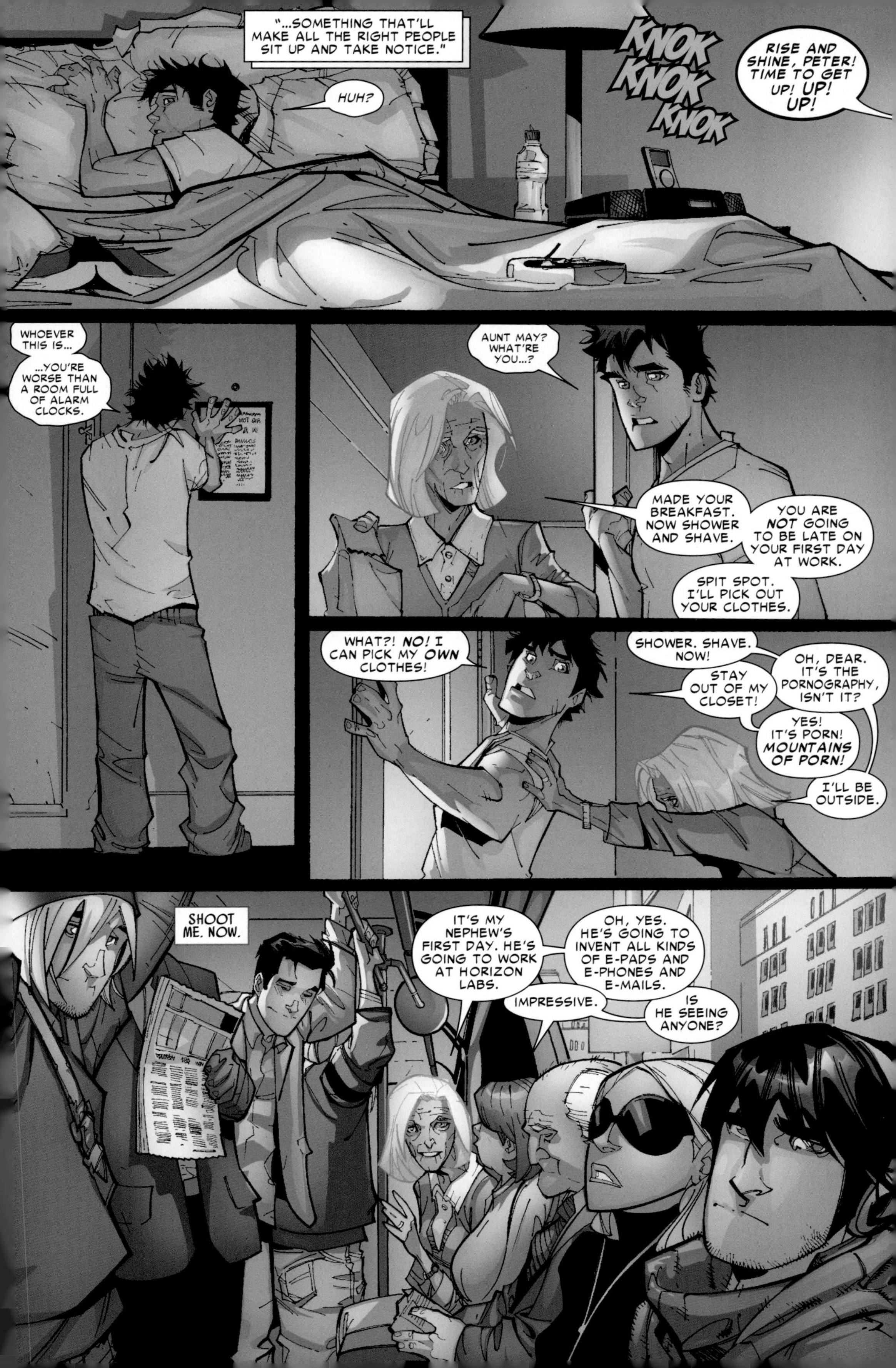
"...SOMETHING THAT'LL MAKE ALL THE RIGHT PEOPLE SIT UP AND TAKE NOTICE."
HUH?
KNOK KNOK KNOK
RISE AND SHINE, PETER! TIME TO GET UP! UP! UP!
WHOEVER THIS IS...
...YOU'RE WORSE THAN A ROOM FULL OF ALARM CLOCKS.
AUNT MAY? WHAT'RE YOU...?
MADE YOUR BREAKFAST. NOW SHOWER AND SHAVE.
YOU ARE NOT GOING TO BE LATE ON YOUR FIRST DAY AT WORK.
SPIT SPOT. I'LL PICK OUT YOUR CLOTHES.
WHAT?! NO! I CAN PICK MY OWN CLOTHES!
SHOWER. SHAVE. NOW!
STAY OUT OF MY CLOSET!
OH, DEAR. IT'S THE PORNOGRAPHY, ISN'T IT?
YES! IT'S PORN! MOUNTAINS OF PORN!
I'LL BE OUTSIDE.
SHOOT ME. NOW.
IT'S MY NEPHEW'S FIRST DAY. HE'S GOING TO WORK AT HORIZON LABS.
OH, YES. HE'S GOING TO INVENT ALL KINDS OF E-PADS AND E-PHONES AND E-MAILS.
IMPRESSIVE.
IS HE SEEING ANYONE?

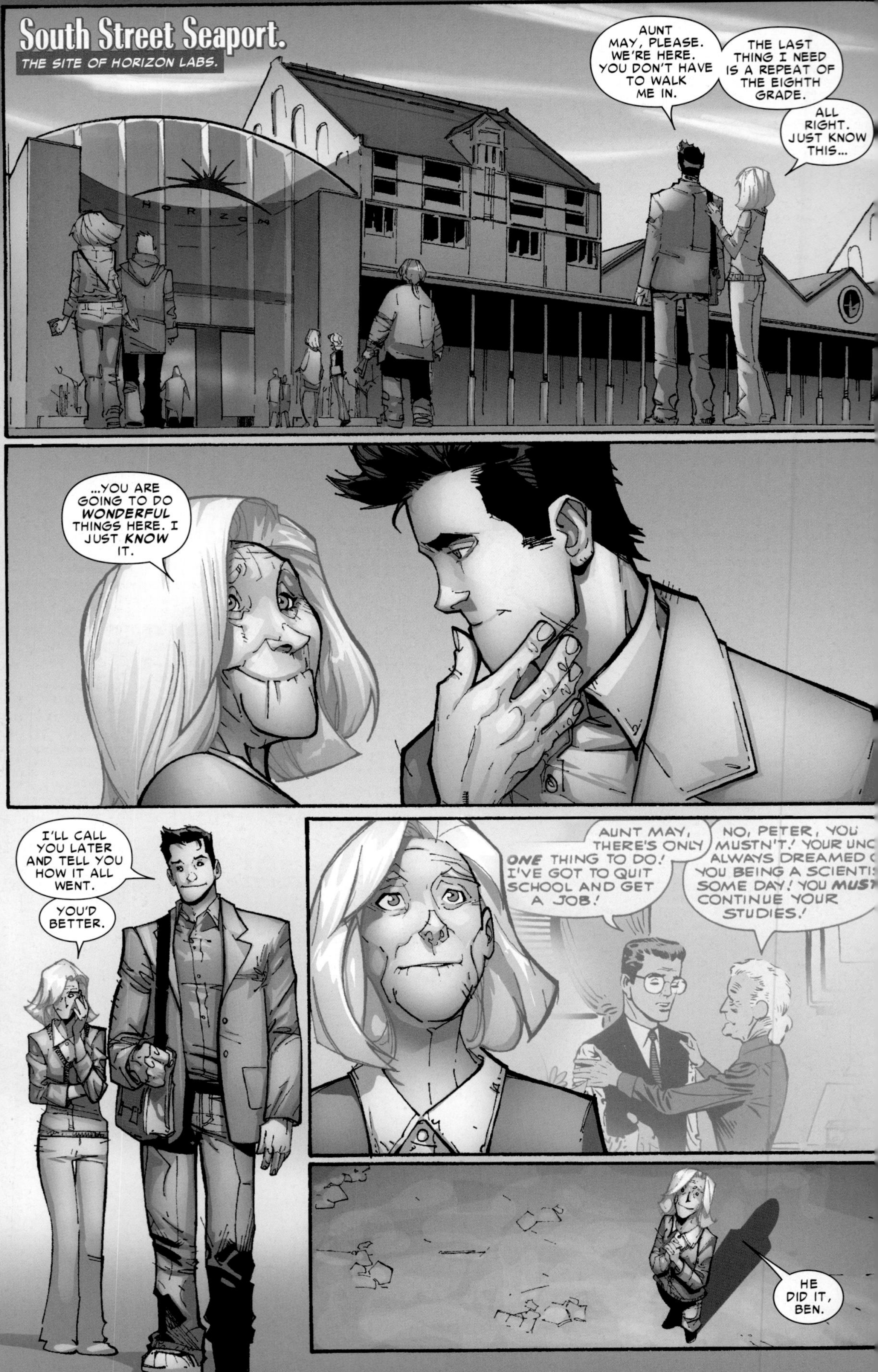
South Street Seaport.
THE SITE OF HORIZON LABS.
AUNT MAY, PLEASE. WE'RE HERE. YOU DON'T HAVE TO WALK ME IN.
THE LAST THING I NEED IS A REPEAT OF THE EIGHTH GRADE.
ALL RIGHT. JUST KNOW THIS...
...YOU ARE GOING TO DO WONDERFUL THINGS HERE. I JUST KNOW IT.
I'LL CALL YOU LATER AND TELL YOU HOW IT ALL WENT.
YOU'D BETTER.
AUNT MAY, THERE'S ONLY ONE THING TO DO! I'VE GOT TO QUIT SCHOOL AND GET A JOB!
NO, PETER, YOU MUSTN'T! YOUR UNC ALWAYS DREAMED YOU BEING A SCIENTI SOME DAY! YOU MUST CONTINUE YOUR STUDIES!
HE DID IT, BEN.

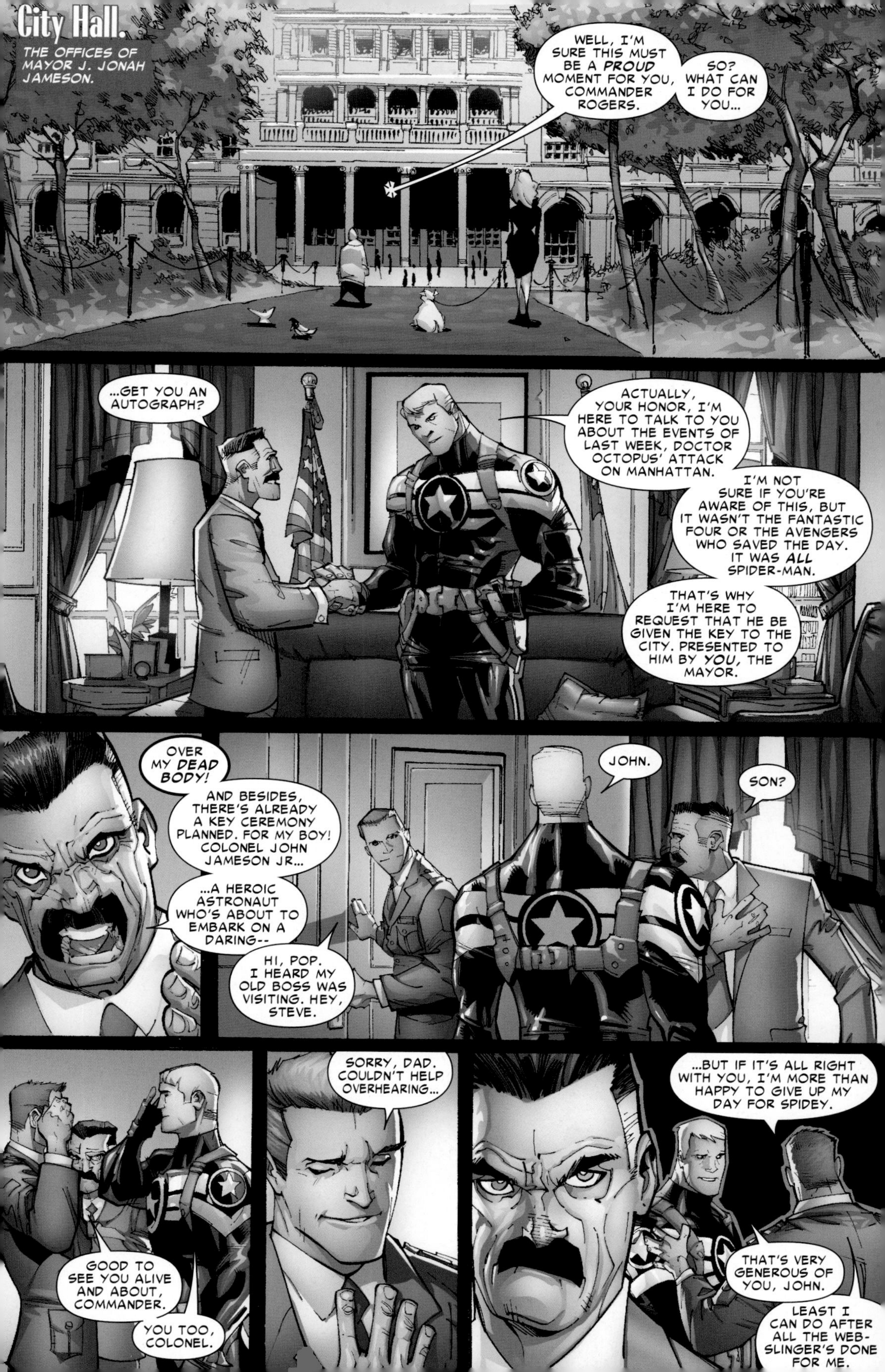
City Hall.
THE OFFICES OF MAYOR J. JONAH JAMESON.
WELL, I'M SURE THIS MUST BE A PROUD MOMENT FOR YOU, COMMANDER ROGERS.
SO? WHAT CAN I DO FOR YOU...
...GET YOU AN AUTOGRAPH?
ACTUALLY, YOUR HONOR, I'M HERE TO TALK TO YOU ABOUT THE EVENTS OF LAST WEEK, DOCTOR OCTOPUS' ATTACK ON MANHATTAN.
I'M NOT SURE IF YOU'RE AWARE OF THIS, BUT IT WASN'T THE FANTASTIC FOUR OR THE AVENGERS WHO SAVED THE DAY. IT WAS ALL SPIDER-MAN.
THAT'S WHY I'M HERE TO REQUEST THAT HE BE GIVEN THE KEY TO THE CITY. PRESENTED TO HIM BY YOU, THE MAYOR.
OVER MY DEAD BODY!
AND BESIDES, THERE'S ALREADY A KEY CEREMONY PLANNED. FOR MY BOY! COLONEL JOHN JAMESON JR...
...A HEROIC ASTRONAUT WHO'S ABOUT TO EMBARK ON A DARING--
HI, POP. I HEARD MY OLD BOSS WAS VISITING. HEY, STEVE.
JOHN.
SON?
GOOD TO SEE YOU ALIVE AND ABOUT, COMMANDER.
YOU TOO, COLONEL.
SORRY, DAD. COULDN'T HELP OVERHEARING...
...BUT IF IT'S ALL RIGHT WITH YOU, I'M MORE THAN HAPPY TO GIVE UP MY DAY FOR SPIDEY.
THAT'S VERY GENEROUS OF YOU, JOHN.
LEAST I CAN DO AFTER ALL THE WEB-SLINGER'S DONE FOR ME.

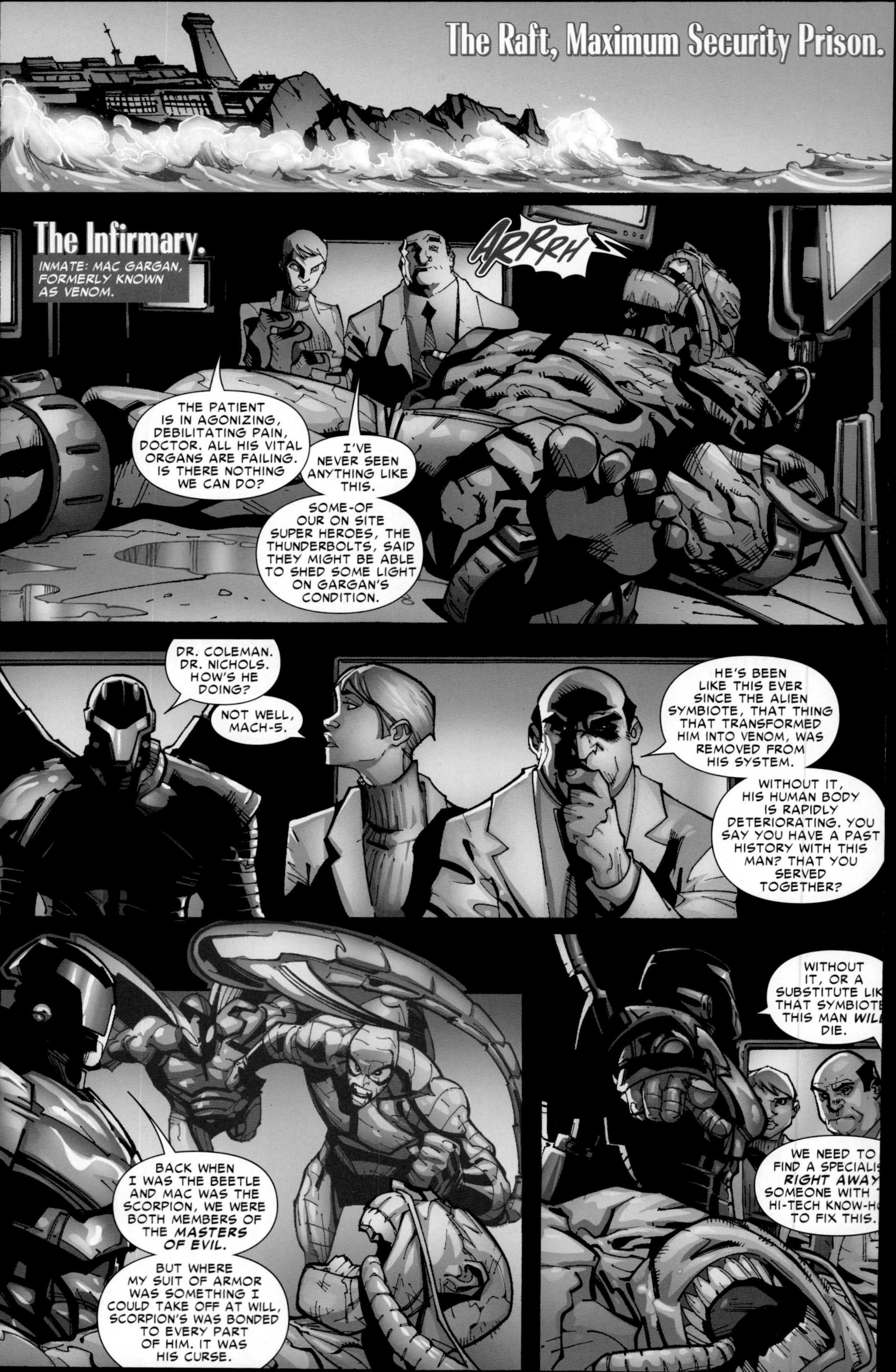
The Raft, Maximum Security Prison.
The Infirmary.
INMATE: MAC GARGAN, FORMERLY KNOWN AS VENOM.
ARRRH
THE PATIENT IS IN AGONIZING, DEBILITATING PAIN, DOCTOR. ALL HIS VITAL ORGANS ARE FAILING. IS THERE NOTHING WE CAN DO?
I'VE NEVER SEEN ANYTHING LIKE THIS.
SOME-OF OUR ON SITE SUPER HEROES, THE THUNDERBOLTS, SAID THEY MIGHT BE ABLE TO SHED SOME LIGHT ON GARGAN'S CONDITION.
DR. COLEMAN. DR. NICHOLS. HOW'S HE DOING?
NOT WELL, MACH-5.
HE'S BEEN LIKE THIS EVER SINCE THE ALIEN SYMBIOTE, THAT THING THAT TRANSFORMED HIM INTO VENOM, WAS REMOVED FROM HIS SYSTEM.
WITHOUT IT, HIS HUMAN BODY IS RAPIDLY DETERIORATING. YOU SAY YOU HAVE A PAST HISTORY WITH THIS MAN? THAT YOU SERVED TOGETHER?
BACK WHEN I WAS THE BEETLE AND MAC WAS THE SCORPION, WE WERE BOTH MEMBERS OF THE *MASTERS OF EVIL.*
BUT WHERE MY SUIT OF ARMOR WAS SOMETHING I COULD TAKE OFF AT WILL, SCORPION'S WAS BONDED TO EVERY PART OF HIM. IT WAS HIS CURSE.
WITHOUT IT, OR A SUBSTITUTE LIK THAT SYMBIOTE THIS MAN *WIL* DIE.
WE NEED TO FIND A SPECIALIS *RIGHT AWAY* SOMEONE WITH HI-TECH KNOW-H TO FIX THIS.

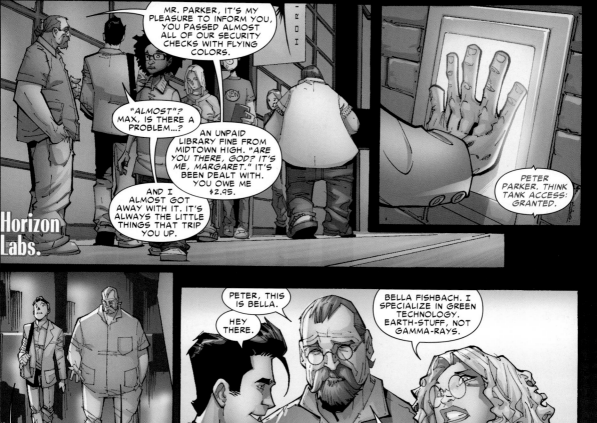

Horizon Labs.

MR. PARKER, IT'S MY PLEASURE TO INFORM YOU, YOU PASSED ALMOST ALL OF OUR SECURITY CHECKS WITH FLYING COLORS.

"ALMOST"? MAX, IS THERE A PROBLEM...?

AN UNPAID LIBRARY FINE FROM MIDTOWN HIGH. "ARE YOU THERE, GOD? IT'S ME, MARGARET." IT'S BEEN DEALT WITH. YOU OWE ME $2.95.

AND I ALMOST GOT AWAY WITH IT. IT'S ALWAYS THE LITTLE THINGS THAT TRIP YOU UP.

PETER PARKER. THINK TANK ACCESS: GRANTED.

PETER, THIS IS BELLA.

HEY THERE.

BELLA FISHBACH. I SPECIALIZE IN GREEN TECHNOLOGY. EARTH-STUFF, NOT GAMMA-RAYS.

AND THIS YOUNG MAN'S OUR ALL-AROUND WUNDERKIND, UATU JACKSON.

I WILL NEVER GET OVER THIS.

LAST TIME YOU WERE HERE, YOU MET TWO OF YOUR FELLOW "LUCKY 7," SAJANI AND GRADY.

ONE MEMBER, JUERGEN IS OFFSITE WORKING ON THE VERTEX SHUTTLE. BUT THE REMAINING THREE ARE ON CALL TODAY.

"UATU"? LIKE THE WATCHER?

MY FOLKS ARE FF FANS. [G]OT ALL THEIR [LIC]ENSED COMICS. [T]HOUGHT THE [NA]ME'D INSPIRE [M]E TO KNOW [EV]ERYTHING.

[I]T INSPIRED [ME] ALL RIGHT. [INS]PIRED ME TO [HU]RRY UP AND [GRA]DUATE OUTTA [DO]GGIE-CENTRAL [BY] THE TIME I WAS TEN.

MAX, YOU'RE NOT INTRODUCING HIM TO NUMBER 6, ARE YOU?

NO. PART OF SIX'S CONDITIONS FOR WORKING HERE IS STRICT ANONYMITY. AND I RESPECT THAT.

SIX? THE MYSTERY MAN IN LAB SIX. I THINK HE'S AN EX-SUPER VILLAIN.

NOPE. IT'S A SHE AND SHE'S SECRETLY AN ATLANTEAN.

STOP THAT, YOU TWO. C'MON, PETER...

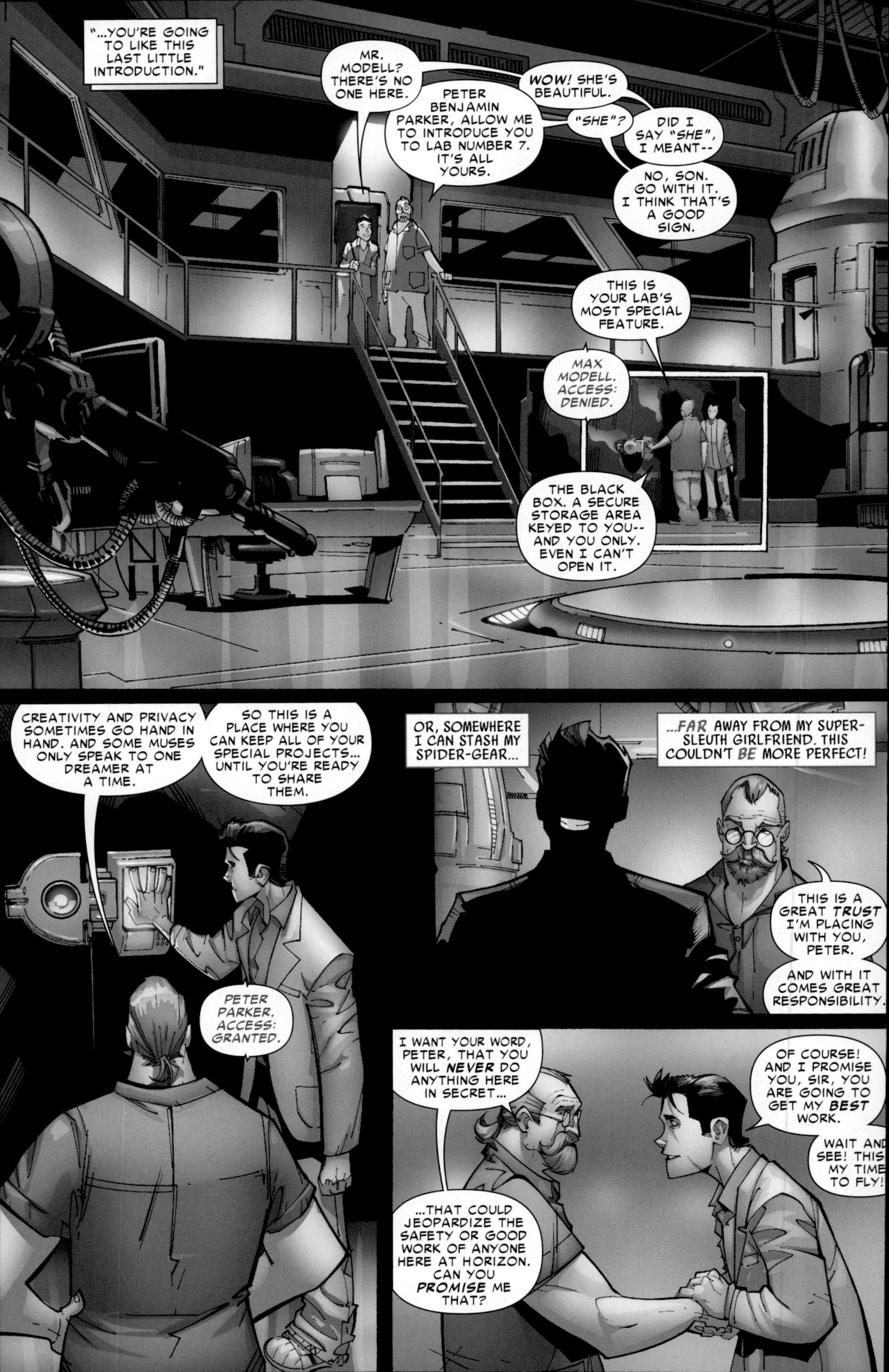
"...YOU'RE GOING TO LIKE THIS LAST LITTLE INTRODUCTION."
MR. MODELL? THERE'S NO ONE HERE.
PETER BENJAMIN PARKER, ALLOW ME TO INTRODUCE YOU TO LAB NUMBER 7. IT'S ALL YOURS.
WOW! SHE'S BEAUTIFUL.
"SHE"?
DID I SAY "SHE", I MEANT--
NO, SON. GO WITH IT. I THINK THAT'S A GOOD SIGN.
THIS IS YOUR LAB'S MOST SPECIAL FEATURE.
MAX MODELL. ACCESS: DENIED.
THE BLACK BOX. A SECURE STORAGE AREA KEYED TO YOU-- AND YOU ONLY. EVEN I CAN'T OPEN IT.
CREATIVITY AND PRIVACY SOMETIMES GO HAND IN HAND. AND SOME MUSES ONLY SPEAK TO ONE DREAMER AT A TIME.
SO THIS IS A PLACE WHERE YOU CAN KEEP ALL OF YOUR SPECIAL PROJECTS... UNTIL YOU'RE READY TO SHARE THEM.
PETER PARKER. ACCESS: GRANTED.
OR, SOMEWHERE I CAN STASH MY SPIDER-GEAR...
...FAR AWAY FROM MY SUPER-SLEUTH GIRLFRIEND. THIS COULDN'T BE MORE PERFECT!
THIS IS A GREAT TRUST I'M PLACING WITH YOU, PETER.
AND WITH IT COMES GREAT RESPONSIBILITY.
I WANT YOUR WORD, PETER, THAT YOU WILL NEVER DO ANYTHING HERE IN SECRET...
...THAT COULD JEOPARDIZE THE SAFETY OR GOOD WORK OF ANYONE HERE AT HORIZON. CAN YOU PROMISE ME THAT?
OF COURSE! AND I PROMISE YOU, SIR, YOU ARE GOING TO GET MY BEST WORK.
WAIT AND SEE! THIS MY TIME TO FLY!

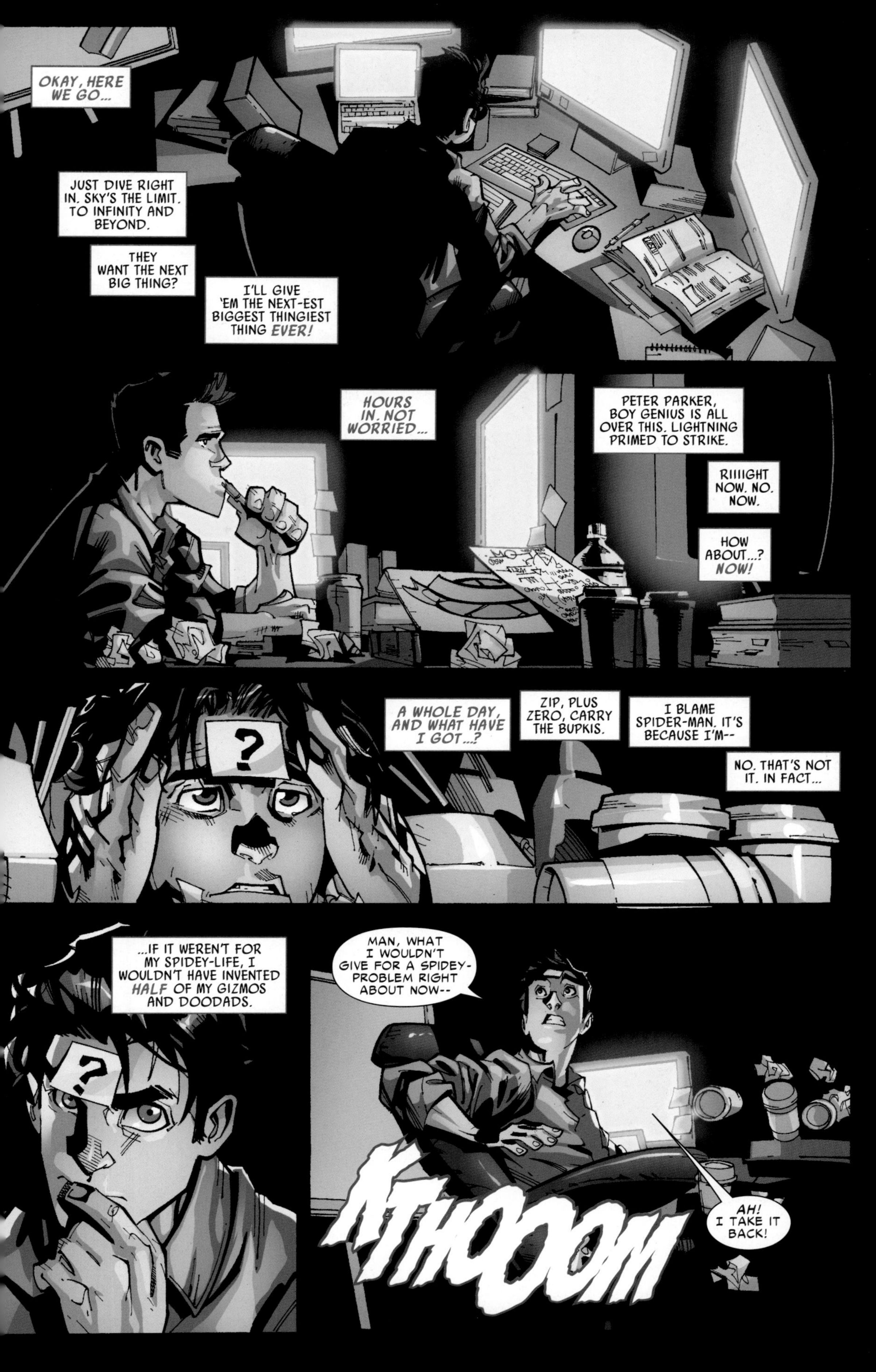
OKAY, HERE WE GO...
JUST DIVE RIGHT IN. SKY'S THE LIMIT. TO INFINITY AND BEYOND.
THEY WANT THE NEXT BIG THING?
I'LL GIVE 'EM THE NEXT-EST BIGGEST THINGIEST THING EVER!
HOURS IN. NOT WORRIED...
PETER PARKER, BOY GENIUS IS ALL OVER THIS. LIGHTNING PRIMED TO STRIKE.
RIIIIGHT NOW. NO. NOW.
HOW ABOUT...? NOW!
A WHOLE DAY, AND WHAT HAVE I GOT...?
ZIP, PLUS ZERO, CARRY THE BUPKIS.
I BLAME SPIDER-MAN. IT'S BECAUSE I'M--
NO. THAT'S NOT IT. IN FACT...
...IF IT WEREN'T FOR MY SPIDEY-LIFE, I WOULDN'T HAVE INVENTED HALF OF MY GIZMOS AND DOODADS.
MAN, WHAT I WOULDN'T GIVE FOR A SPIDEY-PROBLEM RIGHT ABOUT NOW--
KTHOOOM
AH! I TAKE IT BACK!

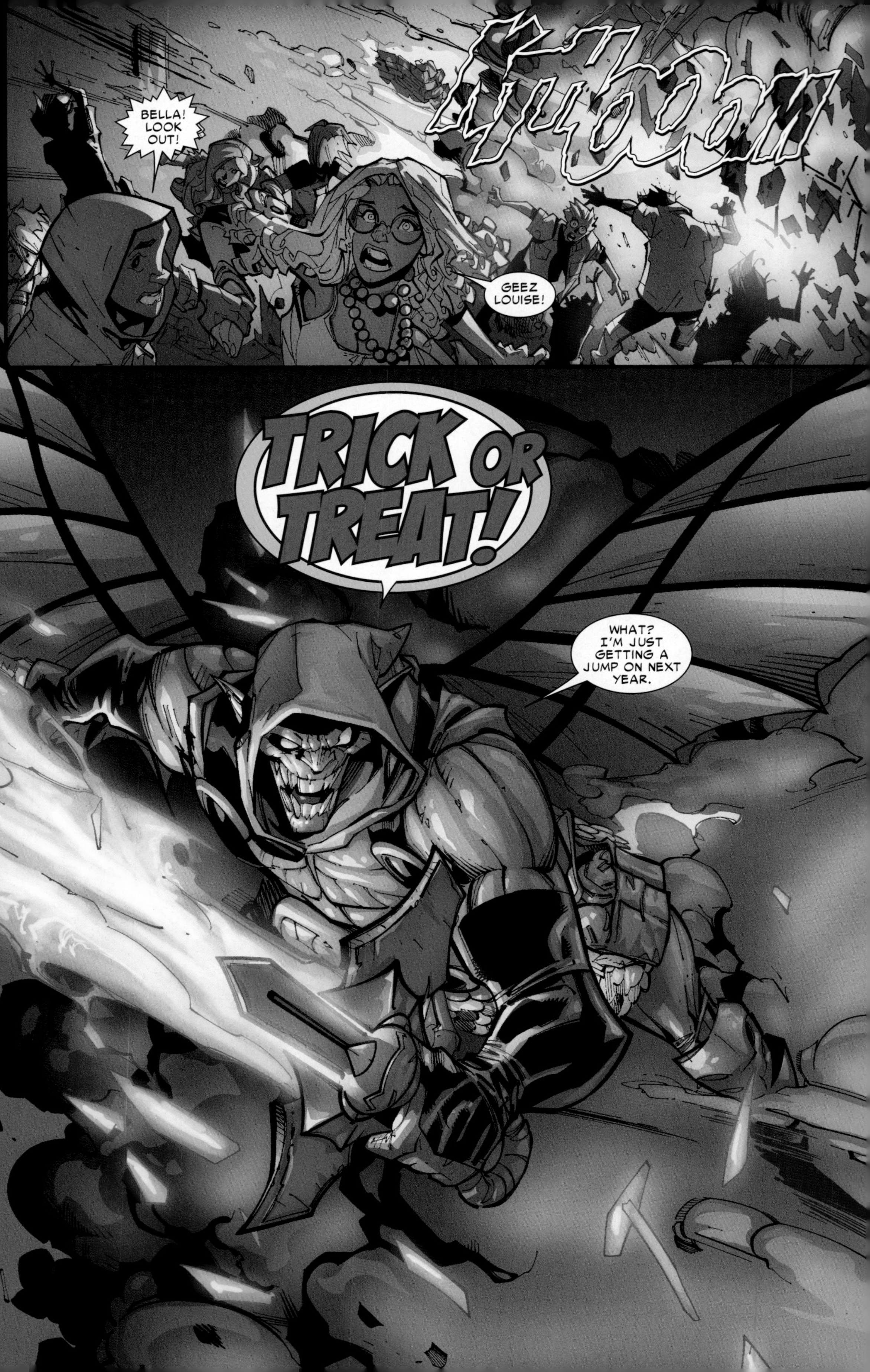
BELLA! LOOK OUT!
GEEZ LOUISE!
TRICK OR TREAT!
WHAT? I'M JUST GETTING A JUMP ON NEXT YEAR.

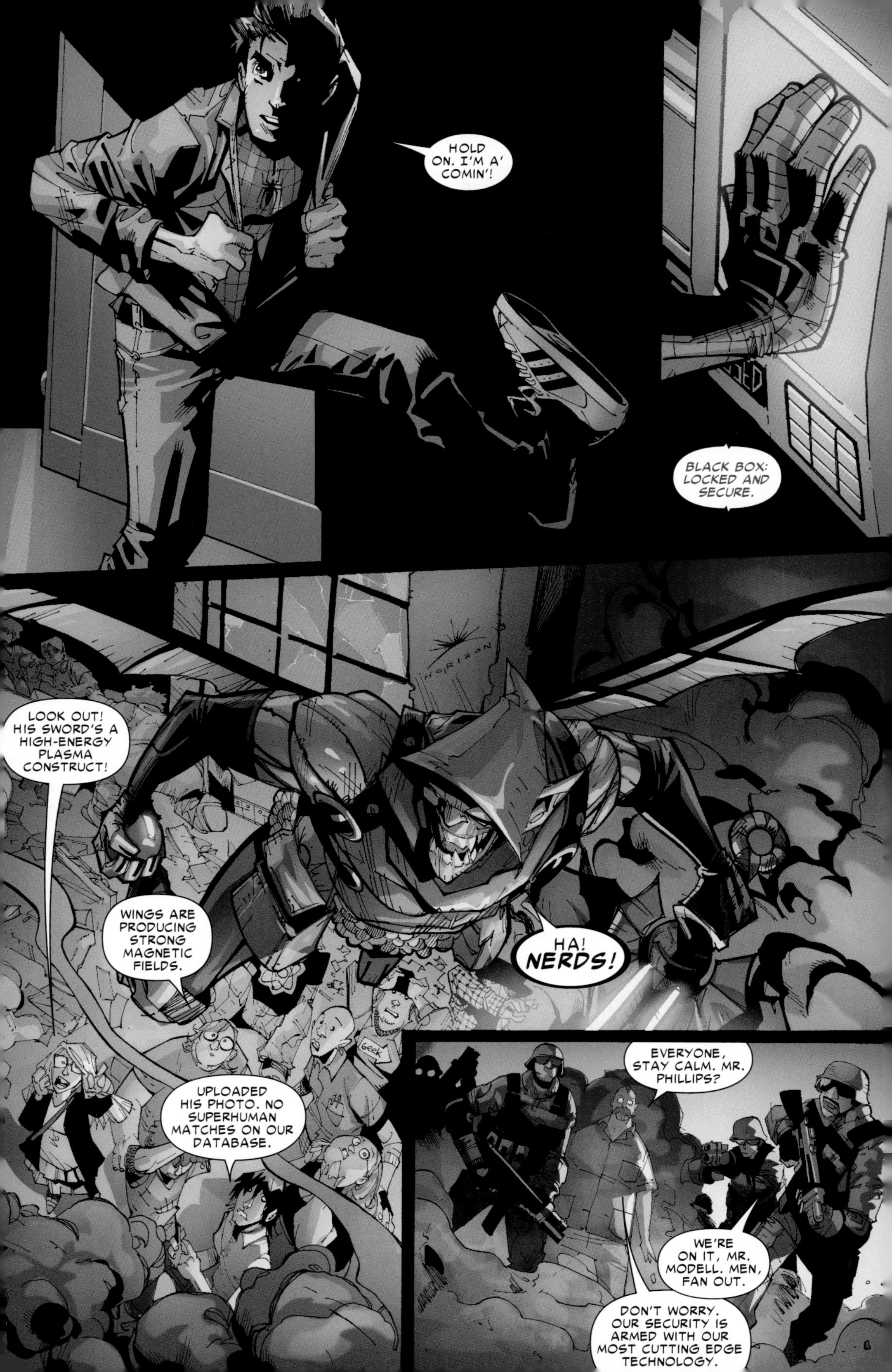
HOLD ON. I'M A' COMIN'!
BLACK BOX: LOCKED AND SECURE.
HORIZON
LOOK OUT! HIS SWORD'S A HIGH-ENERGY PLASMA CONSTRUCT!
WINGS ARE PRODUCING STRONG MAGNETIC FIELDS.
HA! NERDS!
UPLOADED HIS PHOTO. NO SUPERHUMAN MATCHES ON OUR DATABASE.
GEEK
EVERYONE, STAY CALM. MR. PHILLIPS?
WE'RE ON IT, MR. MODELL. MEN, FAN OUT.
DON'T WORRY. OUR SECURITY IS ARMED WITH OUR MOST CUTTING EDGE TECHNOLOGY.

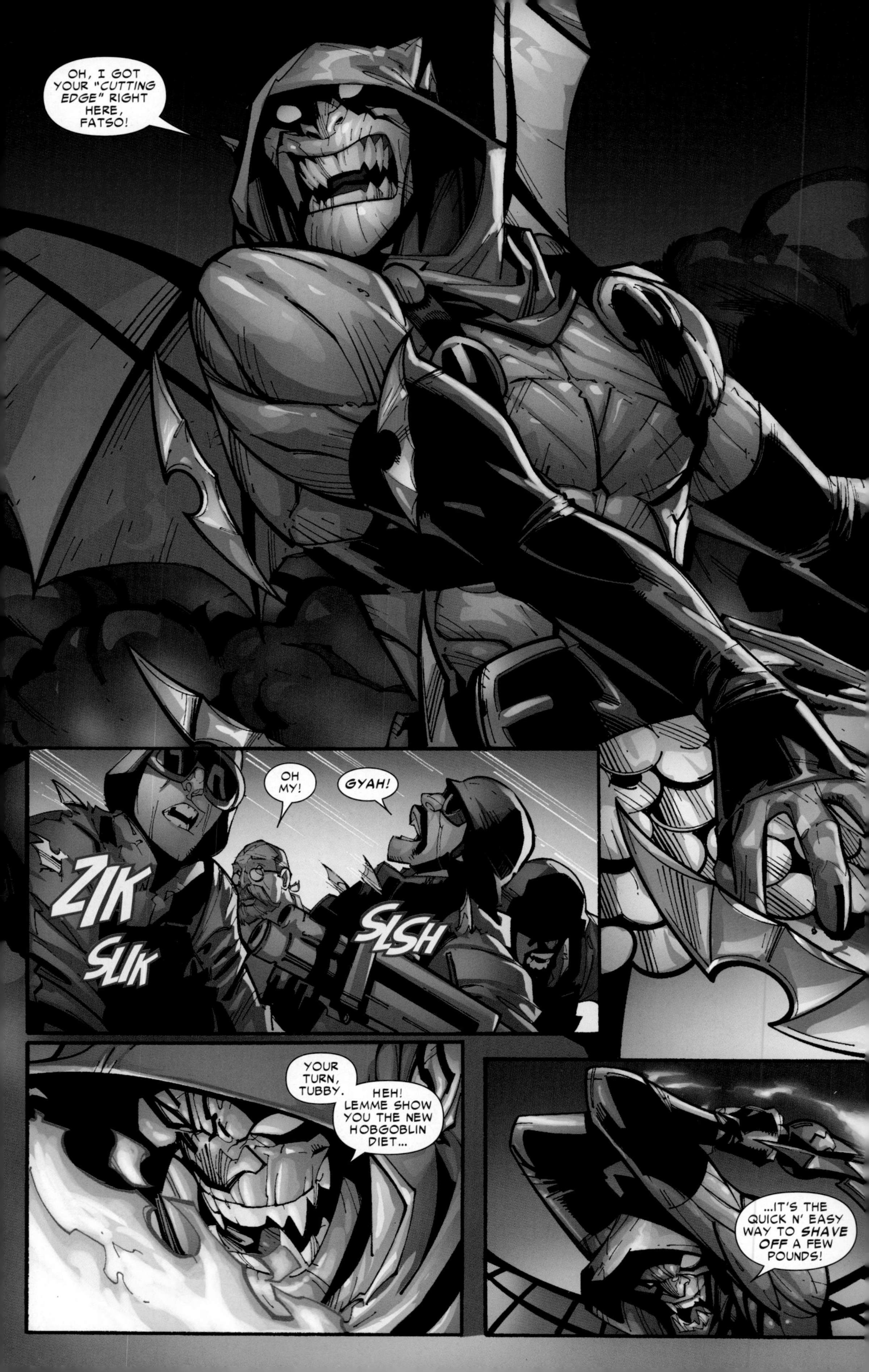
OH, I GOT YOUR "CUTTING EDGE" RIGHT HERE, FATSO!
OH MY!
GYAH!
ZIK
SLIK
SLSH
YOUR TURN, TUBBY.
HEH! LEMME SHOW YOU THE NEW HOBGOBLIN DIET...
...IT'S THE QUICK N' EASY WAY TO SHAVE OFF A FEW POUNDS!

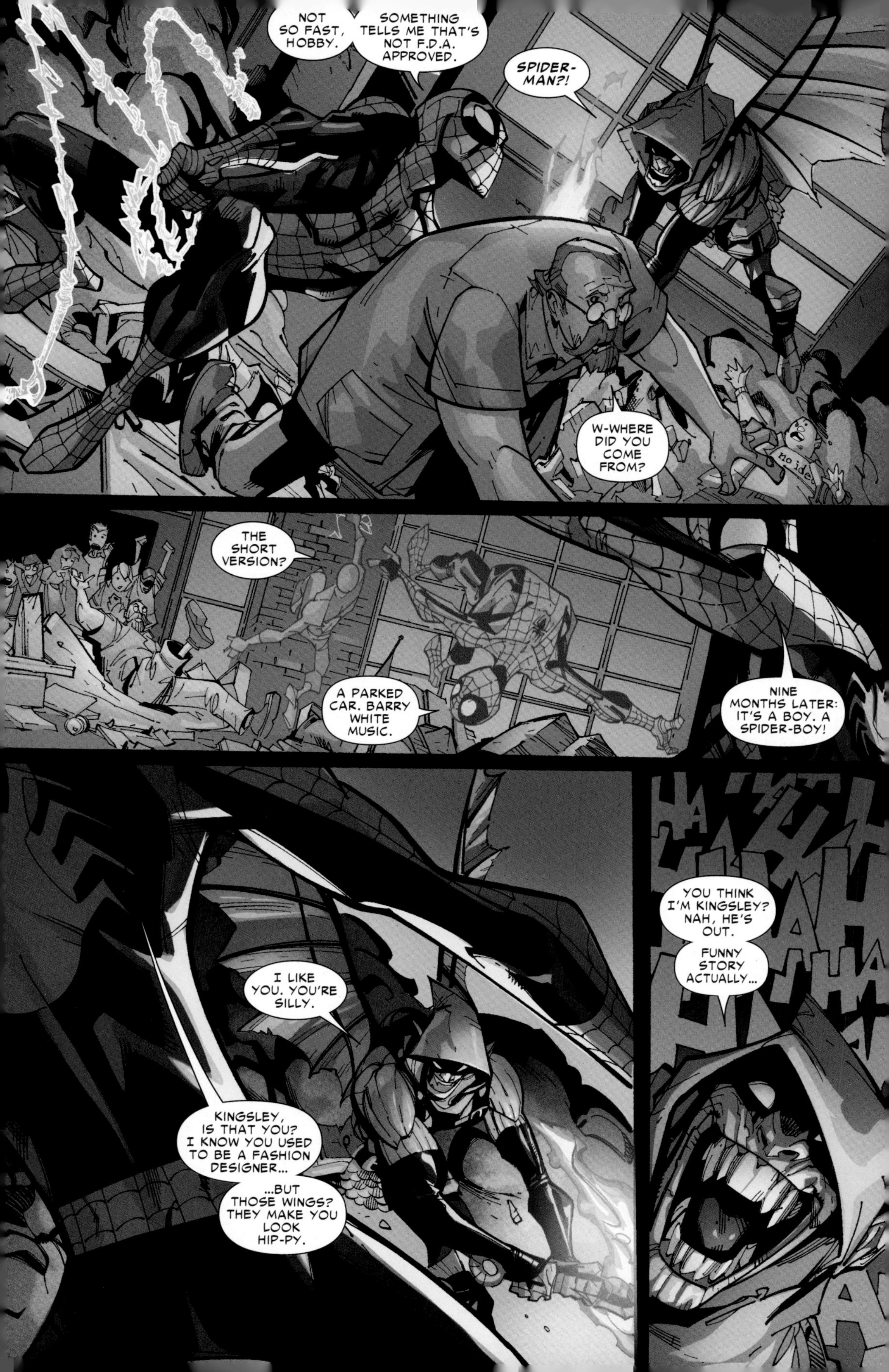
NOT SO FAST, HOBBY.
SOMETHING TELLS ME THAT'S NOT F.D.A. APPROVED.
SPIDER-MAN?!
W-WHERE DID YOU COME FROM?
no ide
THE SHORT VERSION?
A PARKED CAR. BARRY WHITE MUSIC.
NINE MONTHS LATER: IT'S A BOY. A SPIDER-BOY!
I LIKE YOU. YOU'RE SILLY.
KINGSLEY, IS THAT YOU? I KNOW YOU USED TO BE A FASHION DESIGNER...
...BUT THOSE WINGS? THEY MAKE YOU LOOK HIP-PY.
YOU THINK I'M KINGSLEY? NAH, HE'S OUT.
FUNNY STORY ACTUALLY...

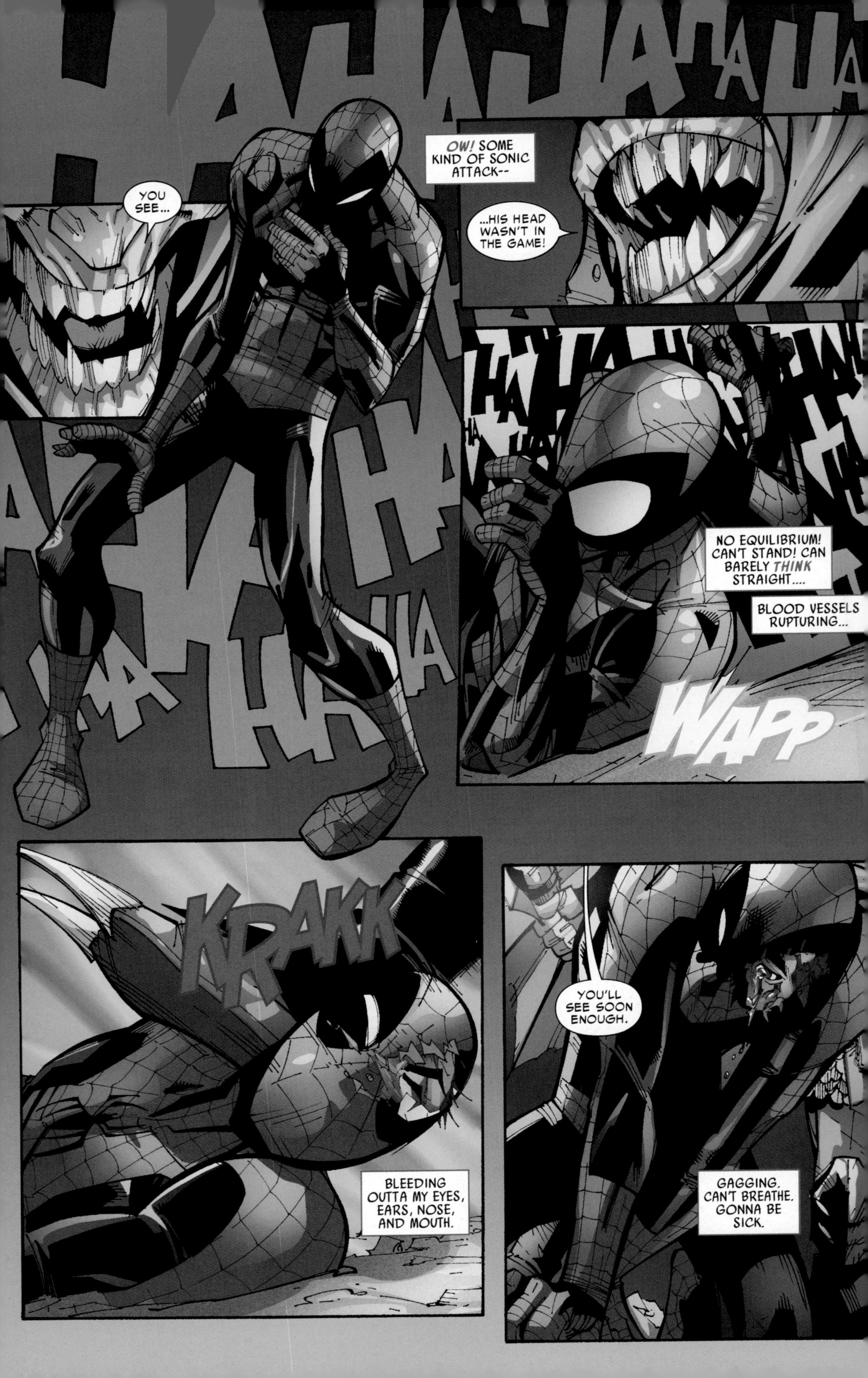

YOU SEE...
OW! SOME KIND OF SONIC ATTACK--
...HIS HEAD WASN'T IN THE GAME!
NO EQUILIBRIUM! CAN'T STAND! CAN BARELY THINK STRAIGHT....
BLOOD VESSELS RUPTURING...
WAPP
KRAKK
BLEEDING OUTTA MY EYES, EARS, NOSE, AND MOUTH.
YOU'LL SEE SOON ENOUGH.
GAGGING. CAN'T BREATHE. GONNA BE SICK.

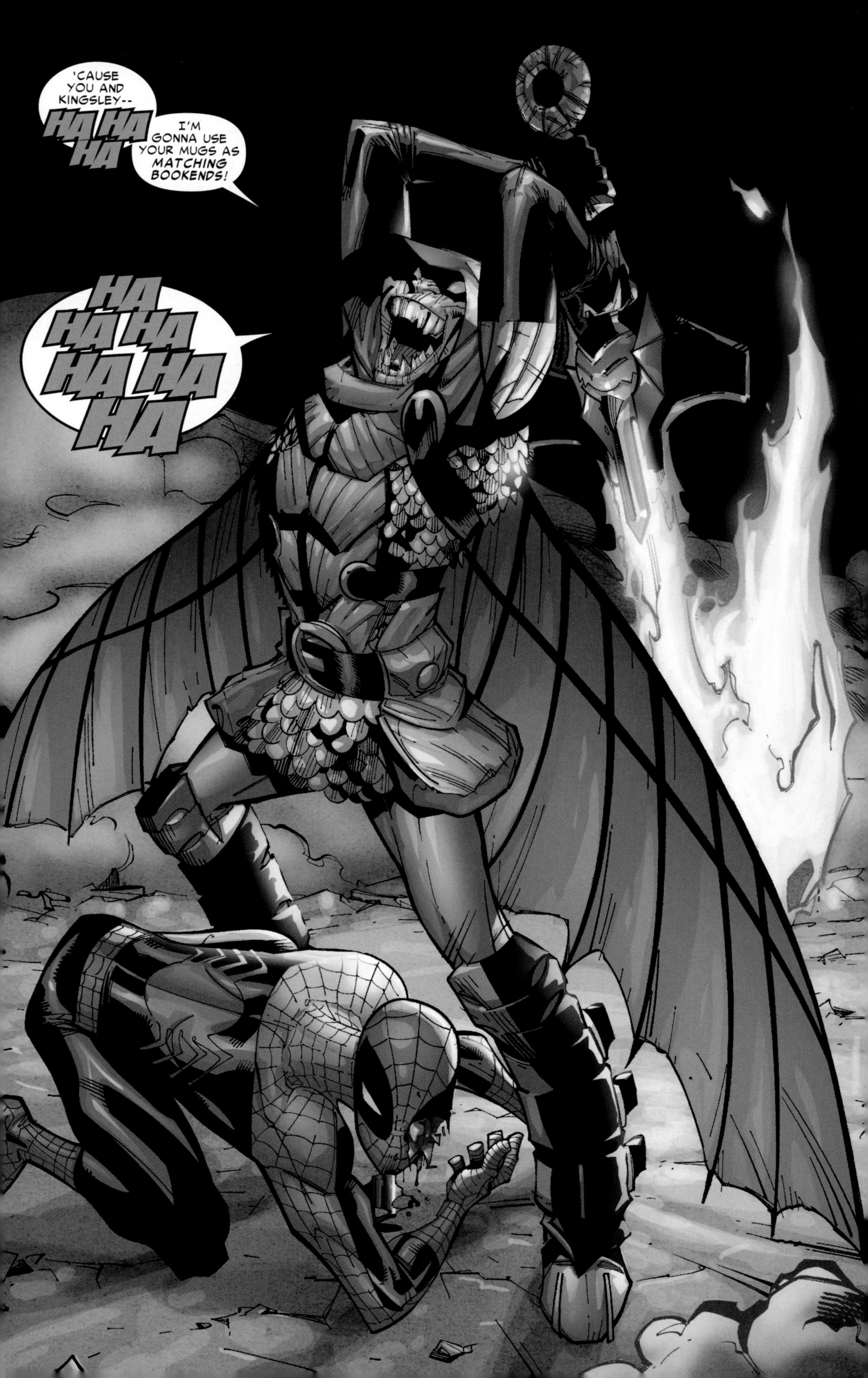
'CAUSE YOU AND KINGSLEY--
HA HA HA
I'M GONNA USE YOUR MUGS AS MATCHING BOOKENDS!
HA HA HA HA HA HA

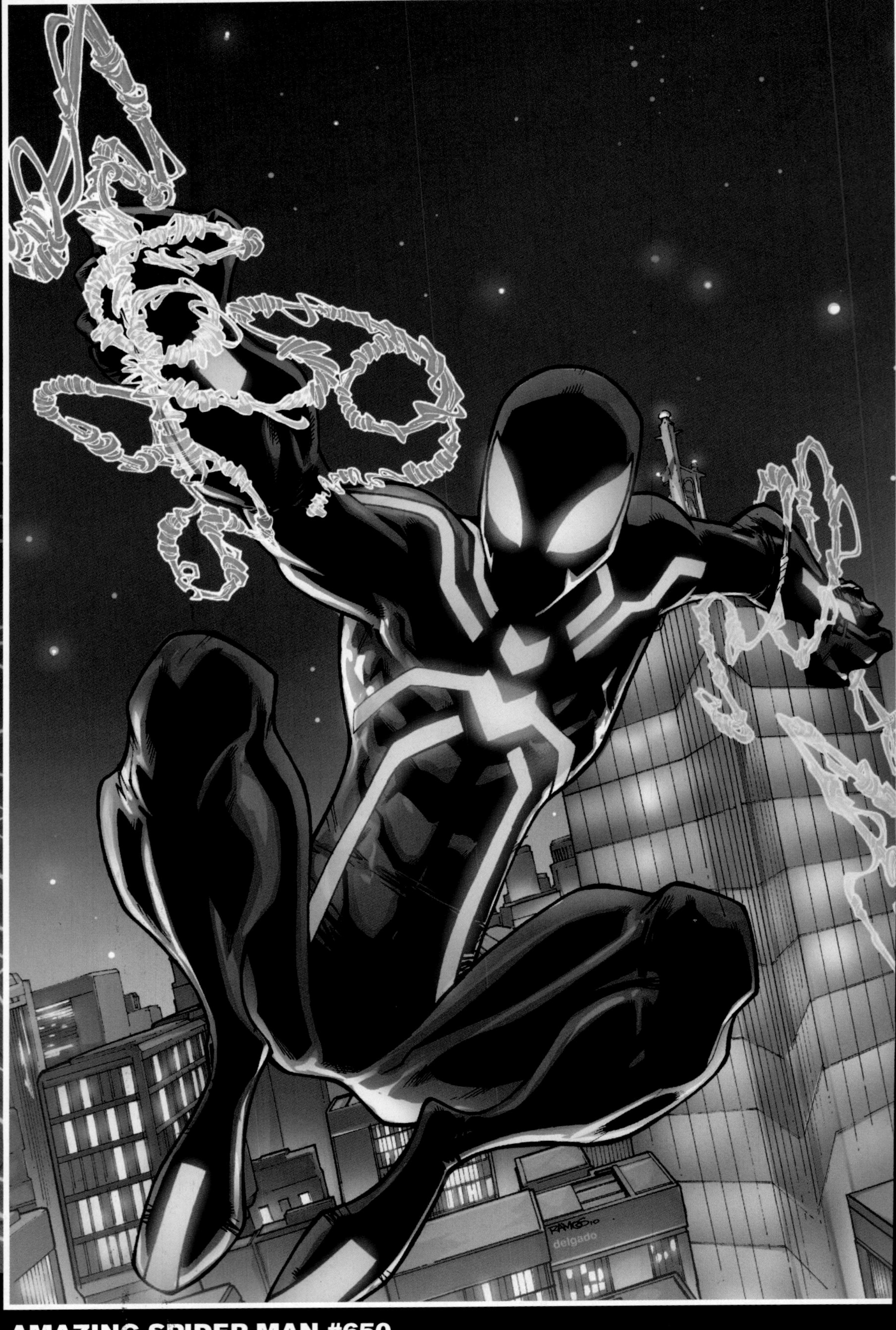

AMAZING SPIDER-MAN #650
COVER BY HUMBERTO RAMOS & EDGAR DELGADO

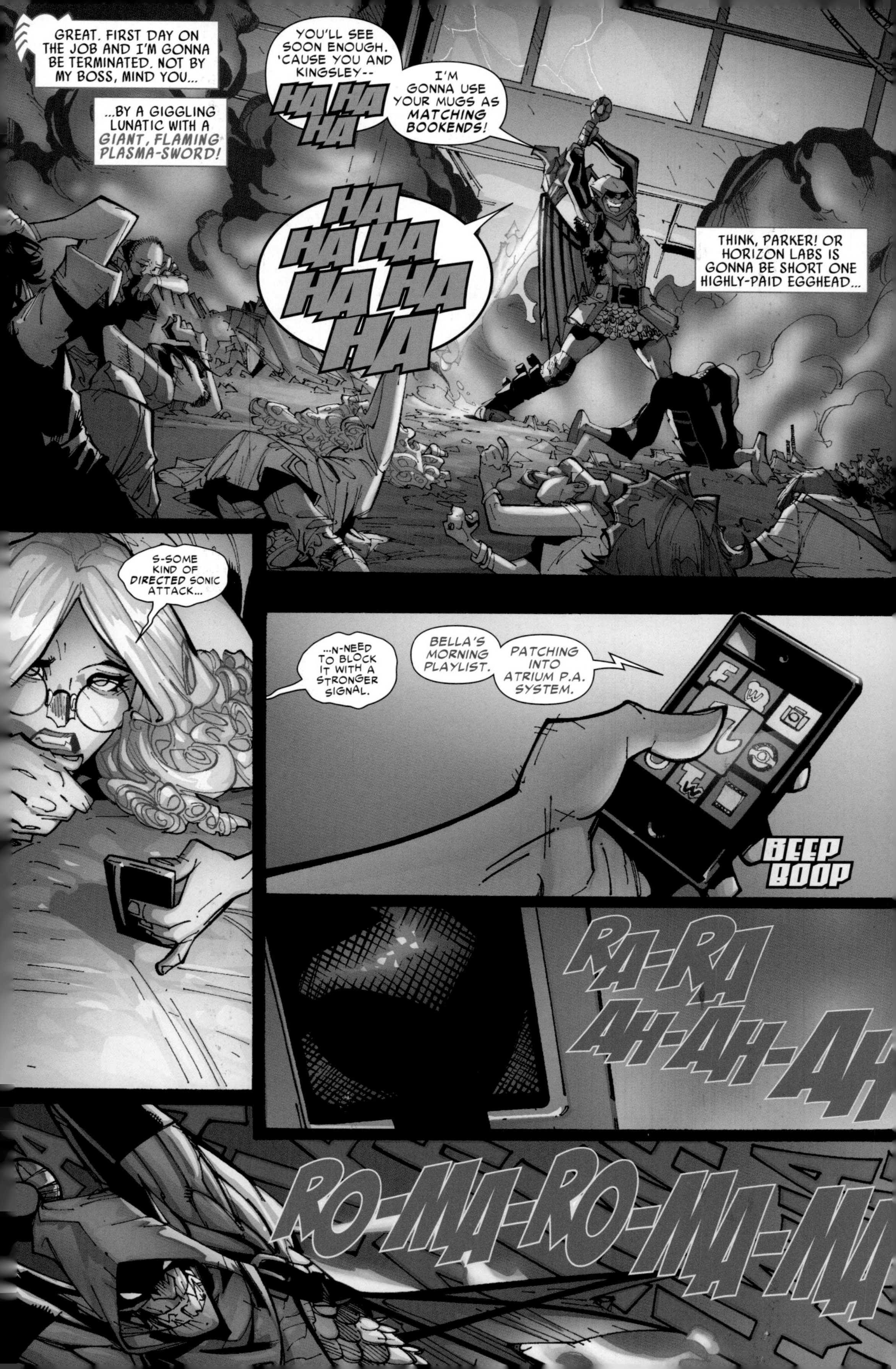
GREAT. FIRST DAY ON THE JOB AND I'M GONNA BE TERMINATED. NOT BY MY BOSS, MIND YOU...
...BY A GIGGLING LUNATIC WITH A GIANT, FLAMING PLASMA-SWORD!
YOU'LL SEE SOON ENOUGH. 'CAUSE YOU AND KINGSLEY--
HA HA HA
I'M GONNA USE YOUR MUGS AS MATCHING BOOKENDS!
HA HA HA HA HA HA HA
THINK, PARKER! OR HORIZON LABS IS GONNA BE SHORT ONE HIGHLY-PAID EGGHEAD...
S-SOME KIND OF DIRECTED SONIC ATTACK...
...N-NEED TO BLOCK IT WITH A STRONGER SIGNAL.
BELLA'S MORNING PLAYLIST.
PATCHING INTO ATRIUM P.A. SYSTEM.
BEEP BOOP
RA-RA AH-AH-AH
RO-MA-RO-MA-MA

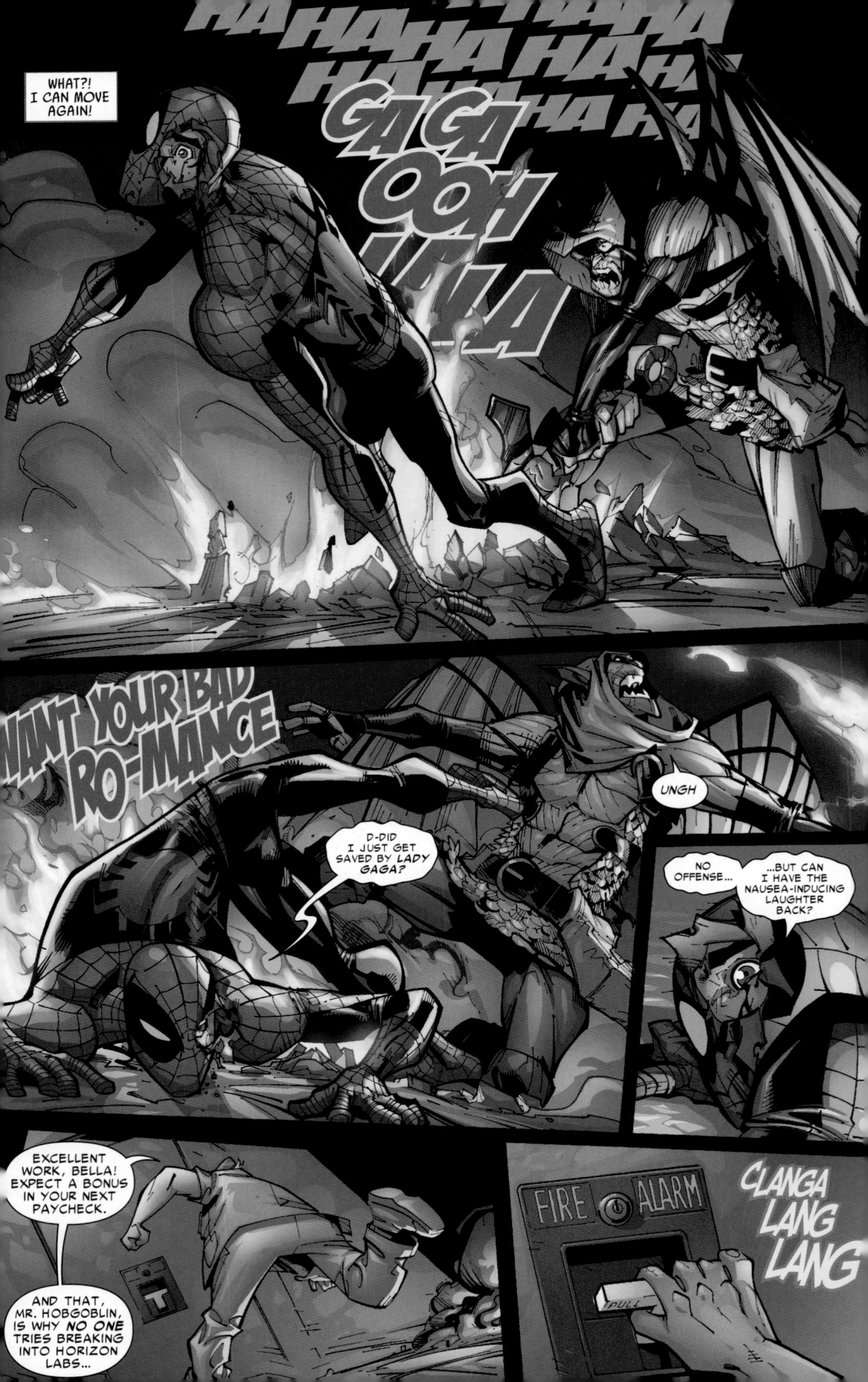
HA HA HA HA HA HA HA HA HA HA HA HA HA
WHAT?! I CAN MOVE AGAIN!
GA GA OOH
RO-MANCE
UNGH
D-DID I JUST GET SAVED BY LADY GAGA?
NO OFFENSE...
...BUT CAN I HAVE THE NAUSEA-INDUCING LAUGHTER BACK?
EXCELLENT WORK, BELLA! EXPECT A BONUS IN YOUR NEXT PAYCHECK.
AND THAT, MR. HOBGOBLIN, IS WHY NO ONE TRIES BREAKING INTO HORIZON LABS...
FIRE ALARM
PULL
CLANGA LANG LANG

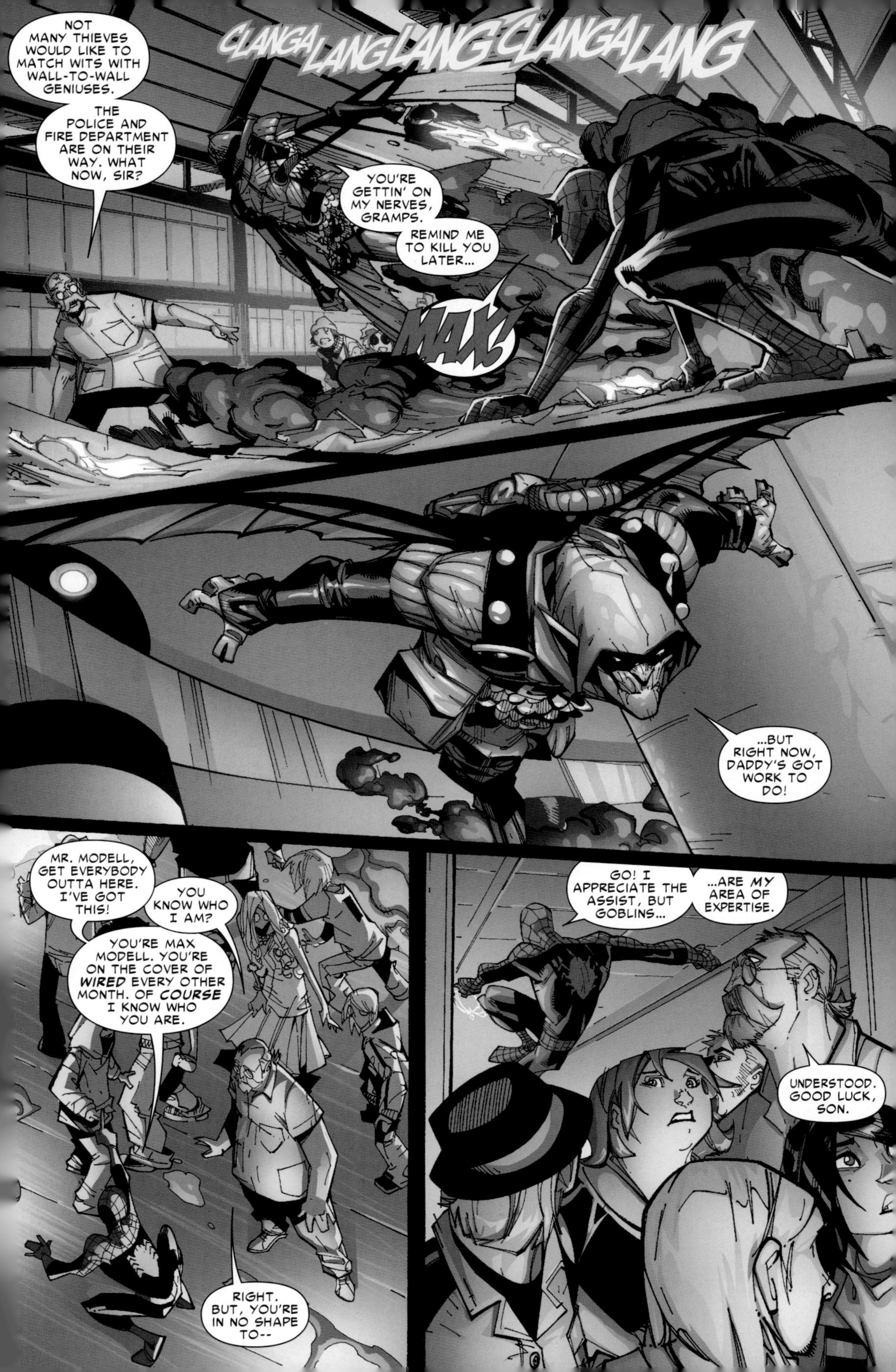
CLANGA LANG LANG CLANGA LANG
NOT MANY THIEVES WOULD LIKE TO MATCH WITS WITH WALL-TO-WALL GENIUSES.
THE POLICE AND FIRE DEPARTMENT ARE ON THEIR WAY. WHAT NOW, SIR?
YOU'RE GETTIN' ON MY NERVES, GRAMPS.
REMIND ME TO KILL YOU LATER...
MAX!
...BUT RIGHT NOW, DADDY'S GOT WORK TO DO!
MR. MODELL, GET EVERYBODY OUTTA HERE. I'VE GOT THIS!
YOU KNOW WHO I AM?
YOU'RE MAX MODELL. YOU'RE ON THE COVER OF WIRED EVERY OTHER MONTH. OF COURSE I KNOW WHO YOU ARE.
RIGHT. BUT, YOU'RE IN NO SHAPE TO--
GO! I APPRECIATE THE ASSIST, BUT GOBLINS...
...ARE MY AREA OF EXPERTISE.
UNDERSTOOD. GOOD LUCK, SON.

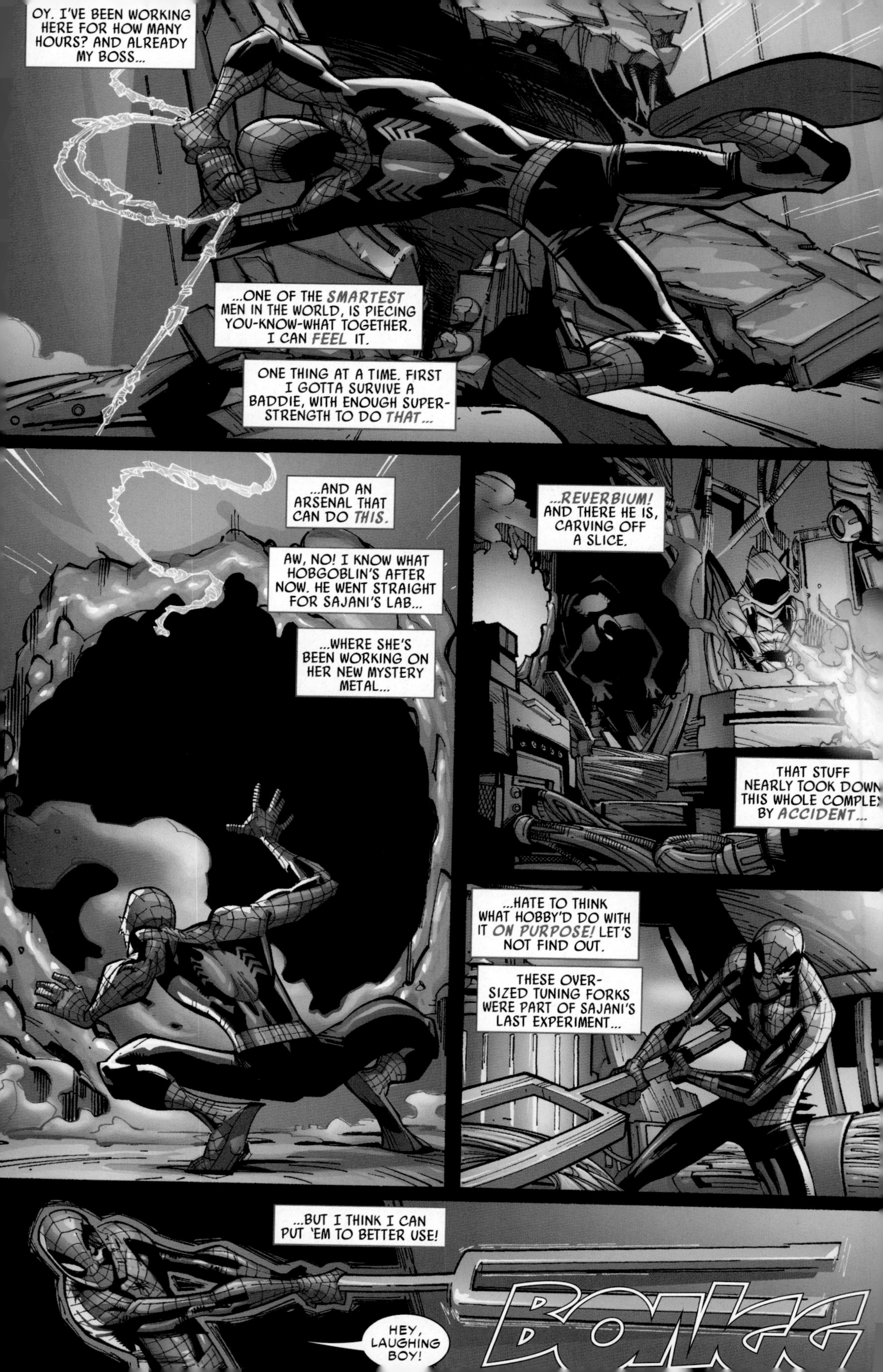
OY. I'VE BEEN WORKING HERE FOR HOW MANY HOURS? AND ALREADY MY BOSS...
...ONE OF THE SMARTEST MEN IN THE WORLD, IS PIECING YOU-KNOW-WHAT TOGETHER. I CAN FEEL IT.
ONE THING AT A TIME. FIRST I GOTTA SURVIVE A BADDIE, WITH ENOUGH SUPER-STRENGTH TO DO THAT...
...AND AN ARSENAL THAT CAN DO THIS.
AW, NO! I KNOW WHAT HOBGOBLIN'S AFTER NOW. HE WENT STRAIGHT FOR SAJANI'S LAB...
...WHERE SHE'S BEEN WORKING ON HER NEW MYSTERY METAL...
...REVERBIUM! AND THERE HE IS, CARVING OFF A SLICE.
THAT STUFF NEARLY TOOK DOWN THIS WHOLE COMPLEX BY ACCIDENT...
...HATE TO THINK WHAT HOBBY'D DO WITH IT ON PURPOSE! LET'S NOT FIND OUT.
THESE OVER-SIZED TUNING FORKS WERE PART OF SAJANI'S LAST EXPERIMENT...
...BUT I THINK I CAN PUT 'EM TO BETTER USE!
HEY, LAUGHING BOY!
BONG

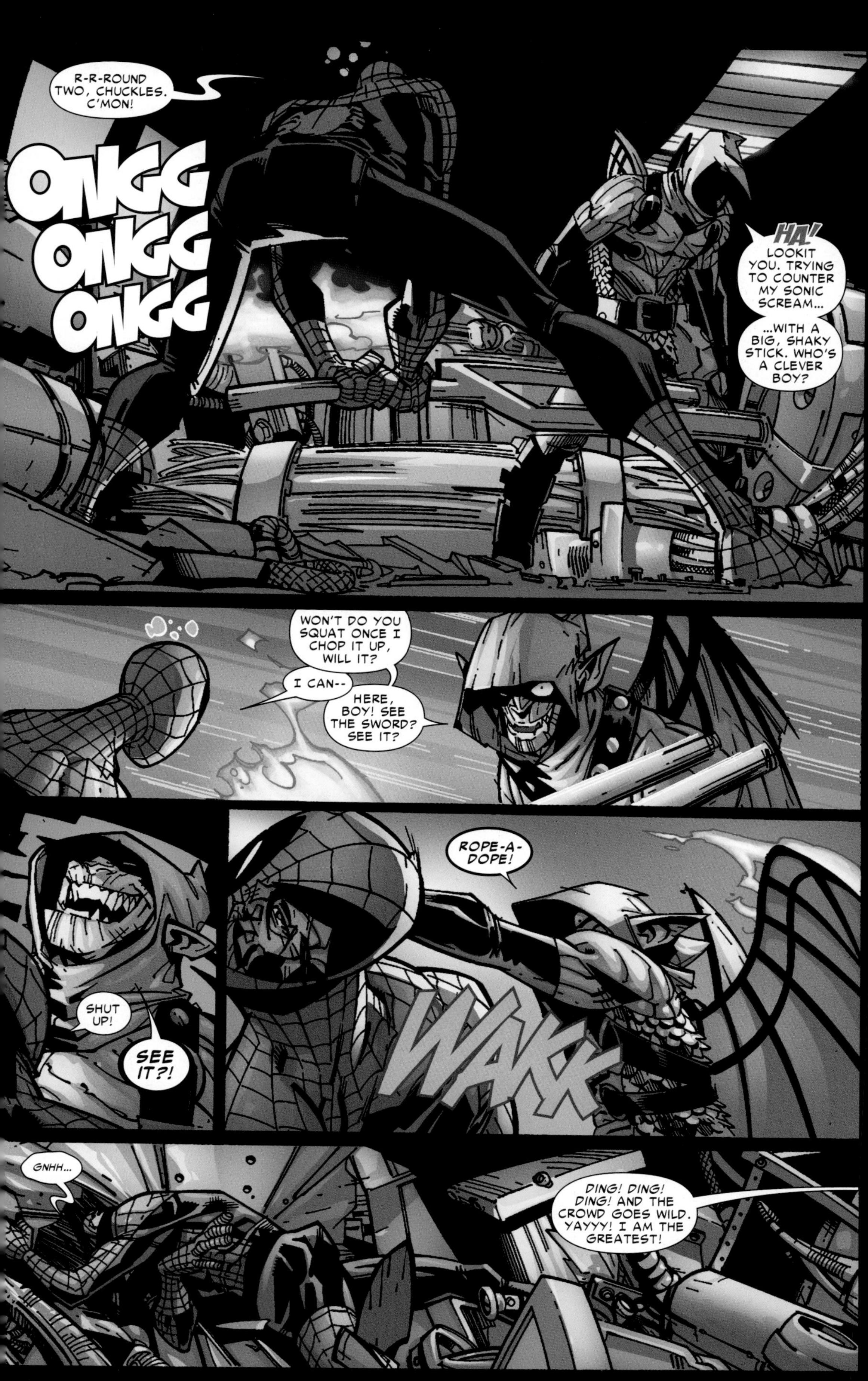
R-R-ROUND TWO, CHUCKLES. C'MON!
ONGG ONGG ONGG
HA!
LOOKIT YOU. TRYING TO COUNTER MY SONIC SCREAM...
...WITH A BIG, SHAKY STICK. WHO'S A CLEVER BOY?
WON'T DO YOU SQUAT ONCE I CHOP IT UP, WILL IT?
I CAN--
HERE, BOY! SEE THE SWORD? SEE IT?
SHUT UP!
SEE IT?!
ROPE-A-DOPE!
WAKK
GNHH...
DING! DING! DING! AND THE CROWD GOES WILD. YAYYY! I AM THE GREATEST!

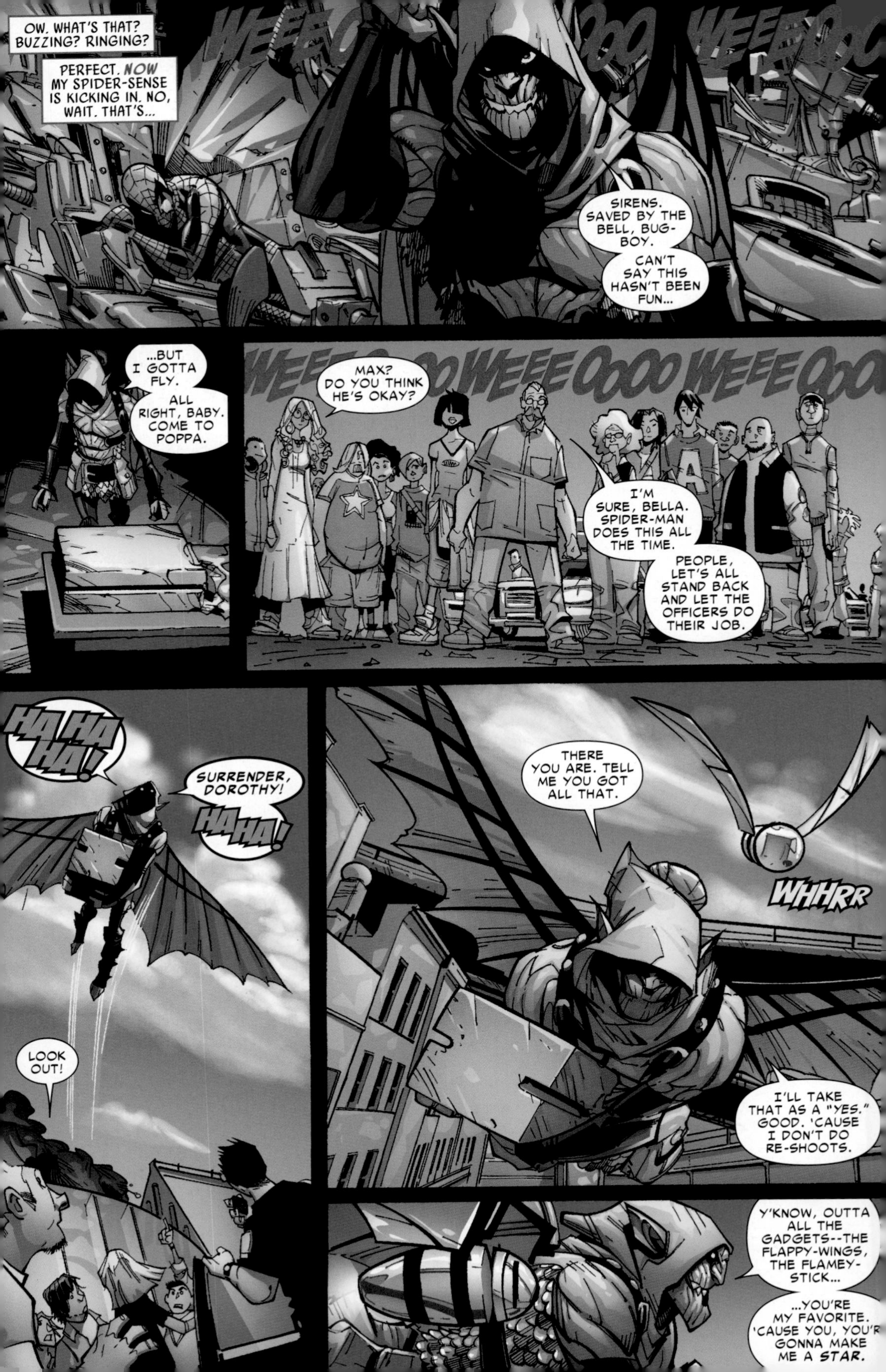
OW. WHAT'S THAT? BUZZING? RINGING?
PERFECT. NOW MY SPIDER-SENSE IS KICKING IN. NO, WAIT. THAT'S...
WEEE OOOO WEEE OOOO
SIRENS. SAVED BY THE BELL, BUG-BOY.
CAN'T SAY THIS HASN'T BEEN FUN...
...BUT I GOTTA FLY.
ALL RIGHT, BABY. COME TO POPPA.
WEEE OOOO WEEE OOOO WEEE OOOO
MAX? DO YOU THINK HE'S OKAY?
I'M SURE, BELLA. SPIDER-MAN DOES THIS ALL THE TIME.
PEOPLE, LET'S ALL STAND BACK AND LET THE OFFICERS DO THEIR JOB.
HA HA HA!
SURRENDER, DOROTHY!
HA HA!
LOOK OUT!
THERE YOU ARE. TELL ME YOU GOT ALL THAT.
WHHRR
I'LL TAKE THAT AS A "YES." GOOD. 'CAUSE I DON'T DO RE-SHOOTS.
Y'KNOW, OUTTA ALL THE GADGETS--THE FLAPPY-WINGS, THE FLAMEY-STICK...
...YOU'RE MY FAVORITE. 'CAUSE YOU, YOU'R GONNA MAKE ME A STAR.

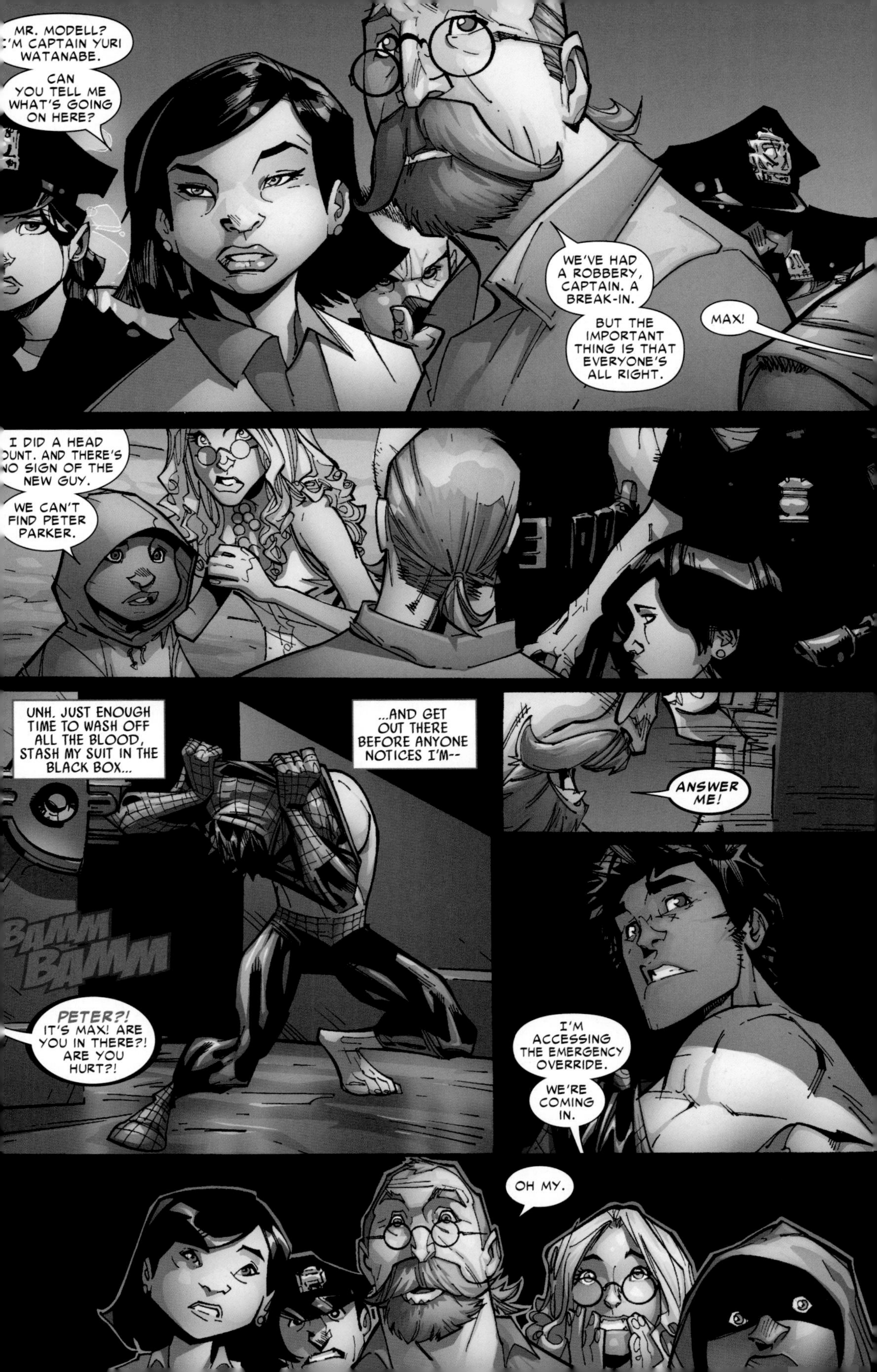
MR. MODELL? I'M CAPTAIN YURI WATANABE.
CAN YOU TELL ME WHAT'S GOING ON HERE?
WE'VE HAD A ROBBERY, CAPTAIN. A BREAK-IN.
BUT THE IMPORTANT THING IS THAT EVERYONE'S ALL RIGHT.
MAX!
I DID A HEAD COUNT. AND THERE'S NO SIGN OF THE NEW GUY.
WE CAN'T FIND PETER PARKER.
UNH. JUST ENOUGH TIME TO WASH OFF ALL THE BLOOD, STASH MY SUIT IN THE BLACK BOX...
...AND GET OUT THERE BEFORE ANYONE NOTICES I'M--
ANSWER ME!
BAMM BAMM
PETER?! IT'S MAX! ARE YOU IN THERE?! ARE YOU HURT?!
I'M ACCESSING THE EMERGENCY OVERRIDE.
WE'RE COMING IN.
OH MY.

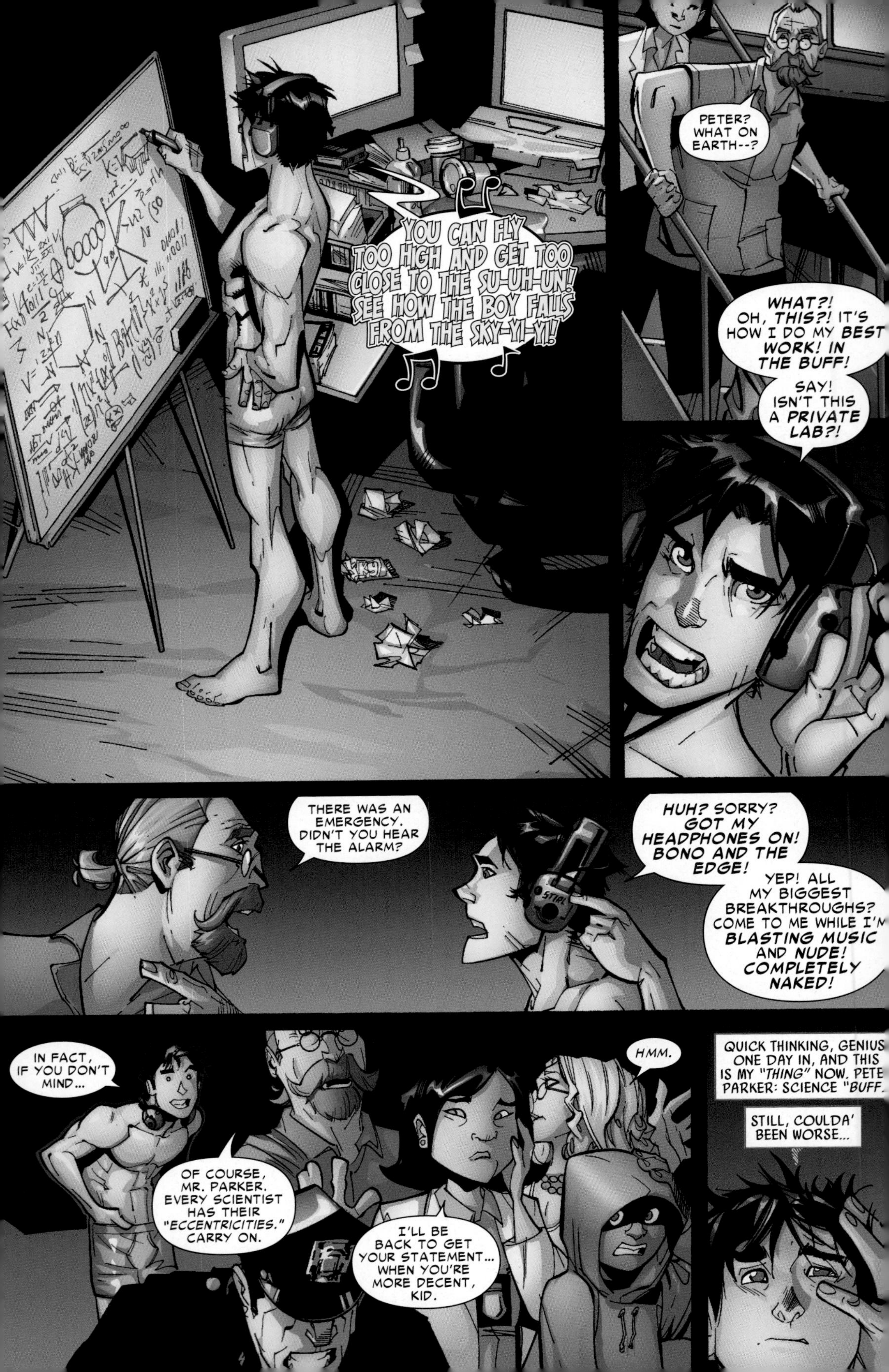
YOU CAN FLY TOO HIGH AND GET TOO CLOSE TO THE SU-UH-UN! SEE HOW THE BOY FALLS FROM THE SKY-YI-YI!
PETER? WHAT ON EARTH--?
WHAT?! OH, THIS?! IT'S HOW I DO MY BEST WORK! IN THE BUFF!
SAY! ISN'T THIS A PRIVATE LAB?!
THERE WAS AN EMERGENCY. DIDN'T YOU HEAR THE ALARM?
HUH? SORRY? GOT MY HEADPHONES ON! BONO AND THE EDGE!
YEP! ALL MY BIGGEST BREAKTHROUGHS? COME TO ME WHILE I'M BLASTING MUSIC AND NUDE! COMPLETELY NAKED!
IN FACT, IF YOU DON'T MIND...
OF COURSE, MR. PARKER. EVERY SCIENTIST HAS THEIR "ECCENTRICITIES." CARRY ON.
I'LL BE BACK TO GET YOUR STATEMENT... WHEN YOU'RE MORE DECENT, KID.
HMM.
QUICK THINKING, GENIUS. ONE DAY IN, AND THIS IS MY "THING" NOW. PETE PARKER: SCIENCE "BUFF."
STILL, COULDA' BEEN WORSE...

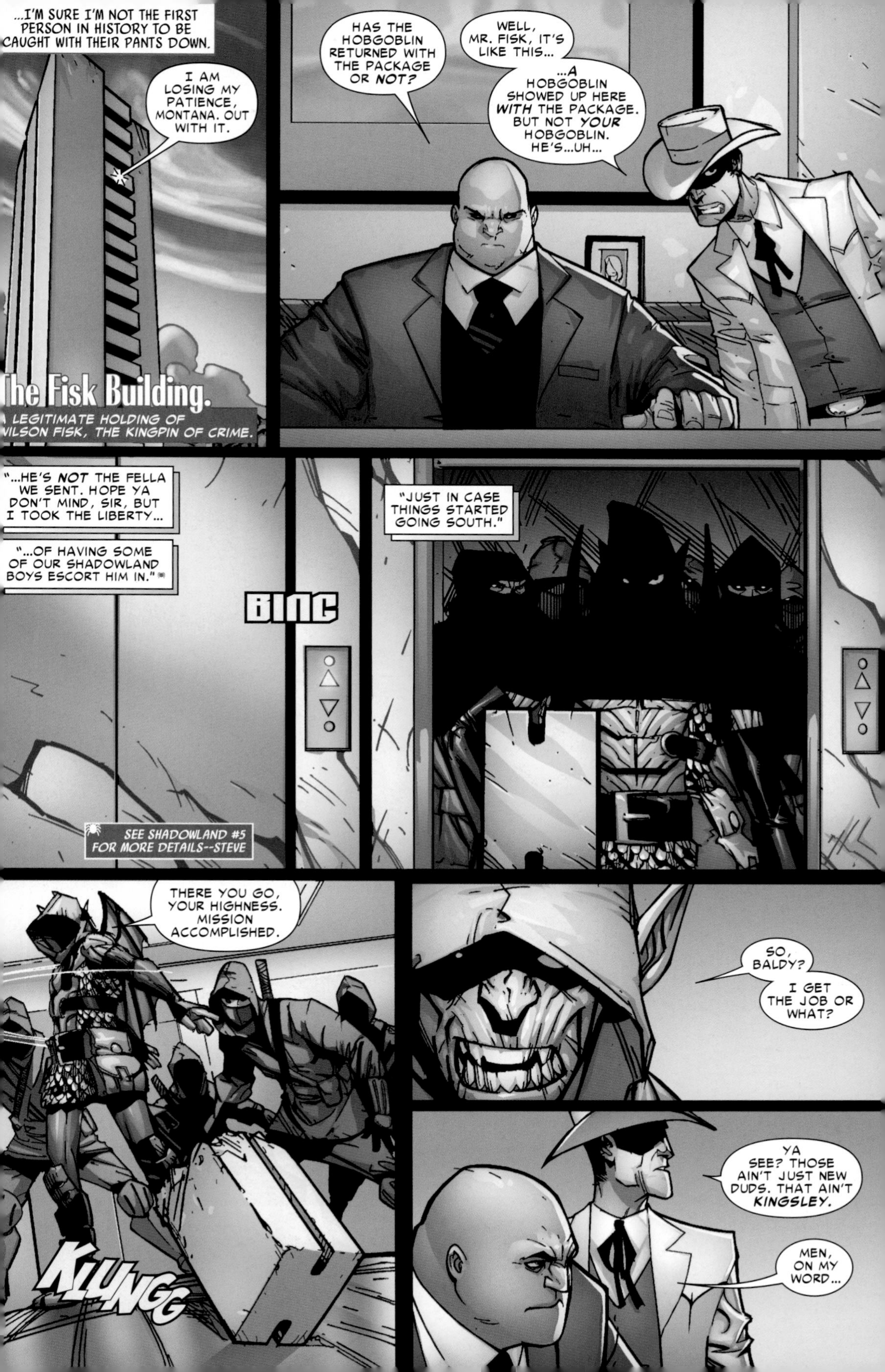
...I'M SURE I'M NOT THE FIRST PERSON IN HISTORY TO BE CAUGHT WITH THEIR PANTS DOWN.
I AM LOSING MY PATIENCE, MONTANA. OUT WITH IT.
The Fisk Building.
A LEGITIMATE HOLDING OF WILSON FISK, THE KINGPIN OF CRIME.
HAS THE HOBGOBLIN RETURNED WITH THE PACKAGE OR NOT?
WELL, MR. FISK, IT'S LIKE THIS...
...A HOBGOBLIN SHOWED UP HERE WITH THE PACKAGE. BUT NOT YOUR HOBGOBLIN. HE'S...UH...
"...HE'S NOT THE FELLA WE SENT. HOPE YA DON'T MIND, SIR, BUT I TOOK THE LIBERTY...
"...OF HAVING SOME OF OUR SHADOWLAND BOYS ESCORT HIM IN."
BINC
SEE SHADOWLAND #5 FOR MORE DETAILS--STEVE
"JUST IN CASE THINGS STARTED GOING SOUTH."
THERE YOU GO, YOUR HIGHNESS. MISSION ACCOMPLISHED.
KLUNGG
SO, BALDY?
I GET THE JOB OR WHAT?
YA SEE? THOSE AIN'T JUST NEW DUDS. THAT AIN'T KINGSLEY.
MEN, ON MY WORD...

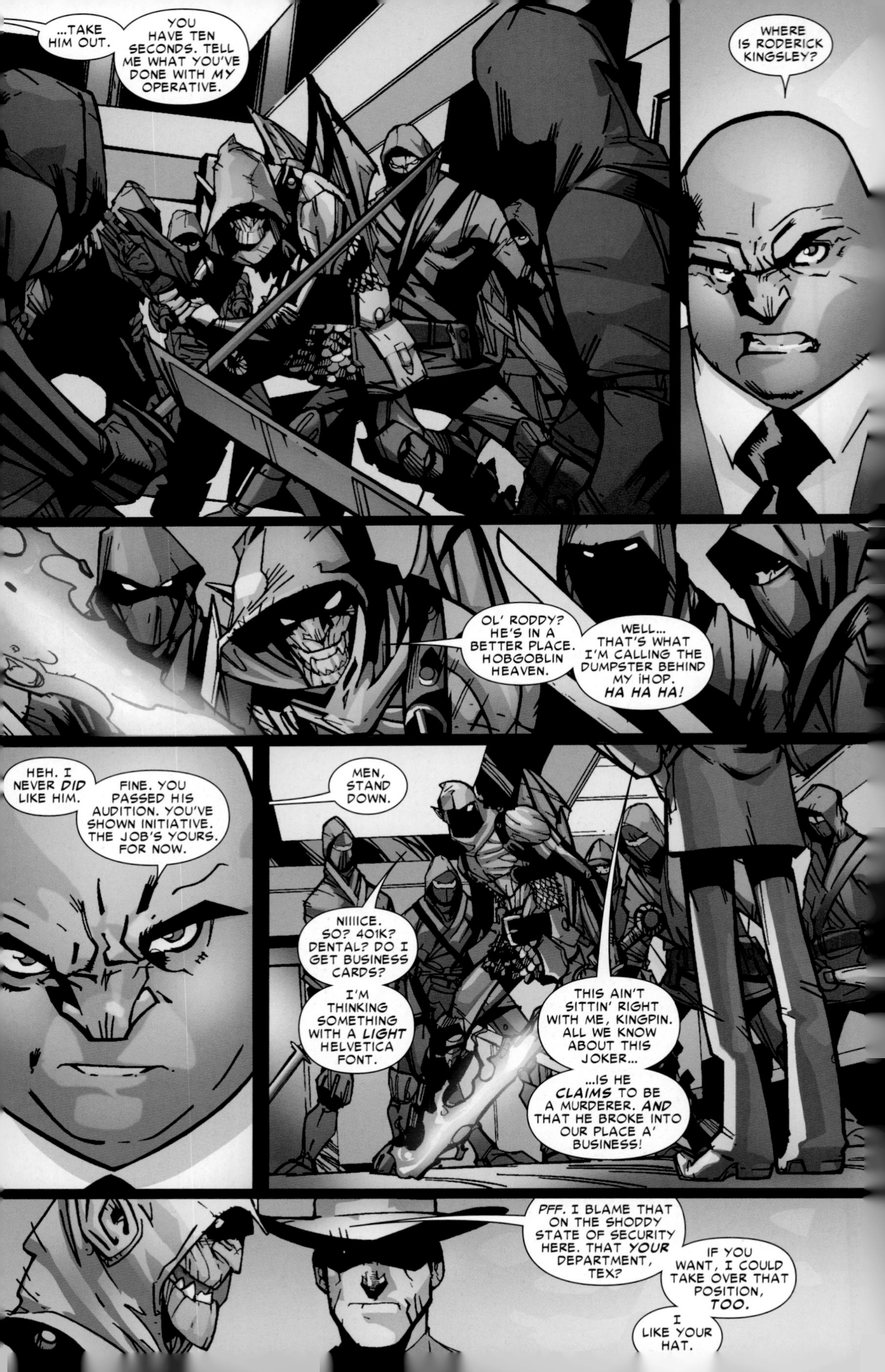
...TAKE HIM OUT.
YOU HAVE TEN SECONDS. TELL ME WHAT YOU'VE DONE WITH MY OPERATIVE.
WHERE IS RODERICK KINGSLEY?
OL' RODDY? HE'S IN A BETTER PLACE. HOBGOBLIN HEAVEN.
WELL... THAT'S WHAT I'M CALLING THE DUMPSTER BEHIND MY iHOP. HA HA HA!
HEH. I NEVER DID LIKE HIM.
FINE. YOU PASSED HIS AUDITION. YOU'VE SHOWN INITIATIVE. THE JOB'S YOURS. FOR NOW.
MEN, STAND DOWN.
NIIIICE. SO? 401K? DENTAL? DO I GET BUSINESS CARDS?
I'M THINKING SOMETHING WITH A LIGHT HELVETICA FONT.
THIS AIN'T SITTIN' RIGHT WITH ME, KINGPIN. ALL WE KNOW ABOUT THIS JOKER...
...IS HE CLAIMS TO BE A MURDERER. AND THAT HE BROKE INTO OUR PLACE A' BUSINESS!
PFF. I BLAME THAT ON THE SHODDY STATE OF SECURITY HERE. THAT YOUR DEPARTMENT, TEX?
IF YOU WANT, I COULD TAKE OVER THAT POSITION, TOO.
I LIKE YOUR HAT.

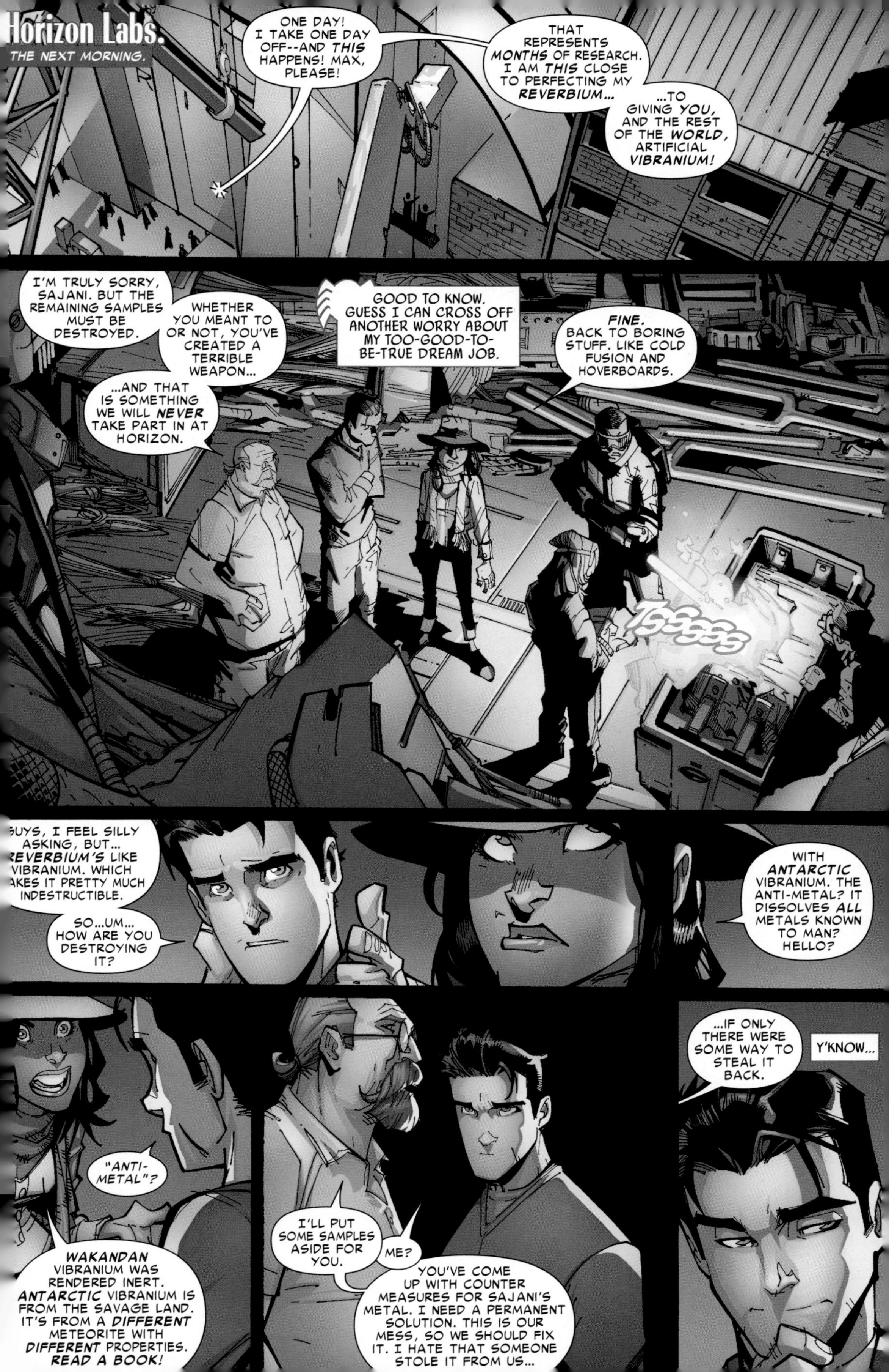
Horizon Labs.
THE NEXT MORNING.
ONE DAY! I TAKE ONE DAY OFF--AND THIS HAPPENS! MAX, PLEASE!
THAT REPRESENTS MONTHS OF RESEARCH. I AM THIS CLOSE TO PERFECTING MY REVERBIUM...
...TO GIVING YOU, AND THE REST OF THE WORLD, ARTIFICIAL VIBRANIUM!
I'M TRULY SORRY, SAJANI. BUT THE REMAINING SAMPLES MUST BE DESTROYED.
WHETHER YOU MEANT TO OR NOT, YOU'VE CREATED A TERRIBLE WEAPON...
...AND THAT IS SOMETHING WE WILL NEVER TAKE PART IN AT HORIZON.
GOOD TO KNOW. GUESS I CAN CROSS OFF ANOTHER WORRY ABOUT MY TOO-GOOD-TO-BE-TRUE DREAM JOB.
FINE. BACK TO BORING STUFF. LIKE COLD FUSION AND HOVERBOARDS.
TSSSSS
GUYS, I FEEL SILLY ASKING, BUT... REVERBIUM'S LIKE VIBRANIUM. WHICH MAKES IT PRETTY MUCH INDESTRUCTIBLE.
SO...UM... HOW ARE YOU DESTROYING IT?
WITH ANTARCTIC VIBRANIUM. THE ANTI-METAL? IT DISSOLVES ALL METALS KNOWN TO MAN? HELLO?
"ANTI-METAL"?
WAKANDAN VIBRANIUM WAS RENDERED INERT. ANTARCTIC VIBRANIUM IS FROM THE SAVAGE LAND. IT'S FROM A DIFFERENT METEORITE WITH DIFFERENT PROPERTIES. READ A BOOK!
I'LL PUT SOME SAMPLES ASIDE FOR YOU.
ME?
YOU'VE COME UP WITH COUNTER MEASURES FOR SAJANI'S METAL. I NEED A PERMANENT SOLUTION. THIS IS OUR MESS, SO WE SHOULD FIX IT. I HATE THAT SOMEONE STOLE IT FROM US...
...IF ONLY THERE WERE SOME WAY TO STEAL IT BACK.
Y'KNOW...

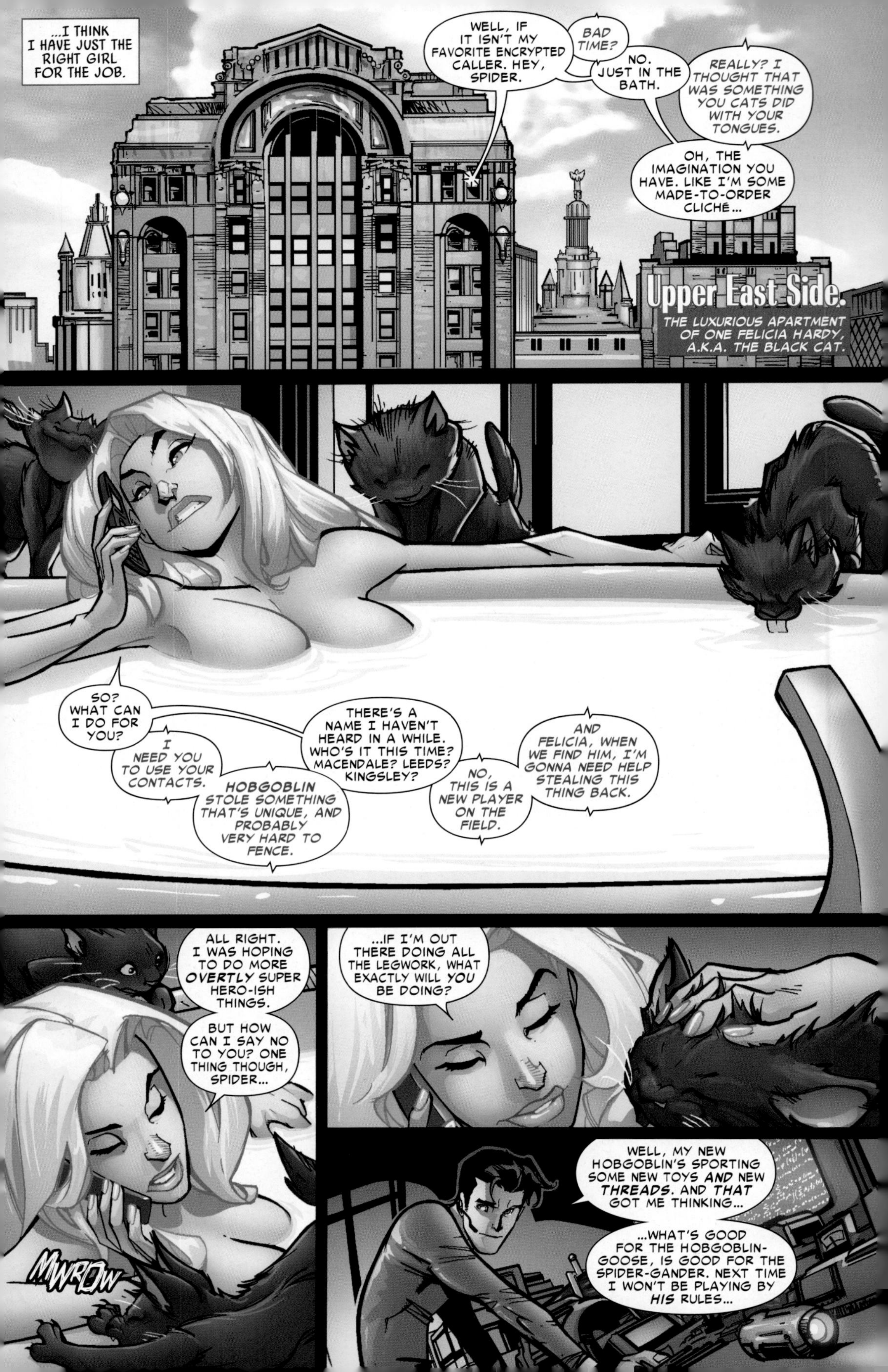
...I THINK I HAVE JUST THE RIGHT GIRL FOR THE JOB.
WELL, IF IT ISN'T MY FAVORITE ENCRYPTED CALLER. HEY, SPIDER.
BAD TIME?
NO. JUST IN THE BATH.
REALLY? I THOUGHT THAT WAS SOMETHING YOU CATS DID WITH YOUR TONGUES.
OH, THE IMAGINATION YOU HAVE. LIKE I'M SOME MADE-TO-ORDER CLICHÉ...
Upper East Side.
THE LUXURIOUS APARTMENT OF ONE FELICIA HARDY, A.K.A. THE BLACK CAT.
SO? WHAT CAN I DO FOR YOU?
I NEED YOU TO USE YOUR CONTACTS.
HOBGOBLIN STOLE SOMETHING THAT'S UNIQUE, AND PROBABLY VERY HARD TO FENCE.
THERE'S A NAME I HAVEN'T HEARD IN A WHILE. WHO'S IT THIS TIME? MACENDALE? LEEDS? KINGSLEY?
NO, THIS IS A NEW PLAYER ON THE FIELD.
AND FELICIA, WHEN WE FIND HIM, I'M GONNA NEED HELP STEALING THIS THING BACK.
ALL RIGHT. I WAS HOPING TO DO MORE OVERTLY SUPER HERO-ISH THINGS.
BUT HOW CAN I SAY NO TO YOU? ONE THING THOUGH, SPIDER...
MWROW
...IF I'M OUT THERE DOING ALL THE LEGWORK, WHAT EXACTLY WILL YOU BE DOING?
WELL, MY NEW HOBGOBLIN'S SPORTING SOME NEW TOYS AND NEW THREADS. AND THAT GOT ME THINKING...
...WHAT'S GOOD FOR THE HOBGOBLIN-GOOSE, IS GOOD FOR THE SPIDER-GANDER. NEXT TIME I WON'T BE PLAYING BY HIS RULES...

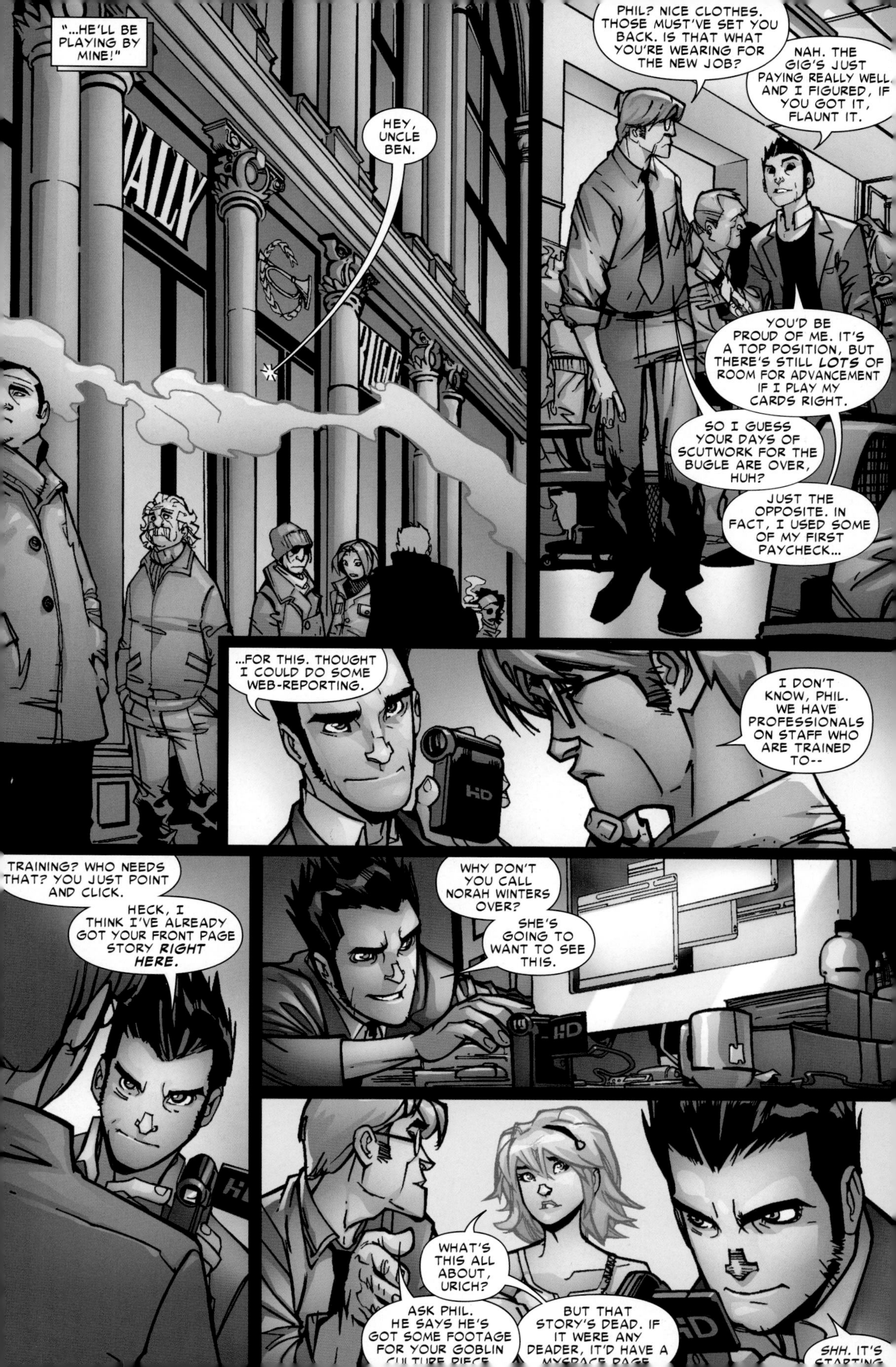
"...HE'LL BE PLAYING BY MINE!"
HEY, UNCLE BEN.
PHIL? NICE CLOTHES. THOSE MUST'VE SET YOU BACK. IS THAT WHAT YOU'RE WEARING FOR THE NEW JOB?
NAH. THE GIG'S JUST PAYING REALLY WELL. AND I FIGURED, IF YOU GOT IT, FLAUNT IT.
YOU'D BE PROUD OF ME. IT'S A TOP POSITION, BUT THERE'S STILL *LOTS* OF ROOM FOR ADVANCEMENT IF I PLAY MY CARDS RIGHT.
SO I GUESS YOUR DAYS OF SCUTWORK FOR THE BUGLE ARE OVER, HUH?
JUST THE OPPOSITE. IN FACT, I USED SOME OF MY FIRST PAYCHECK...
...FOR THIS. THOUGHT I COULD DO SOME WEB-REPORTING.
I DON'T KNOW, PHIL. WE HAVE PROFESSIONALS ON STAFF WHO ARE TRAINED TO--
TRAINING? WHO NEEDS THAT? YOU JUST POINT AND CLICK.
HECK, I THINK I'VE ALREADY GOT YOUR FRONT PAGE STORY *RIGHT HERE.*
WHY DON'T YOU CALL NORAH WINTERS OVER?
SHE'S GOING TO WANT TO SEE THIS.
WHAT'S THIS ALL ABOUT, URICH?
ASK PHIL. HE SAYS HE'S GOT SOME FOOTAGE FOR YOUR GOBLIN
BUT THAT STORY'S DEAD. IF IT WERE ANY DEADER, IT'D HAVE A
SHH. IT'S

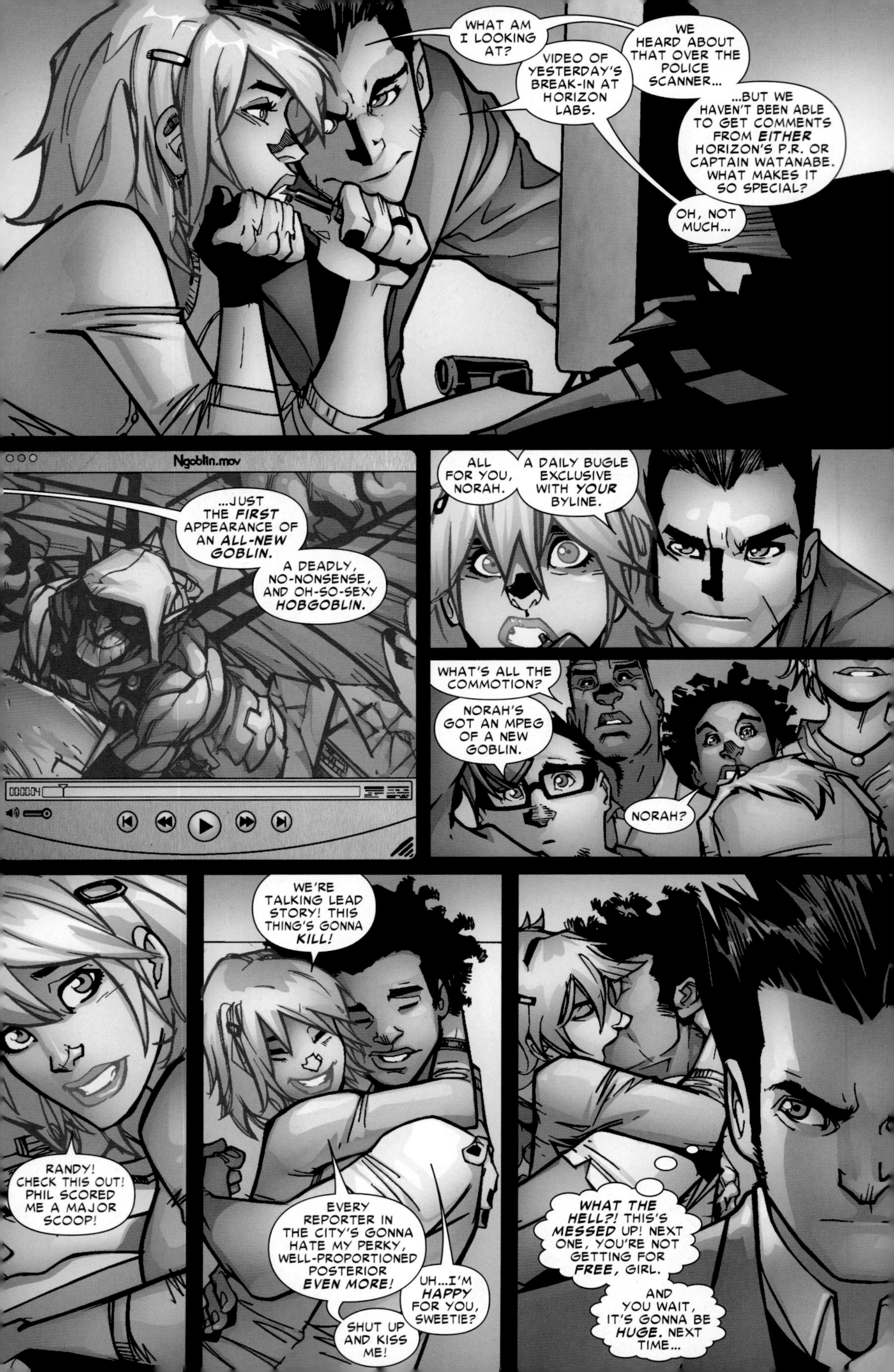
WHAT AM I LOOKING AT?
VIDEO OF YESTERDAY'S BREAK-IN AT HORIZON LABS.
WE HEARD ABOUT THAT OVER THE POLICE SCANNER...
...BUT WE HAVEN'T BEEN ABLE TO GET COMMENTS FROM EITHER HORIZON'S P.R. OR CAPTAIN WATANABE. WHAT MAKES IT SO SPECIAL?
OH, NOT MUCH...
Ngoblin.mov
...JUST THE FIRST APPEARANCE OF AN ALL-NEW GOBLIN.
A DEADLY, NO-NONSENSE, AND OH-SO-SEXY HOBGOBLIN.
00:00:04
ALL FOR YOU, NORAH.
A DAILY BUGLE EXCLUSIVE WITH YOUR BYLINE.
WHAT'S ALL THE COMMOTION?
NORAH'S GOT AN MPEG OF A NEW GOBLIN.
NORAH?
RANDY! CHECK THIS OUT! PHIL SCORED ME A MAJOR SCOOP!
WE'RE TALKING LEAD STORY! THIS THING'S GONNA KILL!
EVERY REPORTER IN THE CITY'S GONNA HATE MY PERKY, WELL-PROPORTIONED POSTERIOR EVEN MORE!
UH...I'M HAPPY FOR YOU, SWEETIE?
SHUT UP AND KISS ME!
WHAT THE HELL?! THIS'S MESSED UP! NEXT ONE, YOU'RE NOT GETTING FOR FREE, GIRL.
AND YOU WAIT, IT'S GONNA BE HUGE. NEXT TIME...

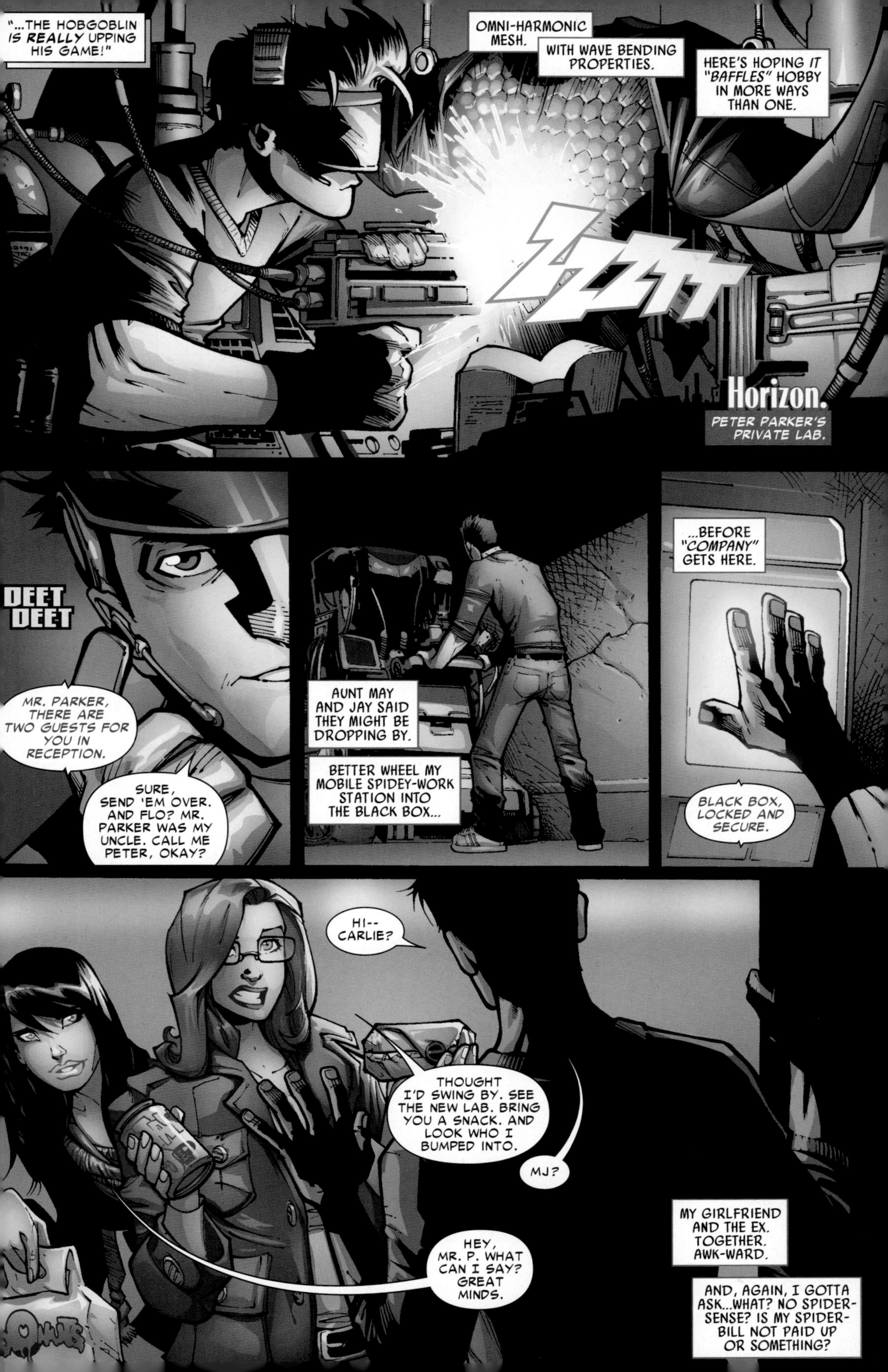
"...THE HOBGOBLIN IS REALLY UPPING HIS GAME!"
OMNI-HARMONIC MESH.
WITH WAVE BENDING PROPERTIES.
HERE'S HOPING IT "BAFFLES" HOBBY IN MORE WAYS THAN ONE.
ZZZTT
Horizon.
PETER PARKER'S PRIVATE LAB.
DEET DEET
MR. PARKER, THERE ARE TWO GUESTS FOR YOU IN RECEPTION.
SURE, SEND 'EM OVER. AND FLO? MR. PARKER WAS MY UNCLE. CALL ME PETER, OKAY?
AUNT MAY AND JAY SAID THEY MIGHT BE DROPPING BY.
BETTER WHEEL MY MOBILE SPIDEY-WORK STATION INTO THE BLACK BOX...
...BEFORE "COMPANY" GETS HERE.
BLACK BOX, LOCKED AND SECURE.
HI-- CARLIE?
THOUGHT I'D SWING BY. SEE THE NEW LAB. BRING YOU A SNACK. AND LOOK WHO I BUMPED INTO.
MJ?
HEY, MR. P. WHAT CAN I SAY? GREAT MINDS.
MY GIRLFRIEND AND THE EX. TOGETHER. AWK-WARD.
AND, AGAIN, I GOTTA ASK...WHAT? NO SPIDER-SENSE? IS MY SPIDER-BILL NOT PAID UP OR SOMETHING?

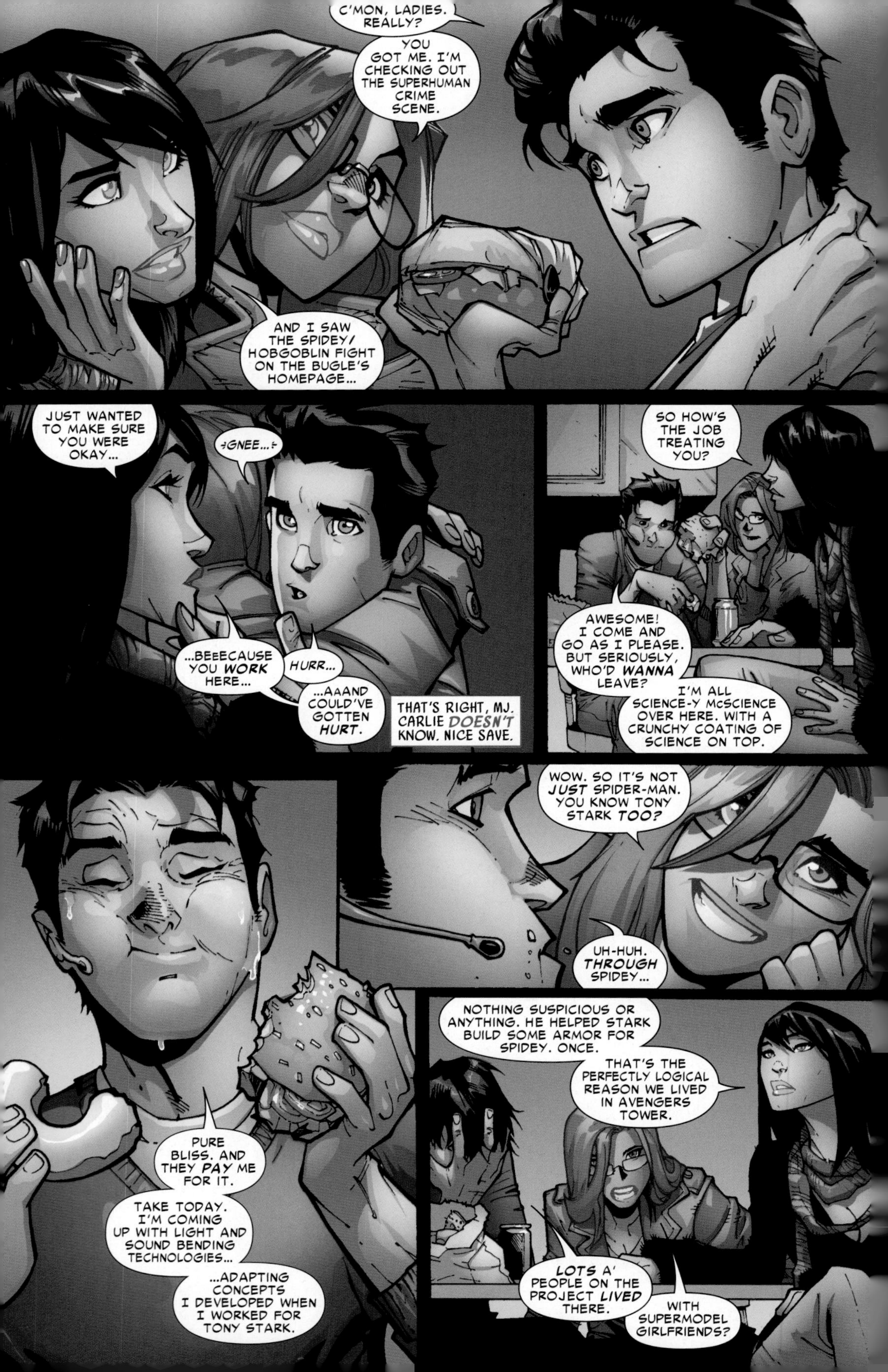

C'MON, LADIES. REALLY?
YOU GOT ME. I'M CHECKING OUT THE SUPERHUMAN CRIME SCENE.
AND I SAW THE SPIDEY/HOBGOBLIN FIGHT ON THE BUGLE'S HOMEPAGE...
JUST WANTED TO MAKE SURE YOU WERE OKAY...
GNEE...
...BEEECAUSE YOU WORK HERE...
HURR...
...AAAND COULD'VE GOTTEN HURT.
THAT'S RIGHT, MJ. CARLIE DOESN'T KNOW. NICE SAVE.
SO HOW'S THE JOB TREATING YOU?
AWESOME! I COME AND GO AS I PLEASE. BUT SERIOUSLY, WHO'D WANNA LEAVE?
I'M ALL SCIENCE-Y McSCIENCE OVER HERE. WITH A CRUNCHY COATING OF SCIENCE ON TOP.
PURE BLISS. AND THEY PAY ME FOR IT.
TAKE TODAY. I'M COMING UP WITH LIGHT AND SOUND BENDING TECHNOLOGIES...
...ADAPTING CONCEPTS I DEVELOPED WHEN I WORKED FOR TONY STARK.
WOW. SO IT'S NOT JUST SPIDER-MAN. YOU KNOW TONY STARK TOO?
UH-HUH. THROUGH SPIDEY...
NOTHING SUSPICIOUS OR ANYTHING. HE HELPED STARK BUILD SOME ARMOR FOR SPIDEY. ONCE.
THAT'S THE PERFECTLY LOGICAL REASON WE LIVED IN AVENGERS TOWER.
LOTS A' PEOPLE ON THE PROJECT LIVED THERE.
WITH SUPERMODEL GIRLFRIENDS?

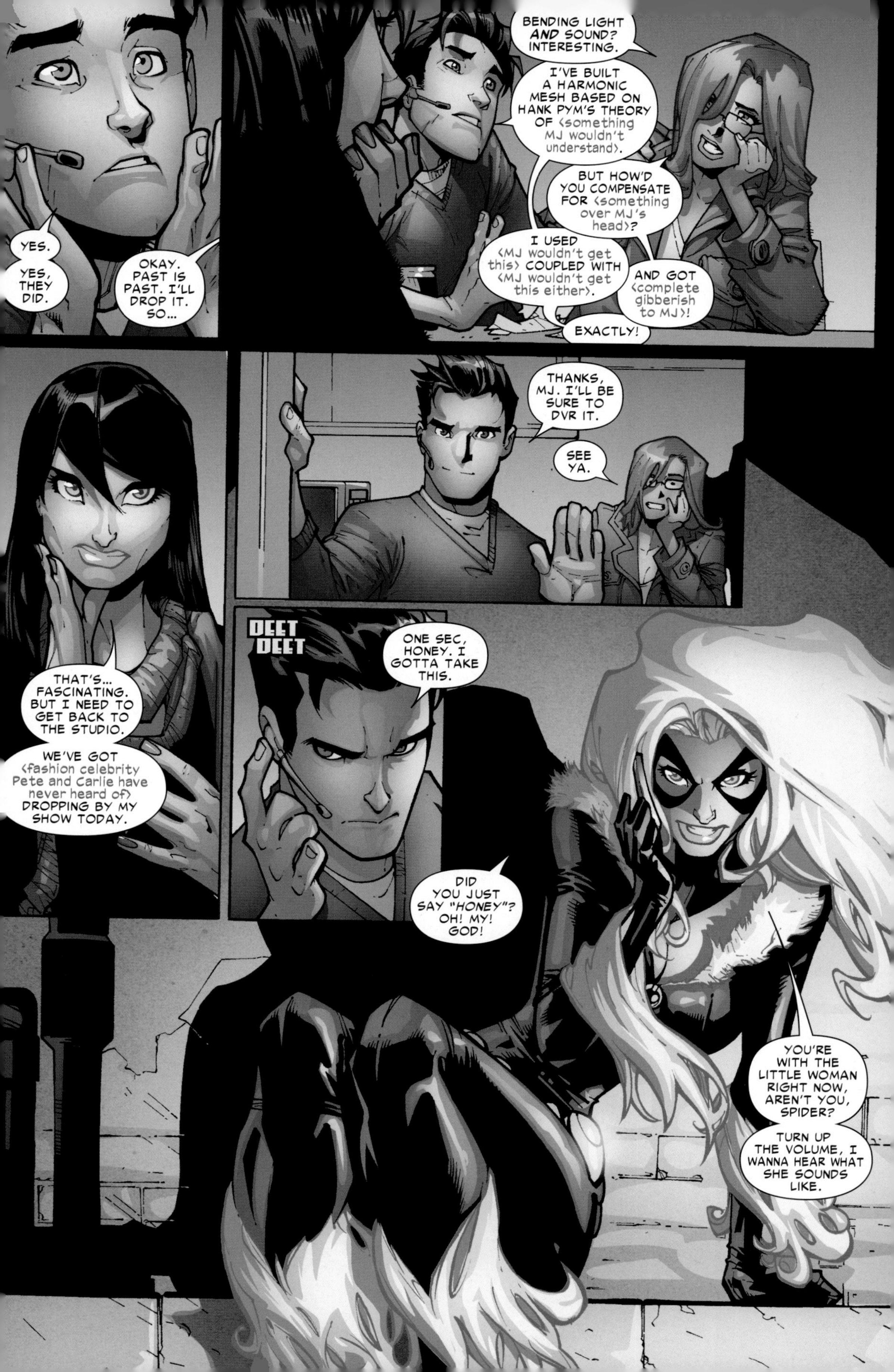
YES.
YES, THEY DID.
OKAY. PAST IS PAST. I'LL DROP IT. SO...
BENDING LIGHT AND SOUND? INTERESTING.
I'VE BUILT A HARMONIC MESH BASED ON HANK PYM'S THEORY OF ‹something MJ wouldn't understand›.
BUT HOW'D YOU COMPENSATE FOR ‹something over MJ's head›?
I USED ‹MJ wouldn't get this› COUPLED WITH ‹MJ wouldn't get this either›.
AND GOT ‹complete gibberish to MJ›!
EXACTLY!
THAT'S... FASCINATING. BUT I NEED TO GET BACK TO THE STUDIO.
WE'VE GOT ‹fashion celebrity Pete and Carlie have never heard of› DROPPING BY MY SHOW TODAY.
THANKS, MJ. I'LL BE SURE TO DVR IT.
SEE YA.
DEET DEET
ONE SEC, HONEY. I GOTTA TAKE THIS.
DID YOU JUST SAY "HONEY"? OH! MY! GOD!
YOU'RE WITH THE LITTLE WOMAN RIGHT NOW, AREN'T YOU, SPIDER?
TURN UP THE VOLUME, I WANNA HEAR WHAT SHE SOUNDS LIKE.

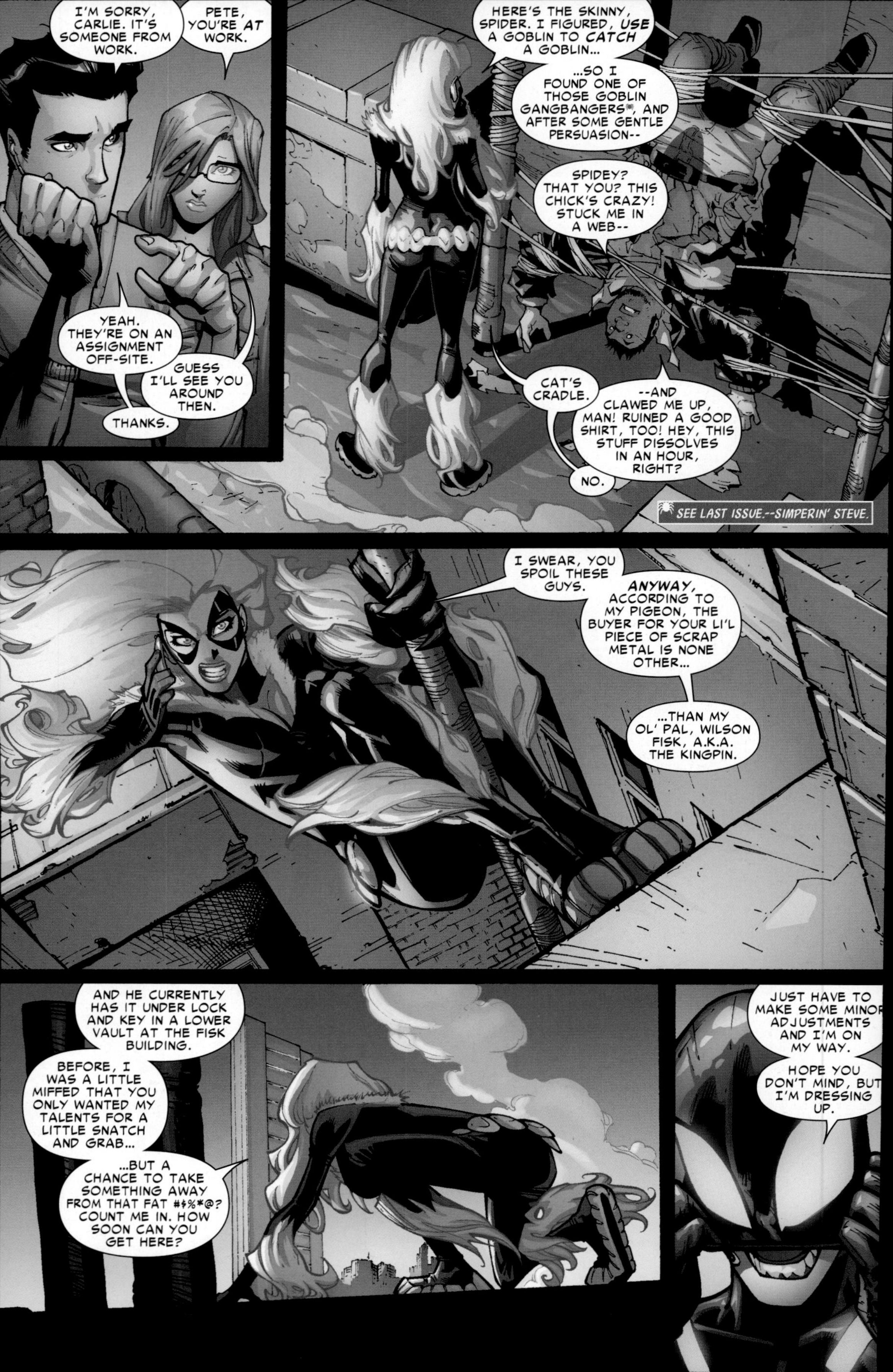
I'M SORRY, CARLIE. IT'S SOMEONE FROM WORK.
PETE, YOU'RE AT WORK.
YEAH. THEY'RE ON AN ASSIGNMENT OFF-SITE.
GUESS I'LL SEE YOU AROUND THEN.
THANKS.
HERE'S THE SKINNY, SPIDER. I FIGURED, USE A GOBLIN TO CATCH A GOBLIN...
...SO I FOUND ONE OF THOSE GOBLIN GANGBANGERS*, AND AFTER SOME GENTLE PERSUASION--
SPIDEY? THAT YOU? THIS CHICK'S CRAZY! STUCK ME IN A WEB--
CAT'S CRADLE.
--AND CLAWED ME UP, MAN! RUINED A GOOD SHIRT, TOO! HEY, THIS STUFF DISSOLVES IN AN HOUR, RIGHT?
NO.
*SEE LAST ISSUE.--SIMPERIN' STEVE.
I SWEAR, YOU SPOIL THESE GUYS.
ANYWAY, ACCORDING TO MY PIGEON, THE BUYER FOR YOUR LI'L PIECE OF SCRAP METAL IS NONE OTHER...
...THAN MY OL' PAL, WILSON FISK, A.K.A. THE KINGPIN.
AND HE CURRENTLY HAS IT UNDER LOCK AND KEY IN A LOWER VAULT AT THE FISK BUILDING.
BEFORE, I WAS A LITTLE MIFFED THAT YOU ONLY WANTED MY TALENTS FOR A LITTLE SNATCH AND GRAB...
...BUT A CHANCE TO TAKE SOMETHING AWAY FROM THAT FAT #$%*@? COUNT ME IN. HOW SOON CAN YOU GET HERE?
JUST HAVE TO MAKE SOME MINOR ADJUSTMENTS AND I'M ON MY WAY.
HOPE YOU DON'T MIND, BUT I'M DRESSING UP.

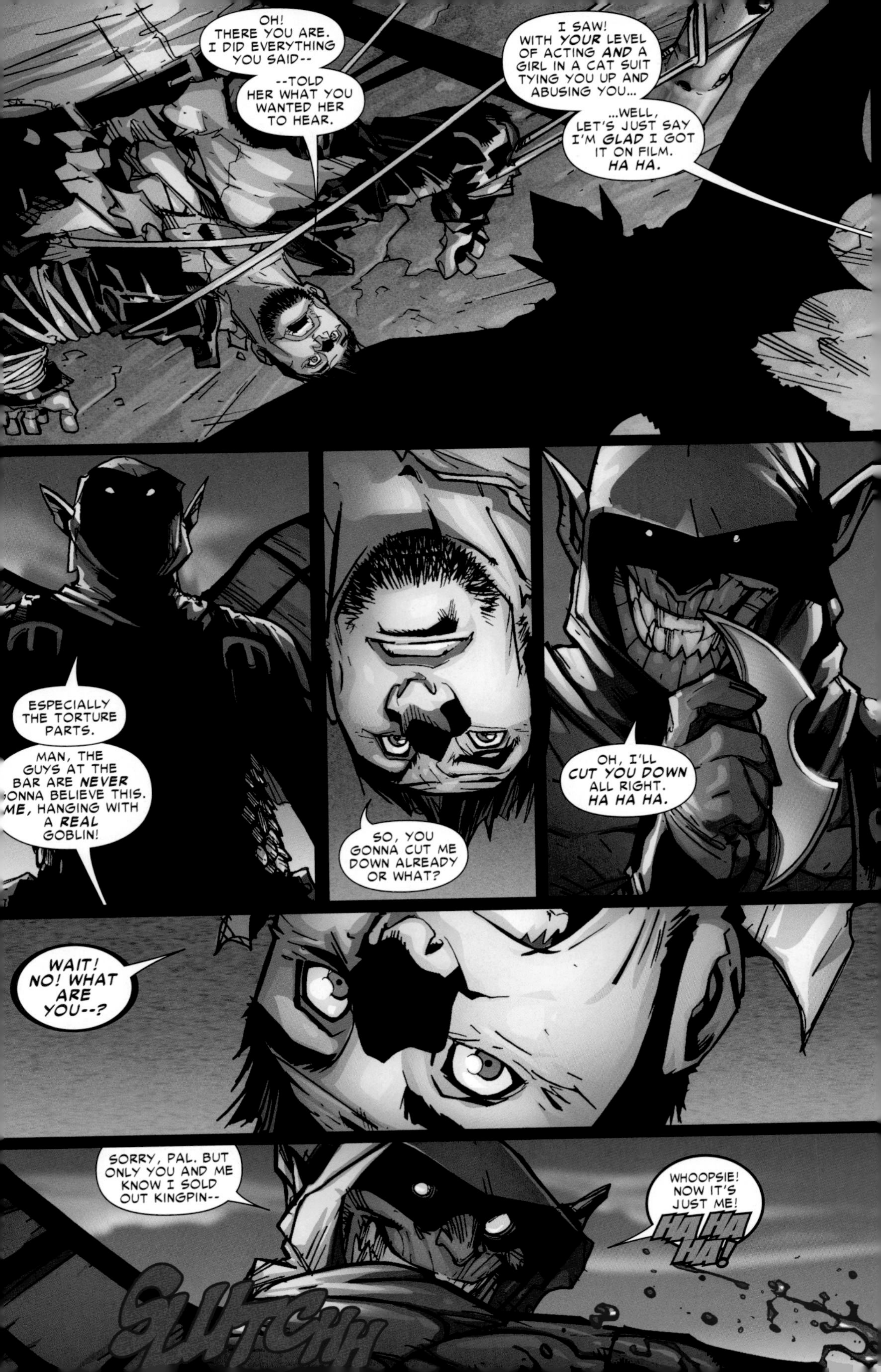
OH! THERE YOU ARE. I DID EVERYTHING YOU SAID--
--TOLD HER WHAT YOU WANTED HER TO HEAR.
I SAW! WITH YOUR LEVEL OF ACTING AND A GIRL IN A CAT SUIT TYING YOU UP AND ABUSING YOU...
...WELL, LET'S JUST SAY I'M GLAD I GOT IT ON FILM. HA HA.
ESPECIALLY THE TORTURE PARTS.
MAN, THE GUYS AT THE BAR ARE NEVER GONNA BELIEVE THIS. ME, HANGING WITH A REAL GOBLIN!
SO, YOU GONNA CUT ME DOWN ALREADY OR WHAT?
OH, I'LL CUT YOU DOWN ALL RIGHT. HA HA HA.
WAIT! NO! WHAT ARE YOU--?
SORRY, PAL. BUT ONLY YOU AND ME KNOW I SOLD OUT KINGPIN--
WHOOPSIE! NOW IT'S JUST ME!
HA HA HA!
SLUTCHH

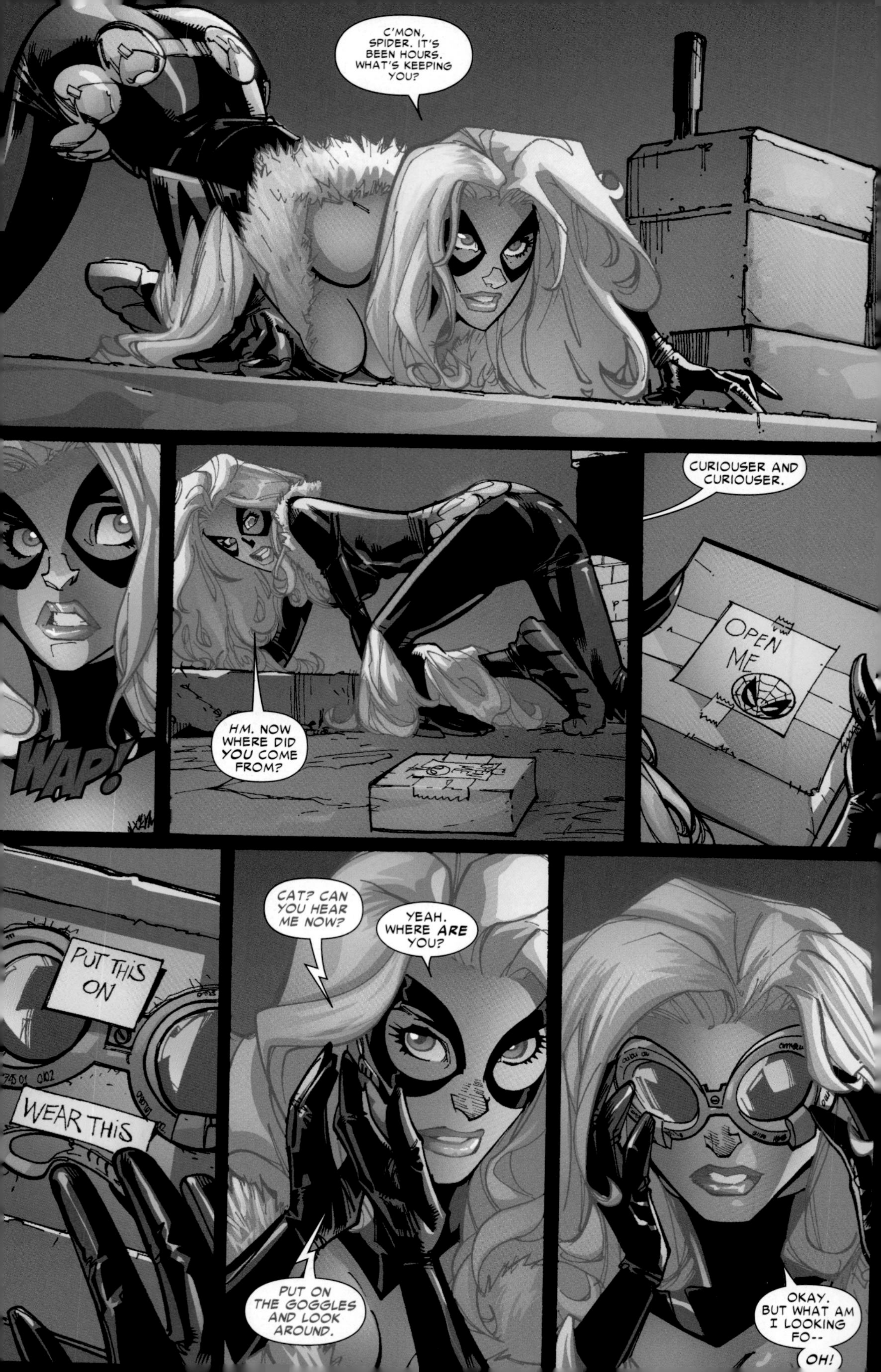
C'MON, SPIDER. IT'S BEEN HOURS. WHAT'S KEEPING YOU?
WAP!
HM. NOW WHERE DID YOU COME FROM?
CURIOUSER AND CURIOUSER.
OPEN ME
PUT THIS ON
WEAR THIS
CAT? CAN YOU HEAR ME NOW?
YEAH. WHERE ARE YOU?
PUT ON THE GOGGLES AND LOOK AROUND.
OKAY. BUT WHAT AM I LOOKING FO--
OH!

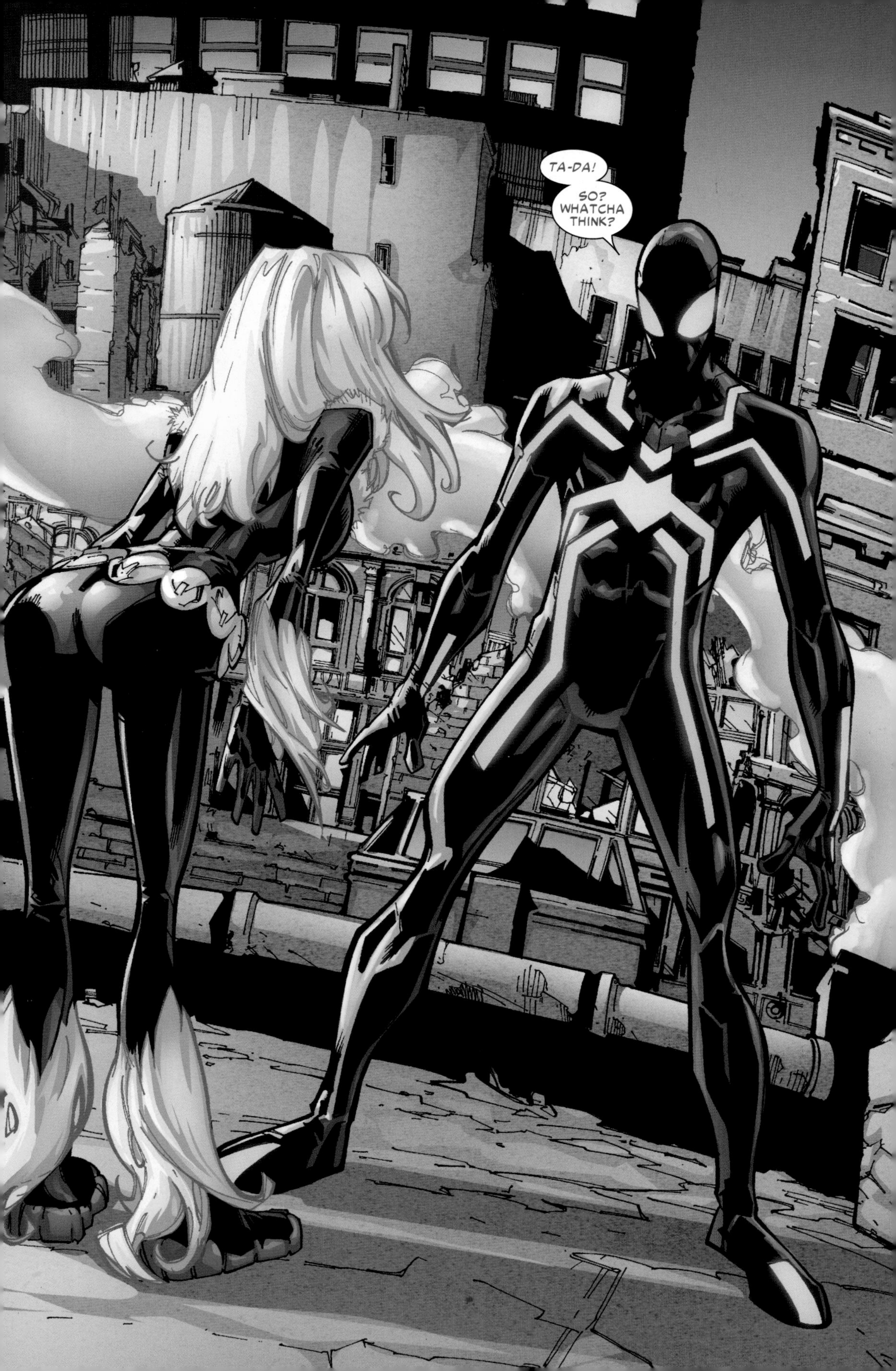
TA-DA!
SO? WHATCHA THINK?

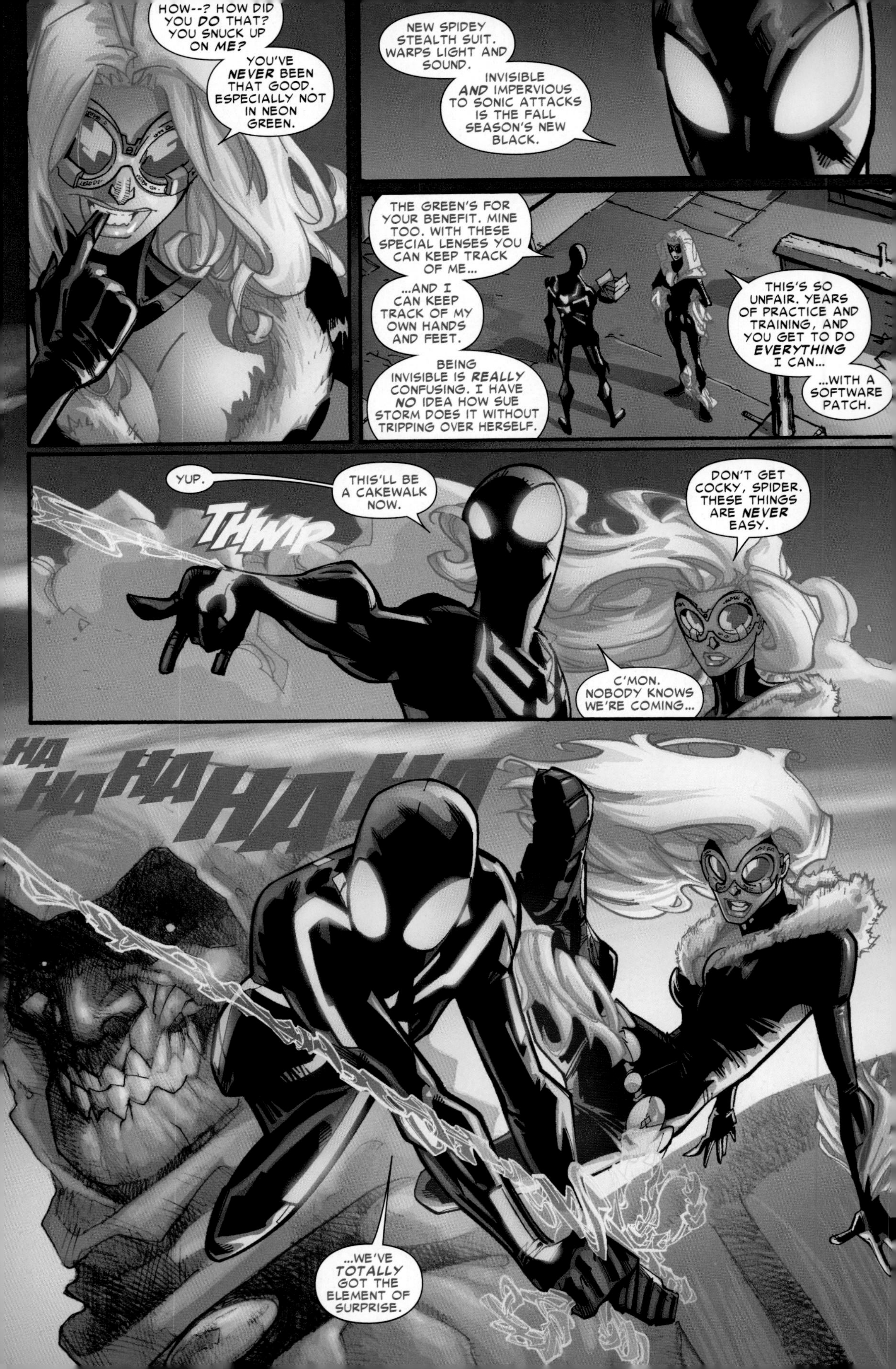
HOW--? HOW DID YOU DO THAT? YOU SNUCK UP ON ME?
YOU'VE NEVER BEEN THAT GOOD. ESPECIALLY NOT IN NEON GREEN.
NEW SPIDEY STEALTH SUIT. WARPS LIGHT AND SOUND.
INVISIBLE AND IMPERVIOUS TO SONIC ATTACKS IS THE FALL SEASON'S NEW BLACK.
THE GREEN'S FOR YOUR BENEFIT. MINE TOO. WITH THESE SPECIAL LENSES YOU CAN KEEP TRACK OF ME...
...AND I CAN KEEP TRACK OF MY OWN HANDS AND FEET.
BEING INVISIBLE IS REALLY CONFUSING. I HAVE NO IDEA HOW SUE STORM DOES IT WITHOUT TRIPPING OVER HERSELF.
THIS'S SO UNFAIR. YEARS OF PRACTICE AND TRAINING, AND YOU GET TO DO EVERYTHING I CAN...
...WITH A SOFTWARE PATCH.
YUP.
THIS'LL BE A CAKEWALK NOW.
THWIP
DON'T GET COCKY, SPIDER. THESE THINGS ARE NEVER EASY.
C'MON. NOBODY KNOWS WE'RE COMING...
HA HA HA HA HA HA
...WE'VE TOTALLY GOT THE ELEMENT OF SURPRISE.

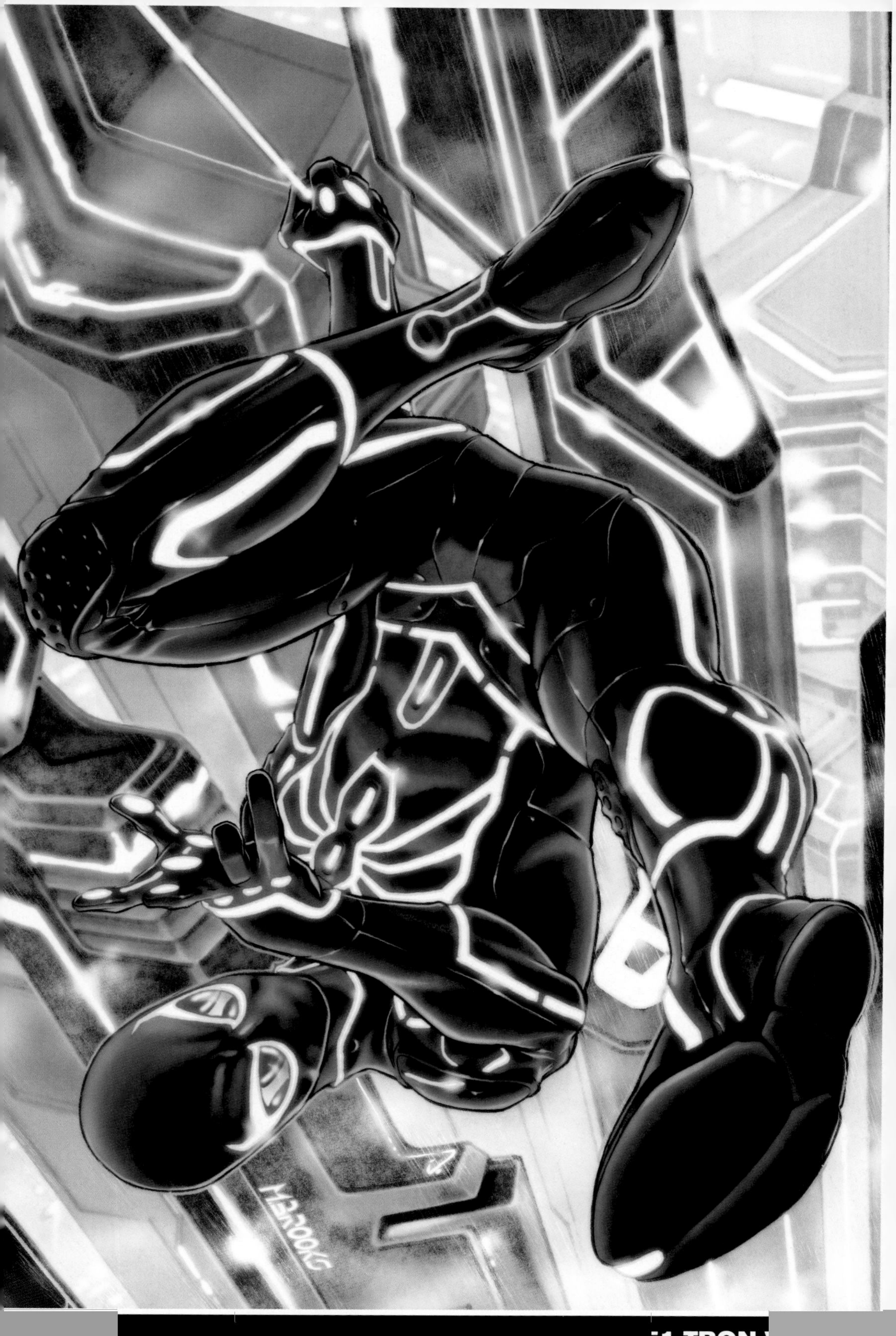

51 TRON V
BY MARK

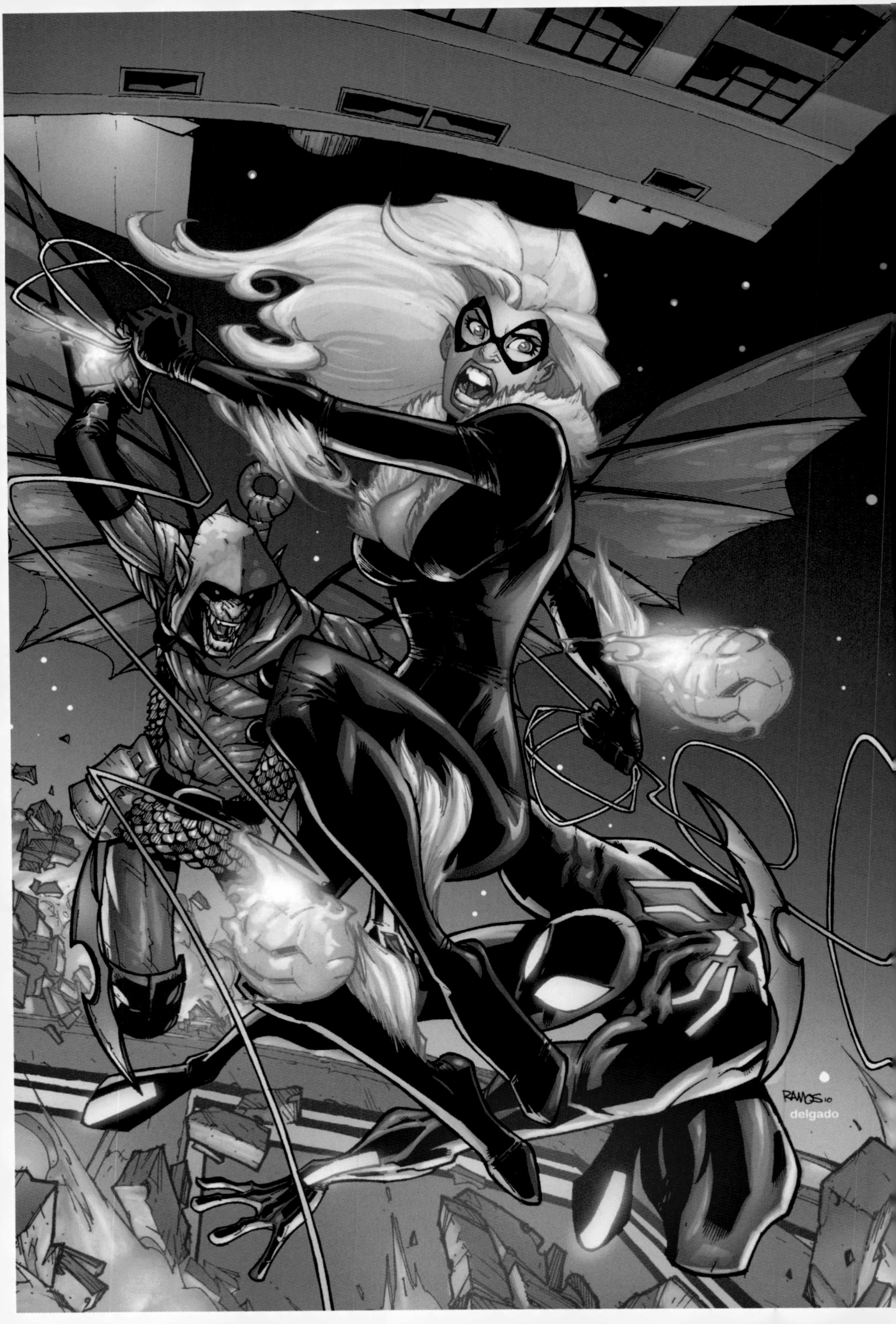
RAMOS'10
delgado

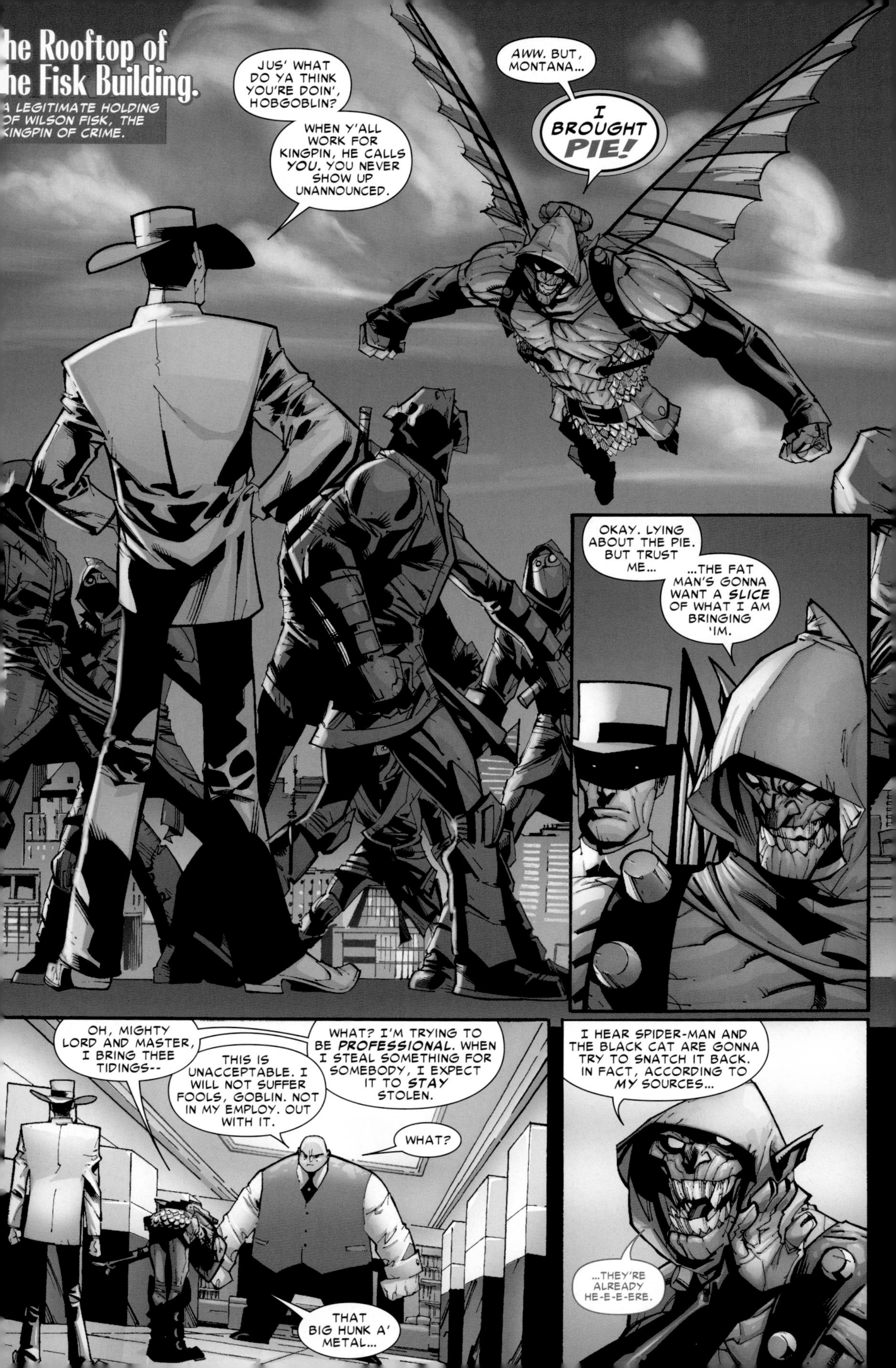

he Rooftop of
he Fisk Building.
A LEGITIMATE HOLDING OF WILSON FISK, THE KINGPIN OF CRIME.
JUS' WHAT DO YA THINK YOU'RE DOIN', HOBGOBLIN?
WHEN Y'ALL WORK FOR KINGPIN, HE CALLS YOU. YOU NEVER SHOW UP UNANNOUNCED.
AWW. BUT, MONTANA...
I BROUGHT PIE!
OKAY. LYING ABOUT THE PIE. BUT TRUST ME...
...THE FAT MAN'S GONNA WANT A SLICE OF WHAT I AM BRINGING 'IM.
OH, MIGHTY LORD AND MASTER, I BRING THEE TIDINGS--
THIS IS UNACCEPTABLE. I WILL NOT SUFFER FOOLS, GOBLIN. NOT IN MY EMPLOY. OUT WITH IT.
WHAT? I'M TRYING TO BE PROFESSIONAL. WHEN I STEAL SOMETHING FOR SOMEBODY, I EXPECT IT TO STAY STOLEN.
WHAT?
THAT BIG HUNK A' METAL...
I HEAR SPIDER-MAN AND THE BLACK CAT ARE GONNA TRY TO SNATCH IT BACK. IN FACT, ACCORDING TO MY SOURCES...
...THEY'RE ALREADY HE-E-E-ERE.

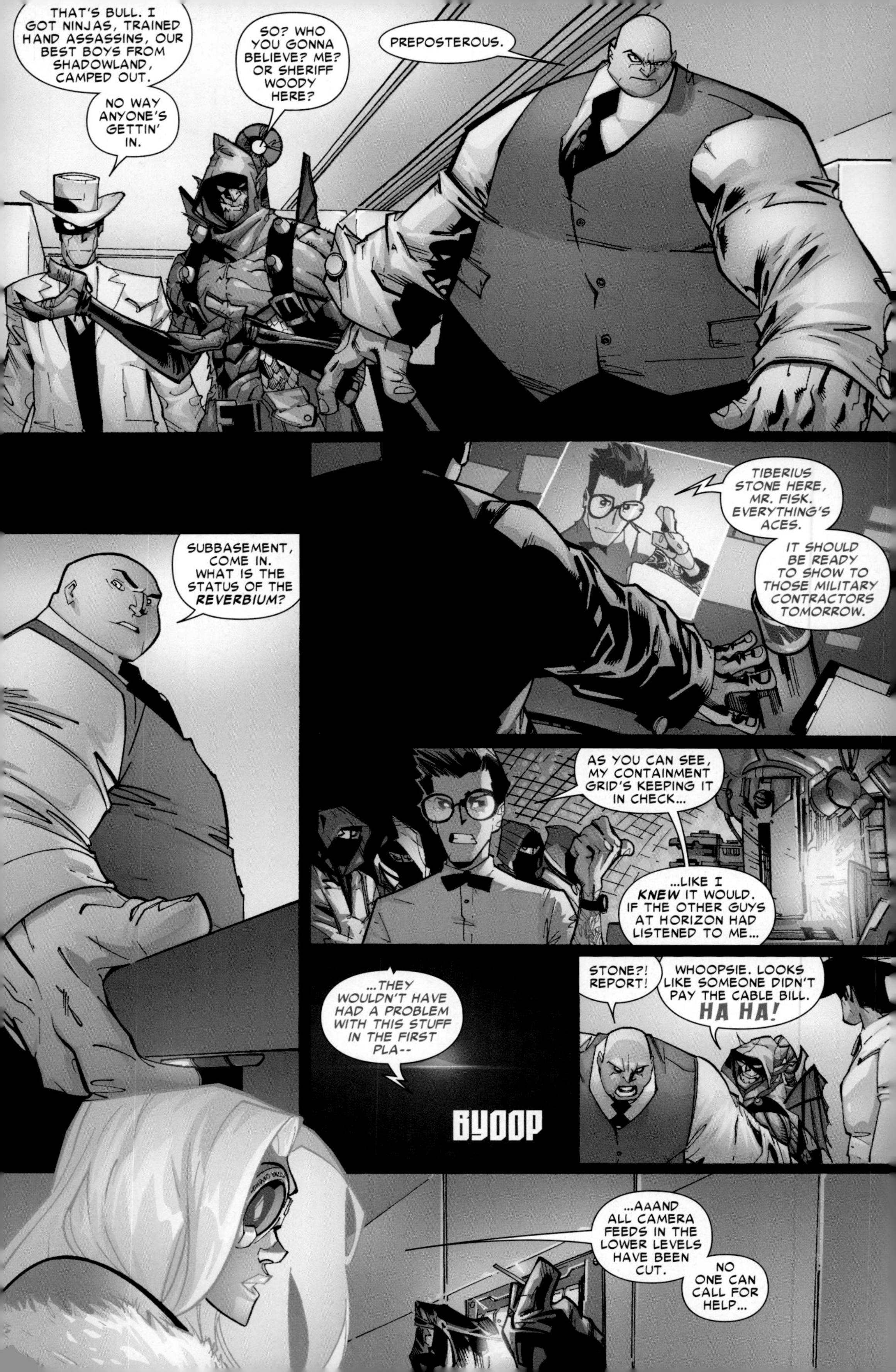

THAT'S BULL. I GOT NINJAS, TRAINED HAND ASSASSINS, OUR BEST BOYS FROM SHADOWLAND, CAMPED OUT.
NO WAY ANYONE'S GETTIN' IN.
SO? WHO YOU GONNA BELIEVE? ME? OR SHERIFF WOODY HERE?
PREPOSTEROUS.
SUBBASEMENT, COME IN. WHAT IS THE STATUS OF THE *REVERBIUM*?
TIBERIUS STONE HERE, MR. FISK. EVERYTHING'S ACES.
IT SHOULD BE READY TO SHOW TO THOSE MILITARY CONTRACTORS TOMORROW.
AS YOU CAN SEE, MY CONTAINMENT GRID'S KEEPING IT IN CHECK...
...LIKE I *KNEW* IT WOULD. IF THE OTHER GUYS AT HORIZON HAD LISTENED TO ME...
...THEY WOULDN'T HAVE HAD A PROBLEM WITH THIS STUFF IN THE FIRST PLA--
BYOOP
STONE?! REPORT!
WHOOPSIE. LOOKS LIKE SOMEONE DIDN'T PAY THE CABLE BILL. HA HA!
...AAAND ALL CAMERA FEEDS IN THE LOWER LEVELS HAVE BEEN CUT.
NO ONE CAN CALL FOR HELP...

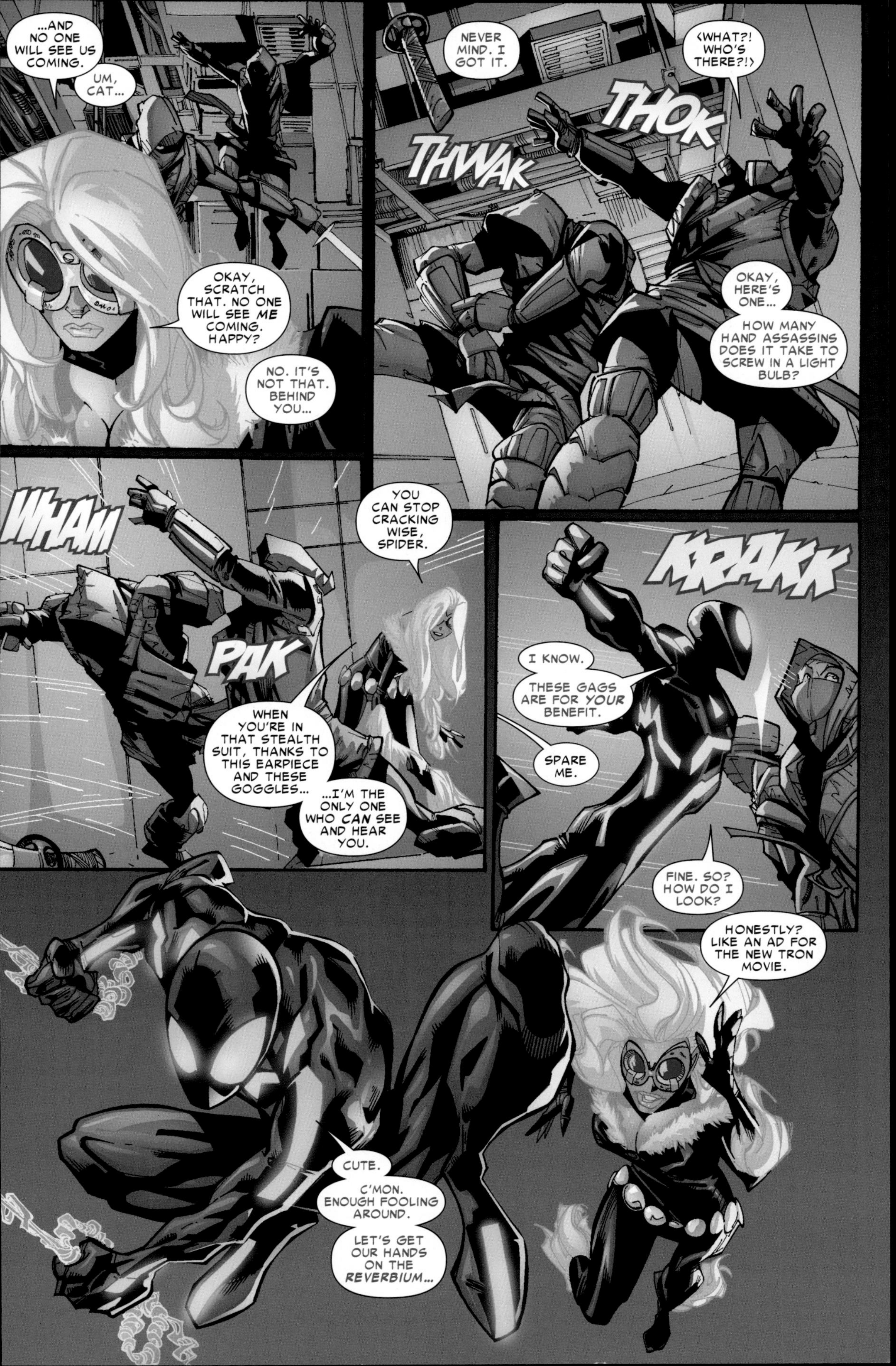
...AND NO ONE WILL SEE US COMING.
UM, CAT...
OKAY, SCRATCH THAT. NO ONE WILL SEE *ME* COMING. HAPPY?
NO. IT'S NOT THAT. BEHIND YOU...
NEVER MIND. I GOT IT.
‹WHAT?! WHO'S THERE?!›
THOK
THWAK
OKAY, HERE'S ONE...
HOW MANY HAND ASSASSINS DOES IT TAKE TO SCREW IN A LIGHT BULB?
WHAM
YOU CAN STOP CRACKING WISE, SPIDER.
PAK
WHEN YOU'RE IN THAT STEALTH SUIT, THANKS TO THIS EARPIECE AND THESE GOGGLES...
...I'M THE ONLY ONE WHO *CAN* SEE AND HEAR YOU.
KRAKK
I KNOW.
THESE GAGS ARE FOR *YOUR* BENEFIT.
SPARE ME.
FINE. SO? HOW DO I LOOK?
HONESTLY? LIKE AN AD FOR THE NEW TRON MOVIE.
CUTE.
C'MON. ENOUGH FOOLING AROUND.
LET'S GET OUR HANDS ON THE *REVERBIUM*...

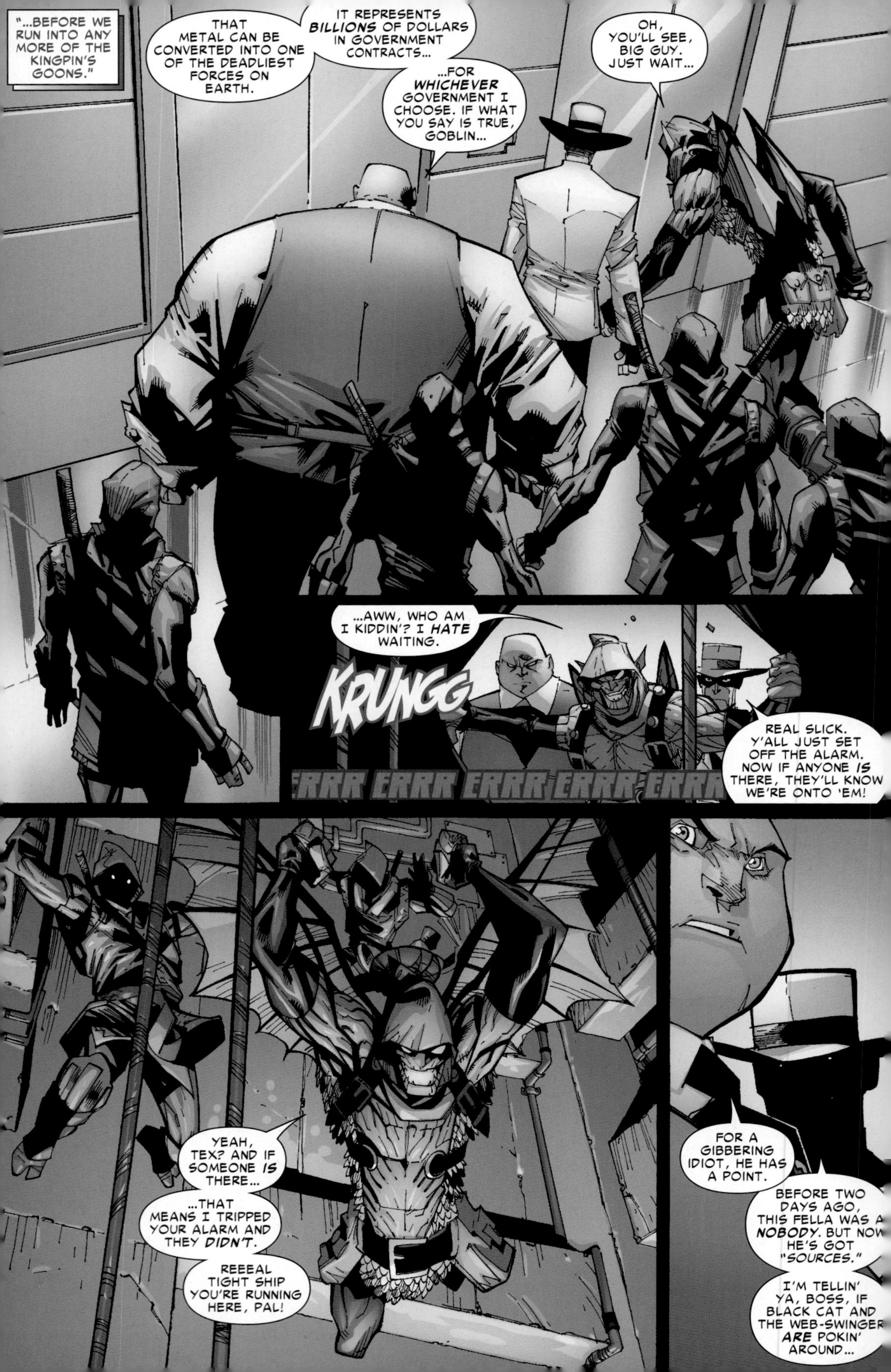
"...BEFORE WE RUN INTO ANY MORE OF THE KINGPIN'S GOONS."
THAT METAL CAN BE CONVERTED INTO ONE OF THE DEADLIEST FORCES ON EARTH.
IT REPRESENTS BILLIONS OF DOLLARS IN GOVERNMENT CONTRACTS...
...FOR WHICHEVER GOVERNMENT I CHOOSE. IF WHAT YOU SAY IS TRUE, GOBLIN...
OH, YOU'LL SEE, BIG GUY. JUST WAIT...
...AWW, WHO AM I KIDDIN'? I HATE WAITING.
KRUNGG
ERRR ERRR ERRR ERRR ERRR
REAL SLICK. Y'ALL JUST SET OFF THE ALARM. NOW IF ANYONE IS THERE, THEY'LL KNOW WE'RE ONTO 'EM!
YEAH, TEX? AND IF SOMEONE IS THERE...
...THAT MEANS I TRIPPED YOUR ALARM AND THEY DIDN'T.
REEEAL TIGHT SHIP YOU'RE RUNNING HERE, PAL!
FOR A GIBBERING IDIOT, HE HAS A POINT.
BEFORE TWO DAYS AGO, THIS FELLA WAS A NOBODY. BUT NOW HE'S GOT "SOURCES."
I'M TELLIN' YA, BOSS, IF BLACK CAT AND THE WEB-SWINGER ARE POKIN' AROUND...

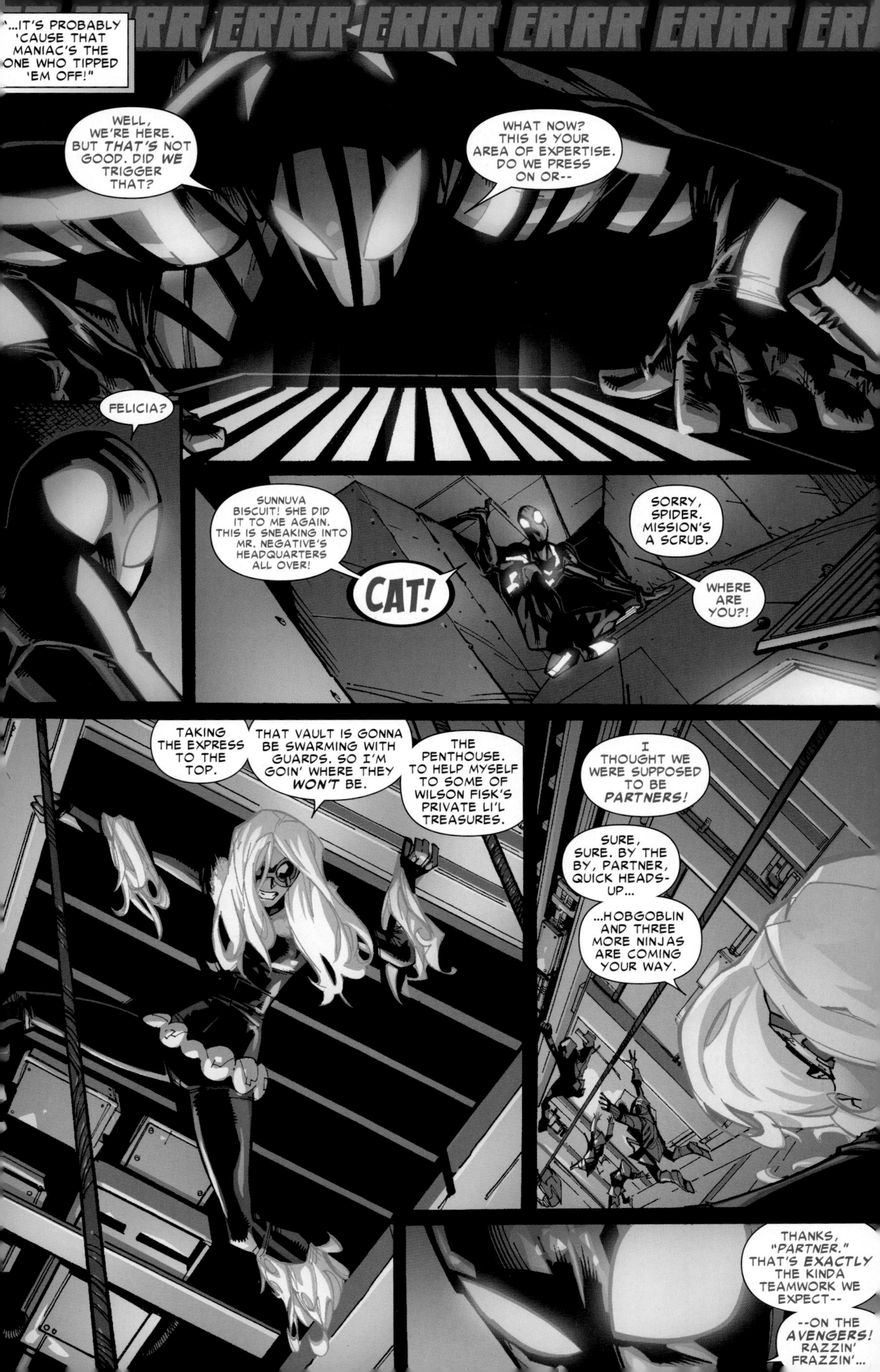
ERRR ERRR ERRR ERRR ERRR ER
"...IT'S PROBABLY 'CAUSE THAT MANIAC'S THE ONE WHO TIPPED 'EM OFF!"
WELL, WE'RE HERE. BUT THAT'S NOT GOOD. DID WE TRIGGER THAT?
WHAT NOW? THIS IS YOUR AREA OF EXPERTISE. DO WE PRESS ON OR--
FELICIA?
SUNNUVA BISCUIT! SHE DID IT TO ME AGAIN. THIS IS SNEAKING INTO MR. NEGATIVE'S HEADQUARTERS ALL OVER!
CAT!
SORRY, SPIDER. MISSION'S A SCRUB.
WHERE ARE YOU?!
TAKING THE EXPRESS TO THE TOP.
THAT VAULT IS GONNA BE SWARMING WITH GUARDS. SO I'M GOIN' WHERE THEY WON'T BE.
THE PENTHOUSE. TO HELP MYSELF TO SOME OF WILSON FISK'S PRIVATE LI'L TREASURES.
I THOUGHT WE WERE SUPPOSED TO BE PARTNERS!
SURE, SURE. BY THE BY, PARTNER, QUICK HEADS-UP...
...HOBGOBLIN AND THREE MORE NINJAS ARE COMING YOUR WAY.
THANKS, "PARTNER." THAT'S EXACTLY THE KINDA TEAMWORK WE EXPECT--
--ON THE AVENGERS! RAZZIN' FRAZZIN'...

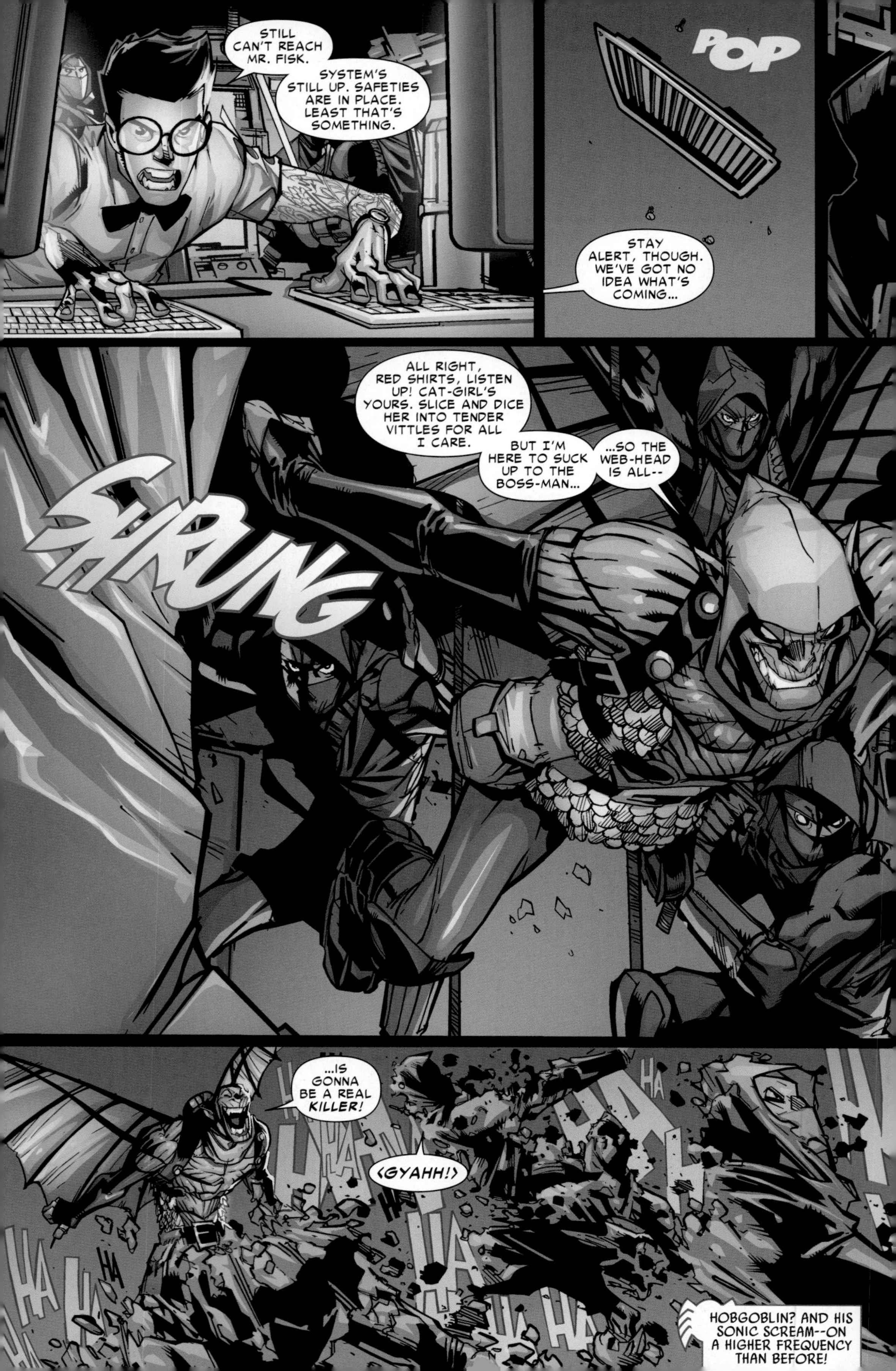
STILL CAN'T REACH MR. FISK.
SYSTEM'S STILL UP. SAFETIES ARE IN PLACE. LEAST THAT'S SOMETHING.
POP
STAY ALERT, THOUGH. WE'VE GOT NO IDEA WHAT'S COMING...
ALL RIGHT, RED SHIRTS, LISTEN UP! CAT-GIRL'S YOURS. SLICE AND DICE HER INTO TENDER VITTLES FOR ALL I CARE.
BUT I'M HERE TO SUCK UP TO THE BOSS-MAN...
...SO THE WEB-HEAD IS ALL--
SHRUNG
...IS GONNA BE A REAL *KILLER!*
<GYAHH!>
HA HA HA HA HA
HOBGOBLIN? AND HIS SONIC SCREAM--ON A HIGHER FREQUENCY THAN BEFORE!

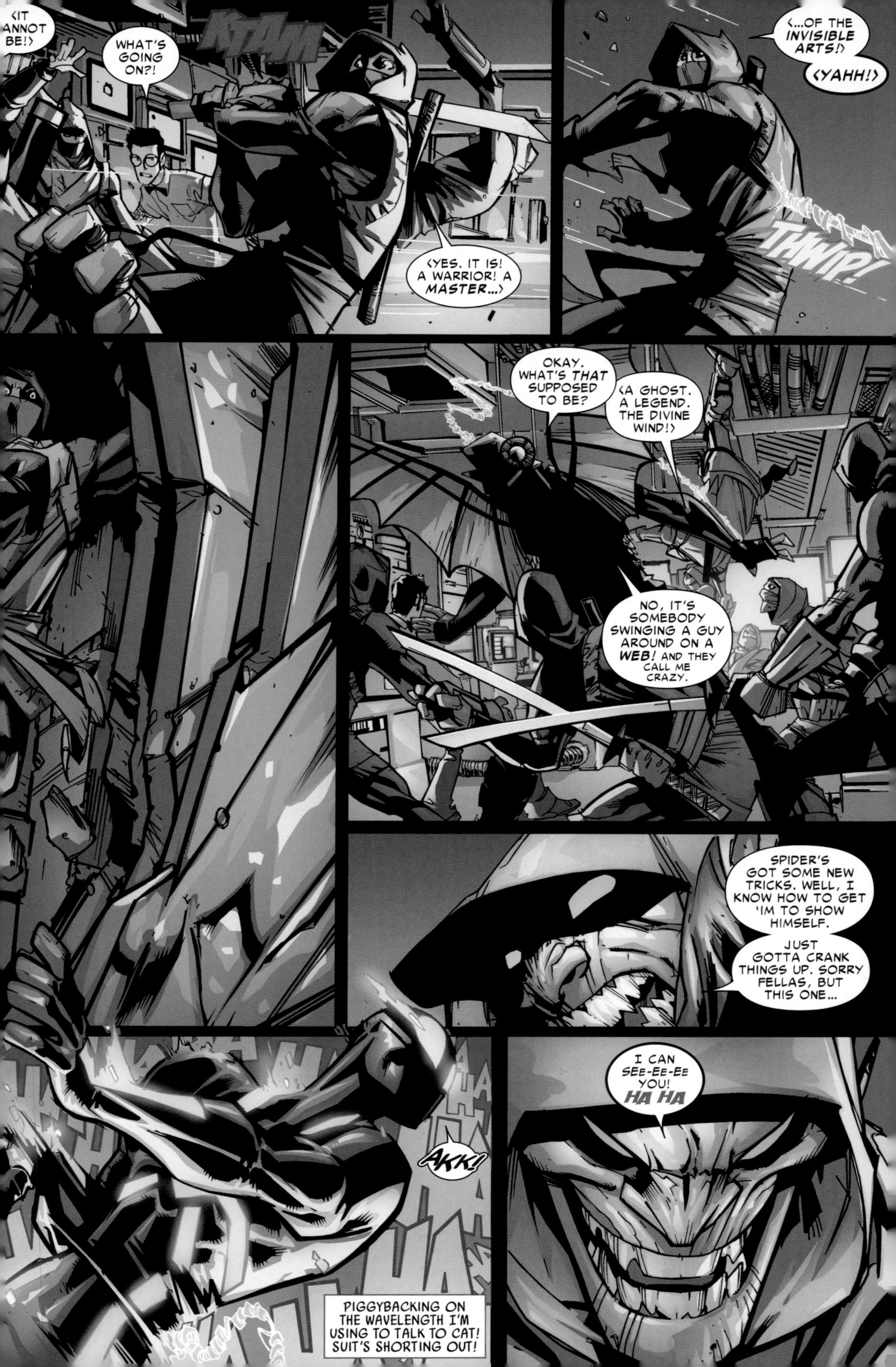

<IT CANNOT BE!>
WHAT'S GOING ON?!
KTAM
<YES. IT IS! A WARRIOR! A MASTER...>
<...OF THE INVISIBLE ARTS!>
<YAHH!>
THWIP!
OKAY. WHAT'S THAT SUPPOSED TO BE?
<A GHOST. A LEGEND. THE DIVINE WIND!>
NO, IT'S SOMEBODY SWINGING A GUY AROUND ON A WEB! AND THEY CALL ME CRAZY.
SPIDER'S GOT SOME NEW TRICKS. WELL, I KNOW HOW TO GET 'IM TO SHOW HIMSELF.
JUST GOTTA CRANK THINGS UP. SORRY FELLAS, BUT THIS ONE...
AKK!
PIGGYBACKING ON THE WAVELENGTH I'M USING TO TALK TO CAT! SUIT'S SHORTING OUT!
I CAN SEE-EE-EE YOU! HA HA

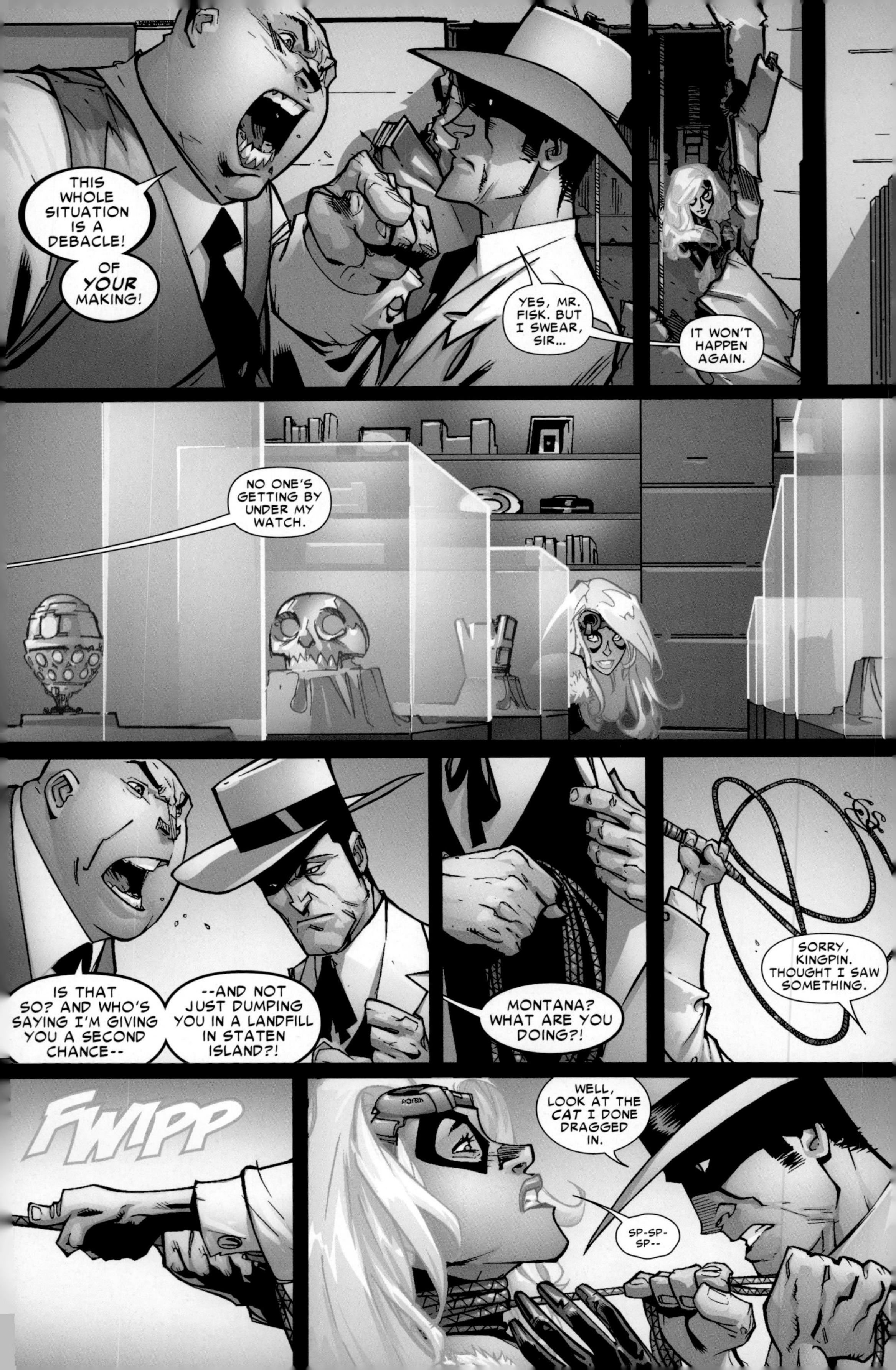
THIS WHOLE SITUATION IS A DEBACLE!
OF YOUR MAKING!
YES, MR. FISK. BUT I SWEAR, SIR...
IT WON'T HAPPEN AGAIN.
NO ONE'S GETTING BY UNDER MY WATCH.
IS THAT SO? AND WHO'S SAYING I'M GIVING YOU A SECOND CHANCE--
--AND NOT JUST DUMPING YOU IN A LANDFILL IN STATEN ISLAND?!
MONTANA? WHAT ARE YOU DOING?!
SORRY, KINGPIN. THOUGHT I SAW SOMETHING.
FWIPP
WELL, LOOK AT THE CAT I DONE DRAGGED IN.
SP-SP-SP--

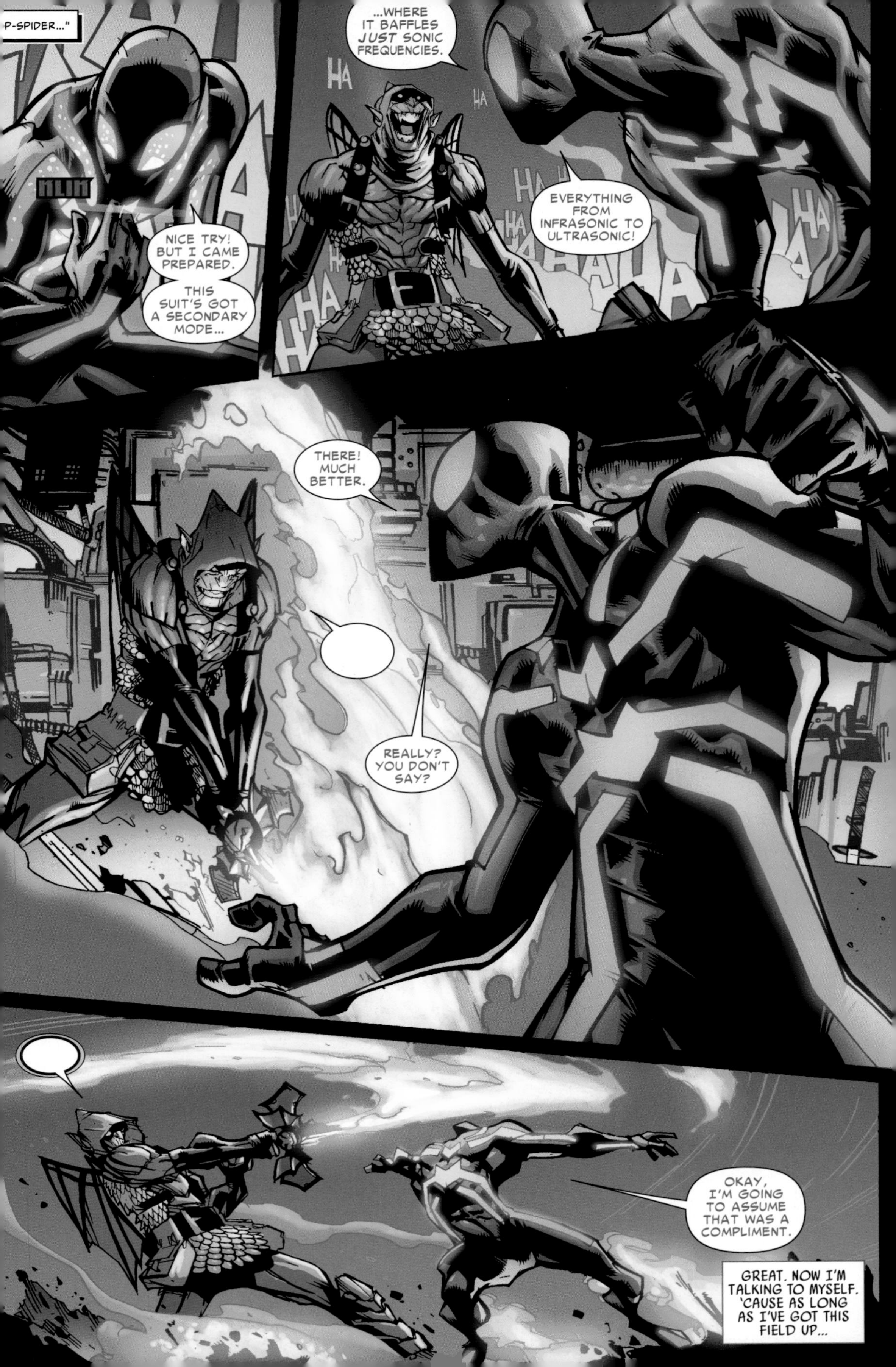

P-SPIDER..."
...WHERE IT BAFFLES JUST SONIC FREQUENCIES.
HA
HA
NICE TRY! BUT I CAME PREPARED.
THIS SUIT'S GOT A SECONDARY MODE...
EVERYTHING FROM INFRASONIC TO ULTRASONIC!
HA HA HA HA HA HA
THERE! MUCH BETTER.
REALLY? YOU DON'T SAY?
OKAY, I'M GOING TO ASSUME THAT WAS A COMPLIMENT.
GREAT. NOW I'M TALKING TO MYSELF. 'CAUSE AS LONG AS I'VE GOT THIS FIELD UP...

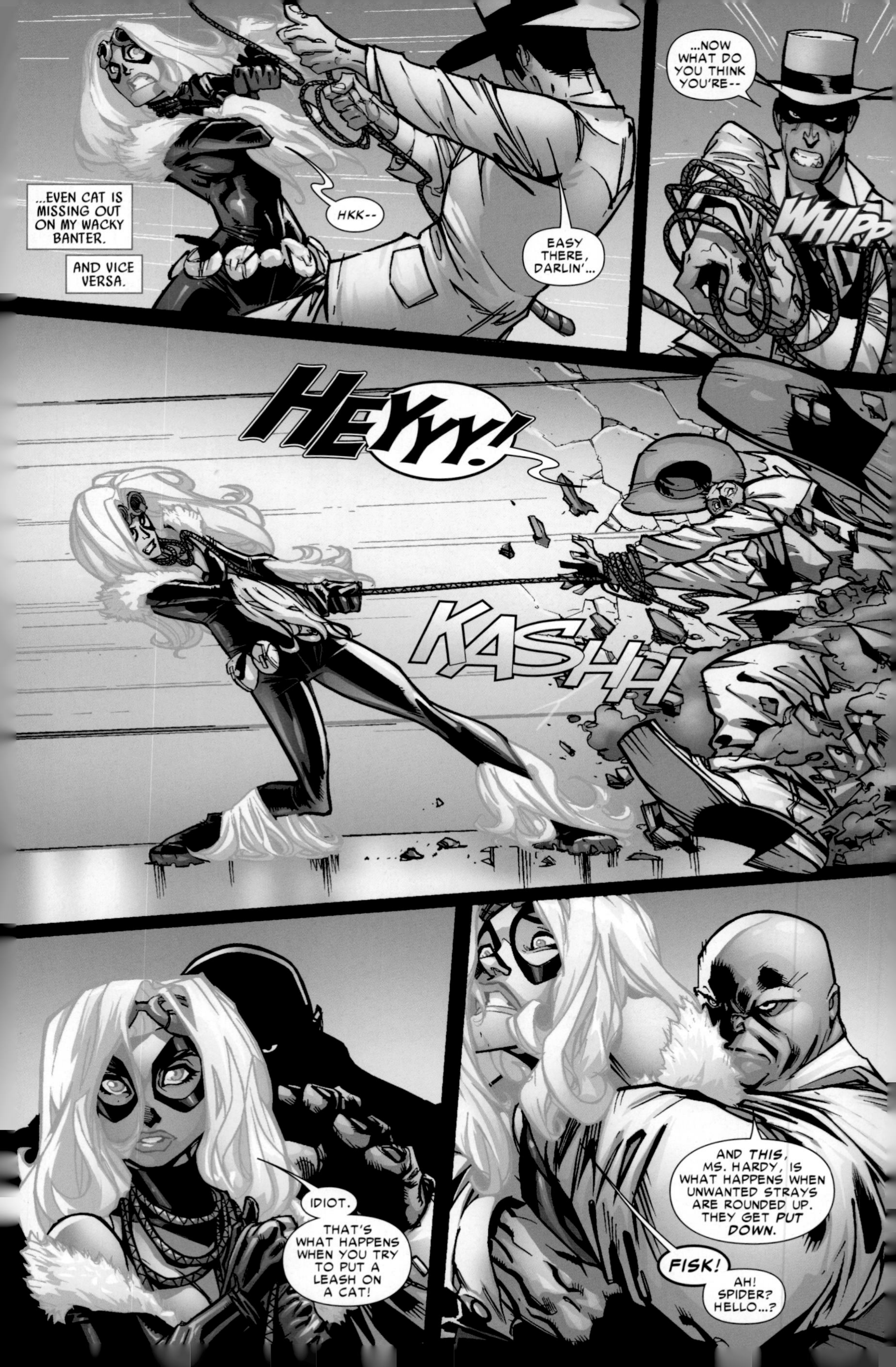
...EVEN CAT IS MISSING OUT ON MY WACKY BANTER.
AND VICE VERSA.
HKK--
EASY THERE, DARLIN'...
...NOW WHAT DO YOU THINK YOU'RE--
WHIPP
HEYYY!
KASHH
IDIOT.
THAT'S WHAT HAPPENS WHEN YOU TRY TO PUT A LEASH ON A CAT!
AND THIS, MS. HARDY, IS WHAT HAPPENS WHEN UNWANTED STRAYS ARE ROUNDED UP. THEY GET PUT DOWN.
FISK!
AH! SPIDER? HELLO...?

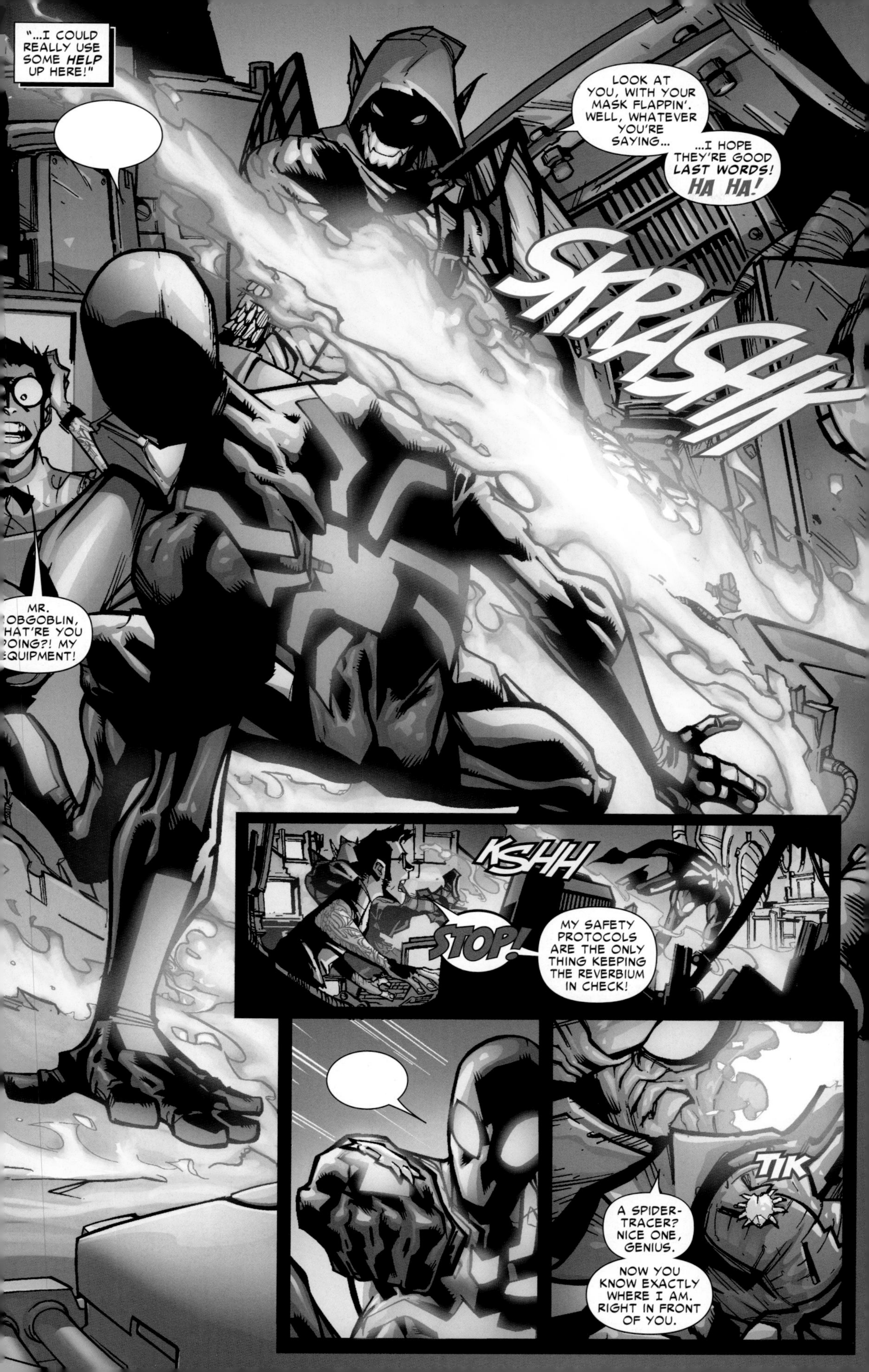

"...I COULD REALLY USE SOME HELP UP HERE!"
LOOK AT YOU, WITH YOUR MASK FLAPPIN'. WELL, WHATEVER YOU'RE SAYING...
...I HOPE THEY'RE GOOD LAST WORDS! HA HA!
SKRASHK
MR. HOBGOBLIN, WHAT'RE YOU DOING?! MY EQUIPMENT!
KSHH
STOP!
MY SAFETY PROTOCOLS ARE THE ONLY THING KEEPING THE REVERBIUM IN CHECK!
TIK
A SPIDER-TRACER? NICE ONE, GENIUS.
NOW YOU KNOW EXACTLY WHERE I AM. RIGHT IN FRONT OF YOU.

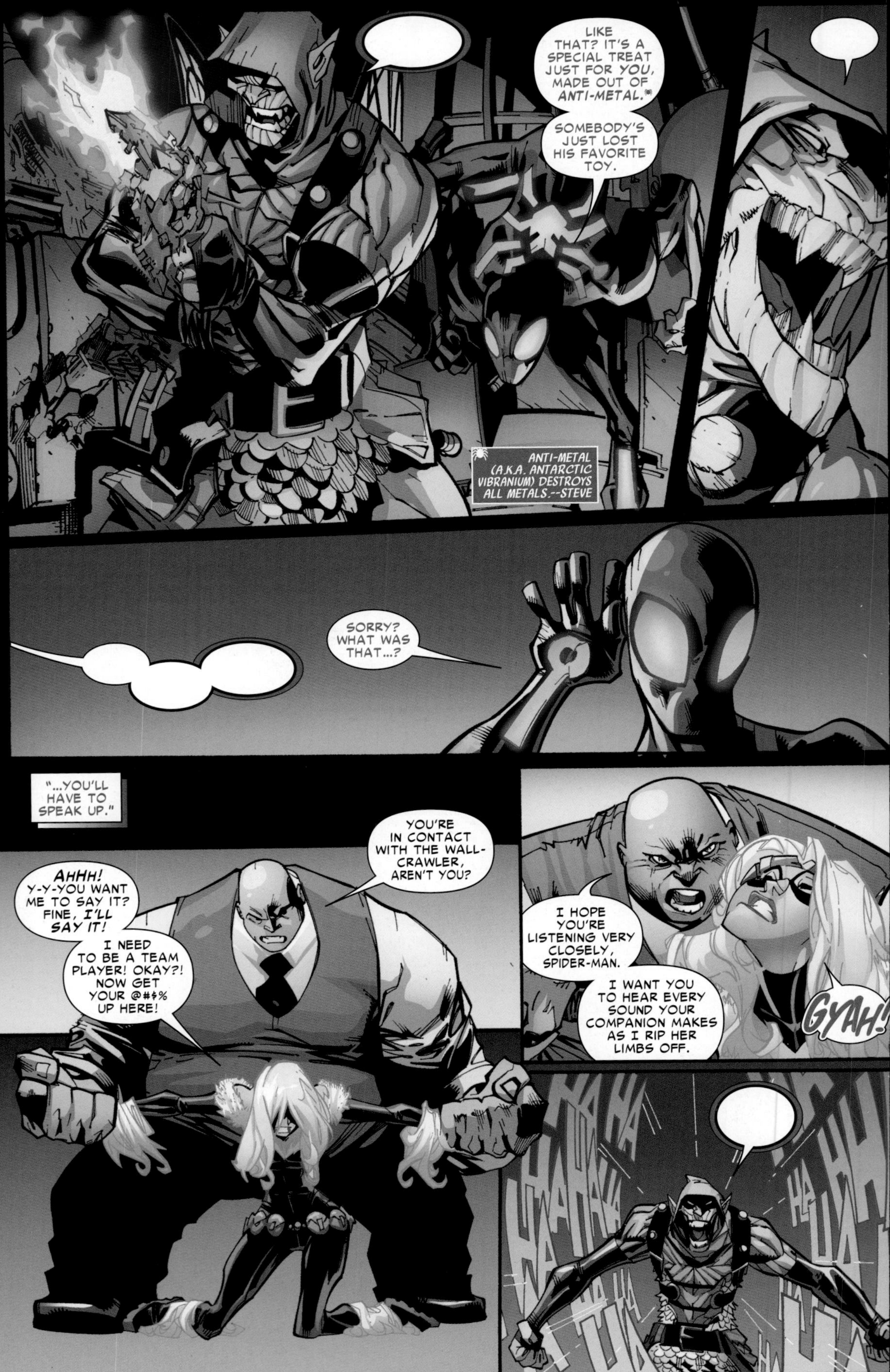
LIKE THAT? IT'S A SPECIAL TREAT JUST FOR YOU, MADE OUT OF ANTI-METAL.
SOMEBODY'S JUST LOST HIS FAVORITE TOY.
ANTI-METAL (A.K.A. ANTARCTIC VIBRANIUM) DESTROYS ALL METALS.--STEVE
SORRY? WHAT WAS THAT...?
"...YOU'LL HAVE TO SPEAK UP."
YOU'RE IN CONTACT WITH THE WALL-CRAWLER, AREN'T YOU?
AHHH! Y-Y-YOU WANT ME TO SAY IT? FINE, I'LL SAY IT!
I NEED TO BE A TEAM PLAYER! OKAY?! NOW GET YOUR @#$% UP HERE!
I HOPE YOU'RE LISTENING VERY CLOSELY, SPIDER-MAN.
I WANT YOU TO HEAR EVERY SOUND YOUR COMPANION MAKES AS I RIP HER LIMBS OFF.
GYAH!

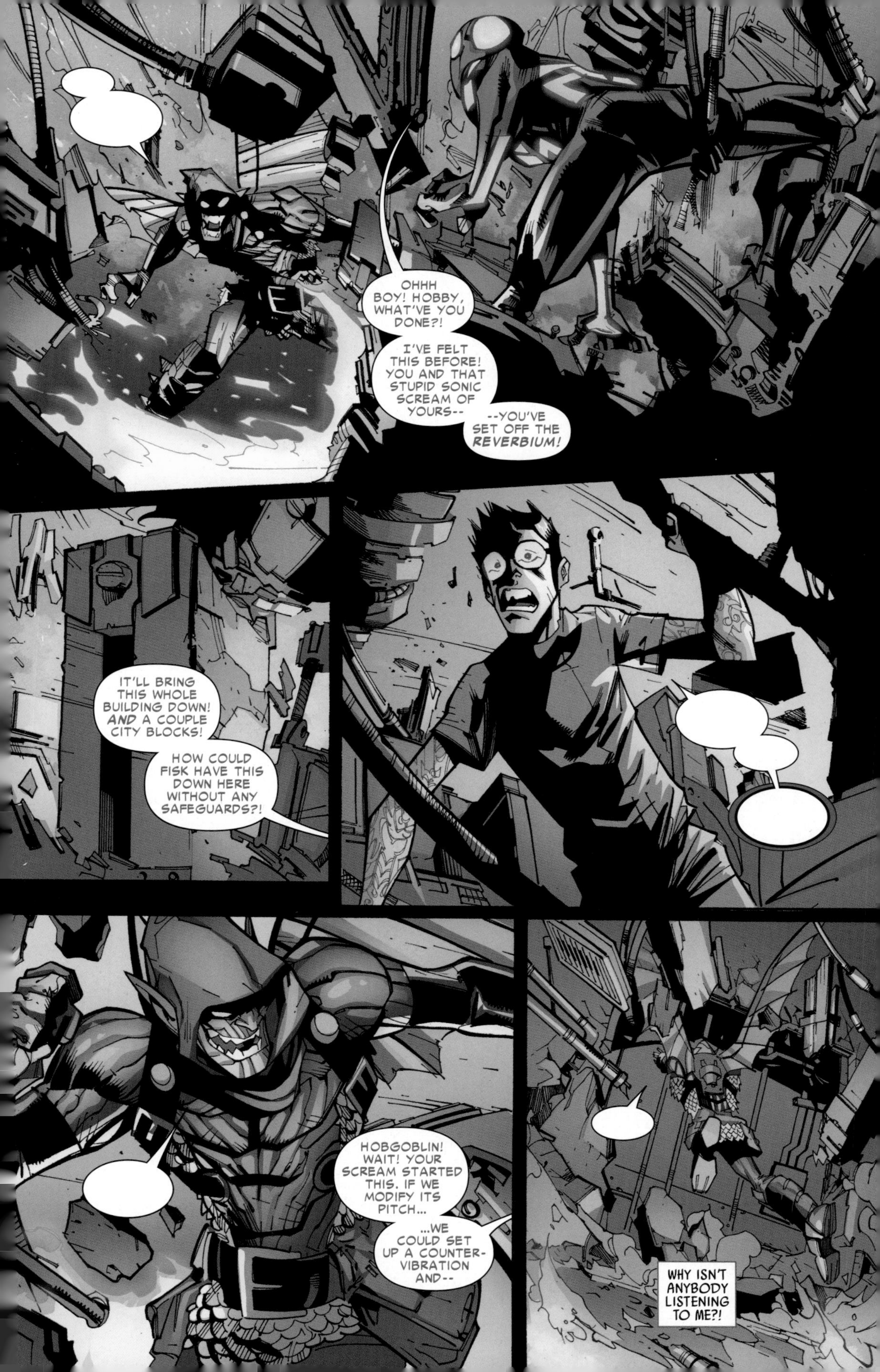
OHHH BOY! HOBBY, WHAT'VE YOU DONE?!
I'VE FELT THIS BEFORE! YOU AND THAT STUPID SONIC SCREAM OF YOURS--
--YOU'VE SET OFF THE REVERBIUM!
IT'LL BRING THIS WHOLE BUILDING DOWN! AND A COUPLE CITY BLOCKS!
HOW COULD FISK HAVE THIS DOWN HERE WITHOUT ANY SAFEGUARDS?!
HOBGOBLIN! WAIT! YOUR SCREAM STARTED THIS. IF WE MODIFY ITS PITCH...
...WE COULD SET UP A COUNTER-VIBRATION AND--
WHY ISN'T ANYBODY LISTENING TO ME?!

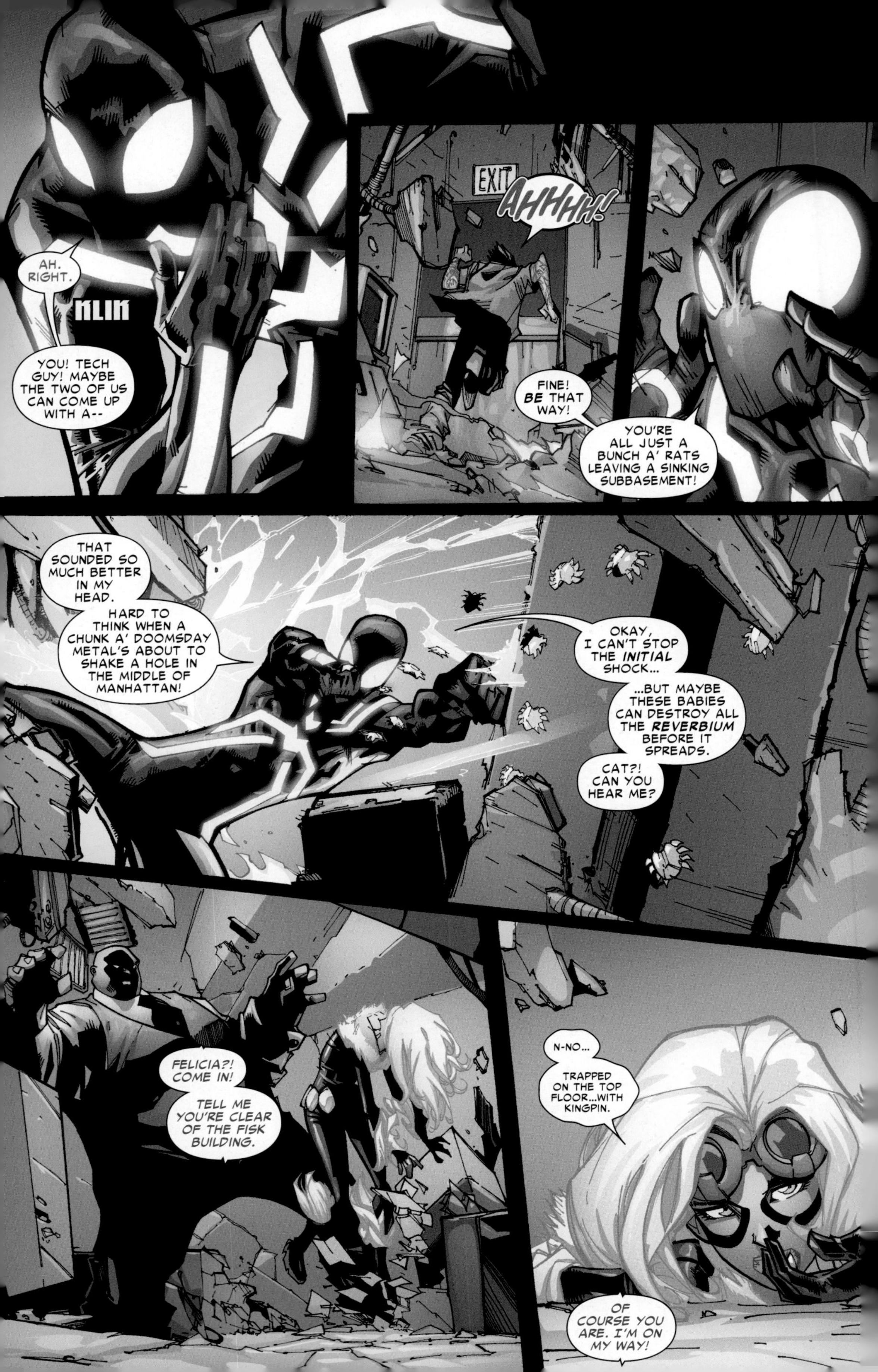

AH. RIGHT.
KLIK
YOU! TECH GUY! MAYBE THE TWO OF US CAN COME UP WITH A--
EXIT
AHHHH!
FINE! *BE* THAT WAY!
YOU'RE ALL JUST A BUNCH A' RATS LEAVING A SINKING SUBBASEMENT!
THAT SOUNDED SO MUCH BETTER IN MY HEAD.
HARD TO THINK WHEN A CHUNK A' DOOMSDAY METAL'S ABOUT TO SHAKE A HOLE IN THE MIDDLE OF MANHATTAN!
OKAY, I CAN'T STOP THE *INITIAL* SHOCK...
...BUT MAYBE THESE BABIES CAN DESTROY ALL THE *REVERBIUM* BEFORE IT SPREADS.
CAT?! CAN YOU HEAR ME?
FELICIA?! COME IN!
TELL ME YOU'RE CLEAR OF THE FISK BUILDING.
N-NO...
TRAPPED ON THE TOP FLOOR...WITH KINGPIN.
OF COURSE YOU ARE. I'M ON MY WAY!

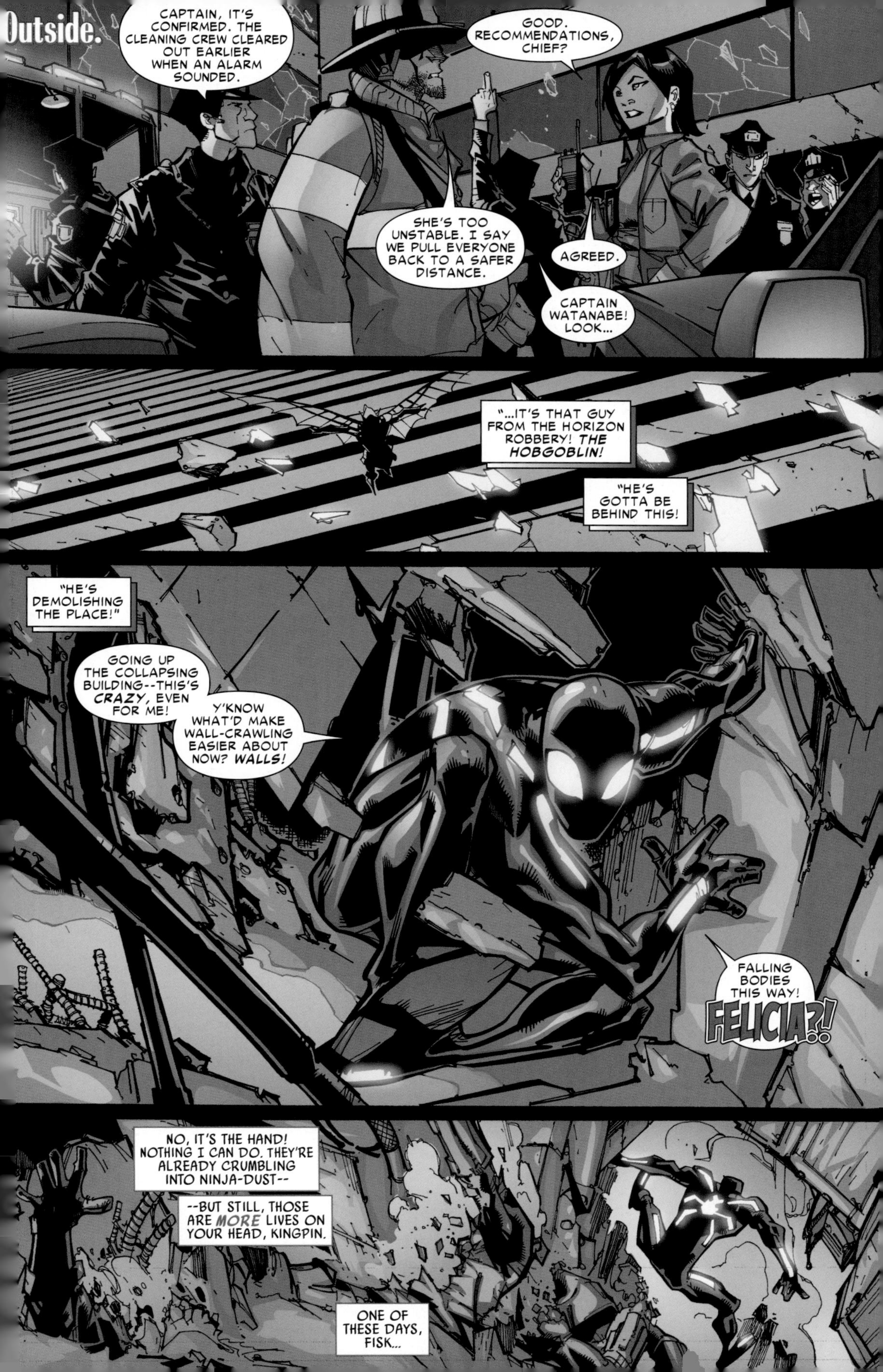
Outside.
CAPTAIN, IT'S CONFIRMED. THE CLEANING CREW CLEARED OUT EARLIER WHEN AN ALARM SOUNDED.
GOOD. RECOMMENDATIONS, CHIEF?
SHE'S TOO UNSTABLE. I SAY WE PULL EVERYONE BACK TO A SAFER DISTANCE.
AGREED.
CAPTAIN WATANABE! LOOK...
"...IT'S THAT GUY FROM THE HORIZON ROBBERY! THE HOBGOBLIN!
"HE'S GOTTA BE BEHIND THIS!
"HE'S DEMOLISHING THE PLACE!"
GOING UP THE COLLAPSING BUILDING--THIS'S CRAZY, EVEN FOR ME!
Y'KNOW WHAT'D MAKE WALL-CRAWLING EASIER ABOUT NOW? WALLS!
FALLING BODIES THIS WAY!
FELICIA?!
NO, IT'S THE HAND! NOTHING I CAN DO. THEY'RE ALREADY CRUMBLING INTO NINJA-DUST--
--BUT STILL, THOSE ARE MORE LIVES ON YOUR HEAD, KINGPIN.
ONE OF THESE DAYS, FISK...

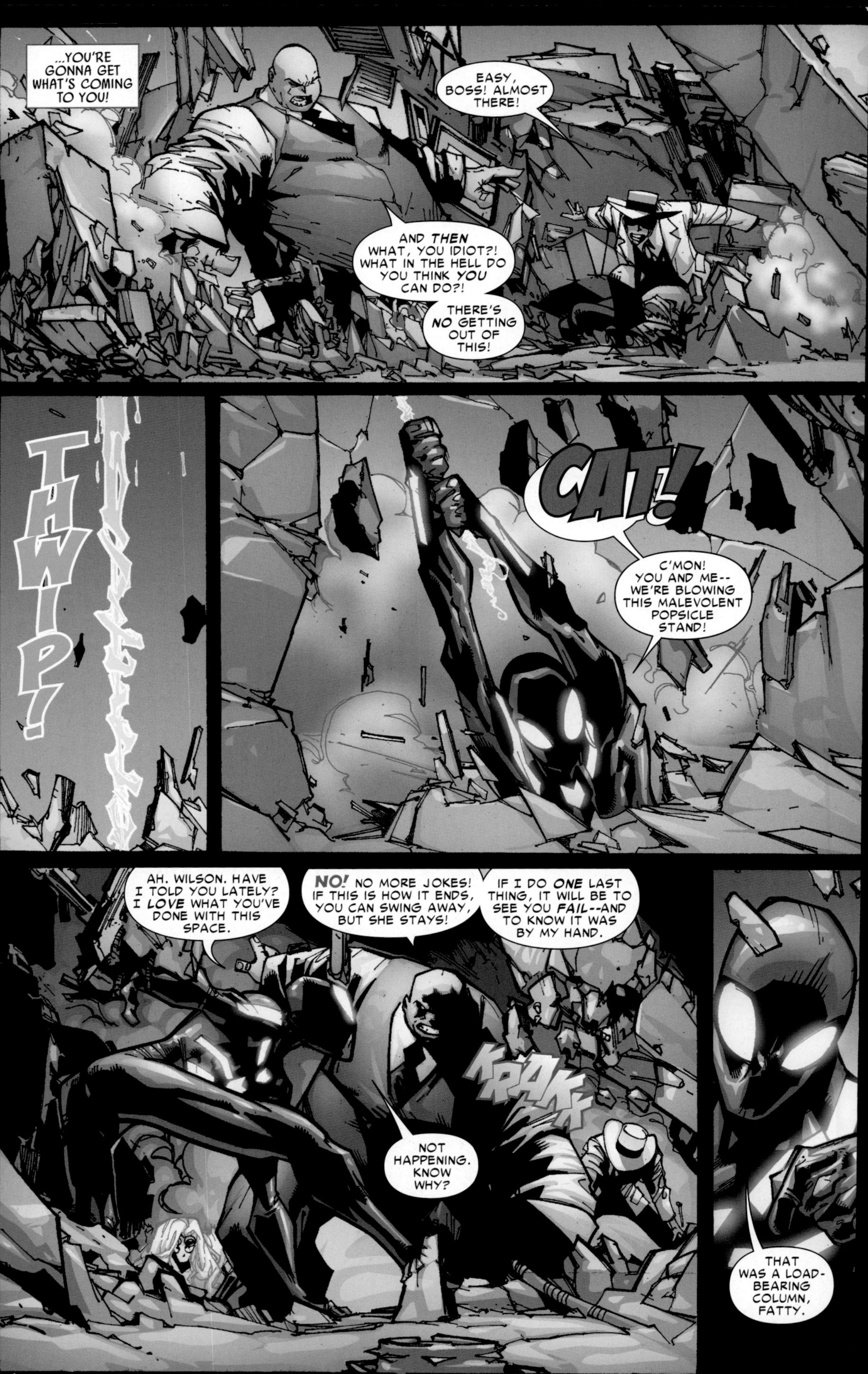
...YOU'RE GONNA GET WHAT'S COMING TO YOU!
EASY, BOSS! ALMOST THERE!
AND THEN WHAT, YOU IDIOT?! WHAT IN THE HELL DO YOU THINK YOU CAN DO?!
THERE'S NO GETTING OUT OF THIS!
THWIP!
CAT!
C'MON! YOU AND ME-- WE'RE BLOWING THIS MALEVOLENT POPSICLE STAND!
AH. WILSON. HAVE I TOLD YOU LATELY? I LOVE WHAT YOU'VE DONE WITH THIS SPACE.
NO! NO MORE JOKES! IF THIS IS HOW IT ENDS, YOU CAN SWING AWAY, BUT SHE STAYS!
IF I DO ONE LAST THING, IT WILL BE TO SEE YOU FAIL--AND TO KNOW IT WAS BY MY HAND.
KRAKK
NOT HAPPENING. KNOW WHY?
THAT WAS A LOAD-BEARING COLUMN, FATTY.

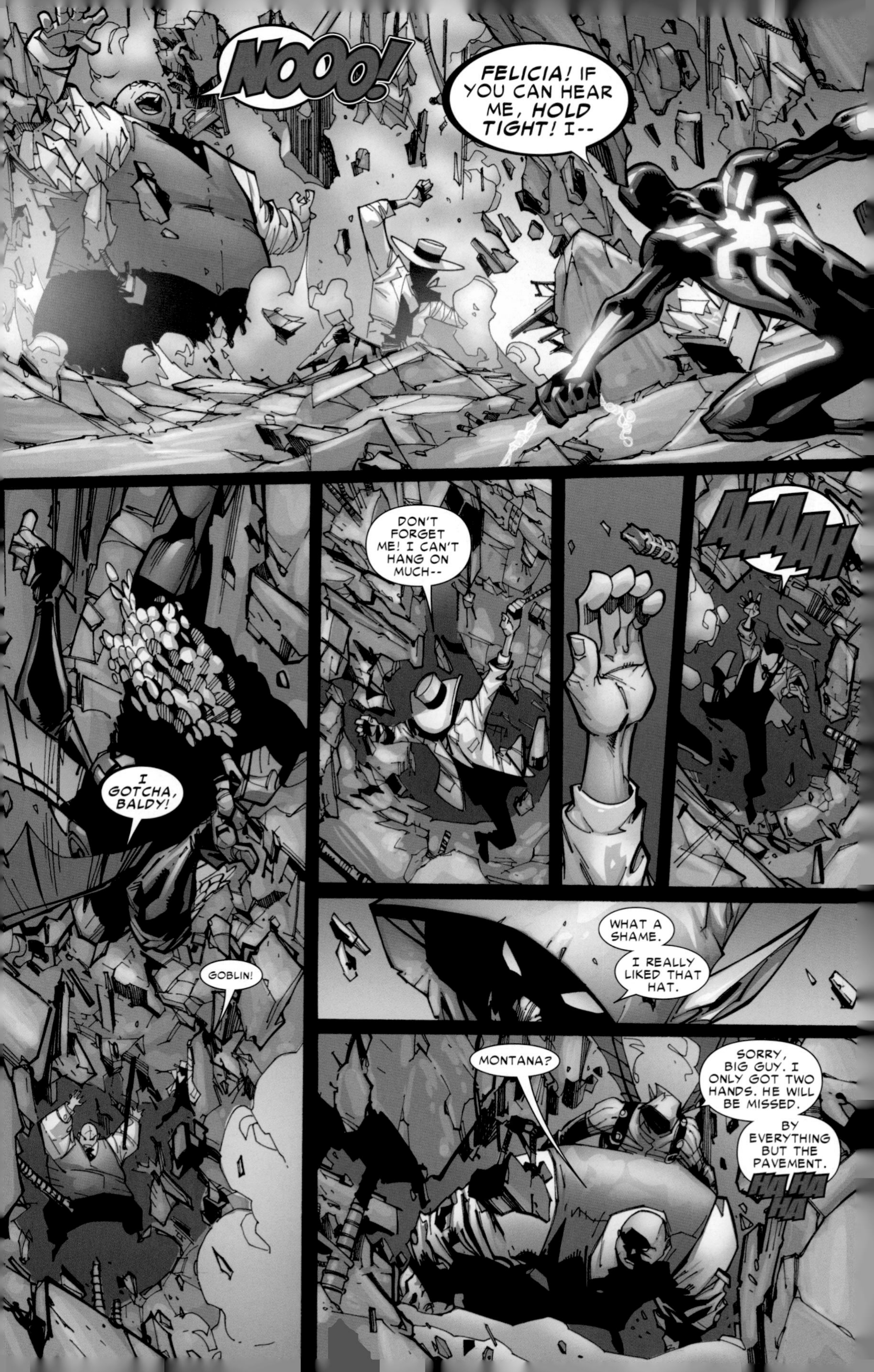
NOOO!
FELICIA! IF YOU CAN HEAR ME, HOLD TIGHT! I--
I GOTCHA, BALDY!
GOBLIN!
DON'T FORGET ME! I CAN'T HANG ON MUCH--
AAAAAH
WHAT A SHAME.
I REALLY LIKED THAT HAT.
MONTANA?
SORRY, BIG GUY. I ONLY GOT TWO HANDS. HE WILL BE MISSED.
BY EVERYTHING BUT THE PAVEMENT.
HA HA HA

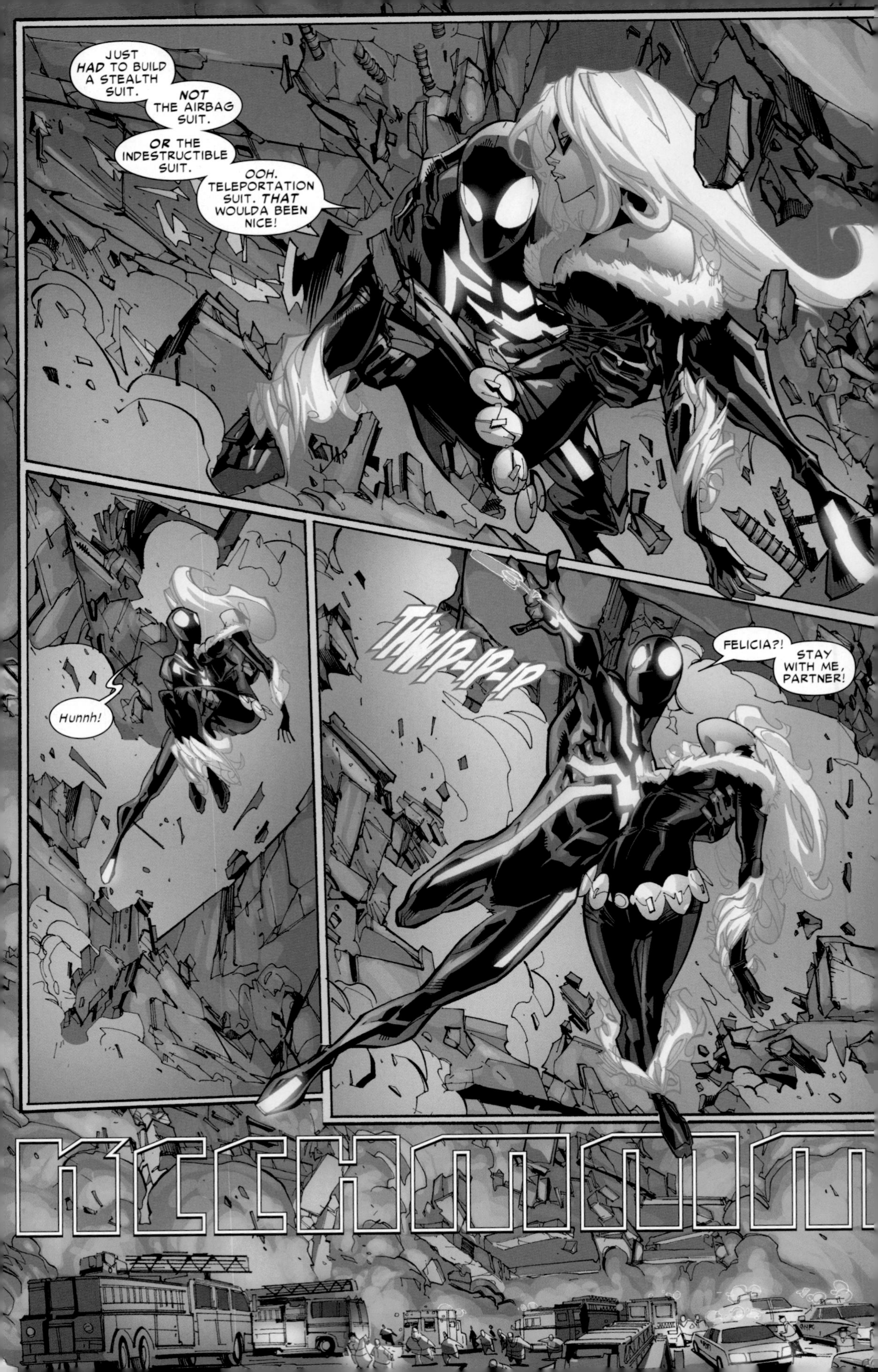

JUST HAD TO BUILD A STEALTH SUIT.
NOT THE AIRBAG SUIT.
OR THE INDESTRUCTIBLE SUIT.
OOH. TELEPORTATION SUIT. THAT WOULDA BEEN NICE!
Hunnh!
THWIP-IP-IP
FELICIA?!
STAY WITH ME, PARTNER!
KRRHOOOOM

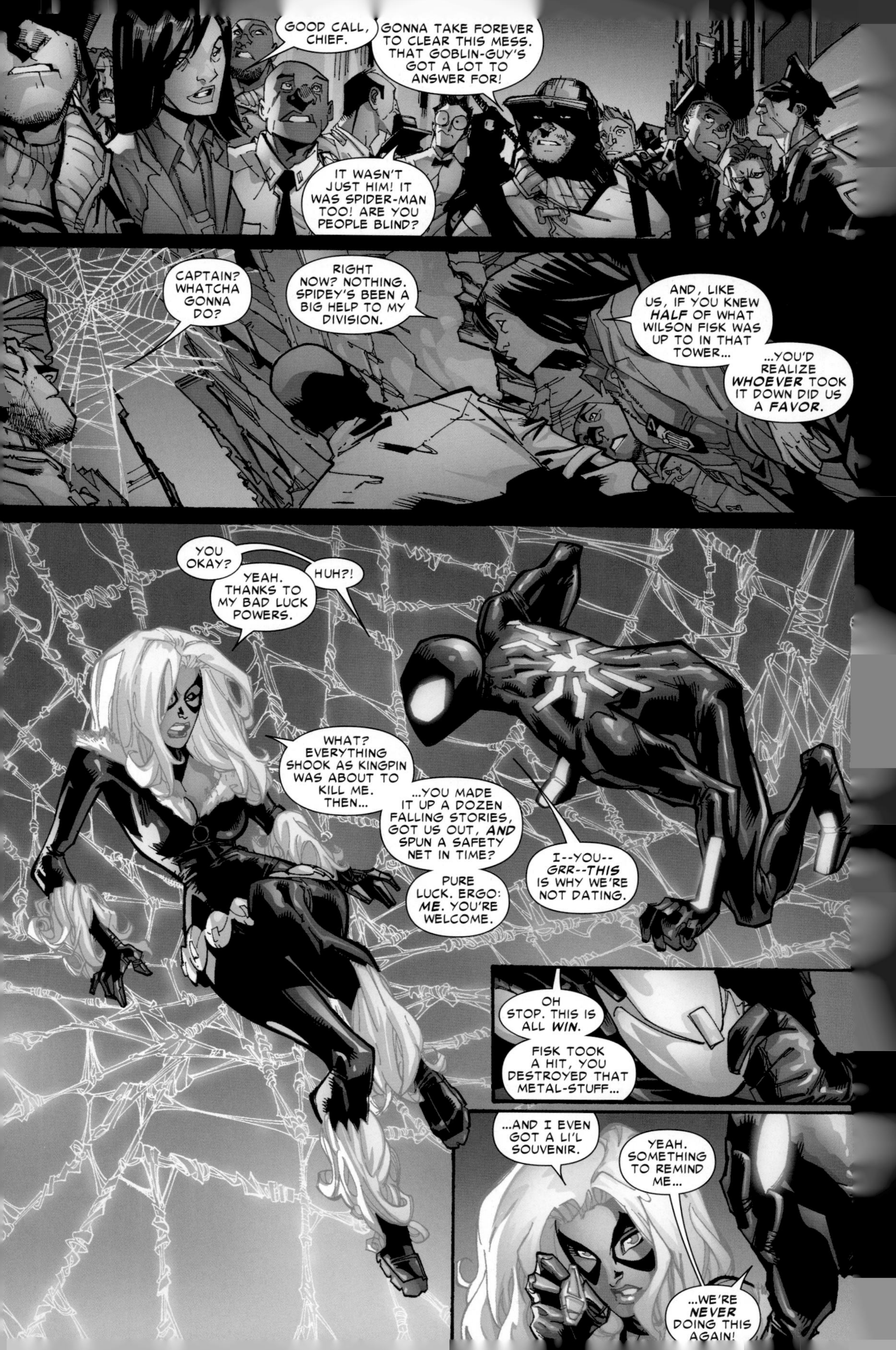
GOOD CALL, CHIEF.
GONNA TAKE FOREVER TO CLEAR THIS MESS. THAT GOBLIN-GUY'S GOT A LOT TO ANSWER FOR!
IT WASN'T JUST HIM! IT WAS SPIDER-MAN TOO! ARE YOU PEOPLE BLIND?
CAPTAIN? WHATCHA GONNA DO?
RIGHT NOW? NOTHING. SPIDEY'S BEEN A BIG HELP TO MY DIVISION.
AND, LIKE US, IF YOU KNEW HALF OF WHAT WILSON FISK WAS UP TO IN THAT TOWER...
...YOU'D REALIZE WHOEVER TOOK IT DOWN DID US A FAVOR.
YOU OKAY?
HUH?!
YEAH. THANKS TO MY BAD LUCK POWERS.
WHAT? EVERYTHING SHOOK AS KINGPIN WAS ABOUT TO KILL ME. THEN...
...YOU MADE IT UP A DOZEN FALLING STORIES, GOT US OUT, AND SPUN A SAFETY NET IN TIME?
PURE LUCK. ERGO: ME. YOU'RE WELCOME.
I--YOU-- GRR--THIS IS WHY WE'RE NOT DATING.
OH STOP. THIS IS ALL WIN.
FISK TOOK A HIT, YOU DESTROYED THAT METAL-STUFF...
...AND I EVEN GOT A LI'L SOUVENIR.
YEAH. SOMETHING TO REMIND ME...
...WE'RE NEVER DOING THIS AGAIN!

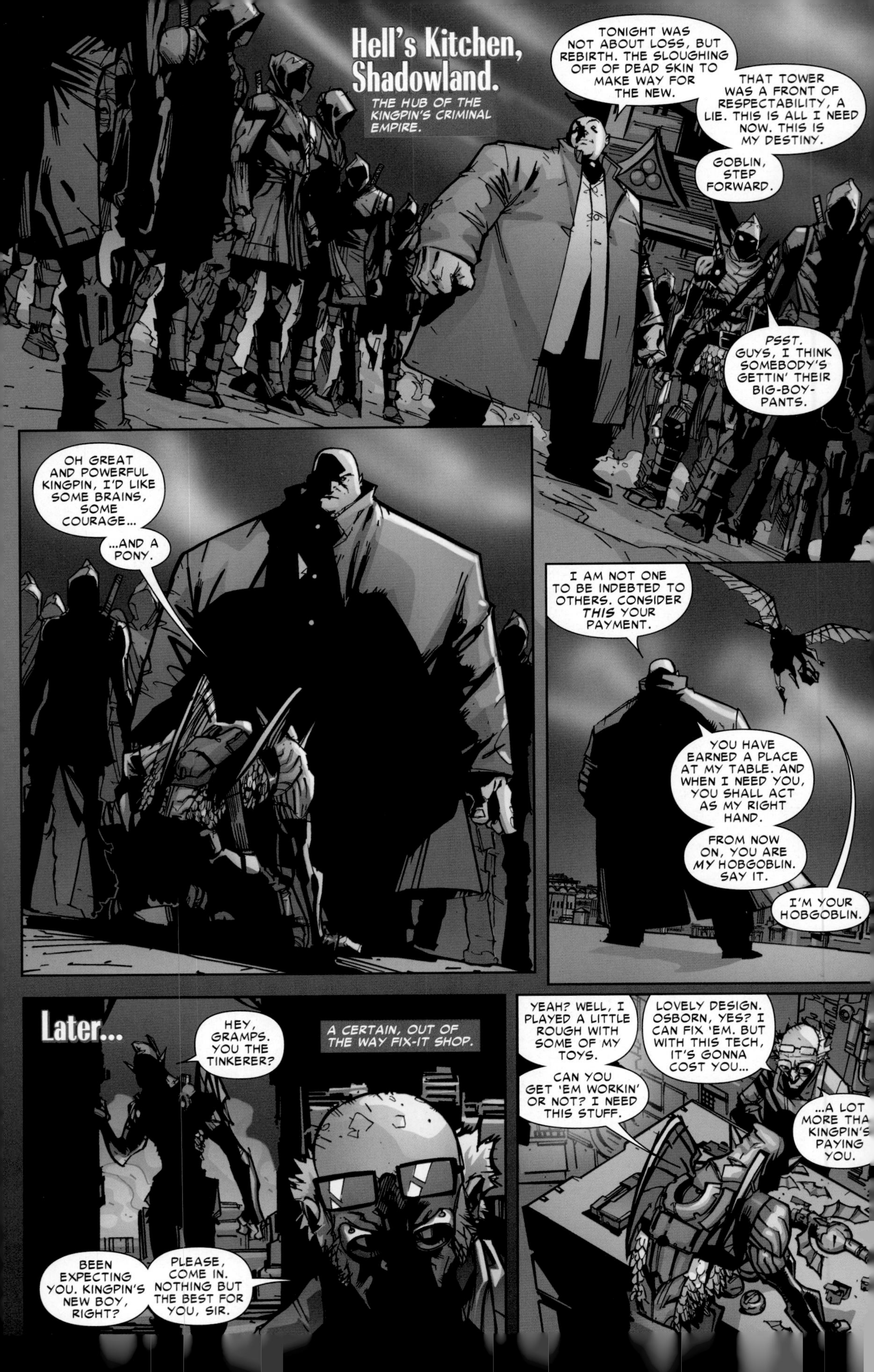
Hell's Kitchen, Shadowland.
THE HUB OF THE KINGPIN'S CRIMINAL EMPIRE.
TONIGHT WAS NOT ABOUT LOSS, BUT REBIRTH. THE SLOUGHING OFF OF DEAD SKIN TO MAKE WAY FOR THE NEW.
THAT TOWER WAS A FRONT OF RESPECTABILITY, A LIE. THIS IS ALL I NEED NOW. THIS IS MY DESTINY.
GOBLIN, STEP FORWARD.
PSST. GUYS, I THINK SOMEBODY'S GETTIN' THEIR BIG-BOY-PANTS.
OH GREAT AND POWERFUL KINGPIN, I'D LIKE SOME BRAINS, SOME COURAGE...
...AND A PONY.
I AM NOT ONE TO BE INDEBTED TO OTHERS. CONSIDER THIS YOUR PAYMENT.
YOU HAVE EARNED A PLACE AT MY TABLE. AND WHEN I NEED YOU, YOU SHALL ACT AS MY RIGHT HAND.
FROM NOW ON, YOU ARE MY HOBGOBLIN. SAY IT.
I'M YOUR HOBGOBLIN.
Later...
HEY, GRAMPS. YOU THE TINKERER?
A CERTAIN, OUT OF THE WAY FIX-IT SHOP.
BEEN EXPECTING YOU. KINGPIN'S NEW BOY, RIGHT?
PLEASE, COME IN. NOTHING BUT THE BEST FOR YOU, SIR.
YEAH? WELL, I PLAYED A LITTLE ROUGH WITH SOME OF MY TOYS.
CAN YOU GET 'EM WORKIN' OR NOT? I NEED THIS STUFF.
LOVELY DESIGN. OSBORN, YES? I CAN FIX 'EM. BUT WITH THIS TECH, IT'S GONNA COST YOU...
...A LOT MORE THA KINGPIN'S PAYING YOU.

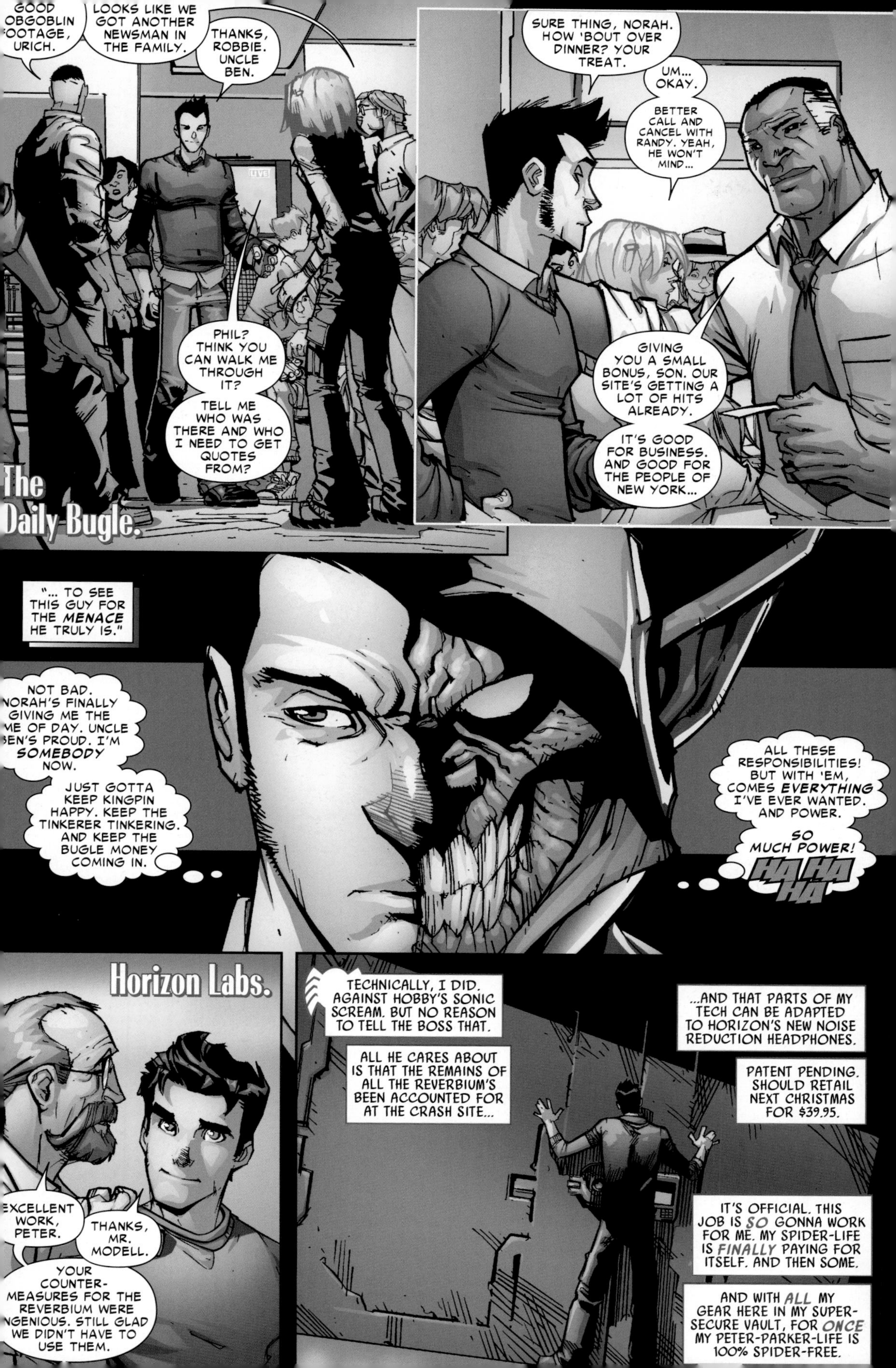
GOOD OBGOBLIN FOOTAGE, URICH.
LOOKS LIKE WE GOT ANOTHER NEWSMAN IN THE FAMILY.
THANKS, ROBBIE. UNCLE BEN.
LIVE
PHIL? THINK YOU CAN WALK ME THROUGH IT?
TELL ME WHO WAS THERE AND WHO I NEED TO GET QUOTES FROM?
The Daily Bugle.
SURE THING, NORAH. HOW 'BOUT OVER DINNER? YOUR TREAT.
UM... OKAY.
BETTER CALL AND CANCEL WITH RANDY. YEAH, HE WON'T MIND...
GIVING YOU A SMALL BONUS, SON. OUR SITE'S GETTING A LOT OF HITS ALREADY.
IT'S GOOD FOR BUSINESS. AND GOOD FOR THE PEOPLE OF NEW YORK...
"... TO SEE THIS GUY FOR THE MENACE HE TRULY IS."
NOT BAD. NORAH'S FINALLY GIVING ME THE ME OF DAY. UNCLE BEN'S PROUD. I'M SOMEBODY NOW.
JUST GOTTA KEEP KINGPIN HAPPY. KEEP THE TINKERER TINKERING. AND KEEP THE BUGLE MONEY COMING IN.
ALL THESE RESPONSIBILITIES! BUT WITH 'EM, COMES EVERYTHING I'VE EVER WANTED. AND POWER.
SO MUCH POWER!
HA HA HA
Horizon Labs.
EXCELLENT WORK, PETER.
THANKS, MR. MODELL.
YOUR COUNTER-MEASURES FOR THE REVERBIUM WERE NGENIOUS. STILL GLAD WE DIDN'T HAVE TO USE THEM.
TECHNICALLY, I DID. AGAINST HOBBY'S SONIC SCREAM. BUT NO REASON TO TELL THE BOSS THAT.
ALL HE CARES ABOUT IS THAT THE REMAINS OF ALL THE REVERBIUM'S BEEN ACCOUNTED FOR AT THE CRASH SITE...
...AND THAT PARTS OF MY TECH CAN BE ADAPTED TO HORIZON'S NEW NOISE REDUCTION HEADPHONES.
PATENT PENDING. SHOULD RETAIL NEXT CHRISTMAS FOR $39.95.
IT'S OFFICIAL. THIS JOB IS SO GONNA WORK FOR ME. MY SPIDER-LIFE IS FINALLY PAYING FOR ITSELF. AND THEN SOME.
AND WITH ALL MY GEAR HERE IN MY SUPER-SECURE VAULT, FOR ONCE MY PETER-PARKER-LIFE IS 100% SPIDER-FREE.

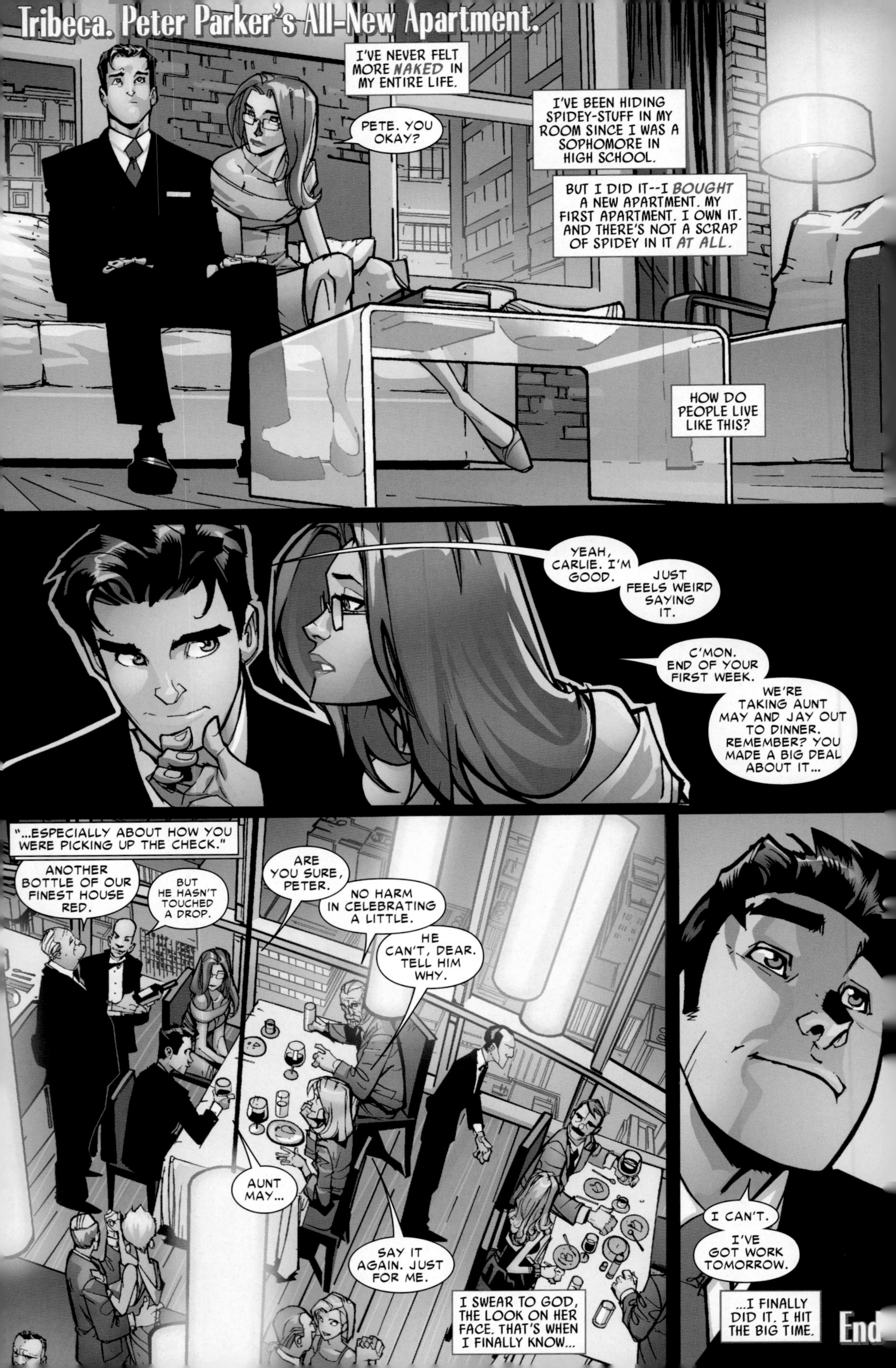
Tribeca. Peter Parker's All-New Apartment.
I'VE NEVER FELT MORE NAKED IN MY ENTIRE LIFE.
PETE. YOU OKAY?
I'VE BEEN HIDING SPIDEY-STUFF IN MY ROOM SINCE I WAS A SOPHOMORE IN HIGH SCHOOL.
BUT I DID IT--I BOUGHT A NEW APARTMENT. MY FIRST APARTMENT. I OWN IT. AND THERE'S NOT A SCRAP OF SPIDEY IN IT AT ALL.
HOW DO PEOPLE LIVE LIKE THIS?
YEAH, CARLIE. I'M GOOD.
JUST FEELS WEIRD SAYING IT.
C'MON. END OF YOUR FIRST WEEK.
WE'RE TAKING AUNT MAY AND JAY OUT TO DINNER. REMEMBER? YOU MADE A BIG DEAL ABOUT IT...
"...ESPECIALLY ABOUT HOW YOU WERE PICKING UP THE CHECK."
ANOTHER BOTTLE OF OUR FINEST HOUSE RED.
BUT HE HASN'T TOUCHED A DROP.
ARE YOU SURE, PETER.
NO HARM IN CELEBRATING A LITTLE.
HE CAN'T, DEAR. TELL HIM WHY.
AUNT MAY...
SAY IT AGAIN. JUST FOR ME.
I SWEAR TO GOD, THE LOOK ON HER FACE. THAT'S WHEN I FINALLY KNOW...
I CAN'T.
I'VE GOT WORK TOMORROW.
...I FINALLY DID IT. I HIT THE BIG TIME.
End

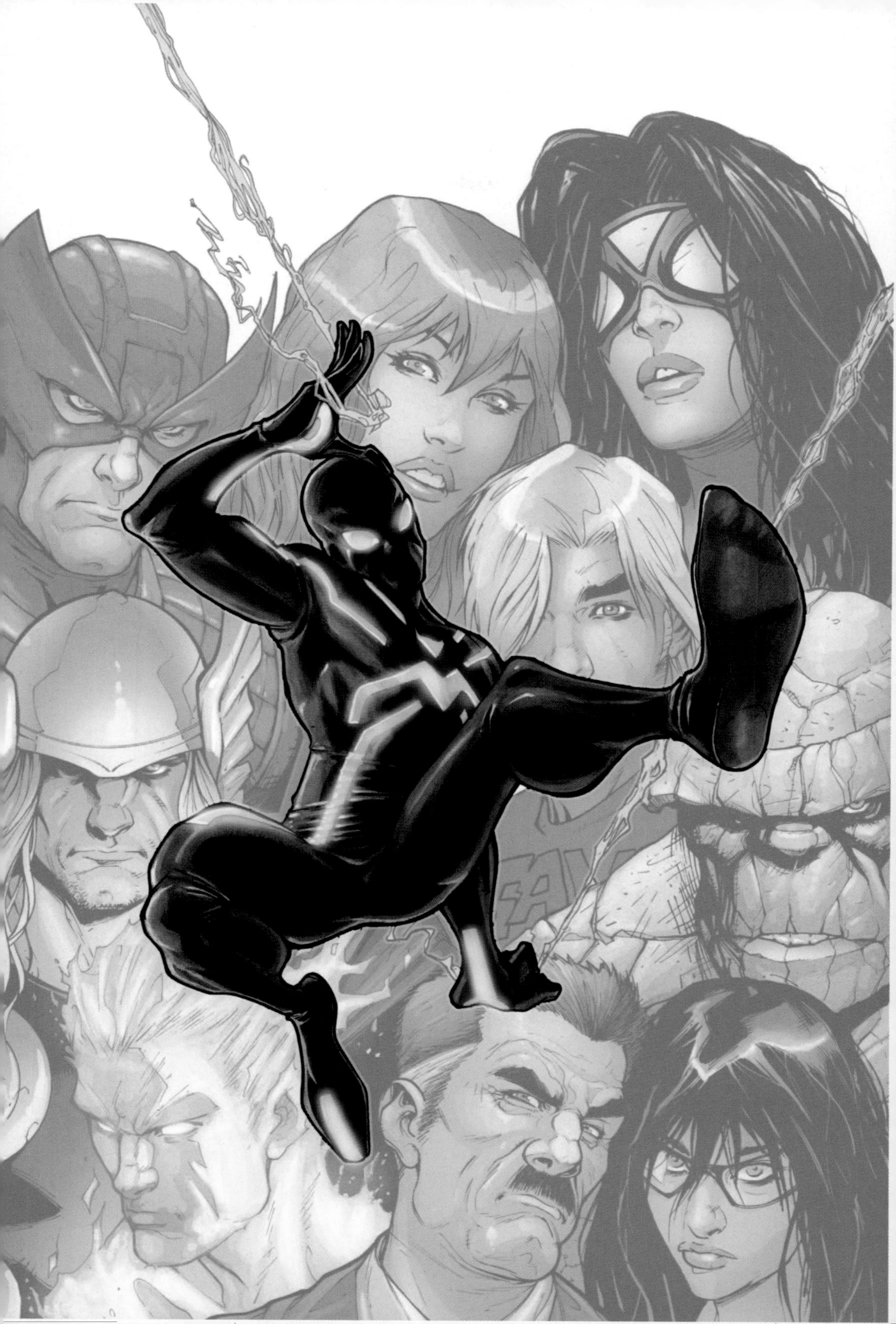

AN #648 V
STEFANC

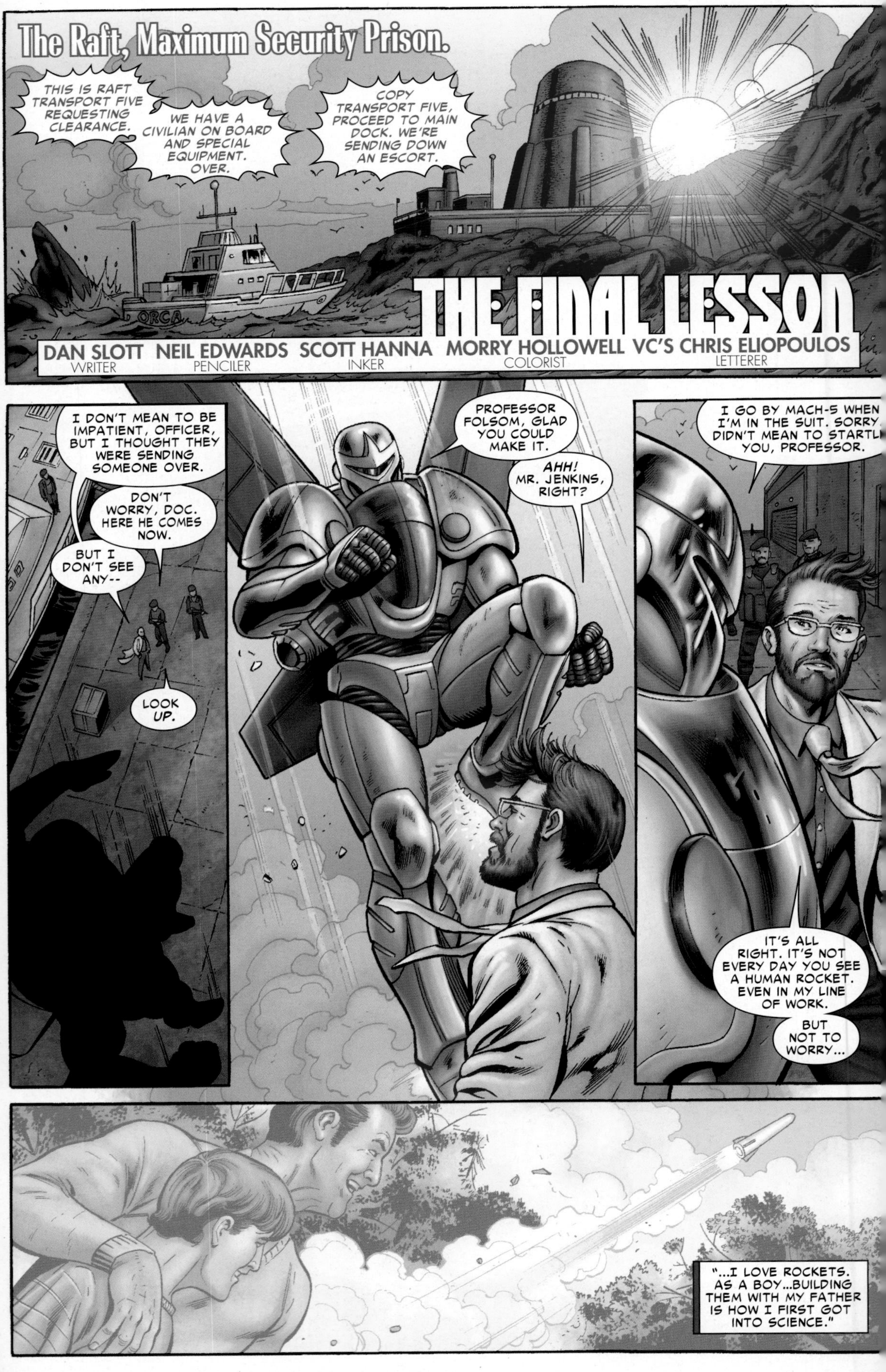
The Raft, Maximum Security Prison.
THIS IS RAFT TRANSPORT FIVE REQUESTING CLEARANCE.
WE HAVE A CIVILIAN ON BOARD AND SPECIAL EQUIPMENT. OVER.
COPY TRANSPORT FIVE, PROCEED TO MAIN DOCK. WE'RE SENDING DOWN AN ESCORT.
ORCA
THE FINAL LESSON
DAN SLOTT WRITER
NEIL EDWARDS PENCILER
SCOTT HANNA INKER
MORRY HOLLOWELL COLORIST
VC'S CHRIS ELIOPOULOS LETTERER
I DON'T MEAN TO BE IMPATIENT, OFFICER, BUT I THOUGHT THEY WERE SENDING SOMEONE OVER.
DON'T WORRY, DOC. HERE HE COMES NOW.
BUT I DON'T SEE ANY--
LOOK UP.
PROFESSOR FOLSOM, GLAD YOU COULD MAKE IT.
AHH! MR. JENKINS, RIGHT?
I GO BY MACH-5 WHEN I'M IN THE SUIT. SORRY. DIDN'T MEAN TO STARTLE YOU, PROFESSOR.
IT'S ALL RIGHT. IT'S NOT EVERY DAY YOU SEE A HUMAN ROCKET. EVEN IN MY LINE OF WORK.
BUT NOT TO WORRY...
"...I LOVE ROCKETS. AS A BOY...BUILDING THEM WITH MY FATHER IS HOW I FIRST GOT INTO SCIENCE."

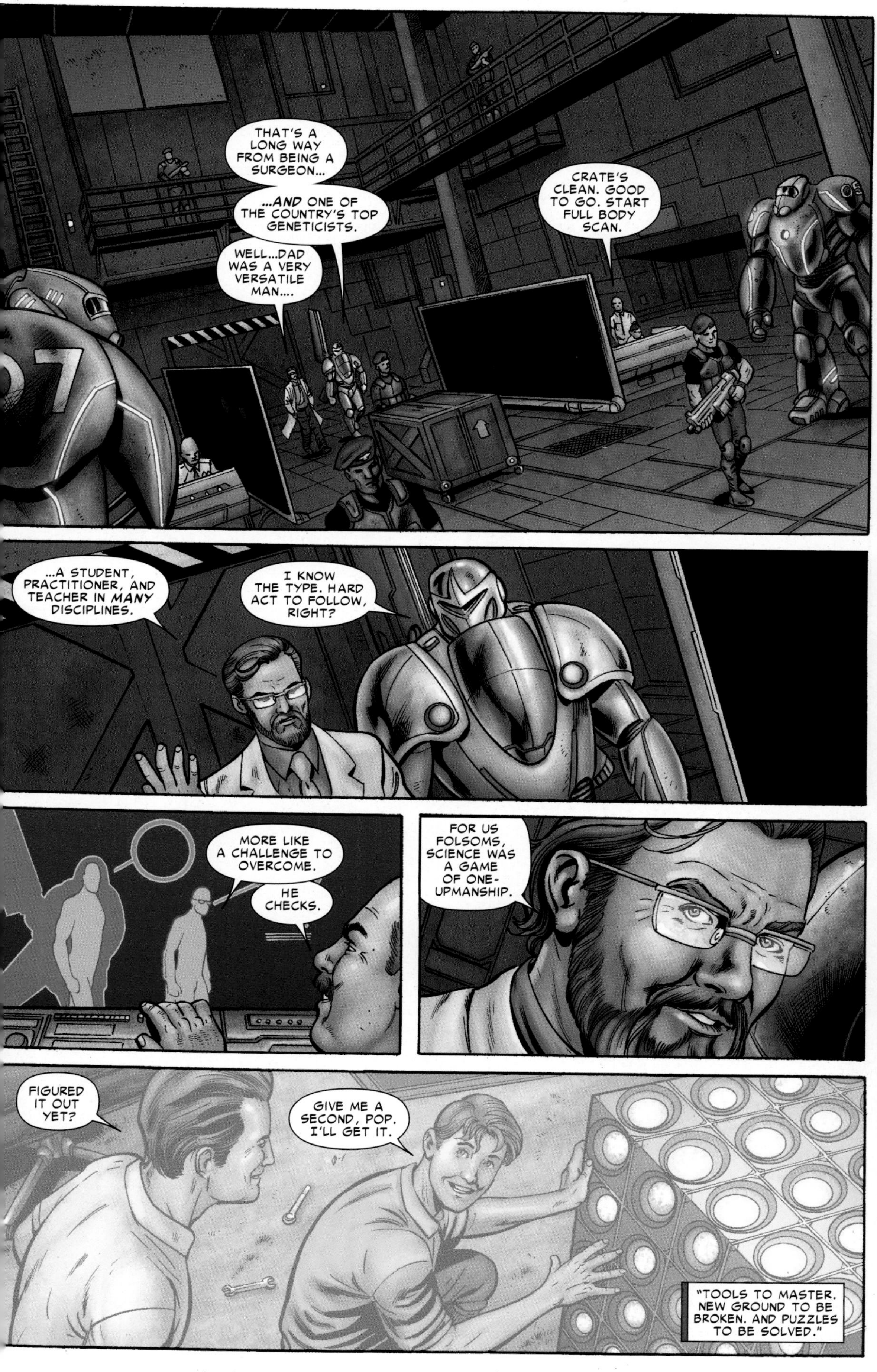
THAT'S A LONG WAY FROM BEING A SURGEON...
...AND ONE OF THE COUNTRY'S TOP GENETICISTS.
WELL...DAD WAS A VERY VERSATILE MAN....
CRATE'S CLEAN. GOOD TO GO. START FULL BODY SCAN.
...A STUDENT, PRACTITIONER, AND TEACHER IN MANY DISCIPLINES.
I KNOW THE TYPE. HARD ACT TO FOLLOW, RIGHT?
MORE LIKE A CHALLENGE TO OVERCOME.
HE CHECKS.
FOR US FOLSOMS, SCIENCE WAS A GAME OF ONE-UPMANSHIP.
FIGURED IT OUT YET?
GIVE ME A SECOND, POP. I'LL GET IT.
"TOOLS TO MASTER. NEW GROUND TO BE BROKEN. AND PUZZLES TO BE SOLVED."

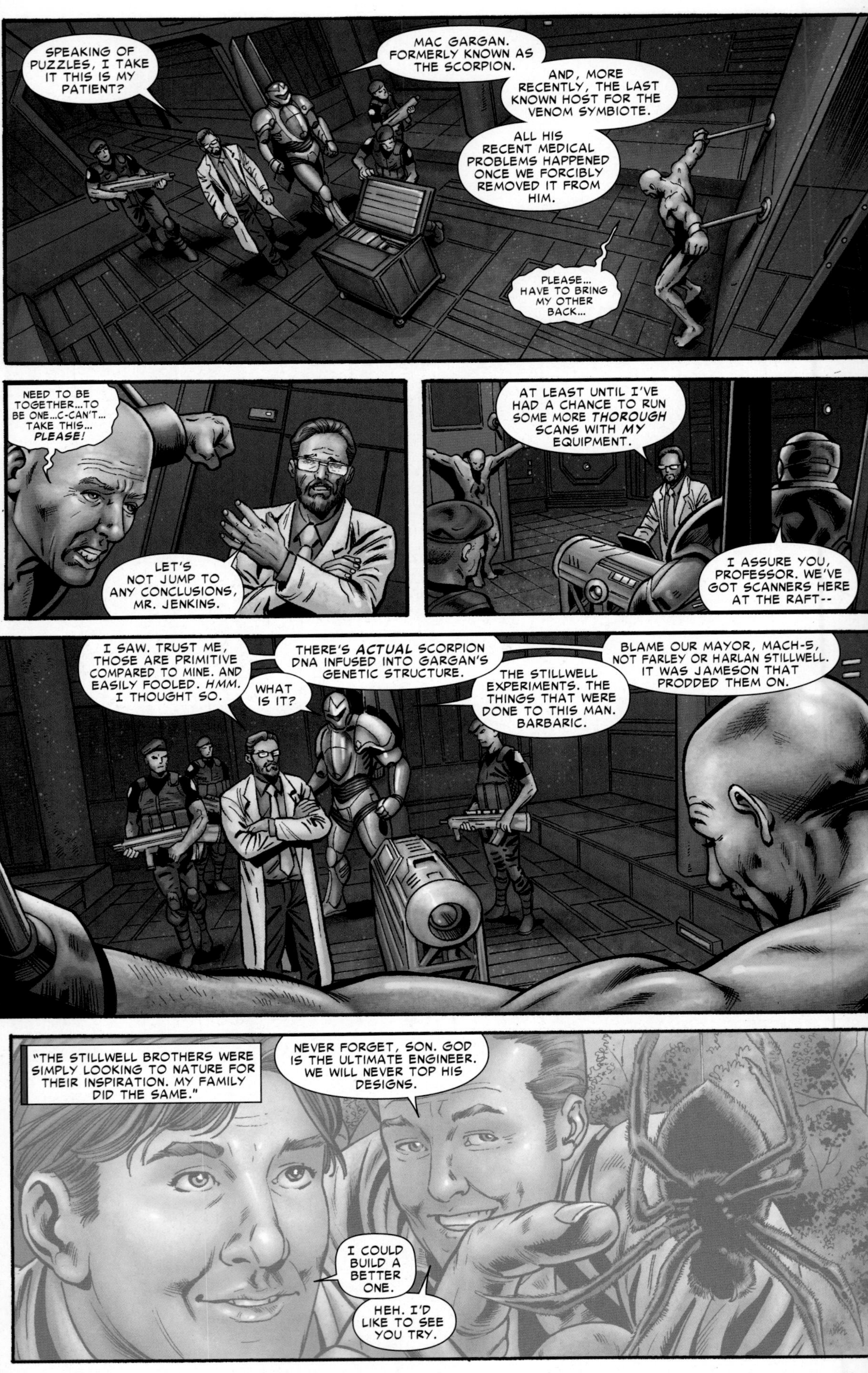
SPEAKING OF PUZZLES, I TAKE IT THIS IS MY PATIENT?
MAC GARGAN. FORMERLY KNOWN AS THE SCORPION.
AND, MORE RECENTLY, THE LAST KNOWN HOST FOR THE VENOM SYMBIOTE.
ALL HIS RECENT MEDICAL PROBLEMS HAPPENED ONCE WE FORCIBLY REMOVED IT FROM HIM.
PLEASE... HAVE TO BRING MY OTHER BACK...
NEED TO BE TOGETHER...TO BE ONE...C-CAN'T... TAKE THIS... PLEASE!
LET'S NOT JUMP TO ANY CONCLUSIONS, MR. JENKINS.
AT LEAST UNTIL I'VE HAD A CHANCE TO RUN SOME MORE THOROUGH SCANS WITH MY EQUIPMENT.
I ASSURE YOU, PROFESSOR. WE'VE GOT SCANNERS HERE AT THE RAFT--
I SAW. TRUST ME, THOSE ARE PRIMITIVE COMPARED TO MINE. AND EASILY FOOLED. HMM. I THOUGHT SO.
WHAT IS IT?
THERE'S ACTUAL SCORPION DNA INFUSED INTO GARGAN'S GENETIC STRUCTURE.
THE STILLWELL EXPERIMENTS. THE THINGS THAT WERE DONE TO THIS MAN. BARBARIC.
BLAME OUR MAYOR, MACH-5, NOT FARLEY OR HARLAN STILLWELL. IT WAS JAMESON THAT PRODDED THEM ON.
"THE STILLWELL BROTHERS WERE SIMPLY LOOKING TO NATURE FOR THEIR INSPIRATION. MY FAMILY DID THE SAME."
NEVER FORGET, SON. GOD IS THE ULTIMATE ENGINEER. WE WILL NEVER TOP HIS DESIGNS.
I COULD BUILD A BETTER ONE.
HEH. I'D LIKE TO SEE YOU TRY.

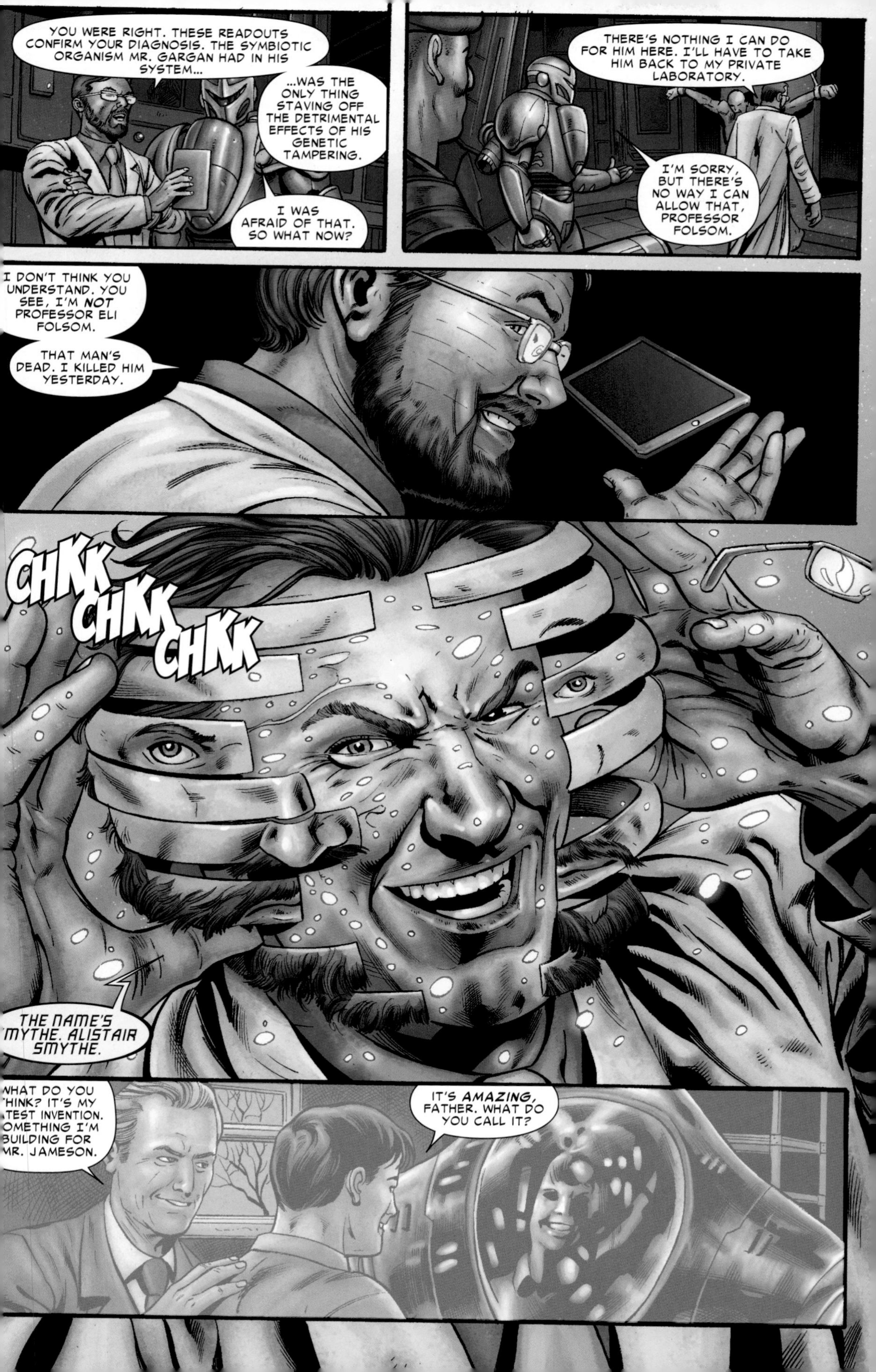
YOU WERE RIGHT. THESE READOUTS CONFIRM YOUR DIAGNOSIS. THE SYMBIOTIC ORGANISM MR. GARGAN HAD IN HIS SYSTEM...
...WAS THE ONLY THING STAVING OFF THE DETRIMENTAL EFFECTS OF HIS GENETIC TAMPERING.
I WAS AFRAID OF THAT. SO WHAT NOW?
THERE'S NOTHING I CAN DO FOR HIM HERE. I'LL HAVE TO TAKE HIM BACK TO MY PRIVATE LABORATORY.
I'M SORRY, BUT THERE'S NO WAY I CAN ALLOW THAT, PROFESSOR FOLSOM.
I DON'T THINK YOU UNDERSTAND. YOU SEE, I'M *NOT* PROFESSOR ELI FOLSOM.
THAT MAN'S DEAD. I KILLED HIM YESTERDAY.
CHKK CHKK CHKK
THE NAME'S SMYTHE. ALISTAIR SMYTHE.
WHAT DO YOU THINK? IT'S MY TEST INVENTION. SOMETHING I'M BUILDING FOR MR. JAMESON.
IT'S *AMAZING*, FATHER. WHAT DO YOU CALL IT?

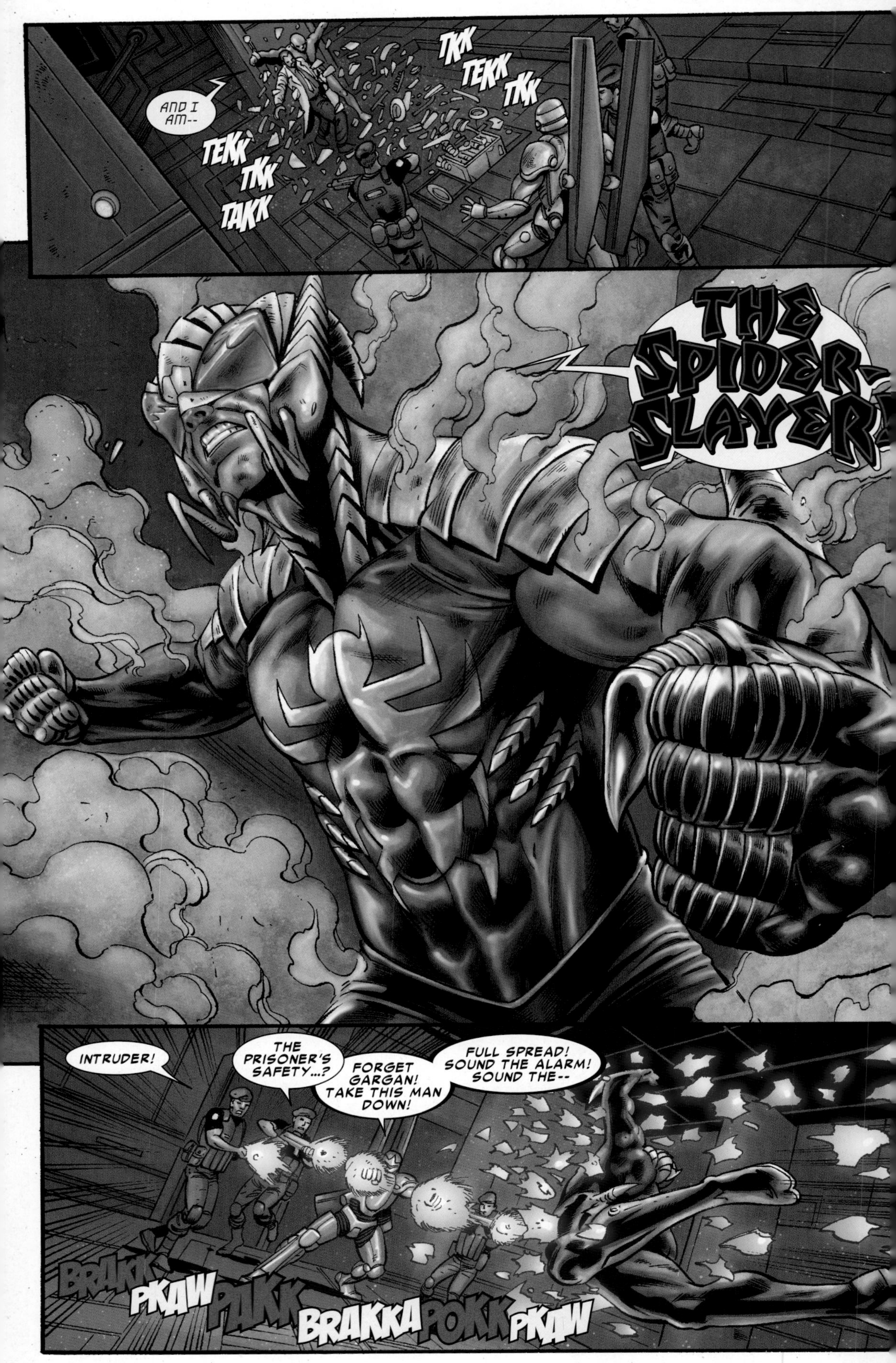
AND I AM--
TEKK
TKK
TAKK
TKK
TEKK
TKK
THE SPIDER-SLAYER!
INTRUDER!
THE PRISONER'S SAFETY...?
FORGET GARGAN! TAKE THIS MAN DOWN!
FULL SPREAD! SOUND THE ALARM! SOUND THE--
BRAKK
PKAW
PAKK
BRAKKA
POKK
PKAW

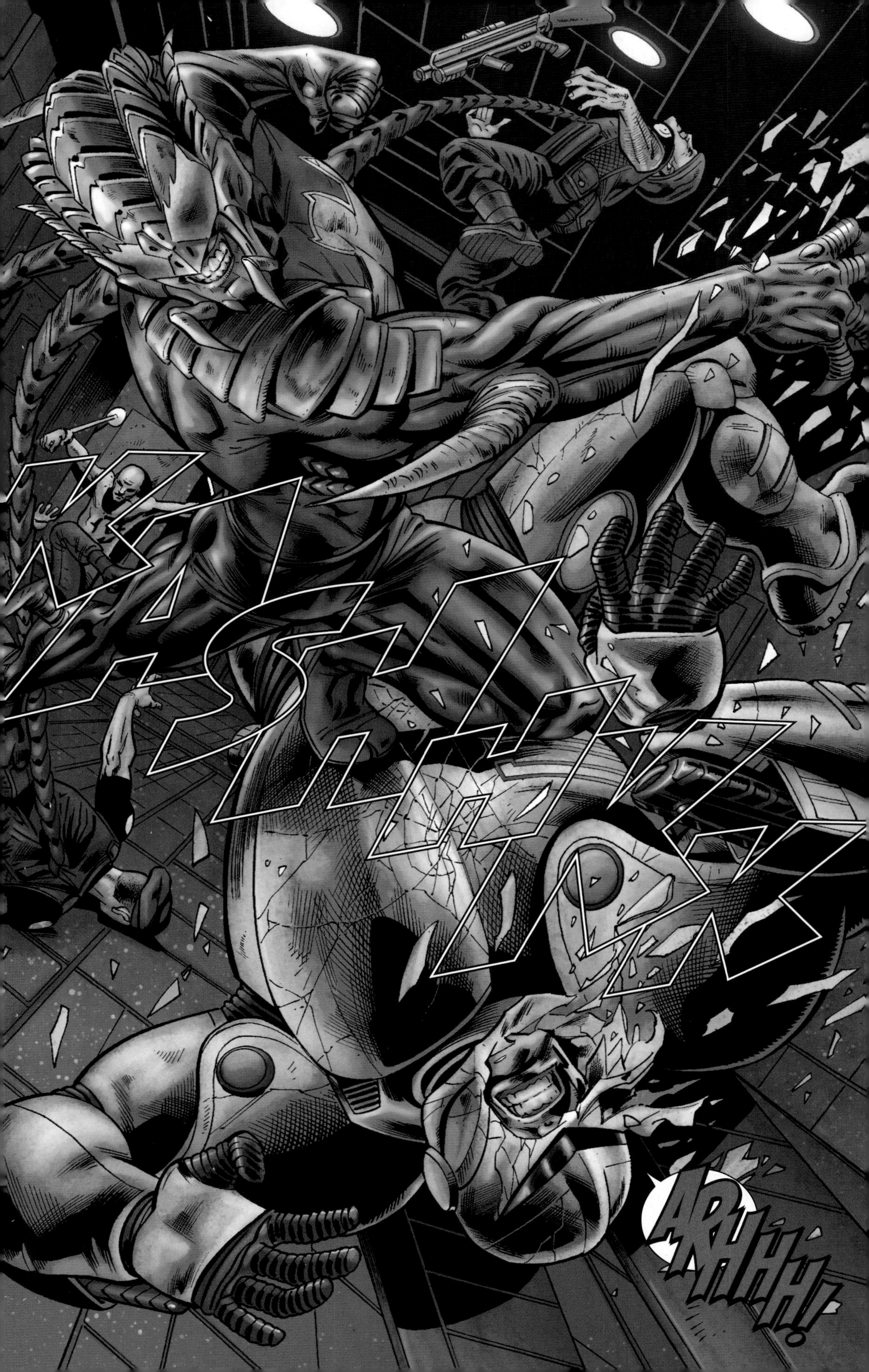
ARHHH!

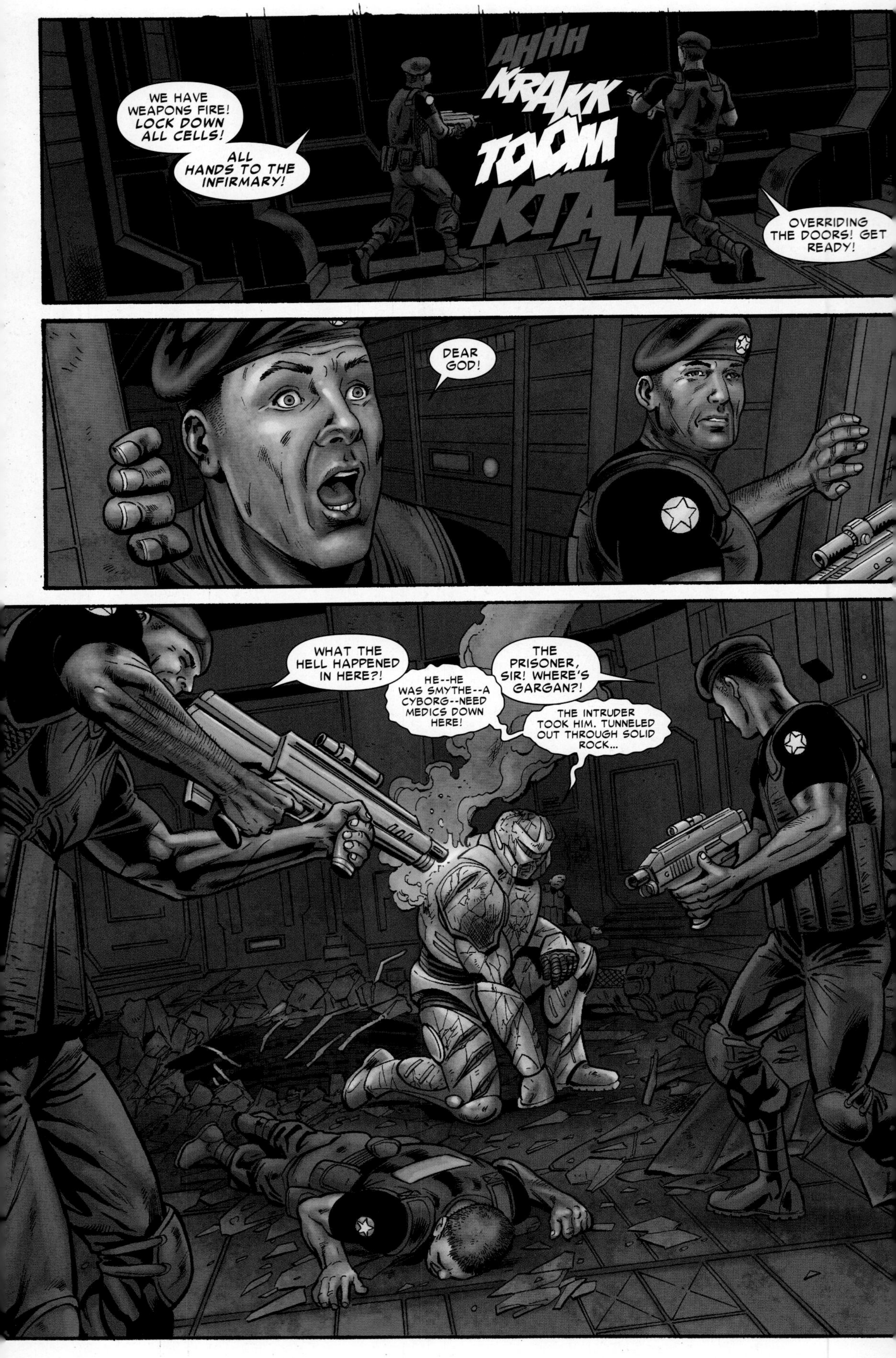
WE HAVE WEAPONS FIRE! LOCK DOWN ALL CELLS!
ALL HANDS TO THE INFIRMARY!
AHHH
KRAKK
TOOM
KTAM
OVERRIDING THE DOORS! GET READY!
DEAR GOD!
WHAT THE HELL HAPPENED IN HERE?!
HE--HE WAS SMYTHE--A CYBORG--NEED MEDICS DOWN HERE!
THE PRISONER, SIR! WHERE'S GARGAN?!
THE INTRUDER TOOK HIM. TUNNELED OUT THROUGH SOLID ROCK...

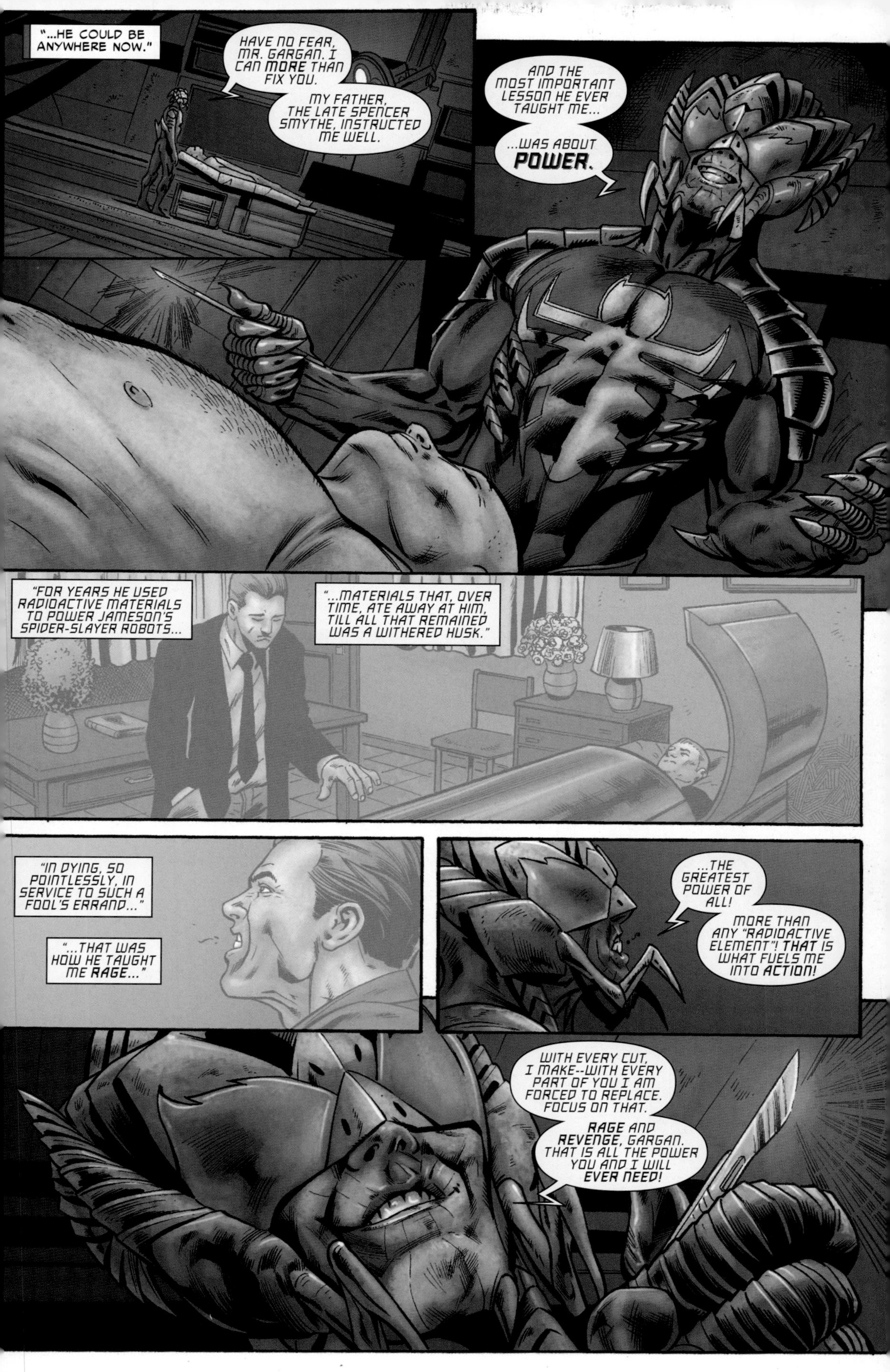
"...HE COULD BE ANYWHERE NOW."
HAVE NO FEAR, MR. GARGAN. I CAN MORE THAN FIX YOU.
MY FATHER, THE LATE SPENCER SMYTHE, INSTRUCTED ME WELL.
AND THE MOST IMPORTANT LESSON HE EVER TAUGHT ME...
...WAS ABOUT POWER.
"FOR YEARS HE USED RADIOACTIVE MATERIALS TO POWER JAMESON'S SPIDER-SLAYER ROBOTS...
"...MATERIALS THAT, OVER TIME, ATE AWAY AT HIM, TILL ALL THAT REMAINED WAS A WITHERED HUSK."
"IN DYING, SO POINTLESSLY, IN SERVICE TO SUCH A FOOL'S ERRAND..."
"...THAT WAS HOW HE TAUGHT ME RAGE..."
...THE GREATEST POWER OF ALL!
MORE THAN ANY "RADIOACTIVE ELEMENT"! THAT IS WHAT FUELS ME INTO ACTION!
WITH EVERY CUT, I MAKE--WITH EVERY PART OF YOU I AM FORCED TO REPLACE. FOCUS ON THAT.
RAGE AND REVENGE, GARGAN. THAT IS ALL THE POWER YOU AND I WILL EVER NEED!

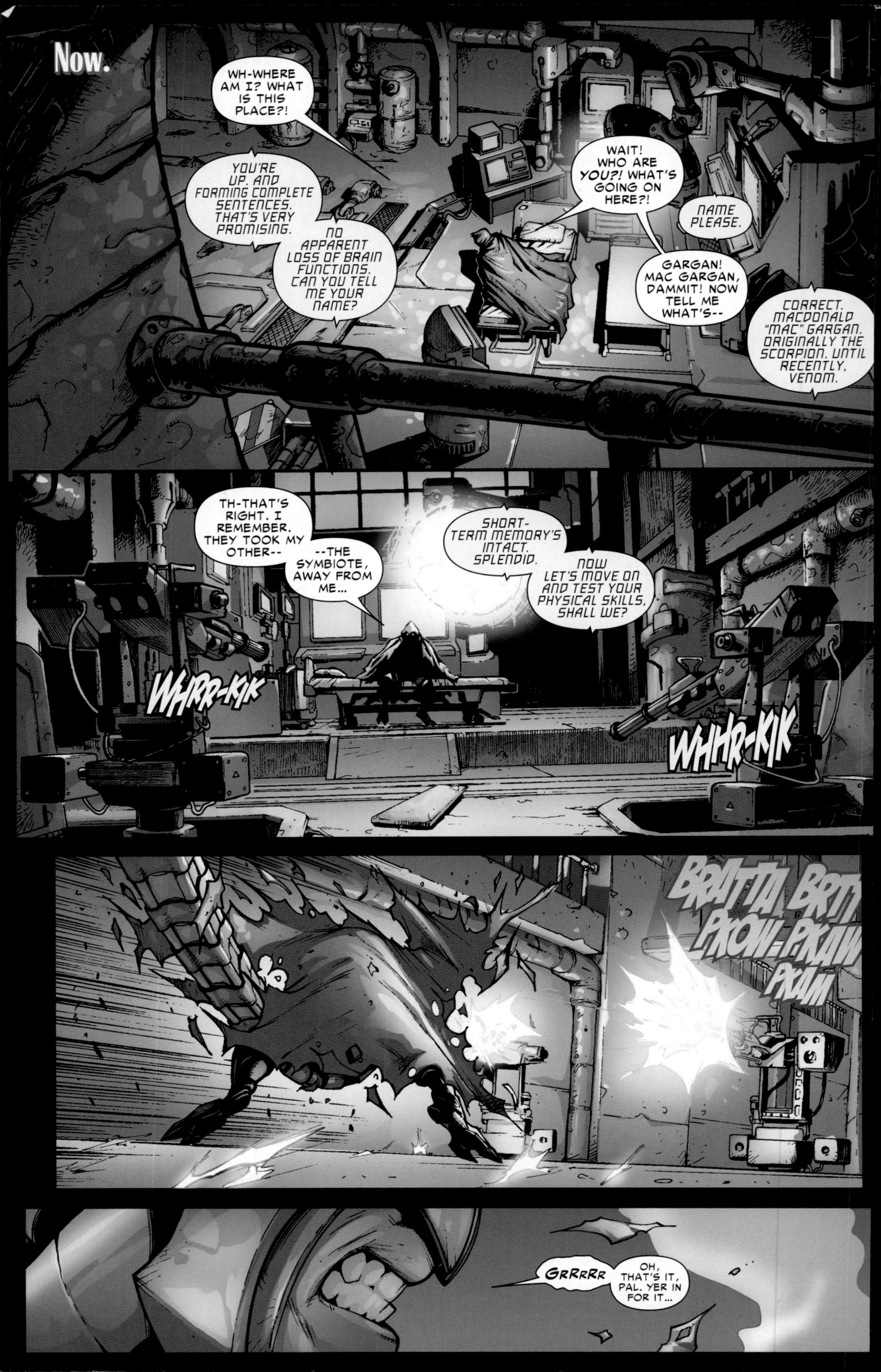

Now.
WH-WHERE AM I? WHAT IS THIS PLACE?!
YOU'RE UP. AND FORMING COMPLETE SENTENCES. THAT'S VERY PROMISING.
NO APPARENT LOSS OF BRAIN FUNCTIONS. CAN YOU TELL ME YOUR NAME?
WAIT! WHO ARE YOU?! WHAT'S GOING ON HERE?!
NAME PLEASE.
GARGAN! MAC GARGAN, DAMMIT! NOW TELL ME WHAT'S--
CORRECT. MACDONALD "MAC" GARGAN. ORIGINALLY THE SCORPION. UNTIL RECENTLY, VENOM.
TH-THAT'S RIGHT. I REMEMBER. THEY TOOK MY OTHER--
--THE SYMBIOTE, AWAY FROM ME...
SHORT-TERM MEMORY'S INTACT. SPLENDID.
NOW LET'S MOVE ON AND TEST YOUR PHYSICAL SKILLS, SHALL WE?
WHRR-KIK
WHRR-KIK
BRATTA BRTT PKOW-PKAW PKAM
GRRRRR
OH, THAT'S IT, PAL. YER IN FOR IT...

THE STING
THAT NEVER GOES AWAY

WHRAKK

'CAUSE YOU HAVE NO IDEA WHAT I'M CAPABLE OF!

DAN SLOTT	STEFANO CASELLI	EDGAR DELGADO	VC'S JOE CARAMAGNA
WRITER	PENCILER	COLORIST	LETTERER

ELLIE PYLE	TOM BRENNAN	STEPHEN WACKER	JOE QUESADA	DAN BUCKLEY	ALAN FINE
ASST. EDITOR	ASSOC. EDITOR	SENIOR EDITOR	EDITOR IN CHIEF	PUBLISHER	EXECUTIVE PRODUCER

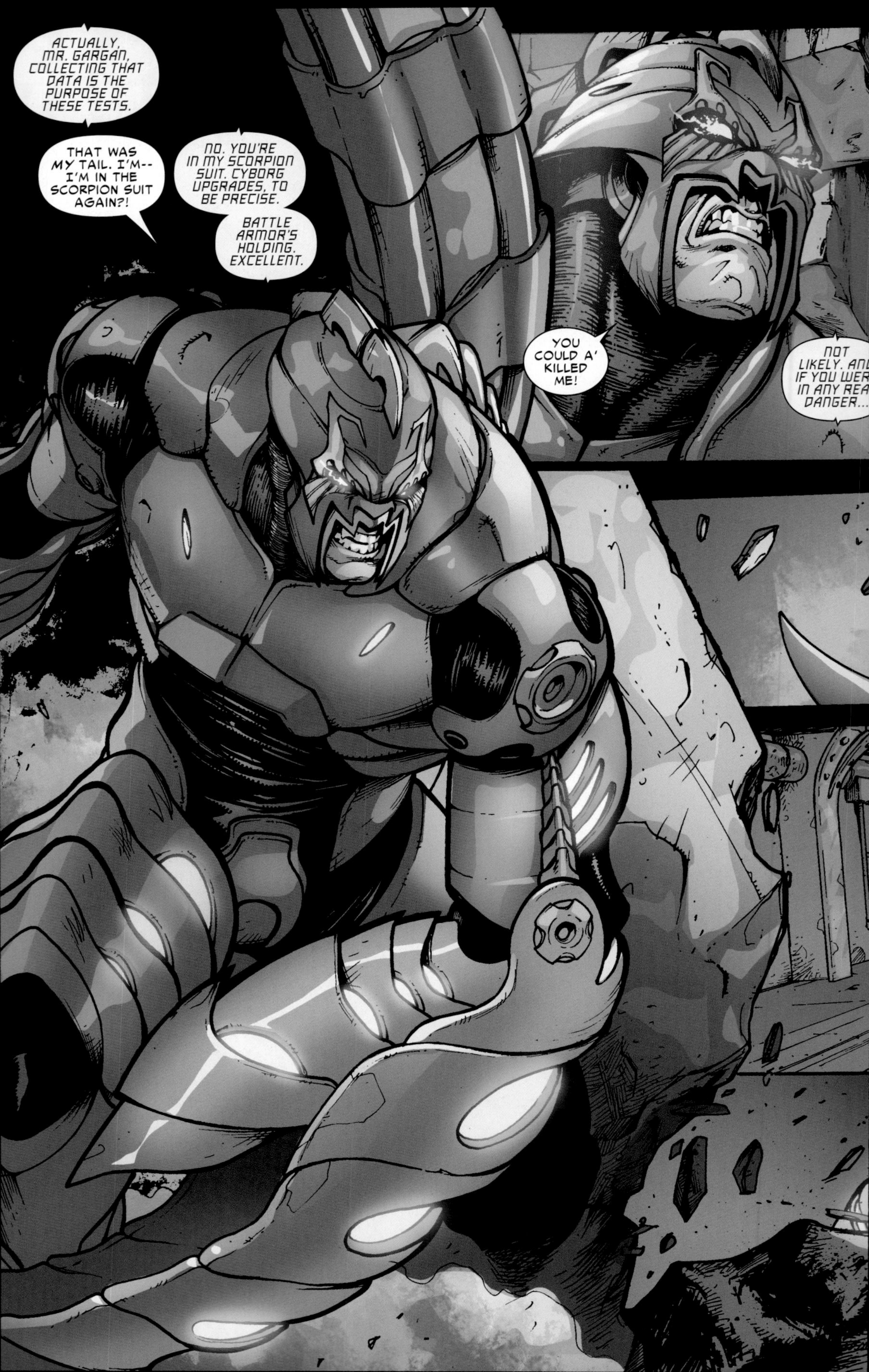
ACTUALLY, MR. GARGAN, COLLECTING THAT DATA IS THE PURPOSE OF THESE TESTS.
THAT WAS MY TAIL. I'M-- I'M IN THE SCORPION SUIT AGAIN?!
NO. YOU'RE IN MY SCORPION SUIT. CYBORG UPGRADES, TO BE PRECISE.
BATTLE ARMOR'S HOLDING. EXCELLENT.
YOU COULD A' KILLED ME!
NOT LIKELY. AN IF YOU WER IN ANY REA DANGER...

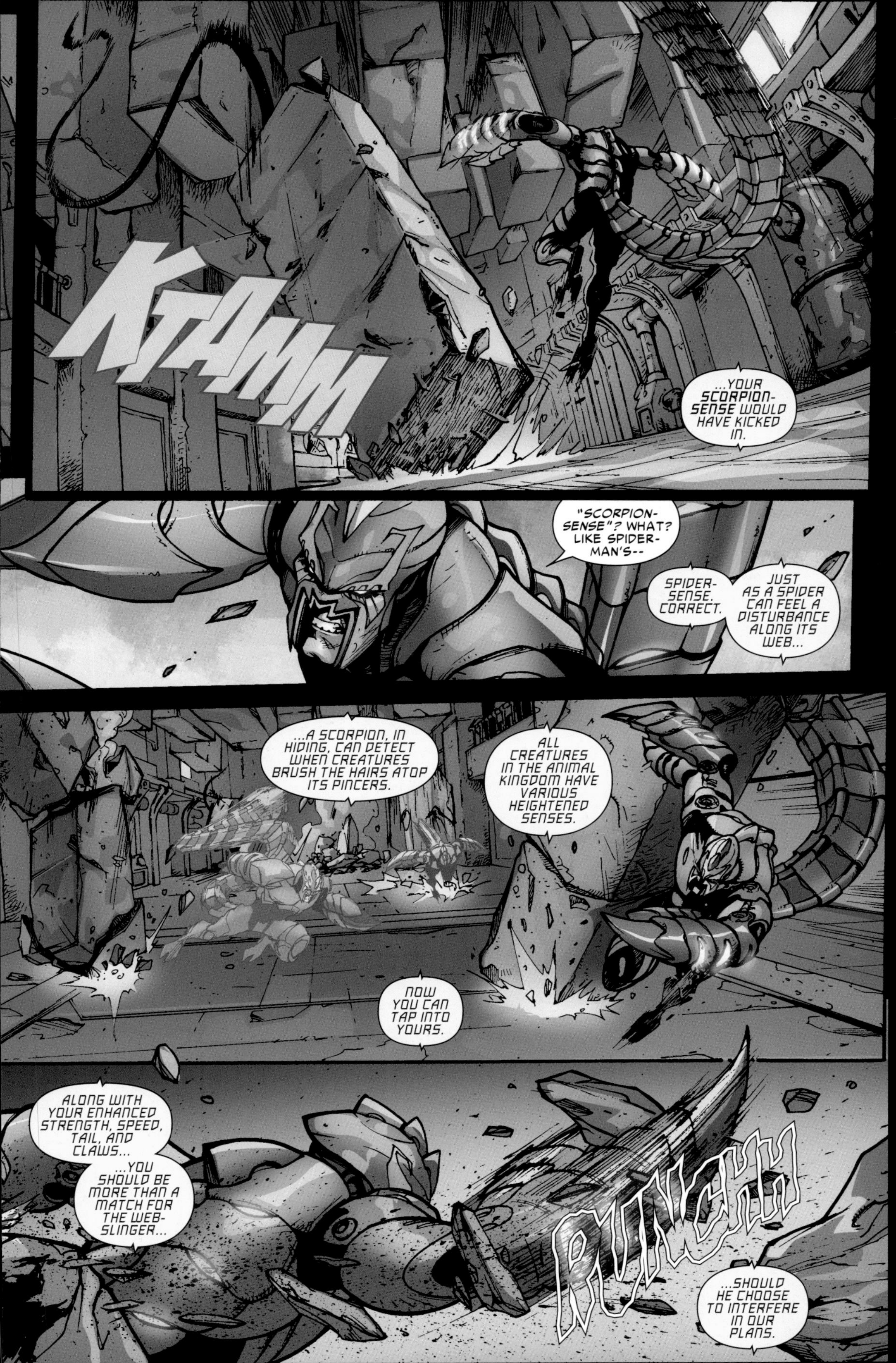
KTAMM
...YOUR SCORPION-SENSE WOULD HAVE KICKED IN.
"SCORPION-SENSE"? WHAT? LIKE SPIDER-MAN'S--
SPIDER-SENSE. CORRECT.
JUST AS A SPIDER CAN FEEL A DISTURBANCE ALONG ITS WEB...
...A SCORPION, IN HIDING, CAN DETECT WHEN CREATURES BRUSH THE HAIRS ATOP ITS PINCERS.
ALL CREATURES IN THE ANIMAL KINGDOM HAVE VARIOUS HEIGHTENED SENSES.
NOW YOU CAN TAP INTO YOURS.
ALONG WITH YOUR ENHANCED STRENGTH, SPEED, TAIL, AND CLAWS...
...YOU SHOULD BE MORE THAN A MATCH FOR THE WEB-SLINGER...
RUNCH
...SHOULD HE CHOOSE TO INTERFERE IN OUR PLANS.

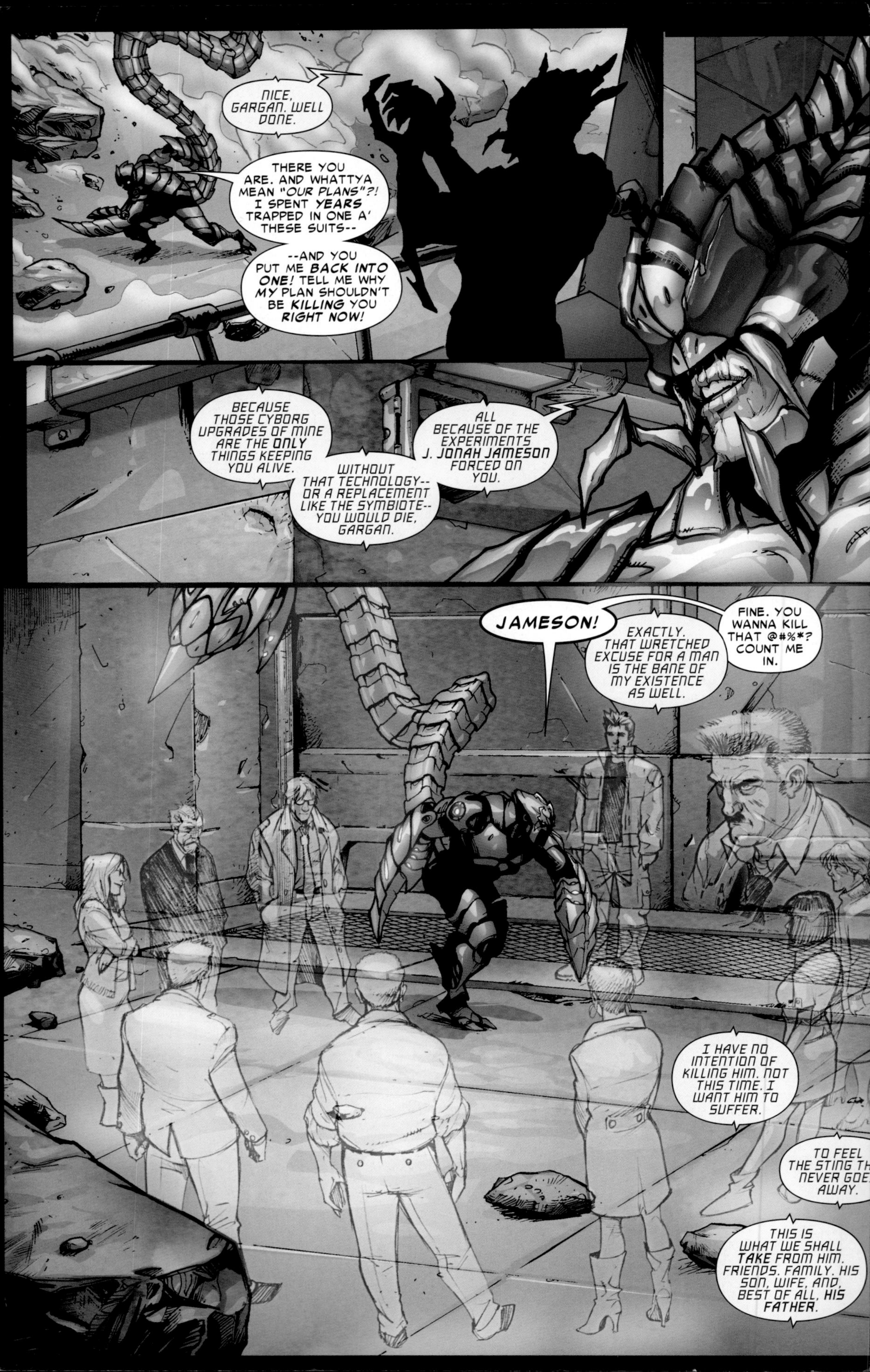
NICE, GARGAN. WELL DONE.
THERE YOU ARE. AND WHATTYA MEAN "OUR PLANS"?! I SPENT YEARS TRAPPED IN ONE A' THESE SUITS--
--AND YOU PUT ME BACK INTO ONE! TELL ME WHY MY PLAN SHOULDN'T BE KILLING YOU RIGHT NOW!
BECAUSE THOSE CYBORG UPGRADES OF MINE ARE THE ONLY THINGS KEEPING YOU ALIVE.
ALL BECAUSE OF THE EXPERIMENTS J. JONAH JAMESON FORCED ON YOU.
WITHOUT THAT TECHNOLOGY-- OR A REPLACEMENT LIKE THE SYMBIOTE-- YOU WOULD DIE, GARGAN.
JAMESON!
EXACTLY. THAT WRETCHED EXCUSE FOR A MAN IS THE BANE OF MY EXISTENCE AS WELL.
FINE. YOU WANNA KILL THAT @#%*? COUNT ME IN.
I HAVE NO INTENTION OF KILLING HIM. NOT THIS TIME. I WANT HIM TO SUFFER.
TO FEEL THE STING TH NEVER GOE AWAY.
THIS IS WHAT WE SHALL TAKE FROM HIM. FRIENDS. FAMILY. HIS SON, WIFE, AND, BEST OF ALL, HIS FATHER.

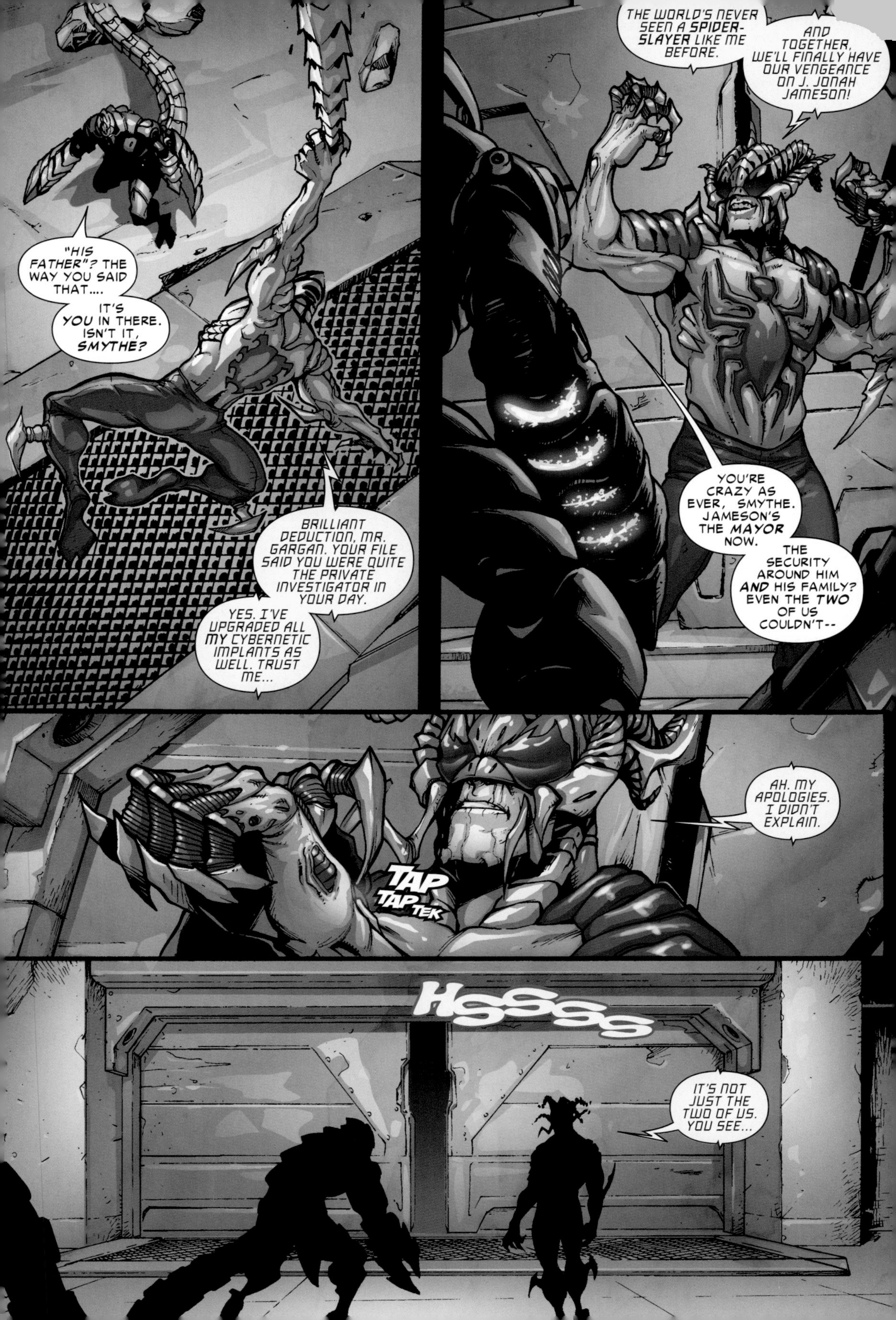

"HIS FATHER"? THE WAY YOU SAID THAT....
IT'S YOU IN THERE. ISN'T IT, SMYTHE?
BRILLIANT DEDUCTION, MR. GARGAN. YOUR FILE SAID YOU WERE QUITE THE PRIVATE INVESTIGATOR IN YOUR DAY.
YES. I'VE UPGRADED ALL MY CYBERNETIC IMPLANTS AS WELL. TRUST ME...
THE WORLD'S NEVER SEEN A SPIDER-SLAYER LIKE ME BEFORE.
AND TOGETHER, WE'LL FINALLY HAVE OUR VENGEANCE ON J. JONAH JAMESON!
YOU'RE CRAZY AS EVER, SMYTHE. JAMESON'S THE MAYOR NOW.
THE SECURITY AROUND HIM AND HIS FAMILY? EVEN THE TWO OF US COULDN'T--
AH. MY APOLOGIES. I DIDN'T EXPLAIN.
TAP
TAP TEK
HSSSSS
IT'S NOT JUST THE TWO OF US. YOU SEE...

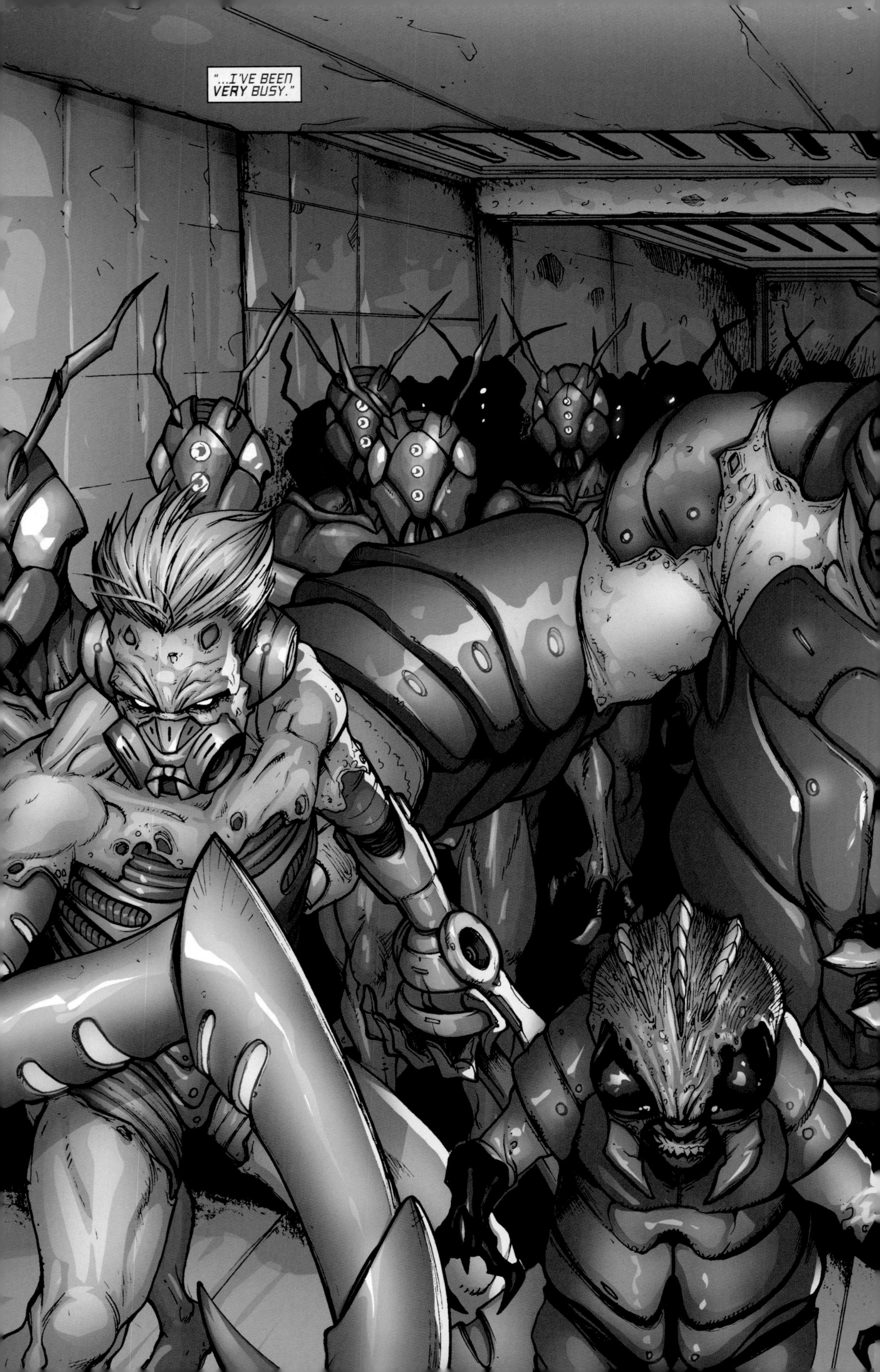
"...I'VE BEEN VERY BUSY."

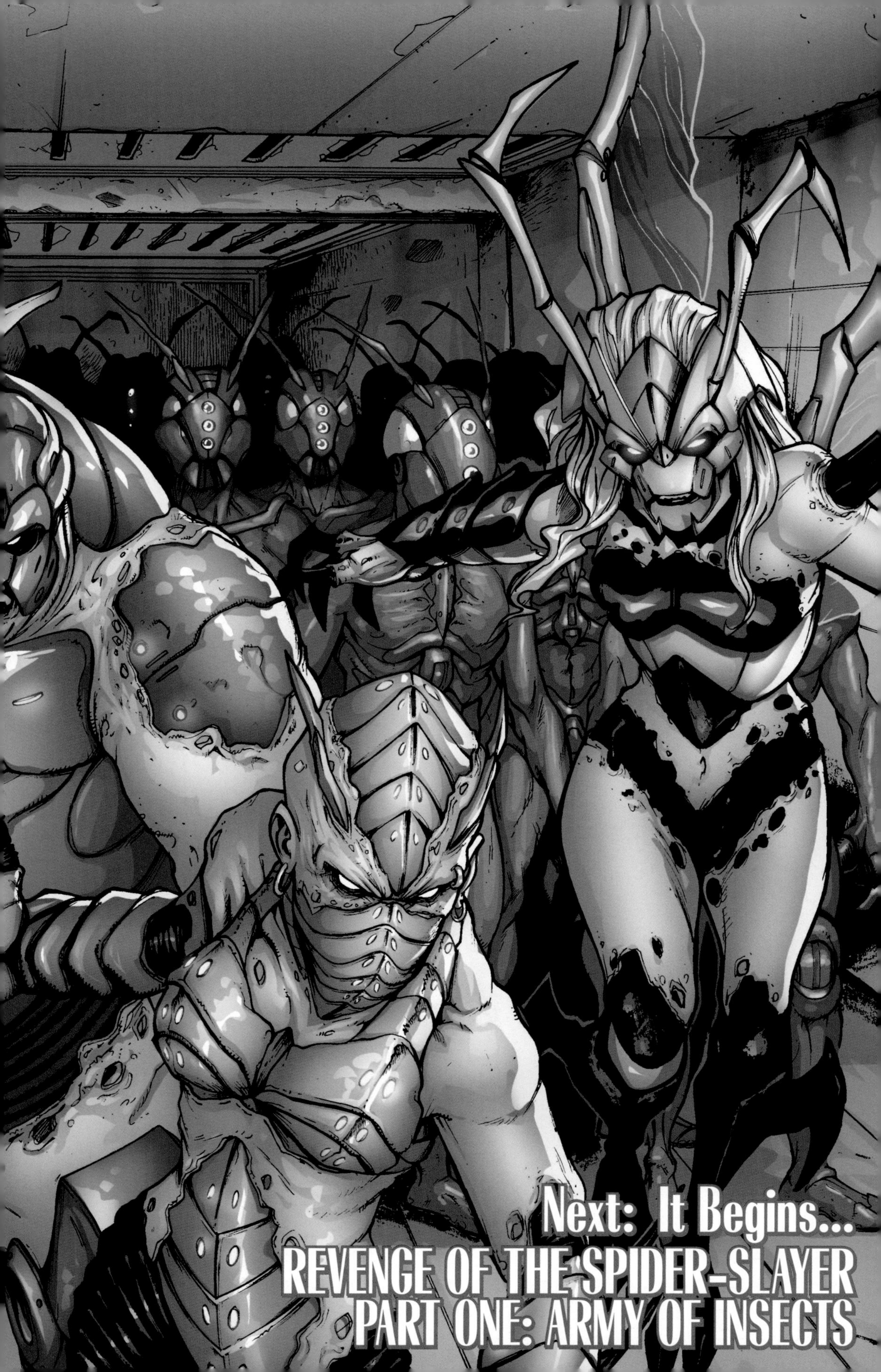
Next: It Begins...
REVENGE OF THE SPIDER-SLAYER
PART ONE: ARMY OF INSECTS

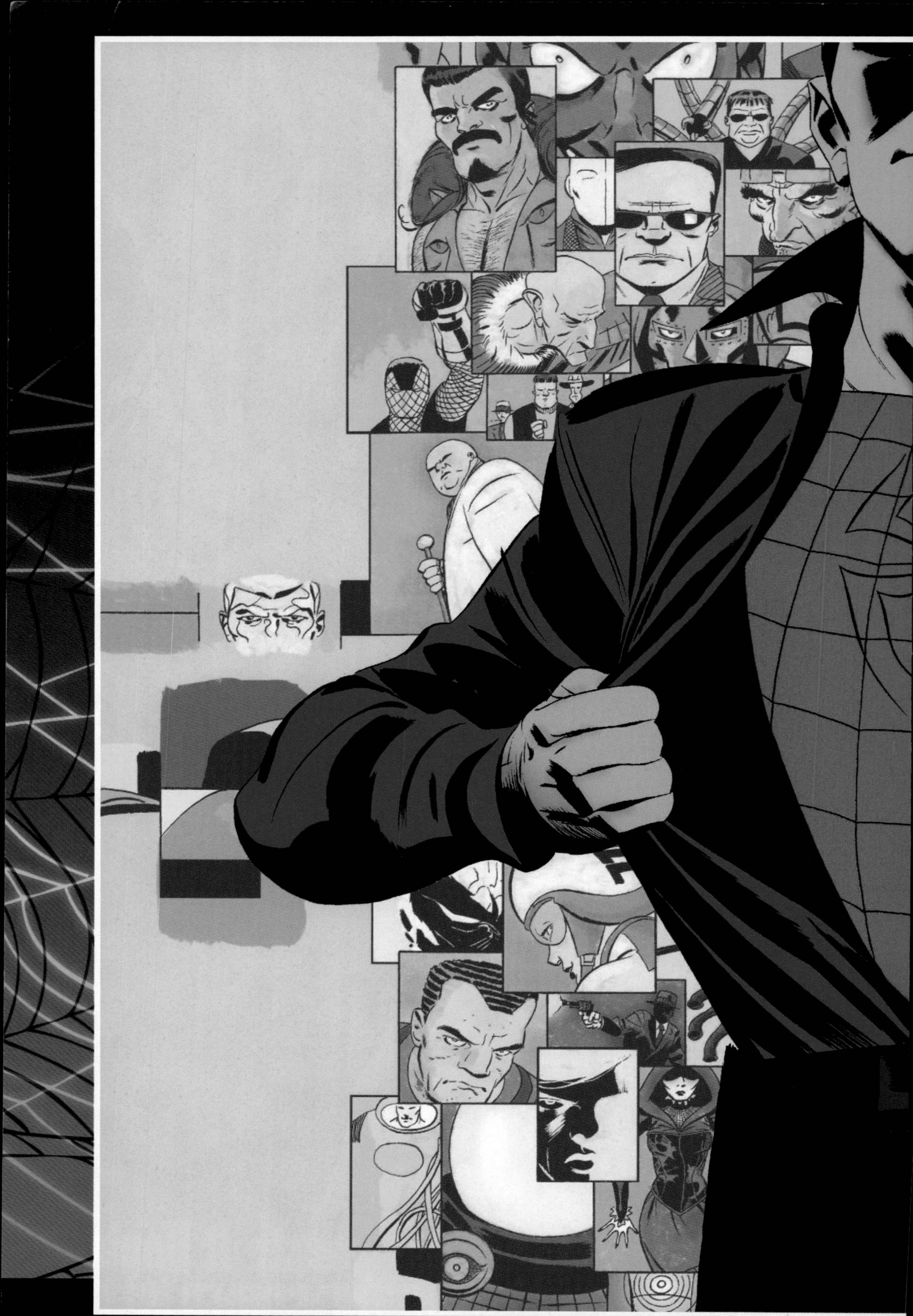

AMAZING SPIDER-MAN #648 VARIANT
COVER BY MARCOS MARTIN

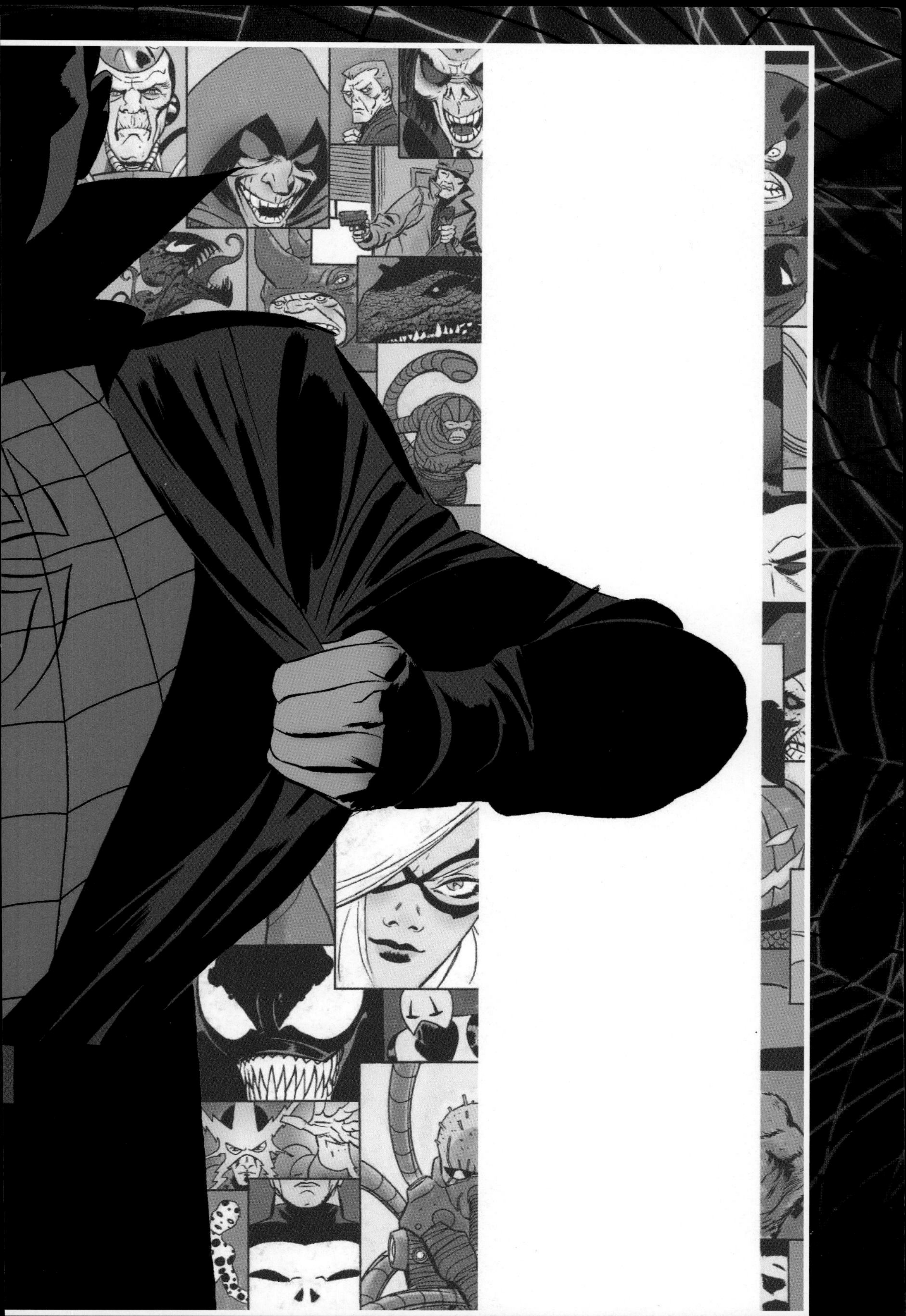

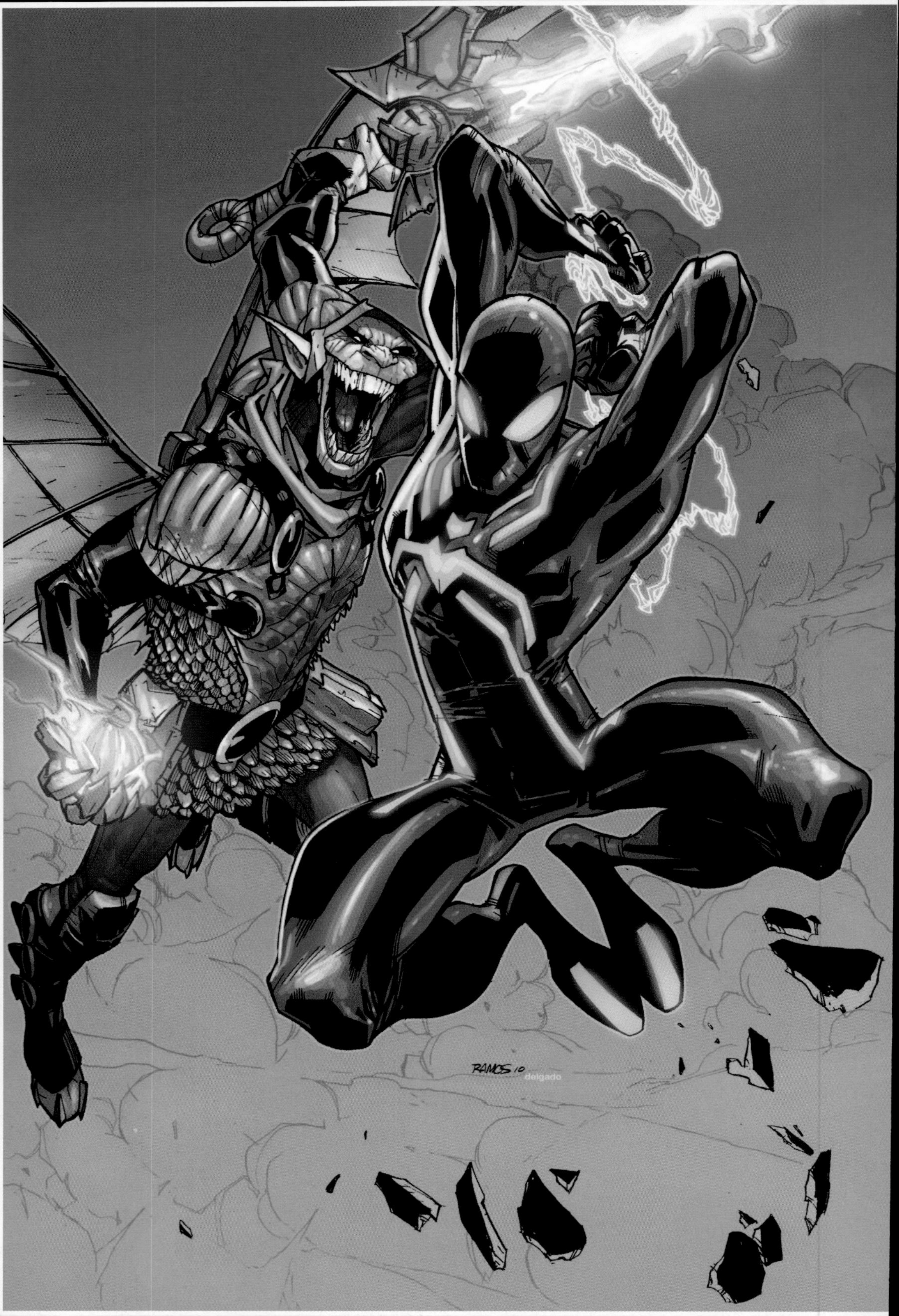
RAMOS 10
delgado

AMAZING SPIDER-MAN PROMOTIONAL ARTWORK
BY HUMBERTO RAMOS & EDGAR DELGADO

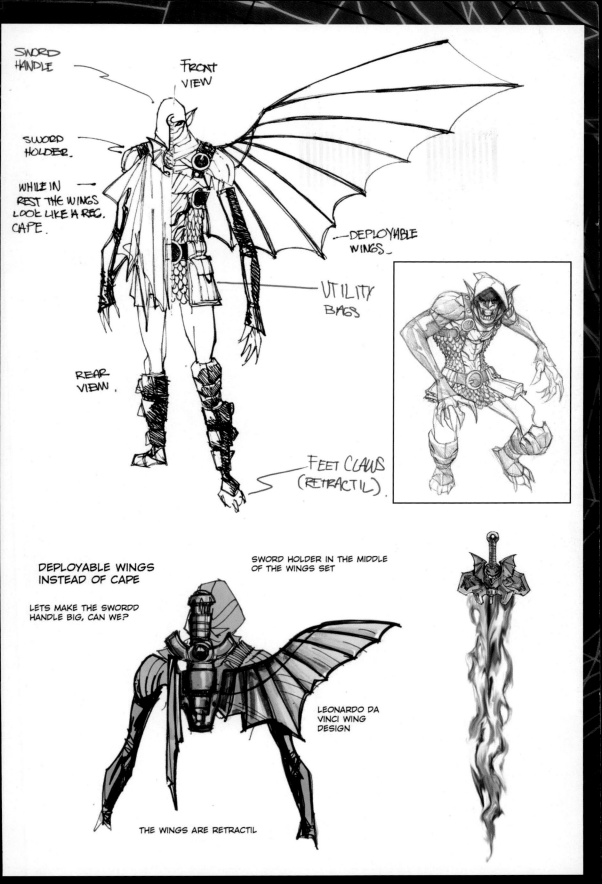

SWORD HANDLE

FRONT VIEW

SWORD HOLDER.

WHILE IN REST THE WINGS LOOK LIKE A REG. CAPE.

DEPLOYABLE WINGS

UTILITY BAGS

REAR VIEW.

FEET CLAWS (RETRACTIL).

DEPLOYABLE WINGS INSTEAD OF CAPE

LETS MAKE THE SWORDD HANDLE BIG, CAN WE?

SWORD HOLDER IN THE MIDDLE OF THE WINGS SET

LEONARDO DA VINCI WING DESIGN

THE WINGS ARE RETRACTIL

HOBGOBLIN DESIGNS
BY HUMBERTO RAMOS

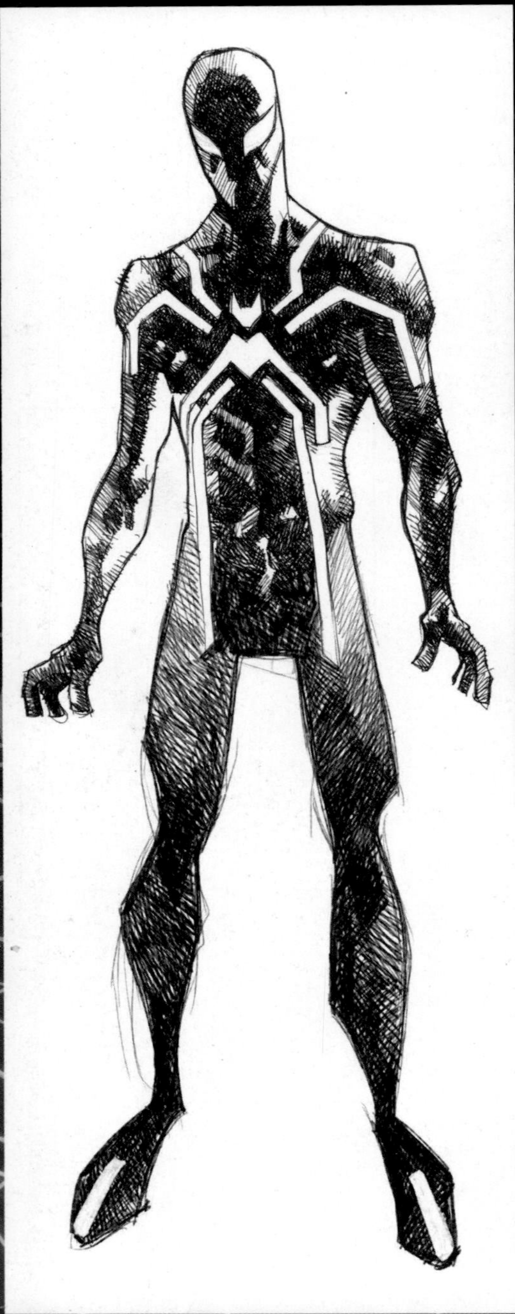

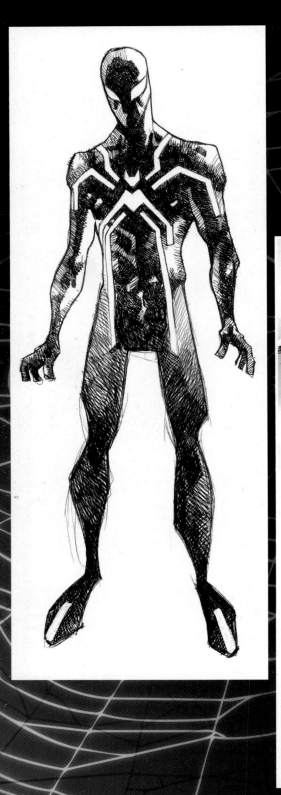

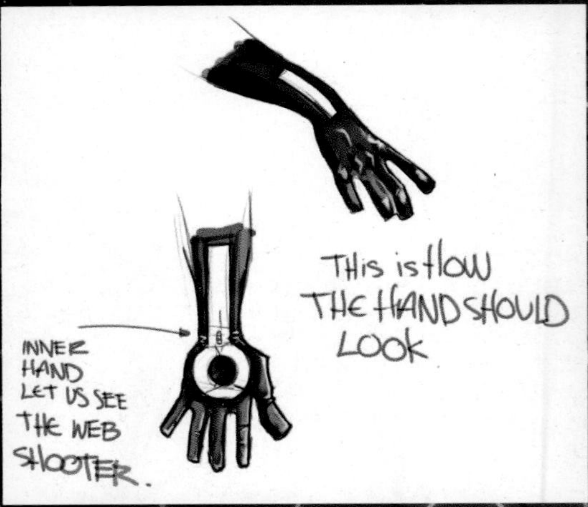
INNER HAND LET US SEE THE WEB SHOOTER.
THIS is HOW THE HAND SHOULD LOOK

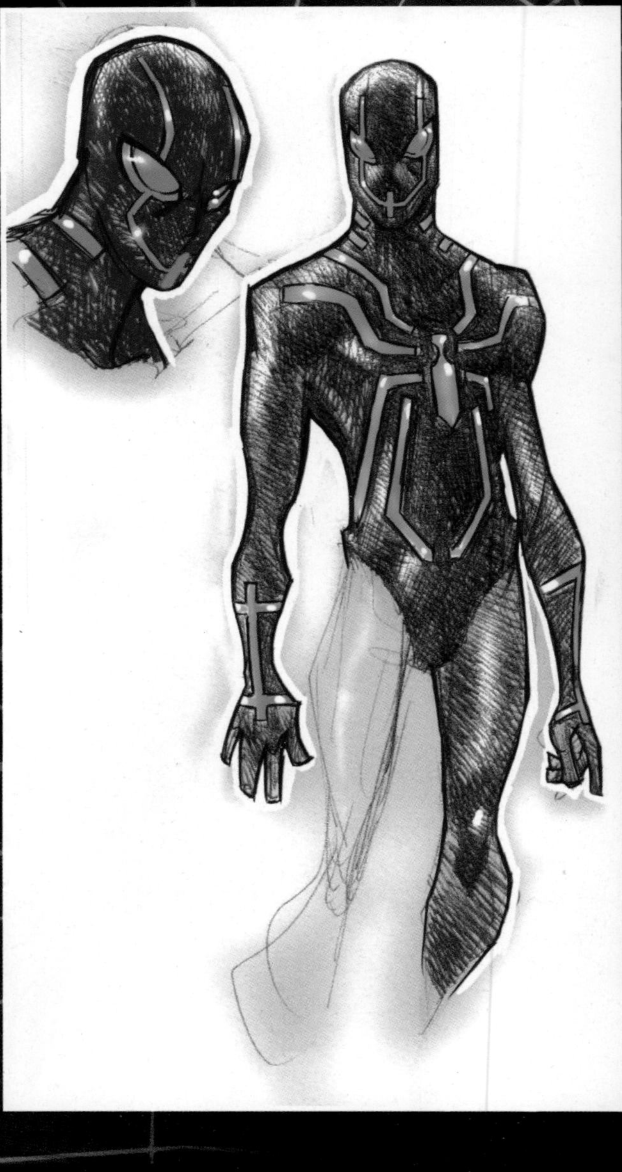

SPIDER-MAN STEALTH COSTUME DESIGNS
BY HUMBERTO RAMOS